ABORIGINAL LAW HANDBOOK

by

SHIN IMAI

With

First edition co-authors Katharine Logan and Gary Stein

Second edition researchers Karry Sandy, Kareena Wilding
and Valerie Nicholls

CARSWELL
Thomson Professional Publishing

Canadian Cataloguing in Publication Data

Imai, Shin
  Aboriginal law handbook

2nd ed.
Includes bibliographical references and index.
ISBN 0-459-23939-2

1. Native peoples — Canada — Legal status, laws, etc. — Popular works.*
I. Title.

KE444.I5 1999   349.71'089'97   C99-932678-3
KF385.I5 1999

CARSWELL
Thomson Professional Publishing

One Corporate Plaza   **Customer Relations:**
2075 Kennedy Road   Toronto 1-416-609-3800
Scarborough, Ontario   Elsewhere in Canada/U.S. 1-800-387-5164
M1T 3V4   Fax 1-416-298-5094

Preface

The title of this book is somewhat of a misnomer. It is not about the laws *of* Aboriginal nations, but rather about laws *in relation to* Aboriginal nations. This distinction is made clear by Brenda Small, a Cree from James Bay, who wrote of her experience at law school in *Native Beat*.

> We cannot study law and go back home and expect that this knowledge will save our people. We cannot pretend that just because we have learned the white man's law, we are in a better position to enhance the survival of our people. In fact, such conclusions are full of a learned arrogance that fails to recognize that the survival of our people has been assured because of our own strengths.
>
> We can be present at the law school but that doesn't mean that we ought to become the instruments or vehicles for the intrusiveness of the white man's law. Instead, we must retain a vision of the world that is based on our own ethics and beliefs. In essence, the laws we need to know best are those presented to us in the wind, in the river and across the skies.

I hope to articulate the growing inter-community law which describes the relationship between Aboriginal and non-Aboriginal communities. Like international law, this inter-community law comes into being both through abstract articulation and through practice or "custom". For the abstract principles, I have drawn freely from the theoretical insights of others. John Borrows of the Chippewas of Nawash, Brian Slattery, and Kent McNeil have all contributed to an understanding of the relation between the Canadian nation and Aboriginal nations.

But this book is not a work of theory. Its aim is primarily practical, attempting to contribute to the development of the inter-community law through "custom" — through the ways that communities find to relate to each other on a day to day basis. It provides both a bridge and a fence between Aboriginal and non-Aboriginal communities. It is a bridge because it shows the ways in which the range of economic, political, and personal relations can be facilitated. It is a fence because it identifies the border between non-Aboriginal law and territory in the domain of Aboriginal nations. This analogy of a fence is not a new one. The Supreme Court of Canada in *R. v. Marshall* recalled how British law was meant to protect rights encompassed in treaties.

> On June 25, 1761, following the signing of the Treaties of 1760-61 by the last group of Mi'kmaq villages, a ceremony was held at the farm of Lieutenant Governor Jonathan Belcher, the first Chief Justice of Nova Scotia. ... Lieutenant Governor Belcher proclaimed:
>
> > The Laws will be like a great Hedge about your Rights and properties, if any break this Hedge to hurt and injure you, the heavy weight of the Laws will fall upon them and punish their Disobedience.

Events in the past decade have shown that there is movement along the right path to the development of both hedges and bridges. Imaginative and thought-provoking ideas have been provided by the Royal Commission on Aboriginal Peoples. Through land claims agreements and informal tripartite arrangements, Aboriginal and non-Aboriginal communities have attempted to tackle challenges together. And the Canadian courts have attempted to give greater recognition to the existence of Aboriginal nations.

Over the next ten years there needs to be a focus on political transition and personal transformation from colonial to co-operative relations. These changes will affect an increasingly large number of Canadians. They will have to be implemented thoughtfully, and with clarity of vision.

How to use this book

The text is written with three goals:

- First, it should be possible to have an overview of the law without referring to the endnotes.
- Second, there is an attempt to organize the topics around situations which are encountered in real life, rather than around legal categories. For example, the chapter on commercial relations includes the law on tax, land surrenders and corporations.
- Third, the endnotes should provide direction for lawyers who need to know where to go for more technical information.

Warning

I have attempted to ensure the accuracy of the material in this book. However, the sheer volume of materials makes absolute accuracy difficult, and there will certainly be many on-going changes to the law and government policy. In addition, the attempt to make this book useful in practical situations means that some chapters integrate law from a variety of sources. The interrelationships can be complex, and the outline provided here cannot serve as a complete statement on the possible permutations. In order to apply the law in specific situations it is necessary to obtain the appropriate legal advice.

Any corrections, or suggestions on improvement would be welcome.

Acknowledgments

I would like to thank those who reviewed chapters of the book, Ellen Murray (Children, Family and Wills), Dianne Martin (Criminal Law) and Mary Truemner (Landlord and Tenant). The co-authors of the first edition, Katharine Logan and Gary Stein have now moved on to other things, but I was reminded of the humour of our early meetings as I reviewed the original chapters. Karry Sandy was a great help on research as we worked hard to meet the deadline in the summer of 1999. Kareena Wilding and Valerie Nicholls provided valuable assistance in previous summers while they were law students. Sarah Payne of Carswell edited and prepared the manuscript.

This book was financially assisted by the Law Foundation of Ontario.

Finally, my three children, who are no longer the babies they were when I began the first edition, have been very patient, as has my partner. So thank you Tosh, Kumi, Mika and Kathy.

Shin Imai
Toronto
November, 1999

Contents

ABORIGINAL GOVERNMENTS

THE COMMUNITY

⚜ THE FAMILY

JUSTICE

Table of Cases

Rights of
Aboriginal Peoples

1

The Constitutional Framework

POINTS TO REMEMBER

1. Aboriginal people have rights to continue to exist as a people with the right of self-determination.

2. The Constitution of Canada recognizes "existing Aboriginal and treaty rights" in section 35(1).

3. Aboriginal people have a special relationship with the Crown. Modern law requires that the Crown act honourably with respect to Aboriginal peoples.

4. The Indians, Métis and Inuit each consist of many distinct nations with different languages and cultures.

1. INTRODUCTION

Canadian policy on Aboriginal people has been based on terrible distortions of history. Here is an account provided in a 1969 university textbook on Canadian history. The view of Aboriginal people espoused by the author leads to an inevitable, and chilling, conclusion:

> The Europeans who came to the shores of North America regarded it as a vacant continent, which lay completely open to settlement from the Old World. In the final analysis this assumption was justified. It is true that the continent was already inhabited by tribes who claimed the land as their own. But in the whole of Canada there were probably no more than 220,000 Indians . . .

> The aborigines made no major contribution to the culture that developed in the settled communities of Canada. . . . They remained a primitive remnant clinging to their tribal organization long after it had become obsolete.

... In the United States, where agricultural settlement was the primary aim, the Indian was not only useless but an active menace whose speedy extermination would be an unqualified boon.[1]

Ronald Wright, in his excellent account of the history of the Americas, *Stolen Continents*[2], estimates that there were 100,000,000 Native Americans in 1492 — one fifth of the world's population. In North America, there were 7-18 million Indians.[3] Some nations relied heavily on agriculture and had large settled communities. Cahokia, near present-day St .Louis, might have had a population of 40,000 in the 1200's.[4] This would have been as large as London or Paris at the same time. Other nations relied more on hunting and gathering, while others served as important trade links among the nations.[5]

Canada is now coming to terms with the reality of history, and, through the Constitution, attempting to address the reality of the existence of Aboriginal nations today.

2. THE CONSTITUTION

The Constitution of any country is the legal foundation for that nation. It determines the relations between individuals and their governments, sets out the authorities of different institutions and provides for the distribution of law-making powers among different levels of government.

In Canada, the view of the Constitution held by many Aboriginal peoples is very different from the view held by the federal and provincial governments. For example, the Haudenosaunee, (the Iroquois Confederacy) in southern Ontario and southern Quebec do not see themselves within the Constitution of Canada at all. Rather, they see themselves as parallel governments. This is an excerpt from an explanation of the relationship which is embedded in the Two Row Wampum (a wampum belt is a belt of beads used by the Haudenosaunee for recording events):

When the Haudenosaunee first came into contact with the European nations, treaties of peace and friendship were made. Each was symbolized by the Gus-Wen-Tah or Two Row Wampum. There is a bead of white wampum which symbolizes the purity of the agreement. There are two rows of purple, and those two rows have the spirit of your ancestors and mine. There are three beads of wampum separating the two rows and they symbolize peace, friendship and respect.

These two rows will symbolize the two paths or two vessels, travelling down the same river together. One, a birch bark canoe, will be for the Indian people, their laws, their customs and their ways. The other, a ship, will be for the white people and their laws, their customs and their ways. We shall each travel the river together, side by side, but in our own boat. Neither of us will try to steer the other's vessel.

The principles of the Two Row Wampum became the basis for all treaties and agreements that were made with the Europeans and later the Americans.[6]

The federal and provincial governments (the Crown governments) have viewed the Constitution as providing powers to only two levels of government. The federal government has the authority to make laws in relation to "Indians and lands reserved for Indians".[7] The provinces also have authority to impose their laws on First Nations through a variety of mechanisms. The Crown governments did not recognize that Aboriginal nations had any independent authority to make laws or preserve their cultures.

A significant change in approach began in 1982. Until then, any changes to Canada's constitution had to be made and approved in Britain. In 1982, Canada rid itself of one of the last remnants of being a British colony when it "patriated" the Constitution. Now, the Canadian government (not the British government) could change the Constitution. It was then that the *Charter of Rights and Freedoms* was introduced to protect individuals against the actions of governments. Just as importantly, the new Constitution set out relationships among different constituents of the country. For example, the right of Catholics to education was recognized, as well as the rights of women and minorities. For Aboriginal nations, the most important provision was section 35(1) which provided:

The existing aboriginal and treaty rights of the aboriginal peoples of Canada is hereby recognized and affirmed.[8]

This provision finally recognized that Aboriginal peoples had constitutional rights as well. The Supreme Court of Canada has stated that these rights reflect an important constitutional value:

The "promise" of s. 35 . . . recognized not only the ancient occupation of land by aboriginal peoples, but their contribution to the building of Canada, and the special commitments made to them by successive governments. The protection of these rights, so recently and arduously achieved, whether looked at in their own right or as part of the larger concern with minorities, reflects an important underlying constitutional value.[9]

The following sections of this chapter describe the six major constitutional provisions:

- The meaning of "Aboriginal" and "Treaty Rights"
- The extent of federal and provincial authority over "Indians"
- Individual rights and the rights of women
- Future changes to the Constitution
- Who are Aboriginal peoples
- Crown fiduciary responsibility

3. THE MEANING OF ABORIGINAL AND TREATY RIGHTS

(a) What are Aboriginal rights?

Aboriginal rights are those rights which the Aboriginal peoples have because of their occupation of North America as sovereign nations before the coming of Europeans. These rights encompass all aspects of their culture, including rights to land, traditions and survival. Aboriginal people were eloquent in their testimony to the Royal Commission on Aboriginal Peoples:

> Aboriginal people have told us of their special relationship to the land and its resources. This relationship, they say, is both spiritual and material, not only one of livelihood, but of community and indeed of the continuity of their cultures and societies.[10]

As you will note from Chapter 2, "Aboriginal and Treaty Rights", there are many differences between Aboriginal nations and the Crown governments over the definition of Aboriginal rights. While Canadian courts have recognized hunting and fishing rights for food, and Aboriginal title, there has been a reluctance to recognize commercial fishing rights, or rights to self-government.

(b) What are treaty rights?

The term "treaty rights" generally refers to the promises which were made when the treaties were signed with First Nations. The idea is that some Aboriginal rights may have been changed or replaced by the terms of a written treaty. For example, Crown governments argue that under a treaty, Aboriginal title was exchanged for small reserves and small treaty payments. Aboriginal nations do not view treaties as real estate deals. They see treaties as creating nation-to-nation relationships. In addition, the Royal Commission on Aboriginal Peoples noted, "one aspect of treaty making that is little understood is the spiritual aspect of treaties. There is no separation between the political and spiritual."[11]

(c) Where do Aboriginal and treaty rights come from?

If you read section 35(1), above, you will note that Aboriginal and treaty rights are *"recognized and affirmed"*. In other words, the rights of Aboriginal people pre-exist the Constitution and are not created by the Constitution. In a way, then, Canadian law now recognizes the basis for the Two Row Wampum — that the governments of the Aboriginal nations were independent entities, and formed relations with the settlers through treaties.[12]

(d) Extinguishment of rights

Finally, it is important to note that the Constitution only recognizes *"existing"* Aboriginal and treaty rights. The Supreme Court of Canada has interpreted this to mean those rights which existed on April 17, 1982, when the new Constitution came into force; rights which had been extinguished before 1982 are not recognized.[13] For example, a court may find that Aboriginal title to land would be extinguished where an Aboriginal nation entered into a treaty, surrendering land in exchange for benefits.

According to the Supreme Court of Canada, federal legislation can still override (or *"infringe"*) Aboriginal and treaty rights. However, the federal government must be able to *justify* the infringement by providing a valid reason for its action.[14]

(These issues are discussed in more detail in Chapter 2, "Aboriginal and Treaty Rights".)

4. EXTENT OF FEDERAL AND PROVINCIAL AUTHORITY OVER "INDIANS"

One purpose of the existing Constitution is to divide law-making authority between the federal government and provincial governments. Federal areas of authority are general national issues such as the military, fisheries and criminal law. Provincial areas include education, property and civil rights in the province, and "matters of a merely local or private nature".

At Confederation in 1867, it was probably thought that the federal government would provide greater protection for Aboriginal people. Because the federal government was farther away than the provincial governments, it would have less incentive and be under less pressure to disregard Aboriginal rights and interests in favour of the desires of local settlers.[15] The federal government has the authority under section 91(24) of the *Constitution Act, 1867* to make laws over "Indians, and Lands reserved for the Indians".

The relationship between the application of federal laws and provincial laws is quite complicated. Here is a simplified explanation[16]:

> 1. The federal government can make a wide range of laws in relation to Indians or Indian lands. One example of a federal law is the *Indian Act*. This law addresses many areas which would normally be under provincial jurisdiction including education, wills and ownership of property on a reserve.

> 2. The general provincial laws which apply to everyone in the province can apply to "Indians" as well, unless those laws relate to something special about being an "Indian". For example, a provincial law about traffic can apply to Indians, even on a reserve, because driving a car has nothing to do with being an Indian.[17] However, a provincial law cannot take away an Indian child's status as a registered Indian.[18]

> 3. The final complication is found in s.88 of the *Indian Act*[19] which makes provincial laws applicable to Indians under certain circumstance. While this section played an important role in the past, its current relevance to the application of provincial laws is in transition.

As you will note in this scheme, section 91(24) does not address the role of the laws of the Aboriginal nations. (These are discussed in more detail in Chapter 7, "Self-government").

5. INDIVIDUAL RIGHTS AND THE RIGHTS OF WOMEN

The *Charter of Rights and Freedoms* was introduced in 1982 with other changes to the Constitution. This *Charter* includes many important rights for people in Canada. It protects the right to free speech, ensures that trials are fair, and provides a remedy against unequal treatment. This last provision, against discrimination, is found in section 15[20] of the *Charter* and could be used to combat racism, or differential treatment between on-reserve and off-reserve Indians.[21]

The rights the *Charter* protects, however, are primarily individual rights. Sometimes, these individual rights may conflict with the collective rights of Aboriginal communities.[22] For example, on remote reserves, it may make sense to have minor crimes reviewed and decided upon by an Elders Panel, with no lawyers present. However, the *Charter's* requirement for lawyers, judges and a complex adversarial proceeding may not allow for this approach. The *Charter's* focus on individual rights may raise obstacles to the community's ability to deal with matters itself, promoting dependence on remote, non-Aboriginal institutions.

(a) Section 25 is a shield to protect rights of Aboriginal peoples

To provide a balance, the *Charter of Rights and Freedoms* includes a special provision. Section 25 protects Aboriginal, treaty and other rights of Aboriginal peoples from being damaged by the inappropriate application of individual rights. For example, non-Aboriginal people may complain about Aboriginal communities' "special" treaty rights to fish. They could argue that the *Charter* in section 15 requires all people to be treated equally. In a case like this, section 25 should operate like a shield to protect the treaty rights of the Aboriginal people from the intrusion of the *Charter*.[23]

(b) Provisions relating to women

The Native Women's Association of Canada and other Aboriginal women's organizations have consistently expressed concerns about the rights of women. They point out the high rate of wife abuse and insensitivity by male leaders.[24]

Some of their concerns are addressed by provisions in the Constitution. For example, section 35(4) of the *Constitution Act, 1982* provides that Aboriginal and treaty rights are guaranteed equally to men and women.[25]

6. FUTURE CHANGES TO THE CONSTITUTION

Although the Constitution contains provisions relating to Aboriginal peoples, only the provincial and federal governments have the power to change the Constitution. However, before making any changes to the constitution which affect Aboriginal people, the Prime Minister must call a First Ministers' Conference and invite representatives of the Aboriginal people to participate in discussions (s. 35.1).[26] This means that Aboriginal peoples do not have an official vote, so that changes can be made without their consent.⟩

7. WHO ARE THE "ABORIGINAL PEOPLES?"

There are as many definitions as there are people doing the defining. Part of the complexity lies in the fact that different descriptions are used for different purposes. But the major part of the confusion is caused by the difference between Aboriginal peoples' own definitions of themselves, and definitions imposed on them by the Constitution or by legislation.

(a) Definitions in the Constitution

There are two different references to Aboriginal people. In section 35, where "existing aboriginal and treaty rights" are recognized, Aboriginal people are described as including "Indians, Inuit and Metis". In section 91(24) the federal government is given authority to make laws regarding "Indians and lands reserved for Indians." The Supreme Court of Canada has held that Inuit are included in "Indians" for the purpose of s. 91(24).[27] Opinion is divided on whether Métis are included.[28]

(b) Indians

The group that is classified as "Indians" are from diverse nations. They range from the Mi'kmaq in the east, to the Iroquois in central Canada to the Cree in the Prairies to the Haida in the west. There are 45 different nations with 56 different languages. These different nations had different rules for deciding membership. Some were matrilineal, and took their family affiliation from their mother. Others were patrilineal.

The federal government ignored these differences, and imposed a registration scheme under the *Indian Act* which made membership dependent on descent down the male line. Indians registered under the *Indian Act* are referred to by the federal government as "status Indians", and their communities are called "Bands". The federal *Indian Act* organizes registered Indians into about 609 Bands. Most Bands have small reserves of about twenty square miles.[29]

Indians who, for one reason or another, are not registered under the *Indian Act* are called "non-status Indians". Before 1985, the largest group of non-status Indians was Indian women who were "de-registered" because they married men without Indian status.

According to Statistics Canada's 1991 National Aboriginal Peoples Survey, the Aboriginal population in Canada was estimated to be approximately 720,000. Within this figure are 438,000 registered Indians and 112,600 Non-Status Indians.[30] (For a fuller description of *Indian Act* membership rules, see Chapter 9, "First Nation Citizenship and Indian Act Registration").

(c) Métis and "Halfbreeds"

Other Aboriginal people who do not have Indian status include Métis and "Halfbreeds". In Alberta, there is legislation which sets up settlements for Métis, and provides for a way of identifying members of the community. However, there is little recognition of Métis by other Crown governments. It is estimated that there are 100,000-200,000 Métis in Canada.[31] (For a fuller discussion of Métis issues, see Chapter 5, "Métis")

(d) Inuit

The Inuit are the smallest Aboriginal group. There are about 37,800 Inuit in Canada.[32] Unlike Indians, there is no national registration scheme for Inuit. However, they are included as beneficiaries in land claims agreements which now cover almost all of their traditional territory. (For a fuller discussion on Inuit issues, see Chapter 6, "Inuit").

8. CROWN FIDUCIARY RESPONSIBILITY

Aboriginal people have a special relationship with the federal Crown and many First Nations feel that, as a matter of principle, they should deal only with the federal government, and not with provincial governments.

The special responsibility of the federal government toward Indians was stated by Lord Denning of the English Court of Appeal in 1981:

> "[T]he discussion in this case will strengthen [the Indians'] hands so as to enable them to withstand any onslaught [by the Government of Canada]. They will be able to say that their rights and freedoms have been guaranteed to them by the Crown . . . No parliament should do anything to lessen the worth of these guarantees. They should be honoured by the Crown in respect of Canada "so long as the sun rises and the river flows". That promise must never be broken.[33]

The English case was followed by two important cases in the Supreme Court of Canada which described the nature of the relationship between the federal Crown and First Nations.[34] The first case, *Guerin v. R.*,[35] held that the Crown could be held accountable for a failure to act in the best interests of the First Nation in a land transaction. The second case, *R. v. Sparrow*,[36] held that the Crown had to exercise its legislative authority to avoid infringing on Aboriginal and treaty rights. If there were to be an infringement, it would only be allowed if there were "compelling and substantial" reasons to do so.[37]

These two cases establish the existence of a fiduciary relationship between the Crown and Aboriginal people. A "fiduciary" responsibility is one where one party (the fiduciary) has the responsibility to ensure that matters are dealt with in the best interests of the other party (the beneficiary).

In *Guerin*, the Musqueam First Nation decided to surrender some of its land to be leased for income. Evidence in that case suggested that the First Nation Council's instructions were not followed by the federal Indian Affairs official, and the land was leased to a golf club for less than its market value. The federal government argued that there was no fiduciary (or trust) relationship between the federal government and a First Nation which could be enforced by the courts. In a precedent-setting decision, the Supreme Court of Canada held that there was an enforceable trust responsibility, and awarded damages of $10 million to the Musqueam.

The *Sparrow* decision was also delivered by the Supreme Court of Canada. In that case, a member of the Musqueam First Nation was fishing in traditional waters with a gill net which was longer than allowed under the federal *Fisheries Act*. Sparrow argued that he had an existing Aboriginal right to fish, and that the regulations on the length of the net did not apply to him. The court agreed. In the judgment, the court stated that section 35(1) of the Constitution carried within it a fiduciary obligation on the part of the federal Crown toward Aboriginal peoples. This fiduciary obligation would require the Crown to act honourably and in keeping with the unique contemporary relationship between Aboriginal people and the Crown. Here, the court held that there was insufficient justification for a law which required that fish for food be caught with nets of a particular length. In coming to this decision, the Chief Justice stated ([1990] 3 C.N.L.R. 160 (S.C.C.) at p. P81):

> Our history has shown, unfortunately all too well, that Canada's aboriginal peoples are justified in worrying about government objectives that may be superficially neutral but which constitute *de facto* threats to the existence of the aboriginal rights and interests.

The federal fiduciary responsibility extends to other areas. For example, the federal government sponsored a referendum for Kahnesetake to resolve a long-standing election dispute in the community. Some members wanted to have *Indian Act* elections for Chief, while others supported the traditional appointment of the chief by clan mothers. The Traditional Council challenged the referendum in court and lost. The court said that the federal government could hold a referendum to find out the views of the community, and that part of the fiduciary duty was to ensure that the reserve was "properly administered".[38]

While the federal fiduciary responsibility is clear, the extent of provincial fiduciary responsibility is still in transition. Arguments that there are no provincial fiduciary responsibilities to Aboriginal peoples are probably no longer correct.[39]

Certainly the province is required to act in a way which is consistent with the "honour of the Crown". For example, a provincial court judge in Ontario criticized the Ministry of Natural Resources for not negotiating with the Kettle Point First Nation. Members of the Kettle Point First Nation were arrested, while they were fishing, by three boatfuls of law enforcement officers carrying sidearms and shotguns. They were charged with commercial fishing without a license. When the case went to court, the judge found that the province had created arbitrary boundaries for Aboriginal fishing and that there was no evidence that the accused people were fishing for commercial purposes. All the accused people were acquitted. What is most remarkable about this judgment is its ringing condemnation of the tactics used by the law enforcement officers:

> In my judgment, the time has long since passed when the Crown should seek to determine its relationship by way of regulation of Indian fishing and hunting rights through the use of the courts particularly in the manner utilized in this case. Surely, the matter of receiving a complaint from the Bluewater Angler's Association, entering upon an investigation of such complaint to the extent of conscripting members of the Ontario Provincial Police, officers of the Department of Natural Resources of the State of Michigan, together with officers of the Ministry of Natural Resources, organizing a pre-dawn raid with boats pursuing and intercepting persons engaged in fishing activities, approaching with guns drawn and boarding and seizing the nets and gear, scarcely can be construed as an activity in which the government's relationship is trust-like rather than adversarial.
>
> Surely, the honour of the Crown in so proceeding is not much in evidence. In that sense I would echo the observation of counsel for the accused, "we are here for all the wrong reasons, we should not be doing what we are doing, the way we are doing it.[40] (at pp. 138-39)

9. HISTORY OF CONSTITUTIONAL CHANGE

From 1980 onwards, Aboriginal issues have been woven through three major constitutional upheavals. While rights of Aboriginal peoples may not always have been appropriately addressed, they could not be ignored.

(a) The Patriation of the Constitution, 1980-1982

When Prime Minister Pierre Trudeau introduced proposals for a new Constitution in October 1980, the proposals did not mention Aboriginal rights. By January 1981, however, pressure from Aboriginal groups and the Canadian public had resulted in the inclusion of an Aboriginal rights clause. But this was a time of confrontation: the provincial and federal governments were in a fierce struggle over the proposed amendments and Quebec began a court case in the Supreme Court of Canada to challenge the way the Constitution was being changed. First Nations, fearing their interests would be neglected or sacrificed in the struggle, travelled to England in an unsuccessful attempt to assert a direct link to the British Crown, and to invoke the British courts' intervention.[41]

The constitutional deadlock dragged on into late 1981, until a sudden secret compromise between the federal and some provincial governments justified the First Nations' fears: new wording for the Constitution had dropped the reference to Aboriginal rights. Further negotiations, public recriminations and public pressure resulted in the present Aboriginal rights clause being included at the last minute.

(b) Constitutional conferences to clarify Aboriginal and treaty rights, and the Meech Lake Accord, 1983-1987

During the next four years, there were four national constitutional conferences. The first conference, in 1983, resulted in a number of changes, including guaranteeing Aboriginal and treaty rights equally to men and women, and providing for Aboriginal participation in future constitutional change. In the remaining conferences, the focus turned toward the recognition of self-government.

The concept of self-government was almost unthinkable for federal and provincial governments in 1983. By 1987, however, most were willing to include self-government in the Constitution. Despite this progress, the parties could not come to an agreement. The federal government would only recognize self-government after an Aboriginal group had successfully negotiated an agreement with the federal and provincial governments. Aboriginal groups refused to accept this condition. They feared that, if the federal and provincial governments refused to negotiate an agreement, then the Aboriginal people would be left with no recognized right of self-government. Aboriginal people called this a "contingent rights" approach (because the rights would be contingent on successful negotiations), an approach fundamentally at odds with the recognition of an "inherent right" (a right that exists outside the Constitution, and does not have to be granted through agreements).

Two months after the failure of the First Ministers to entrench rights to self-government in 1987, Prime Minister Brian Mulroney and the provincial premiers shocked Aboriginal leaders by cobbling together a series of constitutional amendments which recognized Quebec as a "distinct society" while ignoring the status of First Nations. Aboriginal people did not object to the distinct society clause, but did object to Aboriginal issues being shunted aside. Over the three years allowed for ratification of the Meech Lake Accord, opposition mounted from other Canadians as well. As the deadline approached in 1990, two provincial legislatures — Manitoba and Newfoundland — had not ratified the accord. Elijah Harper, a Cree member of the Manitoba Legislature, used a technical objection to the rules of the Legislature to prevent a vote by provincial politicians in Manitoba. The Meech Lake Accord could not be ratified in Manitoba, and Newfoundland also decided not to vote on the Accord. With that, the Meech Lake Accord collapsed.

(c) The Charlottetown Accord, 1990-1992

The third constitutional crisis in a decade began in 1990 after the defeat of the Meech Lake Accord. Quebec reacted to the defeat by passing legislation to hold a referendum in the province on sovereignty by the fall of 1992. Premier Robert Bourassa announced that he would boycott future meetings with other Premiers. Fearing that a vote in favour of sovereignty could lead to the separation of Quebec, the federal government and the provinces began to develop new proposals for constitutional amendments. The new proposals would attempt to address concerns, not only of Quebec, but also of the rest of Canada, including the Aboriginal people.

To meet Quebec's deadline for a vote on sovereignty, the federal government began making plans to draft a set of constitutional amendments for presentation to the rest of the country. The provinces, together with the Aboriginal people objected to a process which would leave major decisions in the hands of the federal government. In March 1992, the provinces succeeded in setting up a multilateral process for negotiations which involved the presence, not only of the federal and provincial governments, but also of the territorial governments and four Aboriginal groups. Quebec initially refused to come to the table.

The four Aboriginal groups involved were those present at the constitutional table in 1987. The Assembly of First Nations was composed mainly of the chiefs of reserves identified under the *Indian Act*. The Inuit Tapirisat of Canada represented the Inuit of northern Canada. The Métis National Council represented the Prairie-based Métis, the descendants of Louis Riel's constituency. And the Native Council of Canada represented a mixed constituency of Métis, urban Aboriginal people, and Indians. The Native Women's Association of Canada was not invited to participate.[42]

In intense weekly meetings from April to July 1992, the sixteen parties at the table drafted a set of amendments that would have dramatically changed Canada's constitutional landscape. An elected Senate, recognition of Quebec's distinct society, a Social Charter and a new division of powers between federal and provincial governments were all parts of the package. One of the most significant sets of provisions recognized the right to Aboriginal self-government and established an extensive framework for negotiations on self-government and on treaties. In August, Quebec agreed to join the process, and, after further negotiations, agreed to the provisions of the Charlottetown Accord on August 28, 1992.

On October 26, 1992 a Canada-wide referendum was held on the Accord. All of the politicians who participated in the negotiations spoke in favour of the Accord. The leaders of the Inuit, the Métis National Council, and the Native Council of Canada also campaigned in favour of the Accord. However, many of the Chiefs of the First Nations were not supportive. In Ontario, the Chiefs held a meeting a week before the vote, and decided that their communities needed more time to look at its provisions. They decided not to endorse the Accord for October 26. A few days later, there was a similar result at a national meeting of the Assembly of First Nations.

On October 26, the people of Canada voted overwhelmingly to reject the Charlottetown Accord. Even the count on the reserves showed that the majority of First Nation voters were opposed.

(d) The Royal Commission on Aboriginal Peoples

The spectacular failure of the constitutional talks was matched by an alarming upheaval in Aboriginal communities. In the summer of 1990, a land dispute between Mohawks of Kahnesetake and the residents of Oka had led to a confrontation that lasted 78 days. The Canadian army was deployed in attempting to quell a rising tide of Aboriginal discontent which eventually spread to Montreal and to blockades across Canada. The financial cost of the Oka crisis was more than $150 million.[43]

The solution for the federal government was to appoint the Royal Commission on Aboriginal Peoples. Seven commissioners, the majority of whom were Aboriginal,[44] met for five years. Their massive five volume report was released in 1996.[45] The ambitious recommendations aim to find a constitutional space for Aboriginal nations in the political and social fabric of Canada. Proposals range from the implementation of self-government, to lands and resources issues, to establishing an elected Aboriginal Parliament to advise on legislation affecting Aboriginal peoples. Even with the twenty-year time frame proposed by the Royal Commission, the task of comprehensive implementation is daunting. The Report is nonetheless enormously influential. Because it is so comprehensive, and so thoughtful, courts and policy makers are turning to it for guidance on new approaches to relations with Aboriginal peoples; new relations which will secure a place for Aboriginal peoples in Canada's constitutional framework.

APPENDIX A

Constitution Act, 1982

    1. *Part I — Canadian Charter of Rights and Freedoms*

25. The guarantee in this Charter of certain rights and freedoms shall not be construed so as to abrogate or derogate from any aboriginal treaty or other rights or freedoms that pertain to the aboriginal peoples of Canada including

    (a) any rights or freedoms that have been recognized by the Royal Proclamation of October 7, 1763; and

    (b) any rights or freedoms that now exist by way of land claims agreements or may be so acquired.

    2. *Part II — Rights of the Aboriginal Peoples of Canada*

35. (1) The existing aboriginal and treaty rights of the aboriginal peoples of Canada are hereby recognized and affirmed.

(2) In this Act, "aboriginal peoples of Canada" includes the Indian, Inuit and Métis peoples of Canada.

(3) For greater certainty, in subsection (1), "treaty rights" includes rights that now exist by way of land claims agreements or may be so acquired.

(4) Notwithstanding any other provision of this Act, the aboriginal and treaty rights referred to in subsection (1) are guaranteed equally to male and female persons.

35.1 The government of Canada and the provincial governments are committed to the principle that, before any amendment is made to Class 24 of section 91 of the "*Constitution Act, 1867*", to section 25 of this Act or to this Part,

(a) a constitutional conference that includes in its agenda an item relating to the proposed amendment, composed of the Prime Minister of Canada and the first ministers of the provinces, will be convened by the Prime Minister of Canada; and

(b) the Prime Minister of Canada will invite representatives of the aboriginal peoples of Canada to participate in the discussions on that item.

ENDNOTES

1 Edgar McInnis, *Canada* (Toronto: Holt Rinehart and Winston, 1969). For a more accurate history, see Olive Patricia Dickason, *Canada's First Nations: A History of Founding Peoples from Earliest Times* (Toronto: McClelland & Stewart, 1992).

2 See Ronald Wright, *Stolen Continents: The "New World" Through Indian Eyes* (Toronto: Penguin, 1993).

3 See Ronald Wright, *supra* note 2 at 123. The higher figure is cited to Henry F. Dobyns, *Their Number Become Thinned* (Knoxville: University of Tennessee Press, 1983) at 42 and Russell Thornton, *We Shall Live Again* (Cambridge: Cambridge University Press, 1986) at 32 for the lower figure. The Trigger cite is 1 million; Thornton says it is absurdly low.

4 See Ronald Wright, *supra* note 2 at 91.

5 For an excellent description of the importance of trade, see Bruce G. Trigger, *The Huron: Farmers of the North*, 2d ed. (Fort Worth: Holt, Rinehart and Winston, 1996).

6 Excerpt quoted in "Indian Self-government in Canada: Report of the Special Committee on Indian Self-government", (Ottawa: Queen's Printer, 1983); for more information on the Great Law of Peace, see A.C. Parker, *The Constitution of the Five Nations or The Iroquois book of the Great Law*, 2m (Ohsweken: Iroqrafts Ltd. Iroquois Publications, 1984); A.C. Parker, *The Code of Handsome Lake, The Seneca Prophet*, 2.5 m (Ohsweken: Iroqrafts Ltd. Iroquois Publications, 1990); and Tehanetorens, *Wampum Belts*, 3m (Ohsweken: Iroqrafts Ltd. Iroquois Publications, 1993).

7 *Constitution Act, 1867*, s. 91(24).

8 *Constitution Act, 1982* R.S.C. 1985, Appendix II, No. 44 En. Canada Act, 1982 (U.K.), c. 11 Am. Constitution Amendment Proclamation, 1983, SI/84-102, Schedule.

9 *Reference re Secession of Quebec* [1998] S.C.J. No. 61, [1998] 2 S.C.R. 217 #82 (p. 262).

10 See Royal Commission on Aboriginal Peoples, *Restructuring the Relationship*, Volume 2, Part Two (Ottawa: Supply and Services, 1996) at 448. [hereinafter RCAP, Vol. 2, Part 2].

11 See RCAP, Vol. 2, Part 2, *supra* note 10 at 129.

12 The fact that Aboriginal and treaty rights pre-existed the Constitution is expressed in *R. v. Vanderpeet*, [1996] 4 C.N.L.R. 177 (S.C.C.), (at para 29) reconsideration refused (January 16, 1997), Doc. 23803 (S.C.C.):

The pre-existence of aboriginal rights is relevant to the analysis of s. 35(1) because it indicates that aboriginal rights have a stature and existence prior to the constitutionalization of those rights and sheds light on the reasons for protecting those rights . . .

These rights do not need the legal recognition of the colonizers to exist. See *R. c. Côté*, (S.C.C.) [1996] 4 C.N.L.R. 26 at para. 48. The same situation exists in the United States. For example see *Johnson v. McIntosh*, 21 U.S. 543 (U.S.Ill., 1823). The highest Court in Australia in *Mabo v. Queensland* (1992), 107 A.L.R. 1 (Australia H.C.), decided that rights of their Aboriginal peoples did not depend on a grant from the Crown.

13 On the subject of "existing" rights see *R. v. Sparrow*, [1990] 3 C.N.L.R. 160 (S.C.C.). [hereinafter *R v. Sparrow*].

14 For the full test on infringement in *R. v. Sparrow*, *supra* note 13, see [1990] 3 C.N.L.R. 160 at pp. 182-187 or the summary of the case in the 1999 edition of the *Annotated Indian Act and Aboriginal Constitutional Provisions* (Shin Imai, Carswell).

15 On the subject of the federal power over Indian affairs, see P.W. Hogg, *Constitutional Law of Canada*, Loose-leaf ed., 4th ed. (Scarborough: Carswell, 1997) Vol. 1 at 27-2 to 27-6. See also D. Sanders, "Prior Claims: Aboriginal People in the Constitution of Canada" in Beck and Bernier, eds., *Canada and the New Constitution: The Unfinished Agenda*, Vol. 1 (Institute for Research on Public Policy, 1983) at 238.

16 Below is an outline which identifies the legal points about federal and provincial authority over Indians. The relationship between federal and provincial authority is very complex. The following is a very general summary of the main issues:

Federal authority
There is an area of exclusive federal authority which cannot be touched by provincial legislation. Among the reasons courts have found provincial laws invalid are impairing the "status and capacities of Indians", affecting "Indianness", regulating Indians *qua* Indians, and regulating a matter which forms an integral part of the primary federal jurisdiction. (See, for example, *Derrickson. v. Derrickson*, [1986] 2 C.N.L.R. 45 (S.C.C.).)

The scope of federal authority is very wide, and includes authority over matters which would otherwise be in the legislative authority of the provinces. (See, for example, *Canada (Attorney General) v. Canard* (1975), [1976] 1 S.C.R. 170 (S.C.C.). All Aboriginal rights are under exclusive federal authority and only the federal government can extinguish those rights. *Delgamuukw v. British Columbia*, [1998] 1 C.N.L.R. 14 (S.C.C.).

Provincial authority
Provincial laws which attempt to legislate about Indians in the area of exclusive federal authority are not valid. (See for example, *R. v. Sutherland*, [1980] 3 C.N.L.R. 71 (S.C.C.). However, provincial laws which fall short

of invading the area of exclusive federal authority may apply to Indians, unless those laws are inconsistent with a federal law. If there is an inconsistency, the federal law is paramount. (See for example, *R. v. Francis*, [1988] 4 C.N.L.R. 98 (S.C.C.).)

Provincial laws of general application which *do* invade the area of exclusive federal jurisdiction may be incorporated into federal law through section 88 of the *Indian Act*. (See for example, *Dick v. R. (R. v. Tenale)*, [1985] 4 C.N.L.R. 55 (S.C.C.).)

17 For a case saying that a provincial traffic law can apply to an Indian on a reserve because traffic laws do not affect "Indianness" see *R. v. Francis*, [1988] 4 C.N.L.R. 98 (S.C.C.).

18 A case saying that a provincial adoption law cannot take away an Indian child's right to be registered is *Birth Registration No. 67-09-022272, Re* (1975), (sub nom. *Natural Parents v. Superintendent of Child Welfare*) [1976] 2 S.C.R. 751 (S.C.C.).

19 See section 88 for a provision which incorporates provincial laws of general application:

> Subject to the terms of any treaty and any other Act of Parliament, all laws of general application from time to time in force in any province are applicable to and in respect of Indians in the province, except to the extent that those laws are inconsistent with this Act or any order, rule, regulation or by-law made thereunder, and except to the extent that those laws make provision for any matter for which provision is made by or under this Act.

> *Indian Act*, R.S.C. 1985, c. I-5, as am. R.S.C. 1985, c. 32 (1st Supp.) R.S.C. 1985, c. 27 (2nd Supp.), s. 10 (Sched.); R.S.C. 1985, c. 17 (4th Supp.); R.S.C. 1985, c. 43 (4th Supp.); R.S.C. 1985, c. 48 (4th Supp.); S.C. 1990, c. 16; 1990, c. 17; 1992, c. 51, s. 54; 1993, c. 28, s. 78 (Sched. III, items 73, 74); 1996, c. 23, s. 187(e); 1998, c. 30, s. 14(j); 1999, c. 3, s. 69.

20 See section 15 in Appendix A.

21 For a case saying that off-reserve people were being discriminated against by the *Indian Act*, see *Corbiere v. Canada (Minister of Indian & Northern Affairs)*, [1999] 3 C.N.L.R. 19 (S.C.C.).

22 For a discussion on the conflict between collective rights, and rights of individuals, see Wendy Moss, "Indigenous Self-government in Canada and Sexual Equality Under the Indian Act: Resolving Conflicts Between Collective and Individual Rights" (1990), 15 Queen's Law Journal 279; B. Schwartz, "A Separate Justice System?" (1990) 19 Manitoba Law Journal (No.1) 77; and M.E. Turpel, "Aboriginal Peoples and the Canadian

Charter: Interpretive Monopolies, Cultural Differences" (1989-90), 6 Canadian Human Rights Yearbook 3.

23 For the text of section 25, see the Appendix. For articles discussing section 25, see William Pentney, "The Rights of the Aboriginal Peoples of Canada and the Constitution, 1982 — Part I: The Interpretive Prism of Section 25" (1987), 22 U.B.C. Law Rev 21; and Bruce Wildsmith, *Aboriginal People and section 25 of the Canadian Charter of Rights and Freedoms.* Saskatchewan: University of Saskatchewan Native Law Centre, 1988.

24 See Theresa Nanahee, "Dancing with a Gorilla: Aboriginal Women, Justice and the Charter" in Aboriginal People and the Justice System, Report on the National Round Table on Aboriginal Justice Issues (Ottawa: Supply and Services, 1993).

25 See Appendix A for the provision. Also relevant are two provisions of the *Charter.* Section 15 prohibits discrimination based on sex, and section 28 provides that the rights and freedoms of the *Charter* are guaranteed equally to male and female persons.

26 See Appendix A for the wording of section 35.1.

27 The case which held that "Indians" includes Inuit is *Reference re Whether the Term "Indians" in s. 91(24) of the B.N.A. Act, 1867, includes Eskimo Inhabitants of Quebec,* [1939] S.C.R. 104 (S.C.C.).

28 Commentators who argue that Métis should be included in 91(24) include C. Chartier, " *'Indian': an analysis of the term as used in section 91(24) of the BNA Act*", (1978-79) 43 Sask. L. Rev. 37, and B. Slattery, "First Nations and the Constitution: A Question of Trust", (1992), 71 Canadian Bar Review 261 at 283. For arguments that section 91(24) should include Métis see RCAP, Vol. 4, at 209. The federal government, however, takes the opposite position.

29 79.3 per cent of Indian reserves are less than 500 hectares in size. See Royal Commission on Aboriginal Peoples, *Restructuring the Relationship,* Volume 2, Part Two (Ottawa: Supply and Services, 1996) at 810.

30 See Royal Commission on Aboriginal Peoples, Volume 1: *Looking Forward, Looking Back.* (Ottawa: Ministry of Supply and Services, 1996) [hereinafter RCAP, Vol.1] at 15.

31 RCAP, Volume 1, *supra* note 30 at 19 estimates that there are an estimated 139,400 self-identifying Métis.

32 See RCAP, Vol. 1, *supra* note 30 at 19.

33 The English case stating that Parliament should not diminish the Crown's guarantees to Indians is found in *R. v. Secretary of State for Foreign & Commonwealth Affairs* (1981), [1981] 4 C.N.L.R. 86 (Eng. C.A.) at p. 99.

34 On the subject of the nature of the relationship between the Crown and the Aboriginal peoples, see also B. Slattery, "First Nations and the Constitution: A Question of Trust" (1992) 71 Can. Bar Rev. 261 in which the author argues that the fiduciary relationship between Aboriginal peoples and the Crown is a special instance of a general doctrine of collective trust that animates the Canadian Constitution as a whole. The article explores the origins and character of the constitutional trust, and considers its application to issues surrounding the inherent Aboriginal right to self-government and Aboriginal land rights. See also Leonard Rotman, *Parallel Paths: Fiduciary Doctrine and the Crown-Native Relationship in Canada* (Toronto: University of Toronto Press, 1996) [hereinafter Leonard Rotman].

35 The case establishing an enforceable fiduciary duty of the Crown to a Band is *Guerin v. R.* (1984), [1985] 1 C.N.L.R. 120 (S.C.C.) [hereinafter *Guerin*].

36 The case establishing a fiduciary relationship in the exercise of legislative authority is *R. v. Sparrow, supra* note 13.

37 On the subject of fiduciary responsibility in the context of land transactions see also *Wewayakum Indian Band v. Canada*, (sub nom. *Roberts v. Canada*), [1989] 2 C.N.L.R. 146 (S.C.C.) in which Madam Justice Wilson affirmed the existence of "the common law relating to aboriginal title which underlies the fiduciary nature of the Crown's obligations. . ."

38 On the federal fiduciary duty to see that a reserve is properly administered, see *Six Nations Traditional Hereditary Chiefs v. Canada (Minister of Indian & Northern Affairs)* (1991), [1992] 3 C.N.L.R. 156 (Fed. T.D.).

39 On provincial fiduciary responsibility see B. Slattery and Leonard Rotman, *supra* note 34.

40 The condemnation of heavy-handed law enforcement tactics is found in *R. v. Jackson*, [1992] 4 C.N.L.R. 121 (Ont. Prov. Div.).

41 The British case holding that Canadian Aboriginal people could not prevent the repatriation of the Constitution is *R. v. The Secretary of State for Foreign & Commonwealth Affairs, supra* note 33.

42 The Native Women's Association of Canada went to court to claim a separate seat at the table. Although the court stated that they had been treated unfairly in the process, their court actions ultimately failed to get them a seat at the negotiation table. See *Native Women's Ass'n of Canada v. R.* (1994), (sub nom. *Native Women's Assn. of Canada v. Canada*) [1995] 1 C.N.L.R. 47, (S.C.C.).

43 See Geoffrey York & Loreen Pindera, *People of the Pines: the Warriors and the Legacy of Oka* (Toronto: Little, Brown & Company, 1991) which provides a detailed chronology of the Oka crisis.

44 The Commissioners were:

Rene Dussault, co-chair:	A judge of the Quebec Court of Appeal.
George Erasmus, co-chair:	Former National Chief of the Assembly of First Nations.
Paul L.A.H. Chartrand:	A prominent Métis academic.
J. Peter Meekison:	Professor of Political Science and Belzberg Chair in Constitutional Studies (Faculty of Law) at the University of Alberta.
Viola Robinson:	Former head of the Native Council of Canada
Mary Sillet:	A founding member and former president of Pauktuutit, the Inuit Women's Association of Canada.
Bertha Wilson:	Former judge of the Supreme Court of Canada.

45 Report of the Royal Commission on Aboriginal Peoples (Ottawa: Ministry of Supplies and Services Canada, 1996).

2

Aboriginal and Treaty Rights

POINTS TO REMEMBER

1. Aboriginal people have Aboriginal rights which derive from their presence in Canada and use of the land since long before the European colonization of Canada. The Royal Commission on Aboriginal Peoples has urged that these rights be given fuller recognition by Canadian courts and Crown governments.

2. Some Aboriginal people also have treaty rights, which are rights provided for in the treaties made between First Nations and the Crown. The exact nature of these rights is often in dispute because of differences between the written text and the text transmitted through oral tradition.

3. Existing Aboriginal and treaty rights are protected under Canada's constitution. However, even these constitutionally protected rights are subject to some government regulation. The extent to which Aboriginal and treaty rights can be regulated is described in the Supreme Court of Canada decision in *R. v. Sparrow*.

1. INTRODUCTION

In the winter of 1763, Nipissing and Algonquin messengers were dispatched across Indian country. They carried strings of wampum and spread word of an important conference to be held at Niagara Falls. Two thousand chiefs gathered the next summer. There were Mi'kmaq from the east coast, Cree from the north, Iroquois from Lake Ontario, Lakota from the west — twenty-four nations in all. They met with William Johnson, Superintendent of Indian Affairs, to negotiate a peace treaty between the British and the First Nations.

There were two treaties exchanged at that time. One, following the convention of the First Nations was an exchange of gifts and wampum belts. One of the belts exchanged was the Two Row Wampum of the Iroquois, affirming the principles that Indian nations and the British were not to interfere in the internal affairs of the other. The second, following British convention, was the Royal Proclamation of 1763.[1] This proclamation recognized the "several Nations or Tribes of Indians" and stated that Indian lands could only be surrendered after a public meeting, to the Crown. In order to prevent "frauds and abuses" individual settlers were not allowed to purchase land directly from the Indians.

In the spring of 1987, there was another historic conference. Representatives of Aboriginal peoples from across Canada arrived in Ottawa to negotiate the amending of the Constitution to recognize the right of Aboriginal peoples to self-government. They met with Brian Mulroney and other first ministers. Under the glare of television lights, an Algonquin Elder gave a reading of three wampum belts. One of the belts showed three figures holding hands with a cross on the right hand side. The Elder explained that the three figures represented the partnership, as equals, among the French, British and the Algonquin people. The cross showed that a priest had witnessed the agreement.

In the two hundred years between these events, economic, social, and legal policies were designed to assimilate Indians and destroy the distinctiveness of their nations. Courts did not recognize rights of Aboriginal peoples, and gave no respect to treaties. The most famous, and for a period of time the most influential statement on treaties, was the decision in *R. v. Syliboy*, which stated, "(t)he savages' right of sovereignty even of ownership were never recognized." Until the change to the Constitution in 1982, courts held that the federal government was free to unilaterally override rights that were contained in treaties.[2]

2. RIGHTS OF ABORIGINAL NATIONS

What the Royal Commission on Aboriginal Peoples found in 1996 was that the assimilationist policies had not succeeded:

> Canadians need to understand that *Aboriginal peoples are nations* . . . To this day, Aboriginal people's sense of confidence and well-being as individuals remains tied to the strength of their nations. Only as members of restored nations can they reach their potential in the twenty-first century.[3]

Aboriginal and treaty rights must be understood, not as privileges extended to individual Aboriginal persons, but rather as institutional arrangements needed for the survival of distinct nations. They are group or collective rights belonging to a community as a whole. This means that Aboriginal individuals may enjoy the benefits of these rights, such as hunting or fishing, but that the rights belong to the community.[4]

3. ABORIGINAL RIGHTS

Aboriginal rights derive from Aboriginal peoples' historical position as self-governing peoples who occupied and used the land before the arrival of the European colonists. Aboriginal people explain that these rights include everything necessary for their survival as Aboriginal peoples, including rights to land, language, economy, culture, law and government.

Canadian courts have had difficulty reconciling concepts of Aboriginal rights with the rest of Canadian law. Previously, there were attempts to classify Aboriginal rights according to pre-existing legal categories derived from English property law. Recently, such attempts have been abandoned. It is now accepted that Aboriginal rights are unique. In legal terms, they are *sui generis*.[5] This perspective provides opportunities to develop sensible understandings of Aboriginal rights. It also means that the definitions will have to develop slowly as courts make decisions on a case by case basis.

(a)   What has the Supreme Court of Canada said about Aboriginal rights?

Canadian courts will not recognize everything that is claimed to be an Aboriginal right, nor will they always give precedence to an Aboriginal right where there is a conflict with an existing Crown law. Nonetheless, in recent years, there has been a growing judicial recognition that Aboriginal rights need to be woven into Canadian law. Chief Justice Lamer stated in the *Delgamuukw* case:

> [Aboriginal rights] are aimed at the reconciliation of the prior occupation of North America by distinctive aboriginal societies with the assertion of Crown sovereignty over Canadian territory. They attempt

to achieve that reconciliation by "their bridging of aboriginal and non-aboriginal cultures."[6]

According to the Supreme Court of Canada, Aboriginal rights cover a spectrum. On the one end is Aboriginal title to land, which gives exclusive possession. On the other end are practices or customs which are "integral to the distinctive cultures of aboriginal peoples" which are not dependent on the existence on Aboriginal title.

There are many technical aspects to the tests applied by the Supreme Court of Canada. What needs to be highlighted here is the point in history that the existence of an Aboriginal right is to be determined. For Aboriginal title claims, the land must have been occupied "at the date of the assertion of British sovereignty".[7] For claims based on a practice or custom, like fishing, the court appears to be saying that the practice or custom must have existed before contact.[8]

Both tests seem counter-intuitive. If this interpretation is taken literally, it would lead to a "reconciliation" between an Aboriginal society as it existed before contact, and contemporary Canadian society: a comparison of two societies separated by as much as five hundred years. A better approach would be to seek an accommodation of *contemporary* Aboriginal society with *contemporary* non-Aboriginal society.

4. TREATY RIGHTS

The source of treaty rights is different from the source of Aboriginal rights. Aboriginal rights are considered "inherent" rights. Aboriginal peoples had those rights before the arrival in North America of Europeans: they are not derived from grant or negotiation. Treaty rights, by contrast, are those rights set out in a treaty which has been negotiated between First Nations and the Crown.

Most of the treaties in Canada were signed between 1800 and the early 1900s. The written text of most treaties in Ontario and the Prairies provides that Aboriginal peoples give up their title to large tracts of land. In exchange, First Nations get small reserves, small annual payments to individuals, and the right to hunt and fish off the reserve in certain circumstances. Other treaties may not refer to land surrenders but may provide for other things such as protection of religion.[9]

The First Nations' views on the meaning of treaties are different from the views of non-Aboriginal peoples[10]. In general, Aboriginal people argue that they did not understand or were misled about what the written words of the treaties meant for their way of life. They argue that the Crown does not honour the spirit and intent of the treaties.

Treaty No. 9, signed in northern Ontario, offers an example. According to the written text of this treaty, the Aboriginal people signed away all their rights to land in northern Ontario, in return for small reserves. They were left with one square mile for every 400 square miles surrendered, $8 each on signing of the treaty, plus a yearly treaty payment of $4 per person per year. The written text was drawn up in Ottawa in complex legal language. Federal Treaty Commissioners brought these texts for signing at a variety of Hudsons Bay posts across the north. Although the Aboriginal people expressed concern about their hunting rights, and were assured their hunting rights would be respected, the written version of the treaty contained many clauses limiting these rights. The participation of the provincial representative ensured that the reserves were located on unfavourable land, far from any rivers with hydro-electric potential.

The terms of the treaty were so unfair to the Indians that in 1978 an Ontario District Court Judge said:

> When Treaty No. 9 was negotiated, the parties to the Agreement were on grossly unequal footings. Highly skilled negotiators were dealing with an illiterate people, who, though fearful of losing their way of life, placed great faith in the fairness of His Majesty, as represented by federal authorities. As a matter of fact, a careful reading of the Commissioners' Reports makes it fairly obvious that the Indians thought they were dealing with the King's personal representatives and were relying on the word of His Majesty rather than officials of Government. They agreed to give up their interest in their land for a few reserves (carefully chosen by the Government to be far away from any potential sources of hydro power) and a few dollars per year per family. As a result, approximately 90,000 square miles of resource-rich land was acquired by the Crown, free of any beneficial Indian interest, for an absurdly low consideration (even for that time). It is still not clear whether Indian treaties are to be considered basically as private contracts or as international agreements. If the former, then the very validity of this treaty might very well be questioned on the basis of undue influence as well as other grounds.[11]

Since 1982, Canadian courts have been attempting to take into account the First Nations' perspectives, but treaties do not fit easily into categories recognized by Canadian law. The courts have concluded that treaties are not ordinary contracts because contracts only bind the people who sign them, whereas treaties set out rights which apply to everyone. They are not the equivalent of international treaties, because they do not deal with sovereign nation states. And they are not completely meaningless promises because courts have been willing to enforce them in the right circumstances. The Supreme Court of Canada has decided that they are unique documents, for which unique rules of interpretation and enforcement must be developed by the courts.[12]

A number of modern land claims agreements, beginning with the historic James Bay and Northern Quebec Agreement of 1975, have been signed or are being negotiated. These include the Inuvialuit Agreement of the Western Arctic, the Nunavut Agreement of the eastern Arctic and agreements in the Yukon and the Northwest Territories. These agreements are modern day treaties which are constitutionally protected.[13] The written versions of the treaties are no longer relied on exclusively. Historical evidence of the actual intentions of the First Nations and the Crown will be considered in determining treaty rights.[14]

5. OVERRIDING OR INFRINGING ABORIGINAL OR TREATY RIGHTS

The amendment to the Constitution in 1982 has made it difficult or impossible to extinguish existing Aboriginal rights without the consent of the Aboriginal people. However, in certain circumstances, the Crown can regulate the exercise of an Aboriginal right without the need for the Aboriginal consent.

In *R. v. Sparrow*,[15] a member of a First Nation in British Columbia caught fish off-reserve in traditional waters. He was charged for using a net that was longer than permitted by federal Fisheries Regulations. His First Nation did not have a treaty. The Supreme Court of Canada held that the Aboriginal right to fish for food had not been extinguished. The court then held that a federal law could limit an Aboriginal right only if there were a very good reason for passing the law, and only if that law interferes with the Aboriginal right in the least intrusive way possible. If the law does not meet these tests, the law will be declared unconstitutional.[16]

The same principle applies to treaty rights. Courts have held that the test developed in *R. v. Sparrow* restricts the ability of the federal government to override rights contained in treaties.[17]

6. EXTINGUISHMENT OF ABORIGINAL AND TREATY RIGHTS

Because section 35(1) of the *Constitution Act, 1982* only recognizes *existing* Aboriginal and treaty rights, courts have held that rights could have been extinguished before 1982.

There are two theories on how Aboriginal rights could have been extinguished:

1. By treaty between the Aboriginal people concerned and the Crown.

    Canadian courts have held that a treaty could extinguish Aboriginal title to land,[18] as well as rights to hunt and fish.[19] Many First Nations argue that rights can only be affected through the treaty-making process. Therefore, if a treaty does not specifically refer to rights being given up (such as the right to self-government), it must be assumed that the right still exists.[20] As will be seen below, Canadian courts have held that rights could be extinguished outside the treaty-making process.

2. By the Crown taking some action which demonstrates a "clear intention" to extinguish specific Aboriginal rights.
    An example of such an intention is the taking away of commercial hunting rights in the Prairies by a constitutional amendment called the *Natural Resources Transfer Agreement*.[21] Aboriginal people generally disagree with this method of extinguishment, arguing instead that their consent is required before their rights can be affected.[22]

7. THE TREATY-MAKING PROCESS

In the past, many of the Crown documents were structured like real estate deals — in return for the surrender of land, money and reserves were promised. Modern negotiations on land and self-government, such as the *James Bay and Northern Quebec Agreement*, continued to be based on the same idea — surrender in return for benefits. This policy came under severe criticism because it purported to "extinguish rights that are part and parcel of Aboriginal identity."[23]

In 1996, the Royal Commission on Aboriginal Peoples recommended that a new relationship between Canada and Aboriginal nations be formalized through the treaty making process. Far from "surrendering" land or "extinguishing" Aboriginal rights, the new treaties would affirm existing Aboriginal rights, and provide for mutual recognition of Aboriginal and Crown rights with respect to land and governance. Through mutual recognition, the parties would have clarity with respect to their respective interests, and a mechanism for addressing differences or changes in circumstances as they arise. This process would help focus on the on-going relationship between the parties, and provide for periodic review of the agreement.

The modern treaties would be protected as treaty rights under section 35(1) of the *Constitution Act, 1982*. The advantage of constitutional protection would be that federal or provincial governments cannot override those treaty rights by ordinary legislation.

8. SPECIFIC ABORIGINAL AND TREATY RIGHTS

What follows is an indication of the types of rights that have been recognized. This is not a complete list. Some of the topics are addressed in more detail in other chapters.

(a) Title to Land[24]

In *Delgamuukw v. British Columbia*,[25] the Supreme Court of Canada set down tests for establishing Aboriginal title to land. It appears that a valid treaty or even an adhesion to a treaty might extinguish the Aboriginal title. Courts have not yet clearly decided whether Aboriginal title can be extinguished by the mere intention of government to extinguish such rights. (See Chapter 4, "Land" for more details.)

(b) Hunting and fishing for food and ceremonial purposes

Many treaties contain rights to hunt and fish. However, a treaty may also specifically extinguish a right to hunt or fish.[26] In the Prairie Provinces, the treaty rights to hunt and fish have been affected by a 1930 constitutional amendment (the *Natural Resources Transfer Agreement*) which limited hunting and fishing to food. Where rights to hunt and fish are not addressed in a treaty, they may survive as Aboriginal rights. A British Columbia Aboriginal person was found to have an existing Aboriginal right to fish in traditional territories in *R. v. Sparrow*.

While most cases are about Indians, such Aboriginal rights extend to Inuit, and a growing number of courts have recognized rights of Métis. (For more detail and these rights, see Chapter 3, "Hunting and Fishing," and Chapter 5, "Métis".)

(c) Commercial fishing rights

There is recognition of a limited commercial fishing right in three cases in British Columbia, Ontario and Nova Scotia. The right to sell fish is limited to earning a "modest livelihood." (See Chapter 3, "Hunting, Fishing and Trapping".)

(d) Trapping

Some treaties specifically mention a right to trap. In Ontario, the case of *Cheechoo v. R.*[27] held that a Treaty #9 Indian could not be regulated by provincial trapping legislation because the Treaty protected the right to trap. However, while the matter has yet been settled, there is a question about whether an activity that arose because of European influence, such as commercial trapping or commercial fishing, could be considered an Aboriginal right. (See Chapter 3, "Hunting, Fishing and Trapping".)

(e) Harvesting trees

In New Brunswick, First Nations succeeded at two trial courts in having Aboriginal or treaty rights to harvest trees recognized. However, the New Brunswick Court of Appeal overturned those decisions.[28]

(f) Religious practices

A 1860 Treaty with the Hurons which promised "free exercise of their religion, customs and trade with the English" was upheld by the Supreme Court of Canada.[29] In that case, the court set aside convictions of Hurons who were charged with "cutting down trees, camping and making fires" in contravention of a Quebec provincial law. The convictions were set aside because the Hurons were engaged in a traditional ceremony. However, Spirit Dancing in British Columbia was not accepted as a defence to assault charges when an individual who did not live in the reserve community was held against his will for a number of days.[30]

(g) Taxes and custom duties

A court held that the Mohawks of Akwesasne did not have to pay duty on goods brought in from the United States because they had an Aboriginal right to trade. The Aboriginal right extends to "non-commercial scale trade" with First Nations in Ontario or Quebec and to personal or collective use and consumption in Akwesasne.[31] In British Columbia, a judge found that the Sto:lo Nation had an Aboriginal right to use tobacco for religious purposes, and that such tobacco should not be subject to customs duties or tax.[32] In other cases, however, courts have enforced taxation of tobacco, as well as customs duties.[33]

(h) Right to Apply Customary Law

Canadian courts have recognized the existence of Aboriginal customary law in a number of circumstances. Customary marriage has been recognized in criminal cases when a wife refused to testify against her husband, and customary adoptions were recognized in the North.

However, in other cases, courts have refused to recognize customary law, and have followed federal or provincial law.[34]

(i) Medicine Chest, Education and other rights

Some treaties in force in the prairie provinces provide for a "medicine chest", education and such items as twine for nets.[35] Cases have attempted to "modernize" these concepts. For example, Prairie

Indians argued that the "medicine chest" clause meant that there was a right to medical care.[36] While these cases have met with mixed success in the past, the tendency now is to provide an interpretation that does not freeze centuries-old concepts. In the *Sparrow* case, for example, the Supreme Court of Canada held that Aboriginal rights (the case was not dealing with treaty rights) should be seen in a modern way, and not be frozen in time. The court quoted Professor Brian Slattery who said that the rights are "affirmed in a contemporary form rather than in their primeval simplicity and vigour."[37]

(j) Gaming

Arguments that First Nations could run bingos and casinos without provincial authority have been rejected. Courts have held that there were no Aboriginal or treaty rights to such gaming on a commercial scale,[38] although there may be a right to gaming within the Aboriginal community.[39] (See Chapter 17, " Economic Development" for more on gaming.)

(k) Right to Self-Government

Aboriginal people say that right to self-government is already recognized as an existing Aboriginal right under section 35(1) of the Constitution. The federal government, and some of the provinces have followed the view of the Royal Commission on Aboriginal Peoples that self-government rights are protected by the Constitution. While self-government provisions have made it into most agreements, there is still disagreement on the contents of self-government. The Supreme Court of Canada has decided not to rule on its existence or non-existence at the present time. (For more information, see Chapter 7, "Aboriginal Self-government".)

ENDNOTES

1 With the Royal Proclamation of 1763, the Crown protects Indian interests against incursions by settlers and regional government. The Royal Proclamation of October 7, 1763, R.S.C. 1970, App. II, No. 1 reads, in part:

> And whereas it is just and reasonable, and essential to our Interest . . . that the several Nations or Tribes of Indians . . . should not be molested or disturbed in the Possession of such Parts of Our Dominions and

Territories as, not having been ceded to or purchased by Us, are reserved to them . . . as their Hunting Grounds. We do therefore . . . declare . . . that no Governor or Commander in Chief in any of our Colonies . . . do presume, upon any Pretence whatever, to grant Warrants of Survey, or pass any Patents for Lands beyond the Bounds of their respective Governments . . .

And We do further strictly enjoin and require all Persons whatever who have either wilfully or inadvertently seated themselves upon any Lands . . . which, not having been ceded to or purchased by Us, are still reserved to the said Indians . . . forthwith to remove themselves from such Settlements.

And whereas great Frauds and Abuses have been committed in purchasing Lands of the Indians, to the great Prejudice of our Interests, and to the great Dissatisfaction of the said Indians; In order, therefore, to prevent such Irregularities for the future, and to the end that the Indians may be convinced of our Justice and determined Resolution to remove all reasonable Cause of Discontent, We do . . . strictly enjoin and require, that no private Person do presume to make any purchase from the said Indians of any Lands reserved to the said Indians . . . but that, if at any Time any of the Said Indians should be inclined to dispose of the said Lands, the same shall be Purchased only for Us, in our Name, at some public Meeting or Assembly of the said Indians . . .

For a full account of this remarkable occasion, see John Borrows, "Constitutional Law from a First Nation Perspective: Self-government and the Royal Proclamation", (1994) 28 U.B.C. Law Rev. 1.

2 In *R. v. Syliboy* (1928), [1929] 1 D.L.R. 307 (N.S. Co. Ct.) it was held that the Treaty of 1752 was not enforceable by Indians. Judge Patterson stated at pp. 313–14:

The savages' rights of sovereignty even of ownership were never recognized. Nova Scotia had passed to Great Britain not by gift or purchase from or even by conquest of the Indians but by Treaty with France, which had acquired it by priority of discovery and ancient possession and the Indians passed with it.

Indeed the very fact that certain Indians sought from the Governor the privilege or right to hunt in Nova Scotia as usual shows that they did not claim to be an independent nation owning or possessing their lands. If they were, why go to another nation asking this privilege or right and giving promise of good behaviour that they might obtain it?

For cases that determined treaty rights could be overridden see *R. v George*, [1966] S.C.R. 267 (S.C.C.); *R. v. Sikyea*, [1964] S.C.R. 642 (S.C.C.).

3 Royal Commission on Aboriginal Peoples, *People to People, Nation to Nation* (1996), Canada Communications Group, pp. x–xi.

4 The connection between the communal rights on the nation and the benefits enjoyed by individuals is described by the British Columbia Court of Appeal in *Pasco v. Canadian National Railway* (1989), (sub nom. *Oregon Jack Creek Indian Band v. Canadian National Railway Co.*), [1990] 2 C.N.L.R. 85 (B.C. C.A.) at pp. 89–90:

> It is a mistake, in my view, to conclude that aboriginal rights vest in an entity (which clearly does not exist today) and to ignore the historical fact that the rights are communal, and that they are possessed today by the descendants of the persons who originally held them. They are not personal rights in the sense that they exist independently of the community, but are personal in the sense that a violation of the communal rights affect the individual member's enjoyment of those rights. Individuals representing all other persons who can claim those rights must have status to do so if any claim is to be made. To hold that only the nation can make the claims in reality to hold that no claim can be made.

For more discussion of groups rights, see Randy Kapashesit & Murray Klippenstein, "Aboriginal Group Rights and Environmental Protection" (1991), 36 McGill Law Journal 926.

5 An excellent place to begin this re-evaluation is with the article by Michael Asch and Catherine Bell "Definition and Interpretation of Fact in Canadian Aboriginal Title Litigation: An Analysis of *Delgamuukw*" (1994) 19 Queen's Law Journal 503. Other articles include Joel Fortune "Construing Delgamuukw: Legal Argument, Historical Argumentation and the Philosophy of History" (1993) 51 U.T. Fac. L. Rev. 80.; Clay McLeod, "The Oral Histories of Canada's Northern People, Anglo-Canadian Evidence Law, and Canada's Fiduciary Duty to First Nations: Breaking Down the Barriers of the Past" (1992) 30 Alta. L. Rev. (No. 4) 1276; Antonia Mills, *Eagle Down is Our Law: Witsuwit'en Law, Feasts and Land Claims* (Vancouver: U.B.C. Press , 1994); Geoff Sherrott, "The Court's Treatment of the Evidence in *Delgamuukw v. B.C.*" (1992) 56 Sask.L.Rev. 441.

6 At pp. 1047-48. The most important cases for determining the tests used to establish Aboriginal rights are *R. v. Vanderpeet*, [1996] 4 C.N.L.R. 177 (S.C.C.) [hereinafter *R. v. Vanderpeet*]; *R. v. Adams*, [1993] 3 C.N.L.R. 98 (C.A. Qué.), infirmé [1996] 4 C.N.L.R. 1 (C.S.C.) [herinafter *R. v. Adams*]; and *Delgamuukw v. British Columbia*, [1997] 3 S.C.R. 1010 [hereinafter *Delgamuukw v. British Columbia*].

7 The requirements for establishing Aboriginal title are outlined in *Delgamuukw v. British Columbia, supra* note 6, especially at D.L.R. pages 254–259.

8 The requirements for establishing Aboriginal customs or traditions prior to contact are in *R. v. Vanderpeet, supra* note 6.

9 The Murray Treaty addresses religion. See *Sioui v. Quebec (Attorney General)*, (sub nom. *R. v. Sioui*) [1990] 3 C.N.L.R. 127, (S.C.C.).

10 For an account of an indigenous perspective on treaty-making, see Sharon Venne, "Understanding Treaty 6: An Indigenous Perspective" in in Michael Asch, ed. *Aboriginal and Treaty Rights in Canada: Essays on Law, Equity, and Respect for Difference* (Vancouver, British Columbia: University of British Columbia Press, 1997).

11 The case describing the unfairness of Treaty No. 9 is *R. v. Battisse* (1978), 19 O.R. (2d) 145 (Ont. Dist. Ct.). See also Patrick Macklem "The Impact of Treaty 9 on Natural Resources and Development in Northern Ontario" in Michael Asch, ed. *Aboriginal and Treaty Rights in Canada: Essays on Law, Equity, and Respect for Difference* (Vancouver, British Columbia: University of British Columbia Press, 1997) at 97.

12 On treaties, Chief Justice Dickson said in *R. v. Simon*, [1986] 1 C.N.L.R. 153 (S.C.C.) at p. 169:

> An Indian treaty is unique; it is an agreement <u>sui generis</u> which is neither created nor terminated according to the rules of international law.

See also *R. v. Sioui*, [1990] 3 C.N.L.R. 127 (S.C.C.) where the court determined that the relationship between the Huron and the Crown was partly nation to nation; J. Woodward, *Native Law* (Toronto: Carswell, 1989) at pp. 404–405.

13 *Constitution Act, 1982*, section 35(3) provides:

> For greater certainty, in subsection (1) "treaty rights" includes rights that now exist by way of land claims agreements or may be so acquired.

See *Crie (Commission scolaire) c. Canada (Procureur général)*, (sub nom. *Cree School Board v. Canada (Attorney General)*) [1998] 3 C.N.L.R. 24 (C.S. Qué.) where the judge affirmed that rights in the James Bay and Northern Quebec Agreeement were treaty rights.

14 See *R. v. Marshall* (1998), 231 N.R. 325 (note), 223 A.R. 398 (note), 183 W.A.C. 398 (note) (S.C.C.), which found that a treaty covering the Mi'kmaq from 1760 should include rights to catch eel and sell for commercial purposes, even though the written version of the treaty did not specifically provide for such a right.

15 *R. v. Sparrow*, [1990] 3 C.N.L.R. 160 (S.C.C.) [hereinafter *R. v. Sparrow*].

16 A summary of the test used in *Sparrow* to justify interference with an Aboriginal right is as follows:

1. Does the federal law interfere with an activity that is within the scope of the Aboriginal right?

2. If there is an interference, the federal government must show that

(a) there was valid reason for making the law, such as conserving and managing the resource, or preventing the exercise of a right in a way which would cause harm to the general populace or Aboriginal peoples, or other objectives which are "compelling and substantial"

(b) the law upholds the honour of the Crown, and is in keeping with the unique contemporary relationship grounded in history and policy, between the Crown and Canada's Aboriginal peoples. In fishing, this means giving priority fishing to Aboriginal people first, with any excess to non-Aboriginal people

(c) the government has addressed other factors, such as infringing the Aboriginal right as little as possible, providing fair compensation to Aboriginal people affected, and consulting with Aboriginal group concerned.

17 Legislation which infringes treaty rights must be justified using the tests set out in *Sparrow*, see *R. v. Badger*, [1996] 2 C.N.L.R. 77 (S.C.C.), *R. v. Côté*, [1996] 4 C.N.L.R. 26 (R.C.S.), *R. c. Adams*, [1996] 4 C.N.L.R. 1 (R.C.S.), *R. v. Gladstone*, [1996] 4 C.N.L.R. 65 (S.C.C.).

18 Aboriginal title could be extinguished by adhesion to a treaty. See *Ontario (Attorney General) v. Bear Island Foundation*, [1991] 3 C.N.L.R. 79, (S.C.C) [hereinafter *Ontario (A.G.) v. Bear Island Foundation*, 1991]. For an analysis of the consequences of the Bear Island decision, see Kent McNeil, "The High Cost of Accepting Benefits from the Crown: A Comment on the Temagami Indian Land Case" in [1992] 1 C.N.L.R. 40, and pages 62–68 with respect to extinguishment of Aboriginal rights.

19 For an example of a situation in which a court found that a treaty can extinguish an Aboriginal right, see *R. v. Howard*, [1994] 3 C.N.L.R. 146 (S.C.C.). The Supreme Court of Canada found that a 1923 treaty explicitly addressed the right to fish, and extinguished that right off-reserve.

20 In the United States the idea that an Aboriginal right was not relinquished by a treaty unless there was an express intention in the treaty is called the reserved rights doctrine.

21 One example of such a clear and plain intention is found in *R. v. Horseman*, [1990] 3 C.N.L.R. 95 (S.C.C.) in which the Supreme Court of Canada held that Treaty #8 hunting was unilaterally altered by the National Resources Transfer Agreement.

Two views on what is necessary for unilateral extinguishment of an Aboriginal interest in land are raised by the Supreme Court of Canada in *Canadian Pacific Ltd. v. Paul*, [1989] 1 C.N.L.R. 47 (S.C.C.). One view is that "Indian title" to land was extinguished simply by "alienation and other acts inconsistent with the existence of aboriginal title." In other words, the surrender of land to the Crown, and later use of that land in a manner which is inconsistent with the Aboriginal title, is sufficient to extinguish the right.

The second view is that the legislature may extinguish an Aboriginal right to land if the intention to extinguish the right is "clear and plain."

In *R. v. Sparrow*, *supra* note 15 at [1990] 3 C.N.L.R. 160, the Supreme Court of Canada said at pages 174–5 that "the test of extinguishment to be adopted, in our opinion, is that the Sovereign's intention must be clear and plain if it is to extinguish an aboriginal right."

22 On the subject of requiring the consent of Aboriginal people before affecting Aboriginal rights, see Patrick Macklem, "First Nations Self-Government and the Borders of the Canadian Legal Imagination" [1991] 36 McGill Law Journal 382. For example, Macklem states at page 405:

Discovery, properly understood, vests only the exclusive right to acquire title from native people as against other potential nations. This holding is critical to the development of a set of principles governing the common law of Aboriginal title that would facilitate the realization of self-government, for it challenges the assumption that the Crown holds underlying title to native land, and instead suggests that Crown regulation or extinguishment of the native proprietary interest at common law cannot occur absent native consent.

See also Kent McNeil, *Common Law Aboriginal Title*, (Oxford: Clarendon Press, 1989) [hereinafter Kent McNeil] at pages 193–243 and 298–306.

23 For a detailed analysis of the issue of extinguishment in treaty negotiations, see Royal Commission on Aboriginal Peoples, *Treaty Making in the Spirit of Co-existence: An Alternative to Extinguishment* (Ottawa: Canada Communications Group, 1995) at 62. At around the same time that the Royal Commission released this report, the Minister of Indian Affairs and Northern Development, Ron Irwin, appointed the Hon.A.C. Hamilton as a Fact Finder on the same issue. See his report, *A New Partnership* (Ottawa: Minister of Public Works and Government Services, 1995).

24 On the topic of whether Aboriginal possession and use of land constitutes title, see Kent McNeil, *supra* note 22.

25 The leading case on Aboriginal title is *Delgamuukw v. British Columbia, supra* note 6.

26 An example of a court ruling that a treaty surrendered a fishing right is *R. v. Howard, supra* note 19 where the Supreme Court of Canada held that the Hiawatha First Nation gave up their rights through their 1923 Treaty.

27 On the subject of trapping as a treaty right, see *Cheechoo v. R.* (1980), [1981] 3 C.N.L.R. 45 (Ont. Dist. Ct.).

28 For the decision that overturned the decisions that recognized Aboriginal or treaty rights to harvest trees see *R. v. Peter Paul* (1993), [1994] 2 C.N.L.R. 167 (N.B. C.A.).

29 On the subject of religious practices as a treaty right, see *Sioui v. Quebec (Attorney General)*, (sub nom. *R. v. Sioui*), [1990] 3 C.N.L.R. 127 (S.C.C.)

30 *Thomas v. Norris*, [1992] 2 C.N.L.R. 139 (B.C. S.C) where religious practices were rejected as a defence to assault charges.

31 *Mitchell v. Canada (Minister of National Revenue* (1998), (sub nom. *Mitchell v. Canada (Minister of National Revenue))* [1999] 1 C.N.L.R. 112 (Fed.C.A.) the Mohawks of Akwesasne established an Aboriginal right to trade with other Mohawk communities.

32 While the court found an Aboriginal right to use tobacco for religious, ceremonial and healing purposes in *R. v. Jacobs* (1998), [1999] 3 C.N.L.R. 239 (B.C. S.C.) it is important to note that, in this case, the accused were convicted because they were bringing in tobacco for commercial sale.

33 See *Francis v. R.*, [1956] S.C.R. 618 (S.C.C.). A Mohawk brought goods into Canada purchased in the United States, and said that the Jay Treaty exempted Indians from paying duty. The court dismissed his claim stating that the terms of general legislation apply to Indians equally with other citizens of Canada, therefore, customs duties were payable. In *R. v. Murdock* (1996), [1997] 2 C.N.L.R. 103 (N.S. C.A.) the accused were convicted of conspiring to defraud the Nova Scotia government of tobacco tax. Murdock bought tobacco products in the United States and Ontario and sold them to Johnson, a retailer on an Indian reserve. The court held that their Aboriginal rights under section 35 of the *Constitution Act* were not infringed, as the scope of the Aboriginal right to use tobacco did not extend to dealing and trading tobacco between Indian bands and non-natives. It was held that tobacco tax applied. In *Québec (Sous-ministre du Revenu) c. Sioui* (1995), [1996] 1 C.N.L.R. 122 (C.S. Qué.), confirmé (1996), [1997] 3 C.N.L.R. 88 (C.A. Qué.), autorisation de pourvoi refusée (sub nom. *Sioui c. Sous-Ministre du Revenu du Québec)* [1997] 4 C.N.L.R. iv (C.S.C.) the

accused failed to collect sales tax for his business. One of his arguments was that he was exempt from collecting sales tax by virtue of the Murray Treaty of 1760. The court held that the Murray Treaty, under which the Hurons were guaranteed the right to free exercise of their customs, did not exempt them from the obligation to collect taxes.

34 On the subject of courts recognizing customary law, see N.K. Zlotkin, "Judicial Recognition of Aboriginal Customary Law in Canada: Selected Mariage and Adoption Cases" [1984] 4 C.N.L.R. 1. Recent cases include *Casimel v. Insurance Corp. of British Columbia* (1991), [1992] 1 C.N.L.R. 84 (B.C. S.C.), reversed (1993), [1994] 2 C.N.L.R. 22 (B.C. C.A.), in which the court held that a Stellaquo First Nation custom adoption was an Aboriginal right. The court ordered the insurance company to pay benefits to the elderly parents of an adopted child who had died in a car accident.

An Aboriginal right to customary marriage was recognized in *Manychief v. Poffenroth* (1994), [1995] 2 C.N.L.R. 67 (Alta. Q.B.)

35 On the subject of treaty clauses providing particular rights, Treaty No. 3, for example provides that the Queen shall spend $1,500.00 every year "in the purchase of ammunition and twine for nets for the use of the said Indians."

36 On the subject of a right to health care in treaties, a clause in Treaty No. 6 states "a medicine chest shall be kept at the house of each Indian Agent for the use and benefit of the Indians at the direction of such agent". Although a Federal Court judge held that this meant that medicine should be supplied free to the Indians (*Dreaver v. R.* (1935), 5 C.N.L.C. 92 (Can. Ex. Ct.)), two Saskatchewan Court of Appeal cases (*R. v. Johnston* (1966), 56 W.W.R. 565 (Sask. C.A.) and *R. v. Swimmer*, [1971] 1 W.W.R. 756 (Sask. C.A.)) in 1966 and 1970 held that the right did not encompass free hospital care. The appeal court emphasized that the supplies were to be used "at the direction of the agent", thereby suggesting that the government still had the power to supervise the supplies. In *Wuskwi Sipihk Cree Nation v. Canada (Minister of National Health and Welfare)*, [1999] F.C.J. No. 82 (Fed. T.D.) the Federal Court cast doubt on the reasoning in the two Saskatchewan Court of Appeal cases, because they were decided before there was constitutional affirmation of treaty rights. Instead, the court felt that the decision in *R. v. Dreaver* was probably correct.

See also Peter A. Barkwell, "The Medicine Chest Clause in Treaty No. 6", [1981] 4 C.N.L.R. 1.

In Treaty No. 3 the provision on education provides:

Her Majesty agrees to maintain schools for instruction in such reserves hereby made as to Her Government of Her Dominion of Canada may seem advisable whenever the Indians of the reserve shall desire it.

In 1989, Indian students went on a hunger strike to protest against cutbacks on financial assistance for post-secondary education, arguing that provisions like those in Treaty No. 3 should be modernized to reflect a right to financial assistance in education.

37 On the subject of the interpretation of rights in a contemporary fashion, see *R. v. Sparrow, supra* note 13.

38 The leading case on gaming is *R. v. Jones*, (sub nom. *R. v. Pamajewon*), [1996] 4 C.N.L.R. 164 (S.C.C.). See also, *R. v. Jim* (1995), [1996] 1 C.N.L.R. 160, (B.C. C.A.), leave to appeal refused [1996] 3 C.N.L.R. (S.C.C.) The cases which have acquitted Indians for gaming have been because there was an honest belief (*R. v. Bear Claw Casino Ltd.* [1994] 4 C.N.L.R. 81 (Sask. Prov. Ct.) or a violation of section 15 (*R. v. Bob* [1991] 2 C.N.L.R. 104 (Sask. C.A.)

39 *R. v. Nelson* (1997), [1998] 2 C.N.L.R. 137 (Man. Prov. Ct.), affirmed (September 13, 1999), Doc. AR 98-30-03609 (Man. C.A.) found that the evidence supported a right to play in traditional Ojibway games. However, gambling on a commercial scale was not "an integral aspect of the distinctive culture of the Ojibway people prior to contact" and was therefore not protected by the Constitution.

3

Hunting, Fishing and Trapping

POINTS TO REMEMBER

1. Registered Indians and Inuit will not be charged for hunting for food or ceremonial purposes in any season, on their traditional territories. However, principles of safety and conservation must be followed.

2. In recent years, the rights of Métis and non-registered Indians to hunt and fish for food have been recognized.

3. The courts will prevent federal laws from infringing on treaty or Aboriginal rights unless the federal government proves that such laws are necessary for conservation or other valid reasons.

4. Courts have begun to extend recognition to very limited commercial rights to hunt or fish.

5. New gun control regulations require registration, licensing and training, but some subsistence hunters are exempt from some fees.

1. INTRODUCTION

Some of the most bitter struggles have involved hunting and fishing rights. Its importance for Aboriginal people is not restricted to livelihood, but extends to community well-being and continuity of their cultures and societies.[1] To many Aboriginal communities, subsistence is a means of reaffirming Aboriginal identity by passing on traditional knowledge to future generations. Subsistence in this sense moves beyond mere economics, encompassing the cultural, social and spiritual aspects of the communities.[2]

2. SOURCES OF HUNTING AND FISHING RIGHTS

Hunting, fishing and trapping rights come from a variety of sources:

- many treaties mention that Indians will continue to be able to hunt, fish or trap over their traditional territory[3]
- in the Prairie provinces, the Natural Resources Transfer Agreement extended treaty rights to hunt for food, but took away commercial hunting rights
- an Aboriginal right to hunt, fish and trap in traditional territories has been recognized since the *R. v. Sparrow* decision in 1989[4]

These rights conflict with provincial and federal laws, such as the provincial game and fish acts[5], the federal *Fisheries Act*[6] and the federal *Migratory Birds Convention Act, 1994*.[7]

(a) Treaties

When treaties were made with Aboriginal people, hunting and fishing rights were often addressed explicitly. The report of the Treaty Commissioners on the negotiations for Treaty No. 9 includes an exchange that must have been repeated all across Canada. The Treaty Commissioner was Duncan Campbell Scott. He met Missabay, the blind Chief at Osnaburgh in Ontario, in 1905:

> Missabay, the recognized chief of the band, then spoke, expressing the fears of the Indians that, if they signed the treaty, they would be compelled to reside upon the reserve to be set apart for them, and would be deprived of the fishing and hunting privileges which they now enjoy.
>
> On being informed that their fears in regard to both these matters were groundless, as their present manner of making their livelihood would in no way be interfered with, the Indians talked the matter over among themselves, and then asked to be given till the following day to prepare their reply.[8]

The written words of the treaty, unfortunately, gave a different story: hunting, trapping and fishing rights were "subject to such regulations as may from time to time be made by the government of the country," and the activities could not be carried on where land was taken up for "settlement, mining, lumbering, trading or other purposes." Words like these in Treaty No. 9 and other treaties have been used by governments and courts to curtail First Nation rights. It clearly was not the intention of the First Nations that all of the lands would be "taken up" so that hunting would be impossible. However, the provincial and federal governments acted as if they had unilateral authority to remove as much land as they wished from the hunting territory. Now, almost every square inch of land in Canada is subject to many interests — forest licenses, cottages, highway rights of way, mining claims and so forth.

In addition, before the Constitution changed in 1982, the courts permitted the federal government to pass laws which actually contravened the treaty.[9] For example, courts had upheld prosecutions for the spring goose hunt under the federal *Migratory Birds Convention Act*. This was in spite of the fact that the treaty guaranteed the right to hunt and there was no evidence that there was a danger to conservation. Under the *Fisheries Act*, the federal government authorized provinces to pass regulations to restrict fishing rights, which also contravened guarantees in treaties.

After 1982, with the constitutional recognition of treaty rights, the law changed. It is now clear that treaty rights can only be overridden if the legislation meets the test laid out in *R. v. Sparrow*.[10] That is:

- there was a valid legislative objective, such as conservation or resource management;
- government acted in accordance with the special trust relationship which the court found to exist with Indians, and gave priority to the treaty right over other uses, such as sport fishing;
- the degree of infringement of the treaty right was minimized;
- there was consultation with the Aboriginal people affected.

Following *R. v. Sparrow*, some of the earlier decisions have been reversed, including the decisions which prohibited the spring goose hunt.[11]

(b) The Natural Resources Transfer Agreement

In 1930, the federal government transferred control of the natural resources of the three prairie provinces to those provinces. As part of this transfer, the provinces were to honour rights of " . . . hunting, trapping and fishing game and fish for food at all seasons of the year on all unoccupied Crown lands and on any other lands to which the said Indians may have a right of access."[12]

This provision extended the right to hunt for food throughout the province, even outside the treaty area. However, according to the Supreme Court of Canada, it extinguished any commercial hunting rights.[13]

(c) Aboriginal Rights

After the decision in *R. v. Sparrow*, Aboriginal rights to hunt and fish for food and ceremonial purposes have been given greater recognition by courts and Crown governments.

Once an Aboriginal right to food is recognized, it must be given priority over other sports or commercial users. This was the issue in the case of two young men who were members of the Chemainus Band. They were caught early in the morning with 27 chum and eight coho salmon taken in gill nets, which was prohibited by the *Fisheries Regulations*. In deciding to acquit the two, the court held that sufficient priority had not been given to the Indian food fishery. Noting that sports and commercial fishers had depleted the stocks of salmon, the court stated:

> While prohibiting members of the Chemainus Band from fishing by gill net in Ladysmith Harbour, the DFO nevertheless allowed sport fishers to troll for salmon throughout the calendar year within Ladysmith Harbour and also beyond the entrance to Ladysmith Harbour (at 204 [C.N.L.R.]).[14]

Other examples of insufficient priority include a lottery scheme for hunting licenses which gave no priority to Indians[15], and an across-the-board reduction in fishing quotas which did not give priority to Indian food fishing.[16]

Métis hunting and fishing rights are now being recognized as well. (See Chapter 5, "Métis").

3. SCOPE OF RIGHTS

This section describes some issues around activities which are protected by rights to hunt or fish.

(a) Incidental activity

To hunt or fish necessarily involves related activity. Courts have recognized that carrying a gun to the hunting ground,[17] teaching youth how to fish[18] and building a cabin in a park[19] are all included in hunting and fishing rights.

(b) Conservation

There is general agreement among Aboriginal and non-Aboriginal people that the principle of conservation must continue to be paramount. The federal and provincial governments often argue that their laws are needed for conservation. However, enforcement of game laws against Aboriginal people may not coincide with any demonstrated need for conservation.

For example, in 1988, the RCMP laid charges against Moose Factory Crees during their traditional spring goose hunt because the hunt contravened the *Migratory Birds Convention Act*, which only permitted hunting in the fall. As it turned out, provincial Ministry of Natural Resources officials could point out that the goose population was not in danger. As well, it became evident that if a threat to the goose population were to develop, it would be from the massive goose hunt conducted by thousands of sports hunters in the United States, not from a few hundred Crees hunting for food in northern Ontario.[20] The charges were eventually stayed by the Attorney-General of Canada when publicity and First Nation defiance brought the matter to the attention of federal politicians.

In another case a year earlier, a judge commented that the Ministry of Natural Resources had not demonstrated the need for conservation in its decision to restrict the fishers from Kettle Point reserve.[21]

Generally, judges will look for specific evidence on the impact of certain activity on conservation, not generalized statements about the need for conservation. So, in *R. v. Jack*[22] the court acquitted a hereditary chief of the Mowachaht Band for fishing in his traditional territory. In that area, fishing for salmon was prohibited for conservation purposes. The court pointed out, however, that at the same time, sports fishers were allowed to catch two chinook daily in a nearby area. Because the Indian food fishery was not given the appropriate priority, the chief was acquitted. The Neskonlith, on the other hand, went to court to complain that the federal government was not doing enough for conservation by allowing too much salmon to be taken by sports fishers. The court here rejected the attempt by the Neskonlith to restrict sport fishing.[23]

To approach the issue of conservation properly, several initiatives are under way to develop measures jointly between Aboriginal people and the Crown. These steps are in line with the Crown's fiduciary duty to consult Aboriginal peoples about measures which affect them.[24] Courts have shown deference to such arrangements, and there are cases of individual members of an Aboriginal group being convicted for violating the arrangement.[25]

(c) Safety

Although there may be agreement that there should be enforcement when there are safety issues, there could be disagreements about what is meant by safety. The more thoughtful judges will consider the impact of safety in a specific fact situation, as opposed to generalized statements about safety.

An example of the better approach is found in *R. v. Fox*.[26] Here, the accused, an Indian protected by Treaty No. 9, was hunting water fowl from a canoe fitted with an outboard motor. He was charged with unlawfully discharging a firearm from a powerboat. The Ontario *Game and Fish Act*, provides that no person shall have a loaded firearm in or on, or discharge the same from a powerboat. The Crown argued that the provisions were a justifiable infringement of the accused's treaty rights based on safety issues. However, the act also provides that if the Minister is satisfied that the holder of a license is incapable of walking and relies on a wheelchair, the Minister can authorize such person to have a loaded firearm and to discharge from a power-boat, not in motion. The Court stated that if safety was the purpose, it would not make sense to allow some people to hunt from a boat, but not others.

Night hunting is generally considered unsafe.[27] However, in *R. v. Machimity*[28] the court found that non-Aboriginal people could be authorized to hunt at night. Therefore, the question was not whether all hunting at night was dangerous, but whether it was dangerous in that particular circumstance. Machimity was acquitted because the Crown did not prove that he was hunting dangerously.

Because the safety issue might involve an infringement of Aboriginal rights or treaty rights, the governments must adequately consult the Aboriginal peoples affected.[29]

4. TERRITORY

The fact that a right to hunt or fish exists in one area does not mean that it can be exercised anywhere. The territory in which the right can be exercised depends on the source of the right.

(a) Treaty areas

While exercising hunting and fishing rights within the treaty territory is well accepted, courts have more difficulty when those rights are exercised outside the territory.[30] Within the territory, hunting and fishing are not allowed on lands that are occupied. According to the courts, hunting on private land is not covered by treaty because such land has been taken up for settlement, and therefore taken away from hunting territory. Exactly which lands are settled, and therefore taken out of the treaty is the matter of some controversy. The shoulder of a highway, for example, has been found to be land which was still subject to a treaty right to hunt.[31]

(b) Natural Resources Transfer Agreement

Hunting for food throughout the province is recognized.[32] Hunting on private land may be allowed if there are no "visible, incompatible land use."[33]

(c) Traditional territory for exercise of Aboriginal Rights

Aboriginal rights are not necessarily restricted to lands for which Aboriginal title can be established. In *R. v. Adams*[34] the Supreme Court held that Mohawks had an Aboriginal right to fish in territory which they had traversed in times past, but did not occupy until fairly recently.

5. COMMERCIAL ACTIVITY

(a) Commercial fishing

(i) *Treaty rights*

In Nova Scotia, the Supreme Court of Canada acquitted Donald Marshall Jr. for selling $787.10 worth of eels because of rights in a 1760 treaty. However, the right is limited to a "moderate livelihood" for Marshall and his family. The Union of Nova Scotia Indians had argued for a more expansive right to commercial fishing, but the court rejected that position.[35]

(ii) *Natural Resources Transfer Agreement*

Even though the treaties in the Prairie Provinces included a commercial right to hunt[36], and a commercial right to fish,[37] courts have held that they had been extinguished by the NRTA.

(iii) *Aboriginal right*

The Supreme Court of Canada found that the Heiltsuk First Nation had engaged in large scale "commercial" trade before contact with Europeans. This meant that the Heiltsuk should have priority for the commercial fishery, but not exclusive use of the resource.[38] An Ontario court judge found that the Saugeen Ojibway Nation had a right to commercial fishery for Band sustenance.[39] However, other cases have found that Aboriginal nations do not have an Aboriginal right to a commercial fishery.[40]

(iv) *United States and New Zealand*

The United States and New Zealand have already addressed commercial fishing rights by Aboriginal people. In *Washington v. Washington State Commercial, Passenger & Fishing Vessel Assn.,*[41] the United States Supreme Court considered the fishing rights referred to in a treaties of 1854 and 1855. In those treaties Indian tribes surrendered their interest in certain lands, but they also protected the tribal "right of taking fish at usual and accustomed grounds and stations . . . in common with all the citizens of the Territory". Noting that "a treaty, including one between the United States and an Indian tribe, is essentially a contract between two sovereign nations", the court held that the intention was to divide the resource between the tribe and the settlers. The court stated that the tribe could take up to 50 per cent of the fish it needed to "provide the Indians with a livelihood — that is to say, a moderate living".[42]

In New Zealand, the Treaty of Waitangi provided for a Maori right to fish for food. There was a disagreement about the extent to which this right extended to commercial fishing. The matter was settled when New Zealand entered into a joint venture with the Maoris and transferred a 50 per cent interest of Sealords Products Ltd. to them. Sealords, a commercial fishing company, held 26 per cent of the fishing quota. In exchange, legislation extinguished Maori rights to fish commercially but preserved other treaty fishing rights.[43]

(b) Trapping

Some treaties specifically mention a right to trap. In Ontario, the case of *R. v. Cheechoo*[44] held that a Treaty No. 9 Indian could not be regulated by provincial trapping legislation because the Treaty protected the right to trap. However, some judges have raised a question about whether an activity that arose because of European influence, such as commercial trapping or commercial fishing, could be considered an Aboriginal right.[45] The matter is not yet settled.

6. GUN CONTROL

The importance of guns for sustenance hunting has always been recognized. In some cases, a person convicted of weapons offences has been allowed to use a gun for hunting purposes.[46] Although courts have held that the unsafe use of guns cannot be protected by treaty rights to hunt[47], courts have looked at whether or not the actual practice is unsafe.[48]

Gun control legislation was enacted mostly in response to the perception of a rise in urban crime involving firearms. The legislation requires registration of all guns, establishes a licensing scheme for users, and restricts the availability of certain dangerous weapons. In response to concerns raised by Aboriginal people, regulations exempt Aboriginal sustenance hunters from some requirements and some registration fees.

(a) Aboriginal Peoples

The *Aboriginal Peoples of Canada Adaption Regulations (Firearms)*[49] say that "Aboriginal" includes Indian, Inuit and Métis. But not every Aboriginal person can benefit from these special rules. An elder or leader must confirm that the person is a member of the Aboriginal community and engages in "traditional hunting practices."[50]

There is a clause in the Canadian *Firearms Act* which states that the Act does not abrogate or derogate from the Aboriginal and treaty rights recognized in the Constitution.[51]

(b) Registration of Existing Weapons

Registration of long guns began on October 1, 1998. All rifles and shotguns must be registered by January 1, 2003. A registration certificate will be issued for each firearm. It is valid for as long as a person owns the firearm. If the firearm is lent to another person, the registration certificate must also be lent.

To receive or transfer a firearm, a transfer authorization is necessary. At the time of transfer, a transfer authorization number will be issued to both the new and previous owners. This number will serve as a receipt for the previous owner and for the new owner until his or her registration certificate arrives in the mail.

For most people, registration fees are $10 for all firearms registered (rising to $18 by July 1, 2001). Transfer fees are $25. "Sustenance hunters" do not have to pay either fee. Each province and territory has its own definition of a sustenance hunter. Information on the local address and telephone number to find out the definition is available from 1-800-731-4000.

(c) License

Most people will require a license by January 1, 2001. They will usually have to take a Canadian Firearms Safety Course, and pass a test. The license must be renewed every five years, but it is not necessary to take a test each time.

A license may be refused for a number of reasons including, convictions for a weapons-related offence, a drug-related offence, a history of mental illness, or a history of violence. For Aboriginal people, before there is a refusal, the recommendations of an elder or community leader about the importance of engaging in traditional hunting practices will be considered.[52]

Fees for a possession license begin at $10 but by January 21, 2001 will rise to $80 for a five year possession and acquisition license. Fees are waived for sustenance hunters.

In certain very restricted circumstances an elder, or Aboriginal persons who cannot reach a Firearms Safety Course may be given licenses.[53]

(d) Minors

There are more strict restrictions on the use of firearms by minors from 12–18. Most minors must take the Canadian Firearms Safety Course and pass the test. Minors involved in sustenance hunting do not have to take the course or pass the test.

An Aboriginal minor of any age may obtain a possession license to engage in traditional hunting practices.[54]

ENDNOTES

1 See the Report of the Royal Commission on Aboriginal Peoples, *Restructuring the Relationship*, Volume 2, Part Two (Ottawa: Supply and Services Canada, 1996) at 448 [hereinafter RCAP, Vol.2.].

2 See RCAP, Vol. 2, *supra* note 1 at 463.

3 Treaty No. 9 states:

And his Majesty the King hereby agrees with the said Indians that they shall have the right to pursue their usual vocations of hunting, trapping and fishing throughout the tract surrendered as heretofore described, subject to such regulations as may from time to time be made by the government of the country, acting under the authority of His Majesty, and saving and excepting such tracts as may be required or taken up from time to time for settlement, mining, lumbering, trading or other purposes.

The Robinson Treaties state:

And the said William Benjamin Robinson of the first part, on behalf of Her Majesty and the Government of this Province, hereby promises and agrees to make the payments as before mentioned; and further to allow the said chiefs and their tribes the full and free privilege to hunt over the territory now ceded by them, and to fish in the waters thereof as they have heretofore been in the habit of doing, saving and excepting only such portions of the said territory as may from time to time be sold or leased to individuals, or companies of individuals, and occupied by them with the consent of the Provincial Government.

Oral promises can also be read as part of the treaty. In *R. v. Taylor* [1981] 3 C.N.L.R. 114 (Ont. C.A.), the Ontario Court of Appeal held that a member of the First Nation covered under Treaty No. 20 had a right to hunt bullfrogs. The promise that "(r)ivers are open to all you have an equal right to fish hunt on them" was contained at 119 [C.N.L.R.] in the minutes of a meeting, but not in the treaty itself. See also *R. v. Marshall* (1998), 231 N.R. 325 (note), 223 A.R. 398 (note), 183 W.A.C. 398 (note) (S.C.C.).

4 In *R. v. Sparrow*, [1990] 3 C.N.L.R. 160 (S.C.C.) the Supreme Court of Canada found that a member of the Musqueam First Nation had an Aboriginal right to fish for food in his traditional territory. Since then, there have been scores of court decisions discussing this right.

5 Ontario, see *Game and Fish Act*, R.S.O. 1990, c. G-1, as am. 1993, c. 27, Sched.; 1993, c. 31, s. 3; 1994, c. 17, ss. 65-66; 1994, c. 27, s.129; 1996, c. 1, Sched. N, s. 2; 1996, c. 14, s. 2; 1996, c. 17, Sched. E. Act Repealed by 1997, c. 41, s.119.

6 *Fisheries Act*, R.S.C. 1985, c. F-14.

7 *Migratory Birds Convention Act, 1994*, S.C. 1994, c. 22 [Unofficial Chapter No. M-7.01]

8 Patrick Macklem, "The Impact of Treaty 9 on Natural Resource Development in Northern Ontario" in Michael Asch, ed. *Aboriginal and Treaty Rights in Canada: Essays on Law, Equity, and Respect for Difference."* (Vancouver: U.B.C. Press, 1997) at 97–134 for a description of the process.

9 On the subject of federal laws contravening treaties, until the passage of the *Constitution Act, 1982*, a treaty that had not been confirmed by the passage of legislation was not self-executing or enforceable. The only protection for the terms of a treaty was s. 88 of the *Indian Act*: by virtue of this section, any provincial legislation which conflicted with the terms of a treaty was not applicable to Indians. This section did not, however, prevent the application of federal legislation. In three cases decided before 1982, the Supreme Court of Canada made it clear that the federal government could validly enact legislation which breached the terms of a treaty (See *R. v. Sikyea*, [1964] S.C.R. 642, (S.C.C.), *R. v. George*, [1966] S.C.R. 267, (S.C.C.), *Daniels v. White*, [1968] S.C.R. 517, (S.C.C.).

In 1990, the Supreme Court held in *R. v. Horseman*, [1990] 3 C.N.L.R. 95 (S.C.C.), that the Natural Resources Transfer Agreements in the prairies unilaterally restricted treaty hunting rights to food hunting only.

10 *R. v. Badger*, [1996] 2 C.N.L.R. 77 (S.C.C.) holds that treaty rights cannot be contravened without meeting a justification test. See also *R. v. Marshall* (1998), 231 N.R. 325 (note), 223 A.R. 398 (note), 183 W.A.C. 398 (note) (S.C.C.).

11 *R. v. Arcand*, [1989] 2 C.N.L.R. 110 (Alta. Q.B.) Arcand was charged under s. 5(4) of the Migratory Birds Regulations for hunting duck out of season on reserve land. Arcand was acquitted on the basis that s. 35(1) of the *Constitution Act* provided him with a complete defence to the charge.

In *R. v. Flett*, [1989] 4 C.N.L.R. 128 (Man. Q.B.), leave to appeal refused (1990), [1991] 1 C.N.L.R. 140, additional reasons at (1990), [1991] 1 C.N.L.R. 140 (Man. C.A.)), Flett was charged under the *Migratory Birds Convention Act* for hunting out of season and for having possession of two Canada geese. Flett was a member of The Pas Indian Band, a signatory to Treaty 5. The court adopted the original rights thesis, which was the reasoning in *R. v. Arcand*, and held that section 35 recognized and affirmed the treaty right to hunt. Flett was acquitted.

12 See the *Natural Resources Transfer Agreement, Constitution Act, 1930* R.S.C. 1985 Appendix II, No. 26.

13 In *R. v. Horseman*, [1990] 3 C.N.L.R. 95 (S.C.C.) the Supreme Court of Canada said that the *Natural Resources Transfer Agreement* (NRTA) extinguished the right to commercial hunting.

However, in *R. v. Badger*, [1996] 2 C.N.L.R. 77 (S.C.C.), the Supreme Court of Canada said that the NRTA had modified, but not extinguished the treaty right to hunt for food.

14 *R. v. Sampson* (1995), [1996] 2 C.N.L.R. 184 (B.C. C.A.).

15 *R. v. Dick*, [1993] 4 C.N.L.R. 63 (B.C. C.A.)

16 *R. v. Joseph*, [1990] 4 C.N.L.R. 59 (B.C. S.C.).

17 The accused, a Mi'kmaq Indian was stopped by police on a public off-reserve road carrying a rifle and shotgun pellets. He was charged with the illegal possession of hunting equipment during closed season. He argued he was on the way to a hunting area and was entitled to carry the weapon and ammunition pursuant to his hunting rights in the treaty of 1752. The court agreed that the treaty protected the right to carry hunting equipment in order to exercise the right to hunt.

18 In *R. v. Côté*, [1996] 4 C.N.L.R. 26 (C. S.C.) the accused was fishing, not strictly for food, but in order to educate some young people.

19 In *R. v. Sundown*, [1999] 2 C.N.L.R. 289 (S.C.C.) the hunter was allowed to construct a cabin in a park for use as a base for hunting.

20 For the story of the charges laid in relation to the traditional goose hunt, see the Globe and Mail, November 5, 1987, page 1. Aboriginal hunters killed about 31,000 Canada geese and 40,000 Snow geese, compared with American sports hunters who killed about 265,000 Canada geese and 500,000 Snow geese.

21 For a case where there was no proof that enforcement was necessary for conservation, see *R. v. Jackson*, [1992] 4 C.N.L.R. 121 (Ont. Prov. Div.)

See also the criticism of Judge Fairgrieve in *R. v. Jones* [1993] 3 C.N.L.R. 182 (Ont. Prov. Div.)

> What should be stated, however, is that a high-handed and adversarial stance on the part of the Ministry [of Natural Resources] will neither meet the constitutional requirements with which, one would expect, it would consider itself duty-bound to comply, nor will it provide an enforceable regulatory scheme capable of achieving the conservation goals which it seeks. It is self-evident, I think, that s. 35(1) of the *Constitution Act, 1982*, particularly after the judgment of the Supreme Court of Canada in *Sparrow*, dictated that a new approach be taken by the government to ensure that its policies discharge the obligations assumed by its constitutional agreement. I do not think it was ever suggested that there would necessarily be no adjustments required or no costs attached. at 208 [C.N.L.R.]

22 *R. v. Jack* (1995), [1996] 2 C.N.L.R. 113 (B.C. C.A.) was a case where the court looked behind the statement that fishing had to be prohibited for conservation purposes. See also *R. v. Joseph*, [1990] 4 C.N.L.R. 59 (B.C. S.C.).

23 In the case of the Neskonlith, they were allowed 85 coho, but only took 2. The quota for sports fishers was 165,000. See *Neskonlith Band v. Canada (Attorney General)* (1997), (sub nom. *Neskonlith Indian Band v. Canada (Attorney General)*) 136 F.T.R. 202 (Fed. T.D.).

24 For a case in which the court felt that consultation on conservation measures was not sufficient, see *R. v. Jack* (1995), [1996] 2 C.N.L.R. 113 (B.C. C.A.).

25 *R. v. Corbiere* (1996), 38 C.R.R. (2d) 155 (Ont. Gen. Div.) and *R. v. Pine*, [1997] O.J. No. 1004 (Ont. Gen. Div.) for cases in which an individual violated a scheme agreed upon between the province and the Band. In *Yale Indian Band v. Lower Fraser Fishing Authority* (1992), [1993] 1 C.N.L.R. 182 (B.C. S.C.) the court upheld an agreement between Canada and some First Nations against the challenge to the arrangement by a different First Nation. On the other hand, in *R. v. Ned*, [1997] 3 C.N.L.R. 251 (B.C. Prov. Ct.) the court allowed two Bands to successfully challenge

an agreement made between a third band and the Department of Fisheries to prohibit fishing in a river.

26 See *R. v. Fox* [1994] 3 C.N.L.R. 132 (Ont. C.A.).

27 For cases on night hunting, see *R. v. Myran* (1975), [1976] 2 S.C.R. 137 (S.C.C.); *R. v. Paul* (1993), [1994] 2 C.N.L.R. 167 (N.B. C.A.); *R. v. Seward* (1997), [1997] [1998] 3 C.N.L.R. 237 (B.C. S.C.), affirmed [1999] 3 C.N.L.R. 299 (B.C. C.A.).

28 For cases which require an evaluation of safety in a particular circumstance, see *R. v. Fox*, [1994] 3 C.N.L.R. 132 (Ont. C.A.) and *R. v. Machimity*, [1996] O.J. No. 4365 (Ont. Prov. Div.).

29 For a court which says that there should be consultation on safety issues, see *R. v. Noel*, [1995] 4 C.N.L.R. 78 (N.W.T. Terr. Ct.)

30 In *R. v. Jacobs* (1998), [1999] 3 C.N.L.R. 239 (B.C. S.C.) the court held that Indians from other parts of Canada could not seek the protection of the Aboriginal rights of the Sto:lo nation. In *R. v. Quipp*, [1997] B.C.J No. 1205 (B.C. Prov. Ct.) two members of the Sto:lo Nation were charged with hunting on the territory of the Thomson or Okanagan First Nations. But see *R. v. Wolfe* (1996), [1997] 1 C.N.L.R. 171 (B.C. Prov. Ct.) where a person covered by Treaty No. 3, had moved out to British Columbia and shot an elk in the Treaty No. 8 area, and *R. v. Buckner*, [1997] O.J. No. 1165 (Ont. Prov. Div.) where a Mi'kmaq person who moved into the Treaty No. 3 area had hunting and fishing rights in the Treaty No. 3 area.

31 *R. v. Machimity*, [1996] O.J. No. 4365 (Ont. Prov. Div.).

32 In *R. v. Frank*, [1978] 1 S.C.R. 95 (S.C.C.) the Supreme Court of Canada explained that the Natural Resources Transfer Agreement had restricted hunting rights to food hunting, but had extended the boundaries to encompass the entire province.

33 See *R. v. Badger*, [1996] 2 C.N.L.R. 77 (S.C.C.) for a discussion of when hunting on private land may be acceptable.

34 *R. v. Adams*, [1996] 4 C.N.L.R. 1 (C.S.C.). Also see *R. v. Marshall* (1998), 231 N.R. 325 (note), 223 A.R. 398 (note), 183 W.A.C. 398 (note) (S.C.C.). The following guideline is provided to a "moderate livelihood". Bare subsistence has thankfully receded over the last couple of centuries as an appropriate standard of life for aboriginals and non-aboriginals alike. A moderate livelihood includes such basics as "food, clothing and housing, supplemented by a few amenities", but not the accumulation of wealth (*Gladstone, supra*, at para. 165). It addresses day-to-day needs. This was the common intention in 1760. It is fair that it be given this interpretation today [at para.59].

35 See *R. v. Agawa*, [1988] 3 C.N.L.R. 73 (Ont. C.A.), leave to appeal refused (1990), (sub nom. *Agawa v. R.*) [1991] 1 C.N.L.R. vi (note) (S.C.C.).

36 See *R. v. Horseman* [1990] 3 C.N.L.R. 95 (S.C.C.)

37 See *R. v. Gladue* (1995), [1996] 1 C.N.L.R. 153 (Alta. C.A.), leave to appeal refused (1996), 200 A.R. 396 (note) (S.C.C.)

38 *R. v. Gladstone*, [1996] 4 C.N.L.R. 65 (S.C.c.)

39 For a case on commercial fishing for Band sustenance, see *R. v. Jones*, [1993] 3 C.N.L.R. 182 (Ont. Prov. Div.)

40 In *R. v. Vanderpeet* (sub nom. *R. v. Van der Peet*), [1996] 4 C.N.L.R. 177 (S.C.C.), reconsideration refused (January 16, 1997), Doc. 23803 (S.C.C.) the court found that there was no right to commercial fishing by the Sto:lo Nation. See also *R. v. N.T.C. Smokehouse Ltd.*, [1996] 4 C.N.L.R. 130 (S.C.C.) where the court found that the exchange of fish for money was not an integral part of the Seshaht and Opetchesaht nations culture prior to European contact to support a claim to fish commercially and *R. v. Dick*, [1993] 2 C.N.L.R. 137 (B.C. Prov. Ct.) where the Lekwiltok were found not to have a commercial fishing rights.

41 *Washington v. Washington State Commercial, Passenger & Fishing Vessel Assn.*, 99 S.Ct. 3055 (1979), at p. 3069.

42 *Ibid.*, at 3075.

43 Maori fishing rights in New Zealand are described in the *Treaty of Waitangi (Fisheries Claims) Settlement Act, 1992.*

44 On the subject of trapping as a treaty right, see *Cheechoo v. R.* (1980), [1981] 3 C.N.L.R. 45 (Ont. Dist. Ct.)

45 In *R. v. Vanderpeet* (sub nom. *R. v. Van der Peet*) [1996] 4 C.N.L.R. 177 (S.C.C.), reconsideration refused (January 16, 1997), Doc. 23803 (S.C.C.). Mr. Justice Lamer observed:

> The fact that Europeans in North America engaged in the same practices, customs or traditions as those under which an Aboriginal right is claimed will only be relevant to the Aboriginal claim if the practice, custom or tradition in question can only be said to exist because of the influence of European culture. If the practice, custom or tradition was an integral part of the Aboriginal community's culture prior to contact with Europeans, the fact, that practice, custom or tradition continued after the arrival of Europeans, and adapted in response to their arrival, is not relevant to determination of the claim; European arrival and influence cannot be used to deprive an Aboriginal group of an otherwise valid claim to an Aboriginal right. On the other hand, where the practice, custom or tradition arose solely as a response to European

influences then that practice, custom or tradition will not meet the standard for recognition of an Aboriginal right. [at 209-210]

For a criticism of this "frozen rights" approach, see the dissent of McLachlin, J. and also John Borrows, "Frozen Rights in Canada: Constitutional Interpretation and the Trickster." (1997) 22 American Indian Law Review 37.

46 On special sentencing for Aboriginal people who need their rifles, see the case of *R. v. Chief*, [1990] 1 C.N.L.R. 92 (Y.T. C.A.) in which a Yukon Indian was convicted of assault and possession of a weapon dangerous to public peace. According to the *Criminal Code*, a conviction for this offence provided that his gun should automatically be taken away for five years. Chief, however, was a trapper and needed his gun to trap and supply meat for his family. The Yukon Territorial Judge refused to apply the minimum five-year prohibition on weapons to Chief, saying that it was cruel and unusual punishment, in conflict with s. 12 of the *Charter*. This decision has been upheld by the British Columbia Court of Appeal. The court held that the prohibition on guns would have a much more serious impact on Chief than on other people: "Some others may not even be inconvenienced by a five-year prohibition while the respondent is deprived of his livelihood and his lifestyle".

A similar decision has been made by the Ontario District Court in *R. v. Cozy* (May 13, 1989), 1157/88 (Ont. Dist. Ct.). See also *R. v. McGillivary*, [1991] 3 C.N.L.R. 113 (Sask. C.A.); *R. v. E. (P.)*, [1990] N.W.T.R. 246 (N.W.T. S.C.); and *R. c. Chabot* [1999] 1 C.N.L.R. 139 (Court of Quebec, Criminal Division).

But other cases have found that, in the circumstances, a ban on weapons was justified. See *R. v. Tobac* (1985), [1986] 1 C.N.L.R. 138 (N.W.T. C.A.), and *R. v. Johnson* (1994), [1995] 2 C.N.L.R. 158 (Y.T.C.A.).

47 For cases holding that treaty rights do not encompass unsafe hunting practices, see *R. v. Paul* (1993), [1994] 2 C.N.L.R. 167 (N.B. C.A.) and *R. v. McCoy* (1993), [1994] 2 C.N.L.R. 129 (N.B. C.A.) and *R. v. Myran* (1975), [1976] 2 S.C.R. 137 (S.C.C.).

48 For example, the Ontario Court of Appeal in *R. v. Fox*, [1994] 3 C.N.L.R. 132 (Ont. C.A.) acquitted a person for illegally discharging a firearm because there was no actual safety issue in that case, and because the provincial regulations allowed disabled people to use firearms in similar situations.

49 See the *Aboriginal Peoples of Canada Adaption Regulations (Firearms)*, SOR/98-205.

50 An Aboriginal person who qualifies for exemptions is defined in section 2 of the regulations. The declaration from the applicant under section 6 requires the following information:

(a) a declaration that the individual

(i) is a member of one of the Aboriginal peoples of Canada,

(ii) is a member of an Aboriginal community, and

(iii) engages in the traditional hunting practices of the individual's Aboriginal community; and

(b) confirmation from an elder or a leader of the individual's Aboriginal community that the individual is a member of that community and engages in the traditional hunting practices of that community.

51 See the *Firearms Act*, S.C. 1995, c. 39, s. 2(3).

52 See *Aboriginal Peoples of Canada Adaption Regulations (Firearms)*, SOR/98-205, ss. 7, 8, and 9 for the role of an elder or leader in explaining the importance of engaging in traditional hunting practices.

53 For exemptions for Aboriginal people from the Canadian Firearms Safety Course and the test, see the Regulations, *Aboriginal Peoples of Canada Adaption Regulations (Firearms)*, SOR/98-205, s. 12-17.

54 See *Aboriginal Peoples of Canada Adaption Regulations (Firearms)*, SOR/98-205, s. 11.

4

Land and "Land Claims"

1. INTRODUCTION

At the root of many disputes about land is a fundamental difference about the meaning of land. Many First Nations, for example, referred to the land as Mother Earth. They did not view land as something which could be owned or sold. Most Europeans, on the other hand, viewed land as property which could be bought and traded like any other commodity.

This difference in viewpoint was described by Judge James Igloliorte of Labrador. A number of Innu had been arrested and charged after they had blockaded military airport runways. The Innu were protesting against the use of low-flying military jets over their traditional territory. In acquitting the protesters, the judge said:

> Since the concept of land as property is a concept foreign to original people the Court must not assume that a "reasonable" belief be founded

on English and hence Canadian law standards. The Innu must be allowed to express their understanding of a foreign concept on their terms, or simply to express what they believe.

The Crown has presented to me recent cases . . . which only emphasize the concept of land as property from an English law viewpoint. Like the I.Q. tests administered to school children some years ago which simply reflects the understanding of the maker of the test, not the person being tested, there is an inherent bias.[1] (at 120 [C.N.L.R.])

2. ABORIGINAL TITLE

Aboriginal title is difficult to describe because, as noted above, Aboriginal perspectives on their *relation* to the land is so different from Western legal concepts centred on *ownership* of land. While Canadian courts and governments have always recognized that Aboriginal people have a legal right,[2] the courts have had difficulty reconciling that Aboriginal interest with conflicting federal and provincial desires to possess and exploit that land. For example, in the past, most courts would ignore Aboriginal rights if the Crown wanted to authorize mining or forestry.

However, in 1998, the Supreme Court of Canada made an important decision on Aboriginal title in *Delgamuukw v. British Columbia.*[3] While this judgment does not give adequate consideration to the impact of *different* concepts on the relation to the land, it does provide a framework for future developments in this area.

The case was brought by two First Nations in the northern part of British Columbia, the Gitskan and the Wet'suwet'en. They challenged the right of the provincial government to take their lands without their consent, and questioned the legitimacy of the laws made by the provincial legislature in the period when Indians were not allowed to vote. When British Columbia entered Confederation in 1870, at least 70 per cent of the inhabitants of the province were Aboriginal,[4] yet only whites were allowed to vote or participate in the political process. Did this minority have the legitimate authority to pass laws and authorize activities on First Nation lands without the consent of the First Nations? At the trial, the First Nations argued that the white minority did not have that right. The First Nations explained that at that time they were societies with their own history and culture, transmitted through their oral histories, the *adaawk* of the Gitskan and the *kungax* of the Wet'suwet'en. They explained their relationship to over 58,000 square kilometres of their traditional territory and the laws that applied to them.

After one of the longest and most complex trials in Canadian history — a trial that had 374 days of hearings, 35,000 pages of transcripts, 50,000 pages of exhibits and a trial judgment over 400 pages long — the First Nations discovered that much of their evidence had been dismissed by McEachern, C.J., the trial judge, as irrelevant or unreliable. Because First Nations societies did not have the same institutions, governmental structure, or technology as the Europeans, he assumed that Aboriginal people did not have law, or even social fabric:

> [I]t would not be accurate to assume that even pre-contact existence in the territory was in the least bit idyllic. The plaintiffs' ancestors had no written language, no horses or wheeled vehicles, slavery and star-vation were not uncommon, wars with neighbouring peoples were common, and there is no doubt, to quote Hobbs, that aboriginal life in the territory was, at best, "nasty, brutish and short."[5]

The trial judge thought that " [the First Nation people] more likely acted as they did because of survival instincts".[6] This snapshot, which *he* had constructed was as all he felt he needed to know about the Gitskan and Wet'suwet'en to decide on their rights. He concluded "[t]he evidence satisfies me that most Gitksan and Wet'suwet'en people do not now live an aboriginal life."[7]

The Supreme Court of Canada rejected the decision of the trial judge, and made important strides in the right direction. Their decision confirmed the importance of recognizing the existence of legally enforceable rights for Aboriginal peoples.

(a) Three general features of Aboriginal title

The court outlined three general features of Aboriginal title:

1. Aboriginal land can only be alienated to the Crown in the right of Canada.
2. The source of Aboriginal title arises from the prior occupation of Canada.
3. Aboriginal title is held communally by the "aboriginal nation" and decisions are made by that community.[8]

(b) Content of Aboriginal title

Chief Justice Lamer sets out two propositions to describe the content of Aboriginal title:

1. Aboriginal title provides exclusive use and occupation of the land for a variety of purposes.

   Although the Chief Justice seems to imply that this could include a wide range of activities, including mining, the second proposition places an important limitation on the possible uses of the land.[9]

2. The uses of Aboriginal title land must be consistent with the group's attachment to the land.

   The court, in a very perceptive balancing move, puts limits on the use of the land using insights provided by Aboriginal peoples about their special relationship to the land. For example, if land is important for hunting and fishing, then Aboriginal people cannot use the land to destroy their own hunting and fishing areas. These words will clearly be welcomed by those members of Aboriginal communities who favour continuing a special relationship to the land. It is clear that this judgment does not provide the basis for uncontrolled exploitation of Aboriginal lands unless the land is first surrendered to the federal Crown.[10]

(c) Proof of Aboriginal title

Chief Justice Lamer outlines three criteria for establishing the existence of Aboriginal title:

1. The land must have been occupied prior to the assertion of British sovereignty.[11]
2. There must be continuity in the possession between the present and the pre-sovereignty occupation.
3. The occupation must be exclusive

3. LAND COVERED BY TREATIES

The written English words of many treaties say that the Indians surrender and give up all their rights in their territories. Aboriginal people, however, often say that their understanding, as transmitted through oral tradition, is that an agreement of peace and friendship was established in which they agreed to share the land with the Europeans, not sell it.[12] It is easy to see, then, why there are so many disagreements about treaties.

Those treaties that provided for the "surrender" of large tracts of land also provided, in return, for the creation of small reserves, and some rights to continue to use lands that were "surrendered". The most common use was for hunting, fishing and trapping rights. (For more information, see Chapter 3, "Hunting, Fishing and Trapping"). Some Canadian courts have recognized that these off-reserve treaty lands need to be protected in order to allow hunting and other activity to continue. For example, the courts prevented the construction of a marina which would have interfered with treaty fishing rights.[13] In general, however, provincial and federal governments had proceeded to develop the "surrendered" lands as if the Aboriginal people had no right to consent or even be consulted.

A variety of initiatives have begun to provide Aboriginal input into the use and development of off-reserve lands. In some cases, co-management agreements over specific resources are put into place. There are also a number of planning boards being negotiated which would have at least 50 per cent Aboriginal participation in developing land use plans over a traditional territory. In Ontario and British Columbia, some First Nations have entered into agreements with the province so that they are notified of proposed developments, dispositions and activities which may have significant impact in their territories. The Nishnawbe-Aski Nation Interim Measures Agreement, for example, provided that authorities must give 30 days notice, and that a First Nation could have the issue referred for advice to an Interim Measures Group composed of representatives from the federal and provincial governments and the First Nations.[14]

Aboriginal interests in off-reserve lands have also received some recognition in agreements like the James Bay and Northern Quebec Agreement and Manitoba's Northern Flood Agreement. In these agreements, Aboriginal peoples in the territory are compensated for the loss of the use of the land, and they gain a role in future development through participation on advisory boards.

With the decisions in *Delgamuukw v. British Columbia* and *R. v. Marshall* it has become highly unlikely that unilateral taking of treaty lands would be allowed. The importance of oral history, and the significance of the laws of the First Nations themselves should force both federal and provincial governments to tread more cautiously when developing land where there are treaty rights to hunt, fish and trap.[15]

4. RESERVE LAND

Reserves are tracts of land which are defined under the *Indian Act*. The title is in Her Majesty who holds the land for the benefit of a Band.[16] Sometimes, these lands were set aside under a treaty, and sometimes, they were created to make room for expanding non-Aboriginal settlements. There are two important features of reserve lands.

First, the land is not owned by individual Indians. The land is owned by the Band as a whole and can only be alienated to the federal Crown after a process which involves a vote by the Band members as a whole. Second, the *Indian Act* applies to reserve lands, setting out a scheme for permits, leases and certificates of possession for those lands, as well as allowing Bands to make by-laws on land use. Provincial laws on real property, such as the land registration system, do not apply. (See Chapter 17, "Commercial Relations" for information on land surrenders and designations.)

Over the years, the *Indian Act* scheme has been criticized by First Nations for being *paternalistic* because almost all transactions of any type needed the approval of the federal government. In order to meet some of these concerns, the *First Nations Land Management Act* has been enacted which puts greater decision-making in the hands of those Bands which decide to opt into the statute.[17]

But this legislation has highlighted another criticism of the *Indian Act*. Some Native Women's organizations complain that the *Indian Act* is *patriarchal* and places men in positions of power. The present *Indian Act* has, in fact, created some unfairness on marital breakdown. Where provincial law would grant possession of the matrimonial home to the wife who had custody of the children, the operation of the *Indian Act* may leave men in occupation of the matrimonial home. A law suit commenced by the British Columbia Native Women's Society alleges that the *First Nations Land Management Act* will further entrench male-dominated Band Councils, to the detriment of native women.[18]

(See Chapter 14, "Marriage, Separation, Divorce" for more information on the difficulties that arise on marital breakdown.

5. TYPES OF LAND CLAIMS

The term "land claims" covers many different types of disputes over land. On the large scale, the issues may be about jurisdiction and rights over vast territories which have not been formally ceded by the Aboriginal people. The federal government calls these *comprehensive claims*. Examples of such claims are the Nunavut claim for the Eastern Arctic, and the Nisga'a claim in British Columbia.

At the other end of the scale, there may be claims for a few acres of land which were illegally taken away from reserves. These are called *specific claims*. Other examples of specific claims are reserve lands which have been illegally occupied, or reserves which were not surveyed correctly.

There are several types of claims in between these two extremes. One such claim is called *treaty land entitlement*. In Manitoba and Saskatchewan, First Nations were promised a certain amount of land under their treaties, but they never received the land they were promised. A process has been established to provide land and money to compensate for the breach of the treaty promises.

Lawyers for Aboriginal people with land claims generally take two courses of action at the same time. They begin a court case, and they file the claim with the federal and provincial governments. Because of the complex nature of claims, and the danger of waiting too long before filing a claim, it is important to consult a lawyer about a potential claim as soon as possible.

In order to avoid litigation, the federal government has developed a number of policies to negotiate claims. These policies have been criticized by Aboriginal people for being slow and unduly restrictive. However, they do provide some advantages in that funding will be provided to research the claims, and certain legal defences which would be available to the Crown in court are not raised in the negotiation process.[19]

(a) Comprehensive claims

Comprehensive land claims are based on "the assertion of continuing Aboriginal title to lands and natural resources". The federal government will negotiate with Aboriginal groups "in areas where claims to Aboriginal title have not been addressed by treaty or through other legal means."[20]

The claims process begins when the federal government accepts an Aboriginal group's statement of claim and supporting materials. The federal government will accept the claim if the statement confirms the following:

- The Aboriginal group is, and was, an organized society.
- The organized society has occupied the specific territory over which it asserts Aboriginal title since time immemorial. The traditional use and occupancy of the territory must have been sufficient to be an established fact at the time of assertion of sovereignty by European nations.
- The occupation of the territory by the Aboriginal group was largely to the exclusion of other organized societies.
- The Aboriginal group can demonstrate some continuing current use and occupancy of the land for traditional purposes.
- The group's Aboriginal title and rights to resource use have not been dealt with by treaty.[21]
- Aboriginal title has not been eliminated by other lawful means.

Settlements have generally included three elements with respect to land. First, land for exclusive use of the Aboriginal nations, and powers over those lands are identified. These lands usually become reserves if First Nations are involved. Second, there is often a second category of lands over which the Aboriginal nation has some interests, but which may be under the jurisdiction of the federal and provincial government. Third, there are provisions for the ownership of minerals and other resources.

Among the comprehensive claim agreements which have been settled since the announcement of the federal government's claims policy in 1973 are:[22]

- The James Bay and Northern Quebec Agreement (1975);[23]
- The North-eastern Quebec Agreement (1978);[24]
- The Inuvialuit Final Agreement (1984);[25]
- The Gwich'in Agreement (1992);[26]
- The Nunavut Land Claims Agreement (1993);[27]
- The Sahtu Dene and Metis Agreement (1994);[28]

- Six Yukon First Nation Final Agreements[29] based on the Council for Yukon Indians Umbrella Final Agreement (1993)

(b) Comprehensive claims in British Columbia

Almost no treaties have been signed with aboriginal people living in British Columbia, and the province has most outstanding comprehensive claims in Canada.

The Nisga'a of the Nass River Valley in north-western British Columbia launched a legal action in 1968 which was heard by the Supreme Court of Canada in 1973.[30] The Court recognized the existence of Aboriginal title. In 1976, the government re-evaluated its aboriginal claims policy and began negotiations with the Nisga'a peoples. The B.C. government did not join these negotiations until 1990.[31]

Around the same time, the federal and provincial governments and BC First Nations created a Task Force to advise on the scope, organization, and process for negotiation of comprehensive land claims in the province. As a response to the Task Force's report, the BC Treaty Commission (BCTC) was established in September 1992. The BCTC allocates funding to support First Nations in treaty negotiations.[32] In allocating funding, the Treaty Commission set criteria taking into account population, number of communities in the First Nation, size of traditional territory, location and travel requirements, number and complexity of territorial overlaps and the anticipated complexity of the issues to be negotiated.[33] The BCTC uses a six-stage process to negotiate treaties:[34]

1. Statement of Intent
2. Preparation for Negotiations
3. Negotiation of a Framework Agreement
4. Negotiation of an Agreement in Principle
5. Negotiation to Finalize a Treaty
6. Implementation of the Treaty

The first modern agreement is the Agreement reached between the Nisga'a First Nation, the province, and the federal government which was signed on August 4, 1998. It includes land ownership and self-government over 2000 sq. km. in the valley, surface and subsurface rights, and fishing rights.[35]

(c) Specific Claims

Specific claims are for "specific actions and omissions of government as they relate to obligations undertaken under treaty, requirements spelled out in legislation and responsibilities regarding the management of Indian assets."[36] They include the claims for unfulfilled treaty claims, lands surrendered but not sold, and unlawful occupation of reserve lands.

Because of the difficulty and length of time it has taken to resolve specific claims, the federal government created the Indian Claims Commission to provide a forum for hearing disputes over specific claims.[37] The Commission makes recommendations, but the final decision still rests with the Minister.

In Ontario, some specific claims are being facilitated through the Indian Commission of Ontario (ICO). The ICO, if it accepts a claim, will provide a facilitator to assist the First Nation, the federal government, and the provincial government to come to a decision.

(d) Treaty Land Entitlement

Treaty Land Entitlement (TLE) claims are a type of specific claim relating to the failure of the Crown failed to provide First Nations with sufficient reserve lands under the terms of its treaty. The Prairie provinces were under a legal requirement to make land available under the 1930 Natural Resources Transfer Agreement.

The 1992 Saskatchewan TLE Framework Agreement settles the land debt owned to 28 First Nations which did not receive their full land entitlement under Treaties 4, 6, and 10. A total of $516 million is provided to settle the outstanding land debt. The federal government initially provides 70 per cent of the overall costs of the settlement while the provincial government covers 30 per cent. First Nations may purchase federal, provincial or private land anywhere in Saskatchewan.[38]

The 1997 Manitoba TLE Framework Agreement covers 19 First Nations. The Province of Manitoba will provide 399,008 hectares of Crown land, and Canada will contribute $76 million to be applied to the purchase of up to 46,444 hectares of land from private owners. The total amount of land will be 445,452 hectares.[39]

6. MÉTIS CLAIMS

Historically, Métis have been excluded from the federal government's comprehensive land claims policy.[40] Presently, the Minister of Indian Affairs has a mandate to enter into negotiations with Métis groups north of the sixtieth parallel. Negotiations which involve Métis include the following:

- The *Sahtu Dene and Métis Land Claim Settlement Act* which came into effect on June 23, 1994. Land title, financial payments and hunting, fishing, and trapping rights are highlights of the agreement.[41]
- The South Slave Métis Tribal Council framework agreement involving the Government of the Northwest Territories and Canada. Formal negotiations toward an agreement-in-principle began in May, 1997.
- The Labrador Métis Association (LMA) submitted a comprehensive land claim to all southern Labrador and their claim submission is currently being reviewed by the Department of Justice.

Present government policy allows the department's Federal Interlocutor for Métis and Non-Status Indians to enter into negotiations with provinces and Métis groups living south of the 60th parallel and Indian people who live off the land base.[42] At this time, the Department of Indian Affairs is not prepared to enter into any land claim agreements with Métis south of 60th parallel.

7. THE FUTURE PROCESS FOR LAND DISPUTES

In 1991, the Indian Claims Commission was established to inquire into and report on disputes arising out of the specific claims process. The Commission sees its focus as research of relevant historical facts, mediation as opposed to the adversarial courtroom process, and liaison between First Nations and government.[43]

Basically, the ICC is an alternative to court action. Although a First Nation who requests an inquiry or mediation is not precluded from court action, such action may have an impact on the ICC process. For instance, it may be inappropriate for the ICC to schedule a community session at the same time as trial, or the government may request that the First Nation stay either court action or an ICC inquiry to avoid multiple proceedings on the same issue.[44]

In 1994, the Indian Claims Commission criticized the Department of Indian Affairs "for its consistent failure to produce documents quickly, attend meetings, consider mediation and respond to the commissions recommendations in a timely manner. Although intended to help speed the resolution of claims, in practice, the commission has been unable to exercise this part of its mandate because the department appears to treat its operations as an interference with the normal workings of claims policy. Such behaviour is symptomatic of the department's adversarial attitude toward First Nations."[45]

The recent report of the Royal Commission on Aboriginal Peoples recommends that the ICC be replaced by an independent tribunal, called the Aboriginal Lands and Treaties Tribunal.[46] One of the tribunal's principal roles will be to ensure the just resolution of existing specific claims, relating mostly, but not exclusively, to lands and resources. It will have responsibility not only for monitoring the fairness of the bargaining process by which most specific claims should be settled, but also, where no agreement is reached, for adjudicating outstanding substantive issues and making final and binding decisions on the merits of these claims. The jurisdiction of the tribunal with respect to powers to adjudicate specific claims can be conferred by federal legislation. Aboriginal people, federal and provincial governments must be actively involved in the design of the tribunal.

ENDNOTES

1 Judge Igliorte acquitted Innu who blockaded air force runway in *R. v. Ashini*, [1989] 2 C.N.L.R. 119, reversed (1989), 79 Nfld. & P.E.I.R. 318 (Nfld. C.A.)

2 The first case to clearly enunciate this was *St. Catharines Milling & Lumber Co. v. R.* (1888), 14 App. Cas. 46 (Canada P.C.) which said that the interest was "usufuctary" — a burden on title which did not amount to fee simple ownership.

3 The trial judgment by McEachern, C.J. was delivered in 1991: 1, 79 D.L.R. (4th) 185 (B.C. S.C.). The British Columbia Court of Appeal overturned the trial decision in 1993: [1993] 5 C.N.L.R. 1 (B.C. C.A.). The Supreme Court of Canada sent the case back for trial in 1997: [1998] 1 C.N.L.R. 14 (S.C.C.). Much of the theory of the Supreme Court of Canada decision relied on an article by Kent McNeil, "The Meaning of Aboriginal

Title" in Michael Asch, ed. *Aboriginal and Treaty Rights in Canada: Essays on Law, Equity, and Respect for Difference* (Vancouver, British Columbia: University of British Columbia Press, 1997)

4 Of the total population of 36,247, Aboriginal people were 25,661, and another 1,000 were Chinese. The vote was taken away from Indians and Chinese in 1872. Royal Commission on Aboriginal Peoples, *Report* chapter 2, part II, pp. 476-8

5 *Delgamuukw v. British Columbia* (1991) 79 D.L.R. (4th) 185 (B.C. S.C.) at 208.

6 *Ibid.* at 441.

7 *Ibid.* at 256.

8 See *Delgamuukw v. British Columbia* (1997), [1998] 1 C.N.L.R. 14 (S.C.C.) [hereinafter *Delgamuukw*] at paragraphs 114 and 115 and paragraphs 148 and 149 for a discussion on the three features of Aboriginal title. The prior occupation is relevant in two ways:

(i) at common law, occupation is proof of possession; consequently, occupation prior to the assertion of British sovereignty is proof of possession [at para. 114 and para. 149]

(ii) prior to the assertion of British sovereignty, Aboriginal law determined the legitimacy of the occupation; consequently, Aboriginal title must partly rely on "pre-existing systems of Aboriginal at 59 [C.N.L.R.] law." [at para. 114, and para. 148]

9 See *Delgaumuukw, supra* note 8 at 59 for the possible uses of Aboriginal title land.

Aboriginal title encompasses the right to use the land held pursuant to that title for a variety of purposes, which need not be aspects of those Aboriginal practices, cultures and traditions which are integral to distinctive Aboriginal cultures [at 57].

10 See *Delgamuukw, supra* note 8 at 63:

[t]here will exist a special bond between the group and the land in question such that the land will be part of the definition of the group's distinctive culture. It seems to me that these elements of Aboriginal title create an inherent limitation on the uses to which the land, over which such title exists, may be put. For example, if occupation is established with reference to the use of the land as a hunting ground, then the group that successfully claims Aboriginal title to that land may not use it in such a fashion as to destroy its value for such a use (e.g., by strip mining it). Similarly, if a group claims a special bond with the land because of its ceremonial or cultural significance, it may not use the land in such a way as to destroy that relationship (e.g., by

developing it in such a way that the bond is destroyed, perhaps by turning it into a parking lot).

11 The point in time for establishing the existence of an Aboriginal practice or custom was the *point of contact* with the Europeans (see *R. v. Vanderpeet*, (sub nom. *R. v. Van der Peet*) [1996] 4 C.N.L.R. 177 (S.C.C.), reconsideration refused (January 16, 1997), Doc. 23803 (S.C.C.)). In the case of Aboriginal title, the point in time is the date of the assertion of British sovereignty.

12 The Aboriginal concept of land is explained by Iroquois elder Oren Lyons:

> We native people did not have the concept of private property in our lexicon, and the principle of private property was pretty much in conflict with our value system. For example, you wouldn't see "No Hunting", "No Fishing" or "No Trespassing" signs in our territories. To a native person, such signs would have been equivalent to saying "No Breathing" because the air is somebody's private property . . . Well, it made the Indians laugh . . . when the Europeans said "We are going to own the land." How could anyone own the land?

See L. Little Bear, M. Boldt, J. Long (eds.), *Pathways to Self-Determination* (Toronto: University of Toronto, 1986) at 5.

13 In *Saanichton Marina Ltd. v. Claxton*, [1989] 3 C.N.L.R. 46 (B.C. C.A.) the court held that the granting of a license to occupy granted by the province to permit construction of a marina derogated from the treaty rights of the Indians and was therefore of no force and effect. The province could not act in contravention of the treaty rights of Indians, or authorize others to do so.

14 An example of an Interim Measures Agreement is the one signed by federal and Ontario governments and the Nishnawbe-Aski Nation in 1990.

15 See Shin Imai, "Preliminary Thoughts on *Delgamuukw* and Treaty Rights" (October 1998) 6 Canada Watch 4, 5 & 6 at 74.

Courts may follow the example of the Ontario Divisional Court in *TransCanada Pipeline Ltd. v. Beardmore (Township)* (1997), [1998] 2 C.N.L.R. 240 (Ont. Div. Ct.), leave to appeal allowed (May 25, 1998), Doc. CA M21842, CA M21857 (Ont. C.A.). In this case, several municipalities in northern Ontario proposed to amalgamate and annex unorganized territory into a new municipality. TransCanada Pipeline objected because it would have resulted in an increase in taxes. A number of First Nations objected because it could affect land claims and treaty hunting, fishing and trapping rights. The court quashed the final order for the amalgamation on a number of grounds. The court was particularly critical of the Restructuring Commission for failing to take into account the rights of the First Nations. While the court did not base its decision on an infringement of section 35(1), the court found that the failure to consult was fatal to the process. The judge stated, in part,

> In my view, the Commission lost its jurisdiction when it failed to consult at all with [Long Lake 58 First Nation] and failed to properly, adequately and meaningfully consult with [the Nishnawbe-Aski Nation] and the [Ginoogaming First Nation]. These Aboriginal peoples would have been impacted the most by the annexation. "Trust me" as an answer is no justification [at 276].

16 See Section 2(1) of the *Indian Act* which provides:

"reserve"

> (*a*) means a tract of land, the legal title to which is vested in Her Majesty, that has been set apart by Her Majesty for the use and benefit of a band, and

> (*b*) except in subsection 18(2), sections 20 to 25, 28, 36 to 38, 42, 44, 46, 48 to 51, 58 to 60 and the regulations made under any of those provisions, includes designated lands;

R.S.C. 1985, c. I-5, as am. R.S.C. 1985, c. 32 (1st Supp.); R.S.C. 1985, c. 27 (2nd Supp.), s. 10 (Sched.); R.S.C. 1985, c. 17 (4th Supp.); R.S.C. 1985, c. 43 (4th Supp.); R.S.C. 1985, c. 48 (4th Supp.); S.C. 1990, c. 16; 1990, c. 17; 1992, c. 51, s. 54; 1993, c. 28, s. 78 (Sched. III, items 73, 74); 1996, c. 23, s. 187(e); 1998, c. 30, s. 14(j); 1999, c. 3, s. 69.

17 See *First Nations Land Management Act*, S.C. 1999, c. 24.

18 In *British Columbia Native Women's Society v. R.* (1998), (sub nom. *British Columbia Native Women's Society v. Canada*) 143 F.T.R. 153 (Fed. T.D.) the British Columbia Native Women's Society have commenced proceedings against Canada alleging breaches of s. 15 of the *Charter of Rights and Freedoms* and breaches of the Crown's fiduciary duty.

19 The federal land claims policies provide that the federal government will not consider limitations problems in the context of evaluating a claim, although it would raise limitation defences in litigation.

20 Department of Indian & Northern Affairs, "Comprehensive Claims Policy and Status of Claims" 9 September 1997. The federal government has accepted some claims for negotiation as comprehensive claims in areas affected by treaties. For example, the NWT claims of the Dene and Metis in Treaties 8 and 11 were accepted for negotiation on the basis that the land provisions of the treaties had not been implemented. Claims from Treaty 8 and Douglas Treaty First Nations in British Columbia have also been

accepted for negotiation within the British Columbia Treaty Commission process, described below.

21 Department of Indian & Northern Affairs, "Comprehensive Claims (Modern Treaties) in Canada" March 1996.

22 The following descriptions of the claims come from a number of sources, see generally: Department of Indian & Northern Affairs, "Comprehensive Claims (Modern Treaties) in Canada" March 1996; Department of Indian & Northern Affairs, "Comprehensive Claims Policy and Status of Claims" 9 September 1997; Department of Indian & Northern Affairs, *First Nations in Canada* (Ottawa: Minister of Public Works & Government Services Canada, 1997) at 97.

23 The *James Bay and Northern Quebec Agreement*, 1975. This was the first settled comprehensive claim, coming into effect in 1977. The settlement provided for 5,543 square kilometres of settlement land for the 11,088 Cree, and 8,151 square kilometres of settlement land for the 7,268 Inuit; $225 million (1975 dollars) for the Cree and the Inuit; full harvesting rights over 150,000 square kilometres; participation in an environmental and social protection regime; an income security program for hunters and trappers; and self-government under the Cree-Naskapi (of Quebec) Act.

24 The *Northeastern Quebec Agreement*, 1978. In 1978 amended the James Bay and Northern Quebec Agreement to integrate the 602 Naskapi, providing $9 million, as well as settlement lands, rights and benefits equivalent to the JBNQA.

25 The *Inuvialuit Final Agreement*, 1984. The final agreement, effective in July 1984, provided 11,000 square kilometres in fee simple and subsurface land; 91,000 square kilometres in settlement land; and 435,000 square kilometres in settlement area for the 2,500 Inuvialuit and included a financial component of $152 million (1984 dollars) and a one time payment of $10 million to assist social development. It also includes wildlife harvesting rights, socio-economic initiatives, and participation in wildlife and environmental management.

26 The *Gwich'in Agreement*, 1992. This claim provided 2,000 Gwich'in of the Mackenzie Delta Region with approximately 24,000 square kilometres of land including some mineral rights.

27 *Nunavut Land Claims Agreement*, 1993. This claim affects 17,500 Inuit and represents the largest comprehensive claim settlement in Canada. The settlement provides the Inuit with approximately 350,000 square kilometres of land (of which 36,000 square kilometres includes mineral rights); $1.17 billion ($580 million in 1989 dollars plus interest) in financial benefits over 14 years; a share of resource royalties; guaranteed wildlife harvesting rights; and participation in decision-making processes dealing

with land and environmental management. On April 1, 1999, the Territory of Nunavut came into being. It is governed by the *Nunavut Act*, S.C. 1993, c. 28, as am. by S.C. 1998, c. 15, ss. 1-42; 1999, c. 3, ss. 1-12, Sched.; 1999, c. 26, s. 12.

28 The *Sahtu Dene and Metis Agreement*, 1994. The 2000 Sahtu Dene and Metis were the second Dene and Metis group to reach a final agreement with respect to their regional comprehensive land claim. The benefits of the claim include 41,437 square kilometres of land including some mineral rights.

29 The Council of Yukon Indians (CYI) claims relates to the whole of Yukon Territory affecting approximately 8,000 Indians. Thus far, the federal government, the Yukon government, and the CYI have signed an Umbrella Final Agreement (UFA) establishing the basis of negotiation for settlements with each of the 14 Yukon First Nations (YFNs) and final agreements with six YFNs: the Vuntut Gwitchin First Nation; the First Nation of the Nacho Nyak Dun; the Champagne and Aishihik First Nations; the Teslin Tlingit Council; Little Salmon/Carmacks (LSCFN) and Selkirk First Nations (SFN). The final agreements provide the six YFNs (approximately 3,505 beneficiaries) with settlement land of 24,701 square kilometres (5.7 percent of the land mass of the Yukon), including partial ownership of mines and minerals; financial benefits of $112,068,620; fishing and wildlife harvesting rights; as well as negotiation of self-government agreements.

30 *Calder v. British Columbia (Attorney General)*, [1973] S.C.R. 313, 34 D.L.R. (3d) 145, [1973] 4 W.W.R. 1 (S.C.C.).

31 Department of Indian & Northern Affairs, *First Nations in Canada* (Ottawa: Minister of Public Works & Government Services Canada, 1997) at 97.

32 Canada and British Columbia provide the money (80% loan and 20% contribution).

33 British Columbia Treaty Commission, "Fairness in Funding" Annual Report 1997. Available online: www.bctreaty.net/files/fund.html

34 British Columbia Treaty Commission, "The Six Stage Negotiation Process" 1994/95 Annual Report available online: www.aaf.gov.bc.ca/aaf/treaty/process/sixstage.htm

35 See See the *Nisga'a Final Agreement Act*, S.B.C. 1999, c. 2

36 The specific claims policy is described in *Outstanding Business: A Native Claims Policy*, 1981. This has been somewhat revised, and is currently being reviewed by a national Working Group on Specific Claims.

37 The Indian Claims Commission was established by order in Council P.C. 1991-1329, July 15, 1991.

38 Department of Indian Affairs, Backgrounder, "Treaty Land Entitlement", May, 1998.

39 Department of Indian & Northern Affairs, Backgrounder, "Treaty Land Entitlement in Manitoba" 21 June 1996.

40 For a summary of this exclusion, see *Canada and Aboriginal Peoples: A New Partnership* (Fact Finder: Hon. A.C. Hamilton) (Ottawa: Queen's Printer, 1995) at 32-34.

41 *1995–1996 Annual Report of the Implementation Committee: Sahtu Dene and Metis Comprehensive Land Claim Agreement*, 1996.

42 *Federal Policy Guide: Aboriginal Self-Government* (The Government of Canada's Approach to Implementation of the Inherent Right and the Negotiation of Aboriginal Self-Government) (Ottawa: Queens Printer, 1995) at 23.

43 *A Special Issue on Land Claims Reform*, Indian Claims Commission Proceedings [1995] 2 ICCP (Co-chairs: D.J. Bellegarde & P.E. James Prentice).

44 *A Special Issue on Land Claims Reform*, Indian Claims Commission Proceedings [1995] 2 ICCP (Co-chairs: D.J. Bellegarde & P.E. James Prentice) at 9.

45 Royal Commission on Aboriginal Peoples, volume 4, Pt. 5, section 5.4 "The Institutional Interests of the Federal Government."

46 See Recommendation 2.4.29 at Report of the Royal Commission on Aboriginal Peoples, *Restructuring the Relationship*, Volume Two, Part Two (Ottawa: Supply and Services, 1996)

The Commission recommends that:

2.4.29 Federal companion legislation to the royal proclamation provide for the establishment of an independent administrative tribunal, to be called the Aboriginal Lands and Treaties Tribunal.

5

Métis

POINTS TO REMEMBER

1. "Métis" have been called the "forgotten people" because they have received so little recognition of their distinctive culture.

2. The Métis people are diverse, and encompass a number of different historical and cultural situations. In the past, those whose ancestors included French fur traders were called "Métis", while those who were descended partly from English fur traders were referred to as "Half-Breeds".

3. There is now a realization of the importance of Métis in Canadian history, and a growing recognition of Métis peoples in contemporary Canadian society.

4. Many courts have begun to recognize that Métis have hunting rights, similar to Indians.

1. INTRODUCTION

The Métis people are named in the Constitution as one of the Aboriginal peoples of Canada.[1] They have played an important historical role from the days of the fur traders, but their cultures have been largely ignored. The federal government still refuses to recognize Métis as a people under federal jurisdiction. Consequently, Métis have not received the benefits of federal programs, a federal land base, or adequate recognition in the land claims process.

This chapter will outline some of the legal issues which are distinct for Métis people, including identification, and hunting and fishing rights. Please note, however, that many other chapters of this book which address issues relating to Aboriginal peoples in general will also be relevant to the Métis.

2. WHO ARE THE MÉTIS?

The term Métis, like the term "Indian" is difficult to define because there is so much diversity, and those that are Métis have different definitions for themselves. The Métis of the Red River Valley associated with Louis Riel had their own language, Michif, and a vibrant culture which exists to this day. Their parents were generally French-Indian.[2] Those that had British fathers were generally referred to as "half-breeds".[3] In Ontario, there were a number of "half-breed" communities. For example, in James Bay, there was a well documented community around the Hudsons Bay post at Moose Factory.[4] There are also groups of people of mixed heritage who were not born into Métis or "Half-Breed" communities. They were born when their mothers married non-Indians, and lost their Indian status. Many of these people ended up in urban centres. Sometimes, these people identified themselves as "non-status Indians". Many in this group regained their status after 1985 when the *Indian Act* was changed to increase the number of people eligible to be registered. (See Chapter 9, "First Nation Citizenship and Indian Act Registration").

An important issue among the Métis is identification. Because there is no national registry system and because Crown governments have failed to recognize Métis communities, there is no universal agreement on who a Métis person is. This has raised problems in court cases when Métis rights are asserted. Métis organizations have drafted their own definitions, and most issue cards identifying their members.

The definition suggested by the Royal Commission on Aboriginal Peoples follows:

> Every person who —
> (a) identifies himself or herself as Métis and
> (b) is accepted as such by the nation of Métis people with which that person wishes to be associated, on the basis of criteria and procedures determined by that nation,
> is to be recognized as a member of that nation for purposes of nation-to-nation negotiations and as Métis for that purpose.[5]

Over the years, some representatives of the Métis have pushed for an enumeration process to identify and register Métis people in Canada. This demand was supported by the Royal Commission on Aboriginal Peoples,[6] and the federal government has committed itself to this process in Saskatchewan and in the Northwest Territories.[7]

There are two national organizations representing this constituency. The Métis National Council (MNC) represents Métis who are descendants of the Red River Métis nation. The Congress of Aboriginal Peoples (CAP) represents many of the other Aboriginal people who might call themselves Métis. In some provinces there are two organizations which are affiliated with each of these national bodies. In Ontario, for example, the Métis Nation of Ontario is affiliated with the MNC and the Ontario Métis and Aboriginal Association is affiliated with CAP.

The internal affairs of these organizations are not set out in a special statute, unlike Indian bands which are established under the *Indian Act*. Because the Métis representative bodies are usually incorporated under federal or provincial law, they are governed by the constitution of the organization, and the legislation on non-profit corporations.[8] (See Chapter 9, "Elections and Referenda" for a discussion of voting requirements under non-profit corporation legislation.)

3. RECOGNITION OF MÉTIS COMMUNITIES

The federal government does not recognize that Métis are included as peoples with whom the federal government has a constitutional relationship.[9] It has therefore fallen largely on the provinces to deal with Métis and non-status Indian issues. Most provinces provide some funding through Aboriginal programs generally, and the federal government provides some funding for institutions like Friendship Centres. But it is clear that Métis do not receive the same recognition as Indians. Métis have launched a number of court cases arguing that they should receive equal access to programs.[10] For example there was an important challenge to an arrangement in Ontario where the proceeds of the one reserve casino run by the Chippewas of Rama was to be distributed only to *Indian Act* Band Councils. The Ontario Court of Appeal held that the province did not have an obligation to ensure that some of the proceeds were distributed to Métis or Aboriginal organizations that were not recognized under the *Indian Act*.[11]

(a) The Métis Settlements Act of Alberta

Alberta has created Métis settlements and given recognition to its Métis people.[12] The Alberta legislation provides for the protection of a collective land base for Métis settlements, the development of a local government, financial administration, a landholding system, and a Métis settlement appeal tribunal.[13]

There are eight settlements governed by a settlement council. These settlement councils have powers analogous to municipalities, such as by-law authority and policy development.[14]

Generally, Métis title to land is held by an individual member and is limited to an area of 175 acres. However, an additional 167 acres may be allotted if required for business purposes. Further, the holder of Métis title may lease lands to anyone, but leasing to non-settlement members requires approval of the relevant settlement council.[15]

(b) Constitutional protection in Manitoba

In Manitoba the Métis are recognized in the *Manitoba Act, 1870*,[16] which was subsequently accorded Constitutional status by the *Constitution Act, 1871*.[17] A total of 1.4 million acres was allocated for the benefit of the families of the Métis under this law.[18]

Although the *Manitoba Act, 1870* purported to extinguish the Métis Indian title in return for land grants there have been consistent allegations of major irregularities in the process. For example, the 1.4 million acres of land was exhausted before all claims had been accommodated. As a result, many claimants were issued scrip rather than direct land grants.[19] Land allotments and scrip became the target for unscrupulous trading agents. The result was rampant fraud and exploitation of individual Métis.[20] Manitoba Métis are now suing Manitoba and the federal government for failing to live up to their obligations under the Manitoba Act.[21]

4. ABORIGINAL AND TREATY RIGHTS OF MÉTIS

Métis and "Half-Breeds" were not treated as Indians, but neither was their Aboriginal heritage entirely ignored. Prime Minister Wilfred Laurier clearly recognized that their Indian heritage gave them an interest in land.[22]

An example of the range of ways of addressing the rights of Métis is found in Ontario where three approaches were used: a separate treaty with "Half-breeds", inclusion of "Half-breed" individuals in treaties, and granting land or scrip (a payment of money).

The first method took place in the Fort Frances area in Northwestern Ontario in 1875: a "Half-breed" community signed a Half-breed

Adhesion to Treaty No. 3. This meant that they were recognized as a distinct people entitled to treaty benefits, including their own reserve.[23]

The second method was to have "Half-Breeds" sign treaties not as communities but as individuals. In Fort Albany, on James Bay, for example, people known to be "Half-breeds", as distinct from Indians, were signed up to the treaty, and they were treated in law like Indians.[24]

The third method, scrip, was the approach taken in Manitoba and the Northwest Territory between 1870 and 1923. In Ontario, a sizeable and well-established "Half-breed" community in Moose Factory was excluded from Treaty No. 9 in 1905. When they demanded scrip, like other "Half-breeds", they were promised 160 acres by the province. This promise has never been fulfilled, and a claim remains outstanding to this day.

While the Supreme Court of Canada has released several important decisions on the meaning of Aboriginal and treaty rights for First Nations, the court has not decided on the Aboriginal and treaty rights of the Métis. It is clear that there must be some differences because the Métis relationship to Canada was different from the Indian relationship, and because Métis society was distinct from Indian cultures.[25]

5. HUNTING AND FISHING RIGHTS

For many Métis people, especially in rural areas, hunting and fishing were important sources of food and an important aspect of their culture. Unlike Indians, however, Métis rights were not recognized by Canadian courts until recently. There is now a strong line of court cases recognizing the hunting and fishing rights of Métis when a number of elements converge, including Aboriginal heritage,[26] identification with a Métis community,[27] and a tradition in that community of hunting or fishing.[28]

The legal situation is a bit more complicated in the three Prairie provinces. In those provinces, the rights of "Indians" to hunt for food is protected by a constitutional document called the Natural Resources Transfer Agreement.[29] Some cases have had to consider whether Métis were meant to be included as "Indians" . If they were, Métis would have constitutional protection for hunting for food. The courts have gone both ways on this issue.[30]

6. LAND

For many years, the Métis of Alberta were the only ones to have a secure land base. However, recent land claims agreements in the North have included Métis and more are being negotiated. (See Chapter 4, "Land", for more information).

ENDNOTES

1 The Métis are included in section 35(2) of the *Constitution Act, 1982*:

"In this Act, "aboriginal peoples of Canada" includes the Indian, Inuit and Métis peoples of Canada".

For a general discussion of Métis perspectives and history, see Report of the Royal Commission on Aboriginal Peoples, *Looking Forward, Looking Back*, Vol. 4, Chapter 5 (Ottawa: Minister of Supply and Services Canada, 1996) [hereinafter RCAP, Vol. 4].

2 Report of the Royal Commission on Aboriginal Peoples, *Looking Forward, Looking Back*, Vol. 1 (Ottawa: Minister of Supply and Services Canada, 1996) at 151 [hereinafter RCAP, Vol. 1.]. For an introduction to the use of the terms Métis and "Halfbreed", see Paul Chartrand, "Aboriginal Rights: the Dispossession of the Métis" in (1991), 29 O.H.L.J. 457.

3 The term "Half-Breed" is extremely pejorative, although it is being reclaimed by some people. The term is used here in quotes to indicate its historical significance. See an important discussion on the issue by Métis academic, Paul Chartrand, "Terms of Division: Problems of 'Outside-Naming' for Aboriginal People in Canada" (1991) 2 Journal of Indigenous Studies 1.

4 RCAP, Vol. 4, *supra* note 1 at 259. For a History of treaty-making in James Bay see three short works by John Long, *Treaty No. 9: The Negotiations 1901-1928, Treaty No. 9: The Half-Breed Question, 1902-1910*, and *Treaty No. 9: The Indian Petitions, 1889-1927* (Cobalt, Ontario: Highway Book Shop, 1978). [hereinafter John Long].

5 Recommendation 4.5.2 of RCAP, Vol. 4, *supra* note 4 at 203 supports the self-identification of Métis.

In *R. v. Blais*, leave to appeal allowed (1998), [1999] 2 W.W.R. 445 (Man. C.A. [In Chambers]) [1998] 4 C.N.L.R. 103 (Man. Q.B.) the court referred to the definition found in the Métis Nation Accord which was negotiated in 1992 with the provincial and federal governments during the Charlottetown Accord constitutional process:

For the purposes of the Métis nation and this Accord

(a) Métis means an aboriginal person who self-identifies as Métis who is distinct from Indian and Inuit and is a descendant of those Métis who received or were entitled to receive land grants and/or Scrip under the provisions of the *Manitoba Act 1870* or the *Dominion Lands Act* as enacted from time to time.

In *R. v. Buckner*, [1997] O.J. No. 1165 (Ont. Prov. Div.) the Ontario Provincial Court accepted the definition provided by the Métis Nation of Ontario:

Anyone of aboriginal ancestry who self-identifies as Métis; is distinct from Indian or Inuit; has at least one grandparent who is aboriginal and who is accepted by the Métis Nation of Ontario.

6 The RCAP included the Proposed Métis Nation Accord from the Charlottetown Accord, which provides at s. 2 for the establishment of enumeration and a Métis registry, RCAP, Vol. 4, *supra* note 4 at 378.

7 The Department of Indian Affairs and Northern Development, *Gathering Strength — Canada's Aboriginal Action Plan* (Ottawa: Minister of Public Works and Government Services Canada, 1997) at 15.

8 See *Card v. Western Region 2A Regional Council Inc.* (1997), 156 Sask. R. 213 (Sask. Q.B.) where the court resolved a dispute within a Saskatchewan Métis organization by referring to the Constitution of the Métis Nation of Saskatchewan and the provincial *Non-Profit Corporations Act, 1995*, S.S. 1995, c. N-4.2. *Parisien v. Sasknative Economic Development Corp.* [1999] S.J. No. 417 (Sask.Q.B.) was a case in which the court disapproved of the interference of the political leadership in the management of the corporation. The court dealt with the dispute between a provincial Métis association and one of its locals in *North Cariboo Métis Assn. v. Métis Provincial Council of British Columbia*, [1999] B.C.J. No. 2038 (B.C.S.C.).

9 Commentators who argue that Métis should be included in 91(24) include C. Chartier, " *'Indian': an analysis of the term as used in section 91(24) of the BNA Act*," (1978-79) 43 Sask. L. Rev. 37, and B. Slattery, "First Nations and the Constitution: A Question of Trust", (1992), 71 Canadian Bar Review 261 at 283. For arguments that section 91(24) should include Métis see RCAP, Vol. 4, supra note 4 at 209.

10 See *Ardoch Algonquin First Nation & Allies v. Ontario* (1997), (sub nom. *Lovelace v. Ontario*) [1998] 2 C.N.L.R. 36 (Ont. C.A.), leave to appeal allowed (sub nom. *Lovelace v. Ontario*) [1998] 1 C.N.L.R. iv (S.C.C.) which held that the provincially approved arrangement which sent casino revenues only to First Nations did not breach section 15 of the *Charter of Rights and Freedoms*.

11 *Ardoch Algonquin First Nation & Allies v. Ontario* (1997), (sub nom. *Lovelace v. Ontario*) [1998] 2 C.N.L.R. 36 (Ont. C.A.), leave to appeal allowed (sub nom. *Lovelace v. Ontario*) [1998] 1 C.N.L.R. iv (S.C.C.) In *R. v. Perry* (1997), (sub nom. *Perry v. Ontario*) [1998] 2 C.N.L.R. 79 (Ont. C.A.), leave to appeal refused (1997), (sub nom. *Perry v. Ontario*) [1998] 1 C.N.L.R. iv (note) (S.C.C.) the Ontario Court of Appeal held that Indians and Métis could be treated differently under provincial government hunting policies. In *Labrador Métis Assn. v. Canada (Minister of Fisheries & Oceans)* (1997), 126 F.T.R. 115 (Fed. T.D.) the Federal Court dismissed a challenge by the Labrador Métis Association to a federal scheme of issuing communal fishing licenses only to "First Nations". However, in *R. v. Morin*, (1997), [1998] 1 C.N.L.R. 182 (Sask. Q.B.) the Saskatchewan Queen's Bench held that provincial fishing laws could not treat Métis differently from Indians.

12 Alberta has passed extensive legislation to recognize eight Métis settlements and has provided for a $310 million financial package spread out over 17 years. (See The *Constitution of Alberta Amendment Act, 1990,* S.A. 1990, c. C-22.2; *Métis Settlements Land Protection Act,* S.A. 1990, c. M-14.8; *Métis Settlements Accord Implementation Act,* S.A. 1990, c. M-14.5; *Métis Settlements Act,* S.A. 1990, c. M-14.3.)

13 See Catherine Bell, *Alberta's Métis Settlements Legislation: An Overview of Ownership and Management of Settlement lands* (Saskatchewan: Canadian Plains Research Centre, University of Regina, 1994) at 1. A decision of the Métis Settlements Appeal Tribunal was considered in *Paddle Prairie Métis Settlement v. Métis Settlements Appeal Tribunal* [1999] 1 C.N.L.R. 134 (Alta.C.A.) There was a land dispute between two members of the Paddle Prairie Métis Settlement. The matter was decided by the Appeal Tribunal. An application for leave to appeal to the Alberta Court of Appeal was refused. The court found that the Tribunal had relied on the wrong section of the *Métis Settlements Act,* but that the Tribunal could have come to the same conclusion had it relied on the correct section of the *Act.* For more on the Tribunal and copies of its decisions, see Catherine Bell, *Contemporary Métis Justice: The Settlement Way,* Saskatoon: Native Law Centre (1999).

14 See Schedule 1 of the *Métis Settlement Act* for by-law making authority of Settlement Councils. For a detailed description of settlement council powers see Catherine Bell, *supra* note 13.

15 See Métis Settlements General Council Land Policy (G.C.P. 90003), *Alberta Gazette,* 1992, I.2592 (draft 09/12/91), part 4, *Métis Settlement Act,* s. 2.8 and 3.3. Also, Catherine Bell, *supra* note 13 at 42.

16 *Manitoba Act, 1870* (U.K.), 33 Victoria, c. 3, reprinted in R.S.C. 1985, App. II, No. 8.

17 *Constitution Act, 1871* (U.K.) 34-35 Victoria, c. 28.

18 See RCAP, Vol. 4, *supra* note 4 at 324.

19 See RCAP, Vol. 4, *supra* note 4 at 334.

20 See RCAP, Vol. 4, *supra* note 4 at 341 and 347.

21 One example of a lawsuit by Métis against the province of Manitoba is *Dumont v. Canada (Attorney General)* (1991), [1992] 2 C.N.L.R. 34 (Man. C.A.). The statement of claim was struck out at trial, but was restored by the Supreme Court of Canada in [1990] 2 C.N.L.R. 19 (S.C.C.). Pre-trial motions have been fought in (1990), [1991] 3 C.N.L.R. 22 (Man. Q.B.), reversed (1991), [1992] 2 C.N.L.R. 34 (Man. C.A.). As of publication this case had not been tried.

22 Prime Minister Wilfred Laurier signed an Order-in-Council in 1899 dealing with land allocation to the Half-breeds of the Northwest Territory:

> The Minister submits that it seems to him moreover that the Half-Breed of the territory referred to would have good reason to be dissatisfied. . . . Whatever rights they have, they have in virtue of their Indian blood; and the first interference with such rights will be when a surrender is effected of the territorial rights of the Indians. It is obvious that while differing in degree, Indian and Half-Breed rights in an unceded territory must be co-existent, and should properly be extinguished at the same time.

For more discussion of Aboriginal rights of Métis and "Half-breeds", see Richard Hardy, "Métis Rights in the Mackenzie River District of the Northwest Territories", [1980] 1 C.N.L.R. 1 at 17. See also B. Slattery, "The Constitutional Guarantee of Aboriginal and Treaty Rights", (1983), 8 Queen's L.J. 232 at 269 and Paul Chartrand, *supra*, note 2.

For a view arguing that Métis do not have Aboriginal rights, see Thomas Flanagan, "The Case Against Métis Aboriginal Rights", in Boldt and Long, *The Quest for Justice: Aboriginal Peoples and Aboriginal Rights* (Toronto: University of Toronto Press, 1985).

23 In time, this community was recognized as a Band under the *Indian Act* and treated like Indians.

24 For a history of treaty-making in James Bay as it affected both Indians and Métis see three short works by John Long, *supra* note 4.

25 In *R. v. Vanderpeet* (sub nom. *R. v. Van der Peet*) [1996] 4 C.N.L.R. 177 (S.C.C.), reconsideration refused (January 16, 1997), Doc. 23803

(S.C.C.) Mr. Justice Lamer indicated that Métis rights may be considered on a different basis from Indian rights:

> Although s. 35 includes the Métis within its definition of "aboriginal peoples of Canada", and thus seems to link their claims to those of other aboriginal peoples under the general heading of "aboriginal rights", the history of the Métis, and the reasons underlying their inclusion in the protection given by s. 35, are quite distinct from those of other Aboriginal peoples in Canada. As such, the manner in which the Aboriginal rights of other Aboriginal peoples are defined is not necessarily determinative of the manner in which the Aboriginal rights of the Métis are defined. At the time when this Court is presented with a Métis claim under s. 35 it will then, with the benefit of the arguments of counsel, a factual context and a specific Métis claim, be able to explore the question of the purposes underlying s. 35's protection of the Aboriginal rights of Métis people, and answer the question of the kinds of claims which fall within s. 35(1)'s scope when the claimants are Métis. The fact that, for other Aboriginal peoples, the protection granted by s. 35 goes to the practices, traditions and customs of aboriginal peoples prior to contact, is not necessarily relevant to the answer which will be given to that question. It may, or it may not, be the case that the claims of the Métis are determined on the basis of the pre-contact practices, traditions and customs of their Aboriginal ancestors; whether that is so must await determination in a case in which the issue arises [at 207].

26 The question of Aboriginal heritage arises in a number of different contexts. In *R. v. Chevrier*, (1988), [1989] 1 C.N.L.R. 128 (Ont. Dist. Ct.) the court held that although the accused was of 'mixed-blood' and was not a registered Indian, the fact that he could trace his descent to a signatory of relevant treaty was sufficient evidence to exercise his treaty rights and *R. v. Fowler*, [1993] 3 C.N.L.R. 178 (N.B. Prov. Ct.) the court found that the though the accused was not a registered Indian, he was a descendent from signatories to a treaty and that was sufficient proof of Aboriginal heritage. The court found that the individual was eligible to be registered as an Indian, so that was sufficient.

27 *R. v. Powley*, [1999] 1 C.N.L.R. 153 (Ont. Prov. Div.).

28 See *R. v. Buckner*, [1997] O.J. No. 1165 (Ont. Prov. Div.) In this case, the court held that the "Half-Breed Adhesion" of Treaty #3 was a source of rights for Métis. In *R. v. Morin, supra* note 11, the Queen's Bench upheld the trial judge's finding that the Métis in this instance continued to live off the land, further, scrip did not result in extinguishment of the right to hunt and fish.

29 *Constitution Act 1930*, R.S.C. 1985, App. II, No. 26, s. 13 of the Schedule (1) (*Manitoba*), Natural Resources Transfer Agreement provides:

13.   In order to secure to the Indians of the Province the continuance of the supply of game and fish for their support and subsistence, Canada agrees that the laws respecting game in force in the Province from time to time shall apply to the Indians within the boundaries thereof, provided, however, that the said Indians shall have the right, which the Province hereby assures to them, of hunting, trapping and fishing game and fish for food at all seasons of the year on all unoccupied Crown lands and on any other lands to which the said Indians may have a right of access.

30   In Saskatchewan (*R. v. Grumbo*, [1998] 3 C.N.L.R. 172 (Sask. C.A.) and in Alberta, (*R. v. Desjarlais* (1995), [1996] 3 C.N.L.R. 113 (Alta. C.A.)) the courts appear to be favouring the approach that Métis are included in the NRTA, *supra*, while in Manitoba, the court appears to be going in the other direction (*R. v. Blais*, [1998] 4 C.N.L.R. 103 (Man. Q.B.), leave to appeal allowed (1998), [1999] 2 W.W.R. 445 (Man. C.A. [In Chambers]).

6

Inuit

1. INTRODUCTION

For the Inuit, change has been very rapid, from the first real intrusions of settlers in the 1950s to the negotiation of land claims agreements across their territory, culminating in the establishment of Nunavut on April 1, 1999.

In the early years, European disease decimated some communities, and in the 1950s there were dramatic relocations of Inuit from Quebec, Inukjuak and Baffin Island to the High Arctic. Often these communities were relocated for the convenience of government administration and a perceived need to industrialize and assimilate Inuit. The consequences of the relocations included increased dependence on government, declining health, cultural disintegration and loss of self-sufficiency.[1] For example, the Inuit of Hebron and Nutak, Labrador were relocated to three communities:

> Five families would be moved to Nain, 10 families would go to Hopedale, and 43 families would go to Makkovik. Their only choice in the matter was decide how relatives would be separated according to these quotas.[2]

For the Inuit as a whole, Nunavut provided the largest of the pieces of self-government. The first agreement was for the Inuit of James Bay in Québec, and the second for the Inuvialuit of the Western Arctic. Only the Inuit of northern Labrador lack a negotiated agreement. This chapter will provide a brief description of the regime under each of the three major land claims agreements which have been negotiated.

2. NUNAVUT

On April 1, 1999, the new territory of Nunavut[3] came into being after over twenty years of negotiation, and a painful division of the Northwest Territories. The agreement covers 1,900,000 square kilometres of the Eastern Arctic, including seven of Canada's largest islands and two-thirds of the country's coastline. It constitutes one-fifth of Canada's total land mass.

There are two parts to the arrangement for Nunavut. The first part is a land claim agreement which was ratified by Parliament in June of 1993. This agreement protects land and resources of the Inuit. The second part is the creation of the territory of Nunavut, which has an elected government similar to other provinces and territories in Canada.

(a) The Land Claim

Under the land claim, Inuit title is recognized to approximately 352,191 square kilometres of land,[4] of which 35,257 square kilometres include mineral rights.[5] Monetary compensation includes a capital transfer payment of $1.148 billion[6] payable to the Inuit over 14 years,[7] a $13 million Training Trust Fund[8] and a share of federal government royalties from oil, gas and mineral development on Crown lands.[9]

Throughout Nunavut, the Inuit have the right to harvest wildlife on lands and water[10] and the right to the use of the water.[11] Other provisions include:

- the right of first refusal on sport and commercial development of renewable resources in the Nunavut Settlement area.[12]
- rights to carving stone.[13]
- the creation of three new federally funded national parks, including provision for the involvement of the Inuit in the planning and management of parks.[14]

(b) Co-management under the land claim

A number of wildlife management, resource management and environmental boards are established to provide Inuit with a formal role in making recommendations to government decision-makers. The Boards are generally composed of the same number of representatives from the Tunngavik Federation of Nunavut as from the federal and territorial governments. Since the territorial government will be dominated by Inuit, they will likely be a majority on the Boards.

An independent *Surface Rights Tribunal* is established to resolve matters including disputes between Inuit land owners, who occupy Crown lands and persons holding subsurface rights who wish to access those lands. The tribunal will also address disputes concerning loss to Inuit from damage to wildlife by development.[15] If the parties cannot come to an agreement, the tribunal has powers to establish the terms and conditions of a right of access to Inuit-owned lands.[16] If the dispute relates to wildlife, the tribunal may determine liability and amount of compensation to be awarded to Inuit harvesters.[17] At least half the members of any panel in a case dealing with Inuit-owned lands must be residents of the Nunavut Settlement Area.[18]

The *Nunavut Impact Review Board* is the environmental assessment agency for the Nunavut Settlement Area. The Board examines the impact of project proposals on the land, air and water, and on the people of the Nunavut Settlement Area. They rely on traditional Inuit knowledge and recognized scientific methods to assess and monitor the environmental, cultural and socioeconomic impacts of proposals.[19] The Board determines whether project proposals should proceed to develop and, if so, under what conditions.[20]

The *Nunavut Water Board* is responsible for the regulation, use and management of water in the Nunavut Settlement Area.[21] In reviewing water applications the Board determines whether water applications should proceed to development and if so, under what conditions.[22]

The *Nunavut Planning Commission* will give Inuit control over all activities on their settlement lands, as well as a say in what happens on Crown lands.[23] The Commission will work with the territorial government to establish broad planning policies, objectives and goals for the Nunavut Settlement Area,[24] including land use plans that guide resource use and development in the region.[25]

The *Nunavut Wildlife Management Board* is the main instrument for wildlife management in the Nunavut Settlement Area and the main regulator of access to wildlife.[26] The purpose of the Board is to create a system of harvesting rights and priorities and privileges that reflect current and traditional Inuit harvesting.[27] The wildlife management system will be governed by and implement principles of conservation.[28] The exercise of harvesting by Inuit will be overseen by local Hunters and Trappers Organizations and Regional Wildlife Organizations.[29] Generally, the function of these organizations is to manage the harvesting among members.[30] The Inuit have free and unrestricted access to all lands, water and marine areas within the Nunavut Settlement Area for harvesting purposes subject to certain limitations.[31]

(c) Beneficiaries under the land claim agreement

An important part of the land claims agreements is the definition of beneficiaries. In the Nunavut agreement, the Inuit are to determine their membership internally based on criteria developed by them.[32] The agreement generally defines "Inuit" as Aboriginal people, who have traditionally used and occupied, and currently use and occupy, the lands and waters of the Nunavut Settlement Area.[33]

The beneficiaries are represented by the Tunngavik Federation of Nunavut. Only the Inuit beneficiaries can participate in the federation. It is a separate entity from the public government of Nunavut which is described below.

(d) Surrender of Aboriginal rights

The Agreement attempts to provide finality and predictability of interests by requiring a surrender of Aboriginal rights. For the rights and benefits provided to the Inuit by the Agreement, the Inuit agreed to cede, release, and surrender all their aboriginal claims, rights, titles and interests, in and to lands and waters anywhere within Canada and adjacent offshore areas within the sovereignty or jurisdiction of Canada.[34] They also agreed, on behalf of their heirs, descendants and successors not to assert any cause of action, claim or demand of any nature based on any aboriginal claims, rights, title or interests in and to lands and waters.

(e) Government in the Nunavut Territory

The second part of the arrangement for Nunavut is the establishment of a separate territory, created by splitting the Northwest Territories into two. An extra Senate seat has been created for the new territory. The capital is Iqualuit, on Baffin Island.

Any resident of Nunavut, Inuit or non-Inuit, may vote for the elected legislative assembly. The nineteen elected members choose a government leader and ministers by consensus. The assembly will sit at least once every 12 months, and there will be an election every five years.[35]

The government of Nunavut will gradually assume the responsibilities of the Northwest Territories until the transfer is completed in 2009. The legislature has powers to make new laws similar to the other two territories. An important power is the administration of justice in Nunavut, including the organization of territorial courts, and the establishment and maintenance of prisons. The legislature will also have authority to make laws for the preservation, use and promotion of the Inuktitut language.[36]

The Nunavut territory is made up of three distinct regions and twenty-eight communities. The government will have 10 departments in 11 different communities.[37] As a result, the Nunavut government will be very decentralized.

3. JAMES BAY AND NORTHERN QUEBEC AGREEMENT[38]

Like many of the other provinces in Canada, Quebec did not recognize the existence of Aboriginal rights, and treated its northern territory as its own. In the early 1970s it decided to commence a massive hydro-electric project which would change the course of rivers, and flood vast territories occupied by the Cree. The Crees commenced a court case to stop the development. Although the case was ultimately unsuccessful in the courts,[39] it forced the parties to the negotiating table, and resulted in the negotiation of Canada's first modern treaty on land and self-government. An agreement which included the Crees, the Inuit and the Naskapi was concluded in 1975 and in 1977. This agreement is unique, in that the signatories are not only the Crees, the Inuit and the two Crown governments, Canada and Quebec. Three corporations are also parties — the Société d'énergie de la Baie James, Société de développement de la Baie James and Hydro-Québec.

The rights in this agreement are treaty rights protected by the Constitution.[40] This fact plays an important part in discussions on separation for Québec. Although Québec argues that it will claim sovereignty over the territory within the current provincial boundaries, the Crees and Inuit point out that the James Bay and Northern Quebec Agreement (JBNQA) prevents Québec from taking any unilateral action which will change the Agreement. The Supreme Court of Canada has stated that if there were unilateral secession, negotiations would have to take into account the interests of the aboriginal people.[41]

(a) Territory

The territory covered by the agreement is huge, including the majority of the land mass of the province. The territory is divided into three categories of land. In each category, there is a balance between rights for the Inuit, and the rights of the province.

Category I lands are for the exclusive use and benefit of the Inuit.[42] Title to approximately 3,150 square miles is transferred to the Inuit Community Corporation for Inuit community purposes, including commercial, industrial and residential development.[43] These lands, however, remain under provincial jurisdiction. Inuit cannot sell or transfer except to Quebec.[44] There are also Special Category I lands which have somewhat fewer protections from provincial intrusion.[45]

About 35,000 square miles, are set aside as Category II lands.[46] The title to these lands are in the province, and the province has the right to initiate development activities. However, Inuit have exclusive hunting, fishing and trapping rights on these lands.[47] If the land is expropriated by Quebec for development activities, the Inuit have a right to replacement land, or to compensation.[48]

The rest of the land is Category III. Both Native and non-Native people may hunt and fish here subject to regulations adopted in accordance with the Agreement.[49] Aboriginal groups have the exclusive rights to harvest certain aquatic species and fur-bearing mammals and to participate in the administration and development of the land.[50]

(b) Government

Inuit communities are incorporated as municipalities under Quebec law and specific powers are delegated to them by Quebec legislation. A regional government structure has been established under a provincial act concerning the Kativik regional government.[51] The Regional government also administers the Kativik Health and Social Services Council.[52]

The Kativik School Board has responsibility for developing and implementing culturally appropriate educational programs in elementary, secondary and adult education.[53] The Federal government funds 25% of the Inuit budget for education, but responsibility for the management of education rests primarily with Quebec.[54]

(c) Co-management

The participation of Inuit in decision-making on all three categories of land is an important aspect of the Agreement.

A *Hunting, Fishing and Trapping Coordinating Committee* is established to review, manage, supervise and regulate the Hunting, Fishing and Trapping Regime.[55] The committee is composed of representatives from federal and provincial governments, the James Bay Cree, the Inuit and the Cree-Naskapi. It administers, reviews and regulates wildlife harvesting and may also set harvesting limits and advise governments on wildlife management.[56] A predominant number of persons charged with enforcing the Hunting, Fishing and Trapping Regime should be native.[57]

The Inuit are entitled to one representative on the *Environmental Expert Committee* of La Societé d'énergie de la Baie James. The member will participate fully, but may only intervene or submit briefs on matters which affect areas north of the 55th parallel.[58]

The *Environmental Quality Commission* is responsible for the administration and supervision of the environmental and social impact assessment process in the region with respect to matters within provincial jurisdiction. There is a nine member board, with four members appointed by the Kativik Regional government. Two members must be Inuit resident in the region.[59]

A *Federal Environmental and Social Impact Assessment and Review Screening Committee* is established to monitor all development projects or development in the region.[60]

(d) Inuit Beneficiaries

A person is entitled to be enrolled as a beneficiary under the Agreement if on November 15, 1974 he or she was a person of Inuit ancestry born in Quebec, is ordinarily a resident in Quebec, or is recognized as a member by on the Inuit communities, or is the adopted child of a person of Inuit ancestry born in Quebec by November 15, 1974.[61]

Makivik Corporation was created to be the legal entity to receive and administer the compensation monies, oversee the implementation of the JBNQA, and to ensure the integrity of the Agreement.[62] Compensation funding for the Inuit was paid directly to the Makivik Corporation. Title to lands was vested in the individual Inuit community corporations.[63]

(e) Surrender of Aboriginal rights

For the rights and benefits contained within the agreement, the James Bay Crees and Inuit of Quebec, ceded, released, surrendered and conveyed all their Native claims, rights, titles and interests, in and to land in the Territory and in Quebec and Canada.[64] The signatories agreed that consent to the agreement represents the settlement out of court of all legal proceedings, and they agreed not institute any further proceedings relating to the James Bay Project. All litigation in the court at that time was also considered to be settled out of court by virtue of the agreement.[65] The Crees and Inuit of Quebec renounced any claims against Quebec with respect to royalties, mining duties, taxes or equivalent derived from development and exploitation of the territory.[66]

4. INUVIALUIT FINAL AGREEMENT (THE WESTERN ARCTIC CLAIM SETTLEMENT)[67]

The 1984 land claims agreement included six settlements in the northwest of Canada around the Beaufort Sea: Sachs Harbour, Holman Island, Paulatuk, Tuktoyaktuk, Inuvik and Aklavik. Their title was recognized for approximately 91,000 square kilometres out of the 435,000 square kilometre area they traditionally use and occupy.[68] However, they own subsurface rights to only 13,000 square kilometres of their land,[69] while the Crown retains subsurface rights to the remaining land.[70] Compensation included $45 million to be paid over 13 years, a $10 million Economic Enhancement Fund and a $7.5 million Social Development Fund.

The Inuvialuit have the exclusive right to harvest certain animal species and have first priority to harvest fish and marine mammals within the region.[71] They also have a preferential right to harvest, for subsistence use, fish[72] and all other wildlife except migratory non-game and insectivorous birds.[73] Compensation payments will be provided to Inuvialuit harvesters from developers for actual losses that occur as the result of development.[74]

(a) Co-management

There are many bodies established which attempt to provide Inuvialuit input into decisions.

The *Inuvialuit Game Council* represents the collective Inuvialuit interest in wildlife. The Council is made up of representatives from each of the six local Hunters and Trappers Committees.[75] It reviews wildlife research proposals from the Canadian Wildlife Service and the renewable resource departments of both territorial governments. It sets funding priorities for these and other implementation tasks related to wildlife and the environment.[76]

Each settlement community has a *Hunters and Trappers Committee*[77] which is responsible for the sub-allocation of community shares for subsistence and other quotas among individuals. The Committee participates in the regulation of the subsistence harvest and the collection of harvest information.[78]

The *Wildlife Management Advisory Council* advises the government and other appropriate bodies on wildlife conservation, management, regulation, policy and administration matters.[79] The Council has an equal number of government and native representatives plus a chairperson.[80]

Advice to the Minister of Fisheries and Oceans on matters relating to fisheries and marine mammals is provided through the *Fisheries Joint Management Committee*.[81]

The *Environmental Impact Screening Committee* determines whether development proposals could have a significant negative impact on the environment or wildlife harvesting.[82] This committee refers development proposals to the *Environmental Impact Review Board* for public review.[83] The Board recommends whether or not the project should proceed, and if it should, on what terms and conditions.[84]

(b) Government

Unlike the other land claims agreements, there are no special provisions on self-government. Like other settlements, however, there are corporations established to implement the agreement. Title to the lands will be vested in the Inuvialuit Land Corporation, owned and controlled by the Inuvialuit.[85] The six communities each have a non-profit corporation to manage the compensation and benefits, and they control the Inuvialuit Regional Corporation.[86]

(c) Beneficiaries

To qualify for beneficiary status under the Western Arctic Claim Settlement, an individual must be a Canadian citizen[87] and meet the following criteria:

    1. be on the official voters' list used for approving the Final Agreement; or,[88]

    2. be of Inuvialuit ancestry and[89]
        a) born in the Inuvialuit Settlement Region or Inuvik, or[90]

b) a resident of the Inuvialuit Settlement Region or Inuvik for a total of at least ten years, or,[91]
3. be the descendent of a beneficiary.[92]

A person may also be eligible if he or she:

1. is of Inuvialuit ancestry and is accepted by an Inuvialuit
Community Corporation as a member; or[93]
2. is an adopted child of a beneficiary described above.[94]

(d) Surrender of Aboriginal Rights

The Inuvialuit cede, release, surrender and covey all their aboriginal claims, rights, title and interests, whatever they may be, in and
to the Northwest Territory and Yukon Territory and adjacent offshore
areas, within the sovereignty or jurisdiction of Canada.[95] The legislation purports to extinguish all aboriginal claims, rights, title and
interests whatever they may be.[96]

5. LABRADOR INUIT LAND CLAIMS AGREEMENT-IN-PRINCIPLE[97]

The refusal of Newfoundland to participate in land claims negotiations delayed progress on this issue for many years. On May 10,
1999, the Inuit succeeded in signing an Agreement in Principle with
Canada and the government of Newfoundland. The Labrador Inuit
Settlement Area will consist of 28,000 square miles of land,[98] and
17,000 square miles of ocean extending out to 12 miles.[99] Within the
settlement area 6,100 square miles of land will be owned by Labrador
Inuit as Labrador Inuit Lands, excluding subsurface resources.[100] Inuit
will have exclusive right to carving stone.[101]

There are specific provisions with respect to water. Everyone may
use water for personal and domestic purposes throughout the settlement area. New commercial or industrial development on Labrador
Inuit Lands must get a water use permit from the province, subject to
approval by the Inuit Central Government.[102] Any establishment of
marine management plans or development of non-renewable resources in the ocean area adjacent to the Settlement Area extending
out to 12 miles requires prior consultation with the Inuit Central
Government. Inuit Impacts and Benefits Agreements are required.[103]

In addition to receiving 25 per cent of provincial revenues from
subsurface developments in Labrador Inuit Lands,[104] Inuit will receive

50 per cent of the first $2 million and five per cent of any additional provincial revenues from subsurface resources in the Settlement area outside of Labrador Inuit Lands. Revenues will be capped when the amount, distributed equally among all beneficiaries, would result in an average per capita income exceeding the average per capita income of all Canadians.[105] The Inuit Central Government will receive 3 per cent of provincial revenues from subsurface resources from the Voisey's Bay project.[106]

The Torngat Mountains National Park Reserve, of approximately 3,000 square miles will be established in the Labrador Inuit Settlement Area.[107]

Land use planning for the Settlement area will be developed jointly by the Province and the Inuit Central Government.[108]

(a) Co-management boards

The *Torngat Wildlife and Plants Management Board* will be appointed by the Province, the Government of Canada, and the Inuit Central Government. It will be the primary body for making recommendations to governments on the conservation and management of wildlife and plants in the Settlement Area.[109] The relevant provincial or federal Minister will retain overall responsibility for the conservation and management of wildlife and plants in the Settlement Area.[110]

The primary body for making recommendations to governments on the conservation and management of fish in the Settlement Area[111] will be the *Torngat Joint Fisheries Board*.[112] The co-management board will be appointed by the Government of Canada, the Province and the Inuit Central Government. Labrador Inuit will have the right to fish for subsistence purposes throughout the Settlement Area.[113] When considering conservation, limits will be set by the Federal Minister on recommendation by the Inuit Central Government.[114]

(b) Government

The Inuit Central Government will make laws primarily for Inuit in Labrador Inuit Lands for matters such as education,[115] health[116] and social services.[117] The Inuit Central Government will also have jurisdiction over its internal affairs, Inuit citizenship and the management of Inuit rights and benefits under the Agreement.[118] The Labrador Inuit will establish their own Constitution, which will establish two levels of government; an Inuit Central Government (Regional) and five Inuit Community Governments.[119]

(c) Beneficiaries

Beneficiaries will mostly be people who traditionally used and occupied, and currently use and occupy, the lands, waters and sea-ice of the Labrador Inuit Land Claims Area.[120] An individual may be enrolled as a beneficiary if he or she

(a) is a Canadian citizen or a permanent resident of Canada; and

(b) is an Inuk pursuant to Inuit customs and traditions and is of Inuit ancestry, or is a Kablunangajuk; and

(c) is permanently resident in the Labrador Inuit Settlement Area or is permanently resident outside the Labrador Inuit Settlement Area and is connected to a Community.[121]

Others eligible include, those of not less than one-quarter Inuit ancestry, minor adoptees, and individuals under legal disability.[122]

(d) Surrender of Aboriginal rights

The Labrador Inuit have never signed a treaty or a land claims agreement with the Government of Canada, the Province of Newfoundland and Labrador or the British Crown. They have claimed Aboriginal rights and title in and to territory in northern Labrador and northeastern Quebec.[123]

ENDNOTES

1 For a detailed account of the relocation of Aboriginal Communities, see Royal Commission on Aboriginal peoples, *Looking Forward, Looking Back* Vol. 1 (Ottawa: Supply and Services, 1996) at 411 [hereinafter Royal Commission on Aboriginal Peoples, Vol. 1]. For a specific analysis of the High Arctic relocation see, Royal Commission on Aboriginal Peoples, *The High Arctic Relocation: A Report on the 1953-55 Relocation* (Ottawa: Supply and Services, 1994).

2 See the Royal Commission on Aboriginal Peoples, Vol. 1, *supra* note 1 at 427.

3 See *Nunavut Land Claims Agreement* (Ottawa: Minister of Indian Affairs and Northern Development and the Tunngavik).

4 *Ibid.* at Schedule 19-2 to 19-7.

5 *Ibid.* at Article 19.2.2.(a) and Schedule 19-2 to 19-7.

6 *Ibid.* at Schedule 29-1 and 29-2.

7 *Ibid.* at Schedule 29-3.

8 *Ibid.* at Article 37.8.3.

9 *Ibid.* at Article 25.1.1.

10 *Ibid.* at Article 5.6.1.

11 *Ibid.* at Article 20.2.2. and 20.2.4.

12 *Ibid.* at Article 5.8.1.

13 *Ibid.* at Article 19.9.1 to 19.9.8.

14 *Ibid.* at Article 8.3.4.

15 *Ibid.* at Article 21.8.1 (a) — (e).

16 *Ibid.* at Article 21.8.1 (a).

17 *Ibid.* at Article 21.8.1 and 21.8.3.

18 *Ibid.* at Article 21.8.7.

19 *Ibid.* at Article 12.2.2 and 12.2.24 (a)(ii).

20 *Ibid.* at Article 12.2.1 to 12.2.5.

21 *Ibid.* at Article 13.2.1.

22 *Ibid.* at Article 13.7.1–13.7.5 and 13.8.1.

23 *Ibid.* at Article 11.2.1.

24 *Ibid.* at Article 11.4.1.

25 *Ibid.* at Article 11.4.4.

26 *Ibid.* at Article 5.1.2 and 5.2.33.

27 *Ibid.* at Article 5.1.3.

28 *Ibid.* at Article 5.1.3 (b).

29 *Ibid.* at Article 5.7.2.

30 *Ibid.* at Article 5.7.3.

31 *Ibid.* at Article 5.7.16.

32 *Ibid.* at Article 35.2.1.

33 *Ibid.* at Article 35.

34 *Ibid.* at Article 2.7.1(a).

35 *Nunavut Act*, S.C. 1993, c. 28.

36 *Ibid.* at s. 23.

37 See Nunavut Planning Commission, News Release, *"Nunavut Government Structure and Political Development"* (1999).

38 *James Bay and Northern Quebec Agreement*, 1975 [hereinafter, *JBNQA*].

39 The Crees initially succeeded in getting an interim injunction to stop the development, but it was overturned a few days later. See the cases chronicling the James Bay dispute with Quebec: *Gros-Louis v. Société de développement de la Baie James* (1973), 8 C.N.L.C. 188 (Que. C.S.); *James Bay Development Corp. v. Kanatewat* (1973), 8 C.N.L.C. 414; and *Société de développement de la Baie James v. Kanatewat* (1974), 8 C.N.L.C. 373 (Que. C.A.).

40 Section 35(3) of the *Constitution Act, 1982* says that treaty rights includes "rights that now exist by way of land claims agreements or may be so acquired". See *Crie (Commission scolaire) c. Canada (Procureur général)*, (sub nom. *Cree School Board v. Canada (Attorney General)*) [1998] 3 C.N.L.R. 24 ((C.S. Qué.) which confirms treaty status of the JBNQA.

41 The *Reference re Secession of Quebec*, [1998] 2 S.C.R. 217 (S.C.C.) 385 dealt with unilateral secession of Quebec, and addressed the rights of Aboriginal people at pages 422 and 442. According to the Royal Commission on Aboriginal Peoples, Canada will have a role as fiduciary in protecting the interests of the Aboriginal Peoples. See Rene Dupuis and Kent McNeil, *Canada's Fiduciary Obligation to Aboriginal Peoples in the Context of Accession to Sovereignty by Quebec* (Ottawa: Minister of Supply and Services, 1995).

42 See the JBNQA, *supra* note 38 at s. 7.1.1.

43 *Ibid.* at s. 7.1.2.

44 *Ibid.* at s. 7.1.5.

45 *Ibid.* at s. 7.1.6.

46 *Ibid.* at s. 7.2.1.

47 *Ibid.* at s. 7.2.

48 *Ibid.* at s. 7.2.3.

49 *Ibid.* at s. 24.3.32.

50 *Ibid.* see Philosophy of the agreement, xvii.

51 *Ibid.* see s. 12, Schedule 2 and s. 13, Schedule 2).

52 *Ibid.* at s. 15.

53 *Ibid.* at s. 17.

54 *Ibid.* at s. 17.0.2.

55 *Ibid.* at s. 24.4.1.

56 *Ibid.* at s. 24.4.

57 *Ibid.* at s. 24.10.

58 *Ibid.* at s. 8.11.5.

59 *Ibid.* at s. 23.3.

60 *Ibid.* at s. 23.4.

61 *Ibid.* at s. 3.2.4.

62 *Ibid.* at s. 7.1.2.

63 *Ibid.* at s. 7.1.3.

64 *Ibid.* at s. 2.1.

65 *Ibid.* at s. 2.4.

66 *Ibid.* at s. 25.2.1.

67 *Inuvialuit Final Agreement*, 1984.

68 *Ibid.* at s. 7 and s. 9.

69 *Ibid.* at s. 7(1)(a)(i) and (ii).

70 *Ibid.* at s. 7(1)(b).

71 *Ibid.* at s. 14(30).

72 *Ibid.* at s. 14(31).

73 *Ibid.* at s. 14(6)(a) (b) (c) (d).

74 *Ibid.* at s. 13(3).

75 *Ibid.* at s. 14(73); 14(74).

76 *Ibid.* at s. 14(74).

77 *Ibid.* at s. 14(75).

78 *Ibid.* at s. 14(78).

79 *Ibid.* at s. 14(45) and 14(47).

80 *Ibid.* at s. 14(46) and 14(62).

81 *Ibid.* at s. 14(61), 14(64), 14(65).

82 *Ibid.* at s. 11(13).

83 *Ibid.* at s. 11(18).

84 *Ibid.* at s. 11(24).

85 *Ibid.* at s. 6(4)(c).

86 *Ibid.* at s. 6(1)(a)-(f).

87 *Ibid.* at s. 5 (2).

88 *Ibid.* at s. 5(2)(a).

89 *Ibid.* at s. 5(2)(b).

90 *Ibid.* at s. 5(c)(i).

91 *Ibid.* at s. 5(c)(ii).

92 *Ibid.* at s. 5(3).

93 *Ibid.* at s. 5(2)(b).

94 *Ibid.* at s. 5(2)(d).

95 *Ibid.* at s. 3(4).

96 *Ibid.* s. 3(5).

97 *Labrador Inuit Land Claims Agreement-in-Principle*, 1999.

98 *Ibid.* at s. 4.3.3.

99 *Ibid.* at s. 4.3.3.

100 *Ibid.* at s. 3.4.1.

101 *Ibid.* at s. 3.6.

102 *Ibid.* at s. 5.2.1 and 5.5.1.

103 *Ibid.* at s. 6.3.1; 6.74 and 6.75.

104 *Ibid.* at s. 3.3.3 and s. 3.4.1.

105 *Ibid.* at s. 7.4.1 and 7.4.4.

106 *Ibid.* at s. 7.5.1.

107 *Ibid.* at s. 9.2.1.

108 *Ibid.* at s. 10.2.3 and s. 10.3.8.

109 *Ibid.* at s. 12.8.1 and 12.9.1.

110 *Ibid.* at s. 12.9.1.

111 *Ibid.* at s. 13.10.

112 *Ibid.* at s. 13.9.

113 *Ibid.* at s. 13.3.1.

114 *Ibid.* at s. 13.10.

115 *Ibid.* at s. 17.7.24.

116 *Ibid.* at s. 17.7.30.

117 *Ibid.* at s. 17.7.43.

118 *Ibid.* at s. 17.7.

119 *Ibid.* at s. 17.3.1 and 17.3.4.

120 *Ibid.* at s. 22.1.1.

121 *Ibid.* at s. 22.2.1.

122 *Ibid.* at s. 22.2.4.

123 *Ibid.* at Preamble.

Aboriginal Governments

7

Self-government

Points to remember

1. Aboriginal people see self-government and self-determination as related to their continued existence as distinct peoples.

2. While both Canadian law and international law give some recognition to self-government rights, courts and governments are hesitant to apply the principle in practice.

3. Different Aboriginal peoples see "self-government" taking different forms. For many First Nations, self-government means the ability to make laws which can override federal and provincial laws. In other contexts, self-government may be the ability to provide services to the members of the community.

1. INTRODUCTION

It would be difficult to say that the term "self-government" has been misunderstood, for it has so many meanings, almost any understanding would find some adherents. For some nations, it may mean the power to make laws within the framework of the Canadian nation state. For the Inuit of Nunavut, it means a land claims agreement combined with the creation of a new territory in which all residents, Inuit and non-Inuit, can participate. In urban situations, it may mean the establishment of social services or a child welfare agency controlled by native people. For some Haudenosaunee, the concept is an extension of colonialism because it falls short of sovereignty.

In the early years, politicians and government policy makers added to the problem by insisting that "self-government" could only be realized by administering some of the services provided by government; that it could not encompass law-making by the Aboriginal nation. This resulted in something of a semantic tug of war over what was "true" self-government, and what was merely "self-administration". While this debate is still alive in some jurisdictions, for the most part it has been laid to rest with the report of the Royal Commission on Aboriginal Peoples. The Royal Commission has given an expansive and flexible definition to the term, which should help focus energies on what to implement, rather than what to theorize about.

It may be easier to grasp the concept if one avoids trying to look for a static definition based on institutions, and legal concepts which exist in the mainstream system. Self-government may be better understood as a bundle of dynamic legal relationships, political aspirations and affirmations of cultural continuity.

2. THE UNITED STATES –– "DOMESTIC DEPENDENT NATIONS"

Indian tribes in the United States are commonly referred to as "domestic dependent nations". The tribes retain sovereignty and make their own laws for their own people. The authority for this power does not come from the Constitution of the United States, but rather is recognized as existing outside the Constitution. Their sovereignty is not absolute, however, and the federal Congress has power to pass laws affecting the tribes. There are two important principles here: first, the tribes have law making power which does not originate from the Constitution of the United States, but which originates from the recognition of tribal sovereignty. Second, the law-making power of the tribe can only be circumscribed when the federal government passes legislation to circumscribe that power.

In practice, the legal regime governing American tribes is a patchwork. In some cases, the federal government allows state law to apply to tribes, so that there is little left of tribal jurisdiction. In other cases, only a few federal restrictions apply so that tribes can make laws on marriage, divorce, minor criminal matters, and set up their own justice systems with very few federal restrictions.[1]

3. CANADA — THE RIGHT TO SELF-GOVERNMENT

Aboriginal people in Canada say that their right to self-government is recognized and affirmed as an existing Aboriginal and treaty right under section 35(1) of the *Constitution Act, 1982* (see Appendix A, "Declaration of the First Nations" for an example). However, because of the hostility of the Crown governments to this idea,

representatives of Aboriginal people fought for a decade to h.
right of self-government explicitly recognized in the Con:
They finally succeeded in 1992, as extensive provisions, not only
recognizing self-government, but for a process to implement self-government, were contained in the Charlottetown Accord. The proposed
amendments, however, were defeated in a national referendum, and
so they never became law. (See Chapter 1, "The Constitutional Framework", for more details).

There is widespread support from legal academics for the existence of a right of self-government.[2] The main legal points of their
argument are the following:

- before the coming of the Europeans, the Aboriginal peoples
  were organized as self-governing societies;[3]
- the Aboriginal peoples were recognized by the Crown as nations capable of entering into treaties;[4]
- the Aboriginal peoples did not give up their right to self-government;[5]
- although the right to self-government may have been restricted,
  it was never extinguished[6]

The federal government has decided to proceed on the basis that
the Aboriginal people do have an inherent right to self-government.
The federal *Agenda for Action with First Nations*, released in January,
1998, states:

> Aboriginal people enjoyed their own forms of government for thou-
> sands of years before this country was founded and they continue to
> have the inherent right to self-government. The federal government is
> committed to working out government-to-government relationships at
> an agreed-upon pace acceptable to First Nations. These government-
> to-government relationships will be consistent with the treaties, the
> recognition of the inherent right of self-government, Aboriginal title,
> and Aboriginal and treaty rights . . .

Similar statements had been made by the Government of Ontario
in 1991 (see Appendix B). A few years earlier, in March 1985, the
Quebec National Assembly passed a resolution calling for negotiations with First Nations on matters including "self-government within
Quebec . . . so as to enable them to develop as distinct nations having
their own identity and exercising their rights within Quebec" (see
Appendix C).

Canadian courts have not yet decided whether or not the Constitution protects the right to self-government. Some lower courts have said that there is no right of self-government for Aboriginal peoples. For instance, a trial judge in British Columbia held that the right of self-government was extinguished. He felt that the Constitution of Canada mentions only two levels of government capable of making laws — the federal government and the provincial government.[7]

However, the Supreme Court of Canada has left the question open. Mr. Justice Lamer made this comment about self-government in *Delgamuukw v. British Columbia*:[8]

> The degree of complexity involved can be gleaned from the Report of the Royal Commission on Aboriginal Peoples, which devotes 277 pages to the issue. That report describes different models of self-government, each differing with respect to their conception of territory, citizenship, jurisdiction, internal government organization, etc.

4. RECOMMENDATIONS OF THE ROYAL COMMISSION ON ABORIGINAL PEOPLES

So what does it mean for Canada if Aboriginal peoples are recognized as nations with the right of self-government? Can the Canadian nation state remain intact? Similar questions are currently being raised throughout the world, as countries strain to find political accommodation for indigenous peoples within their boundaries.

At the United Nations there has been a remarkable turnaround. Until 1989, the U.N. focused on the importance of assimilation of indigenous peoples.[9] In that year, the International Labour Organization enacted a new Convention which recognized the right of indigenous peoples to maintain their own institutions, cultures and identities within the framework of existing nations.[10]

At around the same time, the United Nations Working Group on Indigenous Populations went further with a draft Declaration on the Rights of Indigenous Peoples. This draft stated that "Indigenous peoples . . . have the right to autonomy or self-government in matters relating to their internal and local affairs."[11]

Until the release of the Report of the Royal Commission, however, there was no comprehensive source of ideas on how to implement the principles being developed at the U.N. In spite of the existence of an extremely complex and diverse situation in Canada,

the Royal Commission has succeeded in developing a set of perceptive proposals which will clarify the implications and guide the debate
on these issues.[12]

Quite wisely, the Royal Commission does not gloss over the challenges created by the diverse circumstances of the Aboriginal peoples.
Instead, the Report provides a flexible and creative array of options for
giving political reality to the existence of Aboriginal nations.

The most interesting proposals revolve around three ways of
structuring a new relationship within the existing nation state:

- the nation model
- the public government model
- the community of interest model

(a) The nation model

Sixty to eighty Aboriginal nations are to replace the scattered
Indian Act Bands, Métis communities and Inuit settlements. It is these
Aboriginal nations that will be able to exercise self-government over
their land base and over their citizens.

Consent of Crown governments will not be necessary for an
Aboriginal nation to exercise its authority in "core areas", such as
citizenship, family matters and administration of justice. Once enacted, Aboriginal laws will override federal or provincial laws on
those matters.

The exercise of Aboriginal authority, however, is circumscribed
in a number of ways. For example, Aboriginal authority cannot be
exercised unilaterally when the Aboriginal laws have a major impact
on neighbouring communities or are the object of transcendent federal
or provincial interest. As well, the exercise of authority must conform
to the *Charter of Rights and Freedoms*.

This is the model that will likely be favoured by most First
Nations and Métis with a land base. However, it will likely be some
time before this model is utilized.

There are enormous practical difficulties with creating larger
nations out of 609 fairly independent Indian Bands. Securing a land
base for the Métis outside of Alberta will be a challenge. And the
hostility of the federal and provincial governments to the exercise of
Aboriginal authority will mean progress will be slow.

The next two models already exist on the Canadian political landscape.

(b) The public government model

The territory of Nunavut has been established in the Eastern Arctic. Although the Inuit will be the majority in Nunavut, their government will permit the participation of all residents of the territory, Inuit and non-Inuit. (See Chapter 6, "Inuit," for more details.)

(c) The community of interest model

In urban areas and communities without an exclusive land base, Aboriginal people may provide education, housing or other social services to their members. The organizations delivering a service, or a bundle of services, will most likely exercise authority delegated to them through federal or provincial legislation.

5. CURRENT INITIATIVES

Self-government will not be exercised in the same way by all groups, and it is unlikely that any single community would be interested in undertaking initiatives in all areas.[13] It is therefore likely that for the immediate future Aboriginal communities will identify and work on priorities, while allowing the federal and provincial laws to continue in other areas.

(a) Special purpose agencies and bodies

These organizations may be set up under existing provincial or federal legislation to undertake specific administrative tasks. Examples include Native Child Welfare Agencies, Native community legal aid clinics, and Native Friendship Centres.

(b) Representative organizations

These organizations would not make laws but would be consulted as necessary to create policies or sign agreements on behalf of groups of Aboriginal peoples. Examples of these organizations are tribal councils, the Assembly of First Nations, the Métis National Council and the Native Women's Association.

(c) General law-making bodies

Most Indian bands exercise their authority under the *Indian Act* (see Chapter 8, "Bands, Band Councils and Reserves" for more on the powers of Band Councils under the *Indian Act*.) The Sechelt Band[14] and the Bands covered by the James Bay and Northern Quebec Agreement[15] have negotiated their way out of the *Indian Act* regime. They now operate under their own statutes, which give them more autonomy. Perhaps the most autonomous First Nations are those in the Yukon which have negotiated self-government agreements and are now making their own laws.

Almost all of the Inuit in Canada are now covered by land claims and self-government arrangements. (See Chapter 6, "Inuit" for a description of those agreements.)

The only Métis bodies which can make laws are the settlement councils in Alberta.[16] (See Chapter 5, "Métis" for a description.)

(d) Other initiatives

There are a number of self-government initiatives which address specific regional issues. For example, in Nova Scotia, the *Mi'kmaq Education Act*,[17] will implement an agreement between Canada, and First Nations in Nova Scotia, on education. Once this Act is proclaimed, sections of the *Indian Act* dealing with education will not apply to a community which opts into the agreement.

The *First Nations Land Management Act*[18] changes several provisions in the land regime on the reserves. It gives First Nations more power to make laws on the environment, and takes away some control from the federal government. Fourteen First Nations have decided to opt into this statute.

6. APPENDICES

A. A Declaration of the First Nations
B. Statement of Political Relationship
C. *Assemblée Nationale Résolution* (motion for the Recognition of Aboriginal Rights in Quebec)

APPENDIX A

A Declaration Of The First Nations

We the Original Peoples of this land know the Creator put us here.

The Creator gave us laws that govern all our relationships to live in harmony with nature and mankind.

The laws of the Creator defined our rights and responsibilities.

The Creator gave us our spiritual beliefs, our languages, our culture, and a place on Mother Earth which provided us with all our needs.

We have maintained our freedom, our languages, and our traditions from time immemorial.

We continue to exercise the rights and fulfill the responsibilities and obligations given to us by the Creator for the land upon which we were placed.

The Creator has given us the right to govern ourselves and the right to self-determination.

The rights and responsibilities given to us by the Creator Cannot be altered or taken away by any other Nation.

Assembly of First Nations Conference
December, 1980

. . . .
Chief, Charles Wood   Delbert Riley, President
Chairman, Council of Chiefs   National Indian Brotherhood

APPENDIX B

Statement of Political Relationship

WHEREAS the First Nations represented by the Chiefs-in-Assembly (hereinafter "the First Nations") exist in Ontario as distinct nations, with their governments, cultures, languages, traditions, customs and territories;

AND WHEREAS the Government of Ontario (hereinafter "Ontario") recognizes that its relationships with the First Nations are to be based on the aboriginal rights, including aboriginal title, and treaty rights of the First Nations recognized and affirmed in the *Constitution Act, 1982*, including those formally recognized in the Royal Proclamation of 1763, and in the treaties and agreements with the Crown;

AND WHEREAS Ontario's commitment to and participation in this Statement of Political Relationship is subject to the limits on provincial constitutional authority;

AND WHEREAS it is desirable to minimize conflicts between Ontario and the First Nations;

AND WHEREAS the First Nations and Ontario recognize the need for a mutual understanding of the government(s) to government relationships between them;

NOW THEREFORE THE FIRST NATIONS AND ONTARIO AGREE AS FOLLOWS:

1. The inherent right to self-government of the First Nations flows from the Creator and from the First Nations' original occupation of the land.

2. Ontario recognizes that under the Constitution of Canada the First Nations have an inherent right to self-government within the Canadian constitutional framework and that the relationship between Ontario and the First Nations must be based upon a respect for this right.

3. The First Nations and Ontario — involving the Government of Canada where appropriate — are committed to facilitate the further articulation, the exercise and the implementation

of the inherent right to self-government within the Canadian constitutional framework, by respecting existing treaty relationships, and by using such means as the treaty-making process, constitutional and legislative reform and agreements acceptable to the First Nations and Ontario.

4. Nothing in this Statement of Political Relationship shall be construed as determining Ontario's jurisdiction or as diminishing Canada's responsibilities towards First Nations.

5. This Statement of Political Relationship expresses the political commitment of the First Nations and Ontario and is not intended to be a treaty or to create, redefine or prejudice rights or affect obligations of the First Nations or Ontario, or the aboriginal and non-aboriginal peoples in Ontario.

Signed at Mount McKay, this 6th day of August, 1991.

APPENDIX C

Assemblée Nationale Résolution (Motion for the Recognition of Aboriginal Rights in Quebec)

ASSEMBLÉE NATIONALE
Résolution

Mr. Lévesque (Prime Minister)

Motion for the recognition of aboriginal rights in Québec:

That this Assembly:

Recognizes the existence of the Abenaki, Algonquin, Attikamek, Cree, Huron, Micmac, Mohawk, Montagnais, Naskapi and Inuit nations in Québec;

Recognizes existing aboriginal rights and those set forth in The James Bay and Northern Québec Agreement and The North-eastern Québec Agreement;

Considers these agreements and all future agreements and accords of the same nature to have the same value as treaties;

Subscribes to the process whereby the Government has committed itself with the aboriginal peoples to better identifying and defining their rights—a process which rests upon historical legitimacy and the importance for Québec society to establish harmonious relations with the native peoples, based on mutual trust and a respect for rights;

Urges the government to pursue negotiations with the aboriginal nations based on, but not limited to, the fifteen principles it approved on 9 February 1983, subsequent to proposals submitted to it on 30 November 1982, and to conclude with willing nations, or any of their constituent communities, agreements guaranteeing them the exercise of:

(a) the right to self-government within Québec;
(b) the right to their own language, culture and traditions;
(c) the right to own and control land;

(d) the right to hunt, fish, trap, harvest and participate in wildlife management;

(e) the right to participate in, and benefit from, the economic development of Québec,

so as to enable them to develop as distinct nations having their own identity and exercising their rights within Québec;

Declares that the rights of aboriginal peoples apply equally to men and women;

Affirms its will to protect, in its fundamental laws, the rights included in the agreements concluded with the aboriginal nations of Québec; and

Agrees that a permanent parliamentary forum be established to enable the aboriginal peoples to express their rights, needs and aspirations.

* * *

Québec, March 20th 1985

ENDNOTES

1 For a good introduction to American law, see Douglas Sanders, *Aboriginal Self-government in the United States* (Kingston: Queen's Institute of Intergovernmental Relations, 1985).

2 There are many articles on self-government. The following list is not complete, but provides a good cross section of what is available.

Menno Boldt, 1993 *Surviving as Indians: The Challenge of Self-government* Toronto: University of Toronto Press.

John Borrows, "A Geneology of Law: Inherent Sovereignty and First Nations Self-government" (1992) 30 Osgoode Hall Law Journal 291.

A. Fleras and J.L. Elliot, 1992 *The Nations Within: Aboriginal-State Relations in Canada, the United States, and New Zealand*. Toronto: Oxford University Press.

Peter Hogg and Mary Ellen Turpel, "Implementing Aboriginal Self-government" (1995) 24 Can. Bar. Rev. 187.

John Hylton, ed. *Aboriginal self-government in Canada: Current Trends and Issues*, Saskatoon: Purich Publishing, 1994.

Randy Kapashesit & Murray Klippenstein, "Aboriginal Group Rights and Environmental Protection" (1991), 36 McGill Law Journal 926.

Patrick Macklem, "First Nations Self-government and the Borders of the Canadian Legal Imagination", (1991), 36 McGill L.J. 308.

Ovide Mercredi, and Mary Ellen Turpel. *In the Rapids: Navigating the Future of First Nations*, Toronto: Viking, 1993.

Brian Slattery, "First Nations and the Constitution: A Question of Trust", (1992) 71 Canadian Bar Review 261.

3 Acknowledgement that Aboriginal people were self-governing was most succinctly stated in the often-quoted American case of *Worcester v. Georgia* (1832), 6 Peter 515 at 542:

> America, separated from Europe by a wide ocean, was inhabited by a distinct people, divided into separate nations, independent of each other and of the rest of the world, having institutions of their own, and governing themselves by their own laws.

The Royal Proclamation of October 7, 1763, R.S.C. 1970, App. II, No. 1, also shows that the British Crown recognized self-governing Indian nations:

> And whereas it is just and reasonable, and essential to our Interest . . . that the several Nations or Tribes of Indians . . . should not be molested or disturbed in the Possession of such Parts of Our Dominions and

Territories as, not having been ceded to or purchased by Us, are reserved to them . . . as their Hunting Grounds. We do therefore . . . declare . . . that no Governor or Commander in Chief in any of our Colonies . . . do presume, upon any Pretence whatever, to grant Warrants of Survey, or pass any Patents for Lands beyond the Bounds of their respective Governments . . .

For an explanation of the historical context of the Royal Proclamation, see John Borrows, "Constitutional Law from a First Nation Perspective: Self-government and the Royal Proclamation" (1994) 28 U. B.C. Law Review 1.

4 With respect to the ability to enter into treaties, Lamer, J. said in *Sioui v. Quebec (Attorney General)*, (sub nom. *R. v. Sioui*), [1990] 1 S.C.R. 1025 (S.C.C.):

The mother countries did everything in their power to secure the alliance of each Indian nation and to encourage nations allied with the enemy to change sides. When these efforts met with success, they were incorporated in treaties of alliance or neutrality. This clearly indicates that the Indian nations were regarded in their relations with the European nations which occupied North America as independent nations.

5 The right to continue to be self-governing under the protection of the British Crown was stated in *Worcester v. Georgia* (US. Ga., 1832) 6 Peter, 515, by Chief Justice Marshall of the U.S. Supreme Court:

Such was the policy of Great Britain towards the Indian nations inhabiting the territory from which she excluded all other Europeans, such her claims, and such her practical exposition of the charters she had granted: she considered them as nations capable of maintaining the relations of peace and war; of governing themselves, under her protection; and she made treaties with them the obligation of which she acknowledged.

6 For an articulation of the continued existence of the right to self-government see the Royal Commisison on Aboriginal Peoples, Volume 2, Part 1, *Restructuring the Relationship*, Chapter 3 (Ottawa: Minister of Supply and Services Canada, 1996).

7 Trial level decisions which said that the right to self-government was extinguished include *Delgamuukw v. British Columbia* (1991), 79 D.L.R. (4th) 185 (B.C. S.C.), varied [1993] 5 C.N.L.R. 1 (B.C. C.A.), reversed in part (1997), [1998] 1 C.N.L.R. 14 (S.C.C.) and *Thomas v. Norris*, [1992] 2 C.N.L.R. 139 (B.C. S.C.). On the other hand, see *Eastmain v. Gilpin*, [1987] 3 C.N.L.R. 54 (Que. C.S.P.) which referred to the "residual sovereignty" the Crees of Quebec.

8 See *Delgamuukw v. British Columbia* (1997), [1998] 1 C.N.L.R. 14 (S.C.C.) [hereinafter *Delgamuukw*] at pragraph 171.

9   International Labour Organization Convention No.107 of 1957.

10   International Labour Organization Convention on Indigenous and Tribal Peoples, Convention No.169 of 1989. Canada has not ratified this Convention.

11   Article 31. This draft was adopted by the U.N. Subcommission on Prevention of Discrimination and Protection of Minorities in August, 1994, but has yet to be ratified by the General Assembly. See M.E. Turpel, "Draft Declaration on the Rights of Indigenous peoples", [1994] 1 C.N.L.R. 40.

For a comprehensive treatment of indigenous rights in international law, see James Anaya, *Indigenous Peoples in International Law* (New York: Oxford University Press, 1996).

12   For a full discussion of governance issues, see the Report of the Royal Commission on Aboriginal Peoples, Volume 2, part 1, Restructuring the Relationship, Chapter 3 (Ottawa: Minister of Supply and Services Canada, 1996).

13   On the subject of self-government models see Report of the Special Parliamentary Committee on Indian Self-Government ("The Penner Report") (Ottawa: Queen's Printer, 1983), L. Little Bear, M. Boldt, J.A. Long, eds., *Pathways to Self-Determination* (Toronto: University of Toronto Press, 1986); J.R. Pointing, ed., *Arduous Journey* (Toronto: McClelland & Stewart, 1988); F. Cassidy and R. Bish, *Indian Government: Its Meaning in Practice* (Lantzville: Oolichan Books, 1989).

14   *Sechelt Indian Band Self-Government Act*, S.C. 1986, c. 27.

15   *Cree Naskapi (of Québec) Acts* S.C. 1984, c. 18.

16   *Métis Settlements Act*, S.A. 1990, c. M-14.3.

17   *Mi'kmaq Education Act*, S.C. 1998, c. 24.

18   *First Nations Land Management Act*, S.C. 1999, c. 24. This statute is being challenged by the British Columbia Native Women's Society who feel that it does not do enough to address the concerns of women who may be in conflict with the Band Councils. See an interlocutory proceeding in *British Columbia Native Women's Society v. R.* (1998), (sub nom. *British Columbia Native Women's Society v. Canada*) 143 F.T.R. 153 (Fed. T.D.).

8

Bands, Band Councils and Reserves

POINTS TO REMEMBER

1. There are over six hundred Indian Bands in Canada. Most have a part of their community residing on a reserve.

2. The *Indian Act* provides that the reserve community is to be governed by a Chief and Council.

3. There are four different procedures for enacting by-laws under the *Indian Act*:
   a) the majority of by-laws are passed by Band Council Resolution, but can be disallowed by the Minister within 40 days
   b) by-laws dealing with taxation, remuneration of Band officials, and other aspects of finance are passed by Band Council Resolution and need the prior approval of the Minister of Indian Affairs
   c) alcohol by-laws must be passed by the majority of Band members attending a meeting
   d) membership or citizenship codes must be passed by the majority of Band members who are eligible to vote.

4. *Indian Act* Bands can enter into contracts, sue and be sued, and be liable for criminal acts and provincial offences.

1. INTRODUCTION

The *Indian Act* homogenized the diverse Aboriginal nations in Canada. After its enactment in 1876, each nation was to be patrilineal, like the Europeans.[1] The leaders were to be selected by secret ballot, and have powers like European legislatures. And almost every aspect of life from land allocation to dog control by-laws needed the approval of the Minister of Indian Affairs.[2]

The *Indian Act* has two sometimes contradictory purposes — paternalism and assimilation — although both end up taking away control from First Nations. The best example of paternalism is the approval powers exercised by the government over by-law making on reserve. Almost by-laws enacted by Chief and Council can still be unilaterally disallowed by government. An illustration of the assimilationist objective is the certificate of possession system. This gives individual Indians private plots of land on the reserve in an ownership pattern familiar to Europeans. This system overrides traditional communal land use rules of many First Nations.

The next two chapters will provide an overview of the main provisions of the *Indian Act*.

2. BANDS

Under the *Indian Act*, the basic governmental unit is the Band. These are communities which range in membership from less than fifty to almost twenty thousand.[3] Each Band is governed by an elected Chief and Council, which has jurisdiction over an Indian reserve.

Bands came into being in a number of ways. Depending on the First Nation, Bands could coincide with family groupings, sub-units of nations, or even groups of a number of nations. They were identified through the treaty process, or a government program associated with the need to expand the settlement of Europeans. The status of Bands is now formalized in the *Indian Act*.

A First Nation is a "band" under the *Indian Act* if one of three criteria applies:[4]

- it has a reserve;
- it has government trust funds for its use; or
- it has been declared to be a band by the federal cabinet.

New bands can be created by the federal cabinet. This has occurred in a number of cases. The Big Trout Lake Band, for example, was split into eight bands in 1972, in recognition that many band members had settled in satellite communities hundreds of miles apart. Six other First Nations in northern Ontario which had settled in communities with no legal status were recognized as bands in the 1980s and provided with reserves in 1992.

However, the federal power to create Bands can be abused. The Lubicon of Alberta had fought for years to have their land claims settled. Following the breakdown of negotiations between the federal government and the Lubicon, the federal government decided to create a competing Band on Lubicon territory. The process of reaching an agreement on the establishment of the new Woodland Cree Band was full of irregularities and controversial methods. For example, prior to voting on the agreement, the Woodland Cree were paid fifty dollars to vote, and were promised an additional one thousand dollars if the agreement passed. On voting day the number of eligible voters increased and the polls stayed open past closing.[5]

(a) Legal Status of First Nations

The term "First Nation" is now recognized in federal legislation[6] but the *Indian Act* refers to "bands". The two terms usually describe the same group, but many First Nations do not refer to themselves as bands to avoid the implication that their existence depends upon the provisions of the *Indian Act*. In this chapter we adopt the *Indian Act* usage for clarity in describing its legal provisions.

A band's legal status is not easy to define. The following quote from Jack Woodward's *Native Law* describes the difficulties which arise in trying to define the band's status:[7]

> The band, as an enduring entity with its own government, is a unique type of legal entity under Canadian law. The rights and obligations of the band are quite distinct from the accumulated rights and obligations of the members of the band. What distinguishes a band from a club is that a band exists apart from any voluntary act of its members. In this respect a band is more like a nation state than a club. But no comparison is totally apt. In law a band is in a class by itself.

It is clear that the Band is more than simply a creation of the *Indian Act*. The Band has inherent powers which it exercises when it holds custom elections.[8] An Ontario court has also held that a provincial government was required to respect the right of self government, and so could not unilaterally impose obligations on a Band Council without its concurrence.[9]

A Band can enter into contracts, can sue and be sued,[10] and can be liable for criminal acts and provincial offences.[11] Like any governmental unit, the Band receives funding to run social programs, can raise taxes and pass by-laws. Because Band Councils are created by federal legislation, they are governed by federal laws and their decisions are reviewed by the Federal Court,[12] As employers, they are governed by federal employment legislation[13] and must contribute to unemployment insurance premiums for its employees. (The duties of the Band as an employer are discussed in more detail in Chapter 22, "Employment Relations".)

(b) Band Councils

The Chief, and a number of Councillors are elected for each Band. The elections are usually by secret ballot, although procedures can be authorized either by "Band custom" or by the *Indian Act*. (The method of election, and disputes about eligible voters, is discussed in Chapter 10, "Elections and Referenda.") It should be noted here that not all members of a Band necessarily accept the authority of the Band councils. On a number of reserves, there are strong traditions of hostility to the governing structure imposed by the *Indian Act*. On reserves like Six Nations in Ontario, for example, the vast majority of people refuse to vote in *Indian Act* elections, and the traditional Haudenosaunee Confederacy has a strong following.[14]

Band Councils act formally by passing resolutions, known as Band Council Resolutions (BCR). These decisions, which are taken when there is a quorum of chief and council present at a meeting, can bind the Band,[15] and may also affect the rights of Band members.[16]

When making decisions which affect residents of the reserve, the Band should observe the rules of natural justice. In *Sheard v. Chippewas of Rama First Nation Band Council*[17] the court found that the Band Council had not treated the individuals fairly. Sheard was a member of the First Nation. She leased a house from the Band Council and resided with her common law spouse, Weston, a non-native, and their children. One day, the Band Council passed a Band Council Resolution ordering Weston off the reserve, citing safety concerns about Weston. The Band claimed that Weston did not have a right to reside on the reserve. The court found that Sheard and Weston had not been given notice of the meeting where the BCR was discussed, had not been given disclosure of the basis for the concerns, and had not been given an opportunity to respond. The court granted the judicial review and quashed the decision.

If the Band has elections held under the *Indian Act*, the Indian Band Council Procedure Regulations apply to determine procedures for Council meetings.[18] If elections for chief and council are held by "band custom", there is no set procedure for council meetings, although Indian Affairs will only recognize BCRs signed by a proper majority of chief and council.[19]

The Chief and Council have a fiduciary duty to Band members. For example, a court ordered a former Chief of the Williams Lake Band to return payments from the Band for her student loan and tuition for her children.[20] However, conflict of interest rules must be relaxed to take into account the reality of some small Bands. In one case, where the Band had only 204 electors, the court held that it was acceptable to hire the common-law spouse of one of the members of Council as a Band Manager, as long as the member of Council left the room when the decision was made.[21]

Some decisions cannot be made by chief and council alone. Land surrender or designation, membership codes and alcohol by-laws all require votes by the membership of the Band before valid decisions can be made. (More information on election and referenda procedures are dealt with in Chapter 10, "Elections and Referenda.")

3. BY-LAW MAKING POWERS OF BAND COUNCILS

Although some of the by-law making powers are very broad, they have not been widely used by First Nations. There are several reasons for this, including the following:

- First Nations must submit the by-laws to the federal Minister, who can disallow a by-law
- the by-law making power is formalistic and derived from the *Indian Act*, making it inappropriate for First Nation use
- most First Nation communities do not have any way of enforcing the by-laws

Even though there are good reasons not to use the *Indian Act* by-law powers, in the absence of something better these powers may nevertheless serve important needs. For example, a properly passed by-law can replace conflicting provincial legislation.[22] The courts have also decided that in some cases by-laws supercede other federal legislation or regulations which conflict with them.[23] Critics point out, however, that no matter how effective these *Indian Act* by-law powers become, they do not represent true self-government because they are based on the *Indian Act* and not on First Nations' inherent rights. The Minister of Indian Affairs still has the power to disallow any by-law at his or her discretion.

There are four different types of by-laws, and the procedures for enactment are different for each.

4. GENERAL BY-LAWS UNDER SECTION 81

Most types of by-laws are created under section 81, and they could address the following:

- health of residents on reserve
- regulation of traffic
- observance of law and order
- prevention of disorderly conduct
- trespass by cattle and other domestic animals
- construction of roads and other local works
- zoning for land use
- regulation of construction and repair of buildings
- surveying and allotting reserve lands to individuals
- control of "noxious weeds"
- regulation of bee-keeping and poultry raising
- control of public games and other amusements
- regulation of salesmen on reserve
- management of game, fish and other game on reserve
- removal and punishment of trespassers on reserve
- residence of Band members
- application of by-laws to spouses and children of Band members who reside on reserve
- allowing all members of the Band to vote on citizenship or membership codes

The steps for making these by-laws under section 81 are as follows:

1. Pass the by-law by the majority of councillors at a Band Council meeting.[24]
2. Mail to the Minister of Indian Affairs within four days.[25]

3. Wait for forty days. If the Minister disallows the by-law within this time period, the by-law is ineffective. If the Minister does nothing, the by-law is effective.[26]
4. If the by-law is effective, inform Indian Affairs District Office or Regional Office for registration under the *Statutory Instruments Act*.[27]

(a) Residence By-laws under Section 81

One by-law made under section 81 which deserves special mention concerns "the residence of band members and other persons on the reserve." When making a by-law about residence, it is important to keep in mind that if a member of a First Nation has a right to reside on the reserve, that right must also extend to dependent children of that First Nation member.[28] Strangely enough, this right does not extend to spouses. An Ontario court has upheld a by-law of the Six Nations Council which prohibited the residence of non-Indian spouses.[29]

(b) Fishing By-laws under Section 81

There is growing court recognition of First Nation fishing by-laws as a valid means of regulating fishing on reserve. These by-laws may supercede both federal and provincial laws.[30] However, they may not extend beyond the reserve boundaries. So, in *R. v. Lewis*,[31] the court found that the river that passed through the reserve was not part of the reserve so that the by-law was inapplicable.

(c) Gaming By-law under Section 81

The federal government routinely rejects by-laws on gambling. The St. Mary's Indian Band lost a court case when they objected to the use of the Minister's power to disallow the by-law.[32]

5. TAXATION BY-LAWS UNDER SECTION 83

Bands may pass by-laws dealing with taxation, spending of money and licensing of business under this section. The procedure for making these by-laws are a little different, because approval of the Minister is necessary before the by-law will be effective.[33]

There is an Indian Tax Advisory Board which advises the Minister on section 83 by-laws. Advice from this Board is needed in order to have a taxation scheme approved by the Minister. The Board helps ensure that the taxing regime is fair, and is harmonized with the taxation schemes in the surrounding area. There are model by-laws and a system for taxation available.[34] The general thrust of these taxation provisions has been approved by the Supreme Court of Canada in *Canadian Pacific Ltd. v. Matsqui Indian Band.*[35] In that decision, six of the judges agreed that promoting the development of Aboriginal self-government was a policy objective which could be considered in evaluating the taxation regimes.

Attempts by Bands to impose tax on utilities and railways passing through their reserves have failed because courts have found that those lands have been surrendered, and therefore are no longer part of the reserve.[36] Some Bands have decided to tax the members of the Band for gasoline and tobacco.[37]

In British Columbia, there is legislation which will withdraw municipal taxation of non-Indians on reserves so that the Band can impose the tax. This prevents reserve residents from being double taxed.[38]

The steps for making by-laws under section 83 are:

1. Pass the by-law with the majority of councillors at a Band Council meeting.[39]
2. Mail to District or Regional office for approval.
3. If the Minister allows the by-law then the by-law is effective.
4. Inform Indian Affairs District Office or Regional Office for registration of the by-law under the *Statutory Instruments Act.*

6. ALCOHOL BY-LAWS UNDER SECTION 85.1

A Band Council may make by-laws "prohibiting the sale, barter, supply or manufacture of intoxicants on the reserve of the band," and prohibit anyone from being intoxicated, or to possess intoxicants, on the reserve.[40]

The penalties for sale or barter could be a fine up to $1,000.00 and/or up to six months imprisonment, or $100.00 fine and/or three months imprisonment for being intoxicated or possessing an intoxicant.[41]

Approval of the members of the Band is necessary for this by-law, but not approval of the Minister. The procedure is as follows:

1. Majority of Band Council approves the draft by-law.
2. A special meeting of Band members is called to vote on the by-law (a person who can vote for Chief and Council can vote on the by-law).
3. The majority of those attending the meeting vote in favour of the by-law.
4. The Band Council meets again to pass the approved by-law.
5. A copy of the by-law is sent to the Minister within the next four days.
6. For by-laws passed under section 85.1, the effective date of the by-law is the date on which the by-law is enacted.[42]

7. MEMBERSHIP CODES OR CITIZENSHIP CODES

In 1985, the *Indian Act* was changed to delete discriminatory provisions against women, and to give Bands more control over their citizenship. Bands may, with the assent of the majority of people who are eligible to vote, pass their own Codes to determine who their citizens are. Over 200 First Nations across Canada have passed such Codes.[43] (The method for enacting these codes is discussed in detail in the Chapter 9, "Indian Act membership and First Nation Citizenship".)

8. HOW IS A BY-LAW WRITTEN?

The Act does not require that the by-law be prepared in any particular form. DIAND suggests:

- the by-law appear on plain paper or on special Band letterhead, but not on the same paper/form used for Band Council Resolutions;[44]
- each by-law should contain five parts:[45]
  i.   a title identifying the subject and purpose of the by-law;
  ii. a preamble outlining the reasons for enactment;
  iii. an enactment clause which identifies the council enacting the bylaw and what is being enacted;
  iv. interpretation clause stating how all definitions should be interpreted;

      v. statement of assent and the date that the by-law was passed by council.
- all by-laws should be accompanied by an affidavit on the face of the by-law or as an attachment to the by-law. The purpose of the affidavit is to prove that the by-law is a true copy of the by-law. Affidavits must be signed in front of a commissioner for the taking of oaths appointed pursuant to provincial law or the *Indian Act*.[46]

9. HOW DO YOU CHANGE A BY-LAW?

By-laws can only be amended by using the same procedure needed to enact them in the first place. Therefore, a Band Council Resolution by itself will not be sufficient.[47]

10. ENFORCEMENT OF BY-LAWS

By-laws are usually enforced by the RCMP, provincial police, First Nation Constables, or First Nation by-law enforcement officers.[48] Charges are usually heard by a judge of the provincial division or a justice of the peace. The penalty for violation of section 81 by-laws is a fine of up to $1,000 or thirty days in jail or both.

11. PROCLAMATION OF FIRST NATION LAW

Some First Nations, claiming an inherent right to self-government, have proclaimed that their own laws are in effect. The Mohawks of Akwesasne, for example, have issued fishing permits for disputed waters on the St. Lawrence River, and Shawanga First Nation enacted their own gaming by-law. Whether or not these proclamations are recognized by the members of the First Nation themselves, or by Canadian governments and courts, depends on a number of factors.

One of the factors is the legal basis for the claim. If the First Nation law clearly contradicts a federal law, such as the Criminal Code, it will have a hard time being recognized. In the case of the Shawanaga First Nation, for example, the courts upheld convictions for operating a bingo without a provincial license.[49] A law which is based on a recognized Aboriginal or treaty right would have a greater chance of success being recognized.[50]

A second factor is the political willingness of the government and parties to live with the *de facto* arrangement. For a period, co-operation of non-Aboriginal people, and the lack of government action, allowed the Mohawk arrangement to continue. In British Columbia The Spallumcheen Indian Band passed a by-law giving it jurisdiction to deal with child custody proceedings. Pursuant to this by-law, the Chief and Band Council became the guardians of all children taken into the Band's care. The Federal and British Columbia government have not challenged the by-law. As a result, Spallumcheen was the first First Nation to have achieved a degree of autonomy in the area of child welfare administration.[51]

12. BANDS UNDER OTHER STATUTES

Gradually, individual agreements are being reached which take Bands out of the *Indian Act* to their own legislation. The basic concepts are the same, but there are differences in such things as the scope of the by-law making powers, and the level of scrutiny required by the Minister of Indian Affairs. The following are the main pieces of legislation.

(a) Cree-Naskapi (of Quebec) Act[52]

This statute covers the Kobac Naskapi-Aeyouch (the Naskapi Band of Quebec) and eight Bands of the Cree covered under the James Bay and Northern Quebec Agreement.

(b) Sechelt Indian Band Self-government Act[53]

The Sechelt Band in British Columbia has its own legislation which focuses on reducing Ministerial involvement in land transactions.

(c) First Nations Land Management Act[54]

There are 14 First Nations which have opted into these provisions. The Act allows for greater control of reserve lands by First Nations, greater by-law making powers, and the power to appoint Justices of the Peace.

(d) Yukon Self-government Areements[55]

A number of First Nations in the Yukon who have signed self-government agreements, and have begun making their own laws under those agreements.

13. OTHER POLITICAL UNITS

Band Councils may be affiliated with larger Tribal Councils which will provide regional services such as housing inspection, as well as political representation. On a provincial level, there may be one or more organizations representing the Chiefs of the Bands. While they may receive federal funding for services, these larger organizations are not established under the *Indian Act* and do not have any powers granted under that Act. They are usually incorporated under federal or provincial law, and are governed by their constitutions and legislation governing non-profit corporations. (See Chapter 10, "Elections and Referenda" for more details).

At the national level, almost all of the Bands are affiliated with the Assembly of First Nations (AFN) based in Ottawa . The AFN has an election every three years to elect a national chief. The voters are chiefs of the Band councils.

14. INDIAN RESERVES

Most First Nations have reserves. These are lands which are set aside for the benefit of the Band. The title is in the federal Crown.[56] Reserves were created in a number of ways. Some treaties designated a certain amount of land, for others, some land was set aside by religious orders for Indian communities, and some were established by government orders. Not all Bands have reserves. In the Yukon, for example, there was a policy against the creation of reserves so that most people live in mixed communities.[57]

Most reserves are very poor: 64.2 per cent of Aboriginal peoples on-reserve have a total income of less than $10 000, with 30.8 per cent of on-reserve Aboriginal peoples unemployed. The result is that 41.5 per cent of on-reserve Aboriginal people depend on social assistance.[58] Education levels on-reserve fall behind that of the Canadian population, with 39.7 per cent possessing less than 9 years of formal education, 8.3 per cent with a secondary certificate, 10.6 per cent with a non-university certificate and 0.9 per cent with a university degree.[59] On-reserve estimated life expectancy for males is 62.0 years compared with 74.6 years for the total male population of Canada; female estimated life expectancy is 69.6 years compared with 80.9 for the total female population of Canada.[60] Housing on-reserve is far below the Canadian standard. In 24.0 per cent of on-reserve homes available water is unsuitable for drinking, 6.5 per cent of homes have no electricity and 11.5 per cent of homes have no bathroom facilities.[61]

A few reserves are relatively wealthy because they have access to revenues from oil or because they are able to rent out their land for shopping plazas or condominiums.

Reserve land cannot be sold. Land can only be alienated after a Band meeting, a Band vote, and the approval of the Governor in Council. Individuals may get certificates of possession which can be sold to other Indians, but cannot be sold to non-Indians. (See Chapter 4, "Land" for more information.)

15. APPLICATION OF PROVINCIAL LAWS

While the complexities of the application of provincial laws to Indians, and Indian lands is a fascinating technical challenge for lawyers, the actual practice is fairly straightforward. In spite of quite vigorous opposition from most First Nations, Canadian courts have found that most provincial laws apply to Indians and Indian reserves. (See Chapter 1, "Constitutional Framework" for some of the constitutional principles.)

The following are examples of provincial laws which apply:

(a) Child welfare law generally applies, although provincial adoption legislation cannot affect the *Indian Act* registration of a child;[62]
(b) Family law generally applies, except for the possession of the matrimonial home;[63]
(c) Highway traffic laws apply on reserve, even though the are traffic regulations under the *Indian Act*;[64]
(d) Provincial labour law applies to enterprises on reserves that do not relate to the Band government or Band projects.[65]

The following are examples of provincial laws which do not apply:

1. Provincial controls on hunting and fishing which apply to Aboriginal title or treaty lands, except laws relating to safety or to conservation;[66]
2. Provincial taxation of gasoline and tobacco do not apply on reserve, except to the extent that quota schemes are imposed to limit consumption to reserve residents;[67]
3. Provincial laws which relate to land, such as zoning laws[68] and possibly landlord and tenant laws,[69] do not apply on reserve;
4. Laws on garnishment and seizure generally do not apply to reserve lands or property situated on a reserve, unless there is a conditional sale;[70]
5. Provincial wills and testamentary dispositions legislation do not apply to Indians on reserve, although they apply to Indians off reserve.[71]

ENDNOTES

1 The Nisga'a, who are matrilineal, are attempting to escape the *Indian Act* scheme by providing for matrilineal descent in Section 20 of the Nisga'a Final Agreement. The *Nisga'a Final Agreement Act*, S.B.C. 1999, c. 2, Sched., Chapter 11, s. 39 provides that the Nisga'a may make laws in respect of Nisga'a citizenship.

2 The authority of the *Indian Act* has been upheld by the Canadian courts. Examples include *Isaac v. Davey*, [1977] 2 S.C.R. 897, (S.C.C.), in which elections under the *Indian Act* were upheld over the Six Nations' customary process, and *Logan v. Canada (Attorney General)* (1959), 20 D.L.R. (2d) 416 (Ont. H.C.), in which the court ruled that the Six Nations were subjects of the Crown and governed by the *Indian Act*.

3 The Six Nations of the Grand River has a band membership of 19,002, of which 9,527 reside on-reserve.

4 On the subject of band status, section 2(1) of the *Indian Act* states:
In this Act,
"band" means a body of Indians
(a) for whose use and benefit in common, lands, the legal title to which is vested in Her Majesty, have been set apart before, on or after September 4, 1951,
(b) for whose use and benefit in common, moneys are held by Her Majesty, or

(c) declared by the Governor in Council to be a band for the purposes of this Act.

5 For a detailed account of the history and process in establishing the Woodland Cree Band see John Goddard, *Last Stand of the Lubicon Cree* (Vancouver, British Columbia: Douglas & McIntyre Ltd., 1991). The Lubicon Cree continue to negotiate a settlement with the government of Canada. There are presently approximately 500 members of the Lubicon Nation. The process continues to be tainted by further distasteful moves by the federal government to recognize the "Little Buffalo Band", another splinter group. For further information contact the volunteer non-profit group: Friends of the Lubicon, 485 Ridelle Ave Toronto, Ontario, M6B 1K6 Tel:416-763-7500 Fax:416-535-7810 Web: www.tao.ca/~fol

6 In Ontario, the term is used in the new *Police Services Act, 1990*, S.O. 1990, c. P.15, s. 54, where the appointment and approval of First Nations Constables is described.

The *First Nations Land Management Act*, S.C. 1999, c. 24 uses the term "first nation". S. 2 (1) of the Act provides that "first nation" means a band named in the schedule; "first nation member" means a person whose name appears on the band list of a first nation or who is entitled to have their name appear on that list. Other federal legislation using the term "First Nation" refer to specific "First Nation" communities, see *York Factory First Nation Flooded Land Act*, S.C. 1997, c. 28; *Split Lake Cree First Nation Flooded Land Act*, S.C. 1994, c. 42; *Nelson House First Nation Flooded Land Act*, S.C. 1997, c. 29; *Yukon First Nations Self-Government Act, S.C.* 1994, c. 35; and the *Yukon First Nations Land Claims Settlement Act*, S.C. 1994, c. 34.

7 On the subject of First Nations' legal status, see Jack Woodward, *Native Law* (Toronto: Carswell, 1998) at 397.

8 See *Bone v. Sioux Valley Indian Band No. 290* [1996] 3 C.N.L.R. 54 (F.C.T.D.):

I do not think that the power of the Band to choose its council in a customary manner is a "power conferred on the Band" as is contemplated [under] the *Indian Act*. Rather it is an inherent power of the Band; it is a power the Band has always had, which the Indian Act only interferes with in limited circumstances, as provided for under section 74 of the Act. Thus, in my view the Band may exercise this inherent power unrestrained by subsection 2(3)(a) of the *Indian Act* (para 32).

9 See *Mushkegowuk Council v. Ontario* [1999] O.J. No. 3170 (Ont. S.C.). The province of Ontario enacted regressive welfare legislation slashing benefits, and imposing workfare on recipients. Municipalities and Band Councils were saddled with obligations to administer these changes under

the *Ontario Works Act*. The seven First Nations of the Mushkegowuk Council in northern Ontario objected to the legislation. They argued that the province had no right to impose obligations on Band Councils.

The judge agreed. He found that the relationship with First Nations required the Crown to respect inherent rights of self-government. By unilaterally imposing obligations on Bands, the provincial legislation "offends the spirit of the current and evolving reality of Aboriginal peoples in Canada" [at para. 26].

10 On the subject of a First Nation's ability to sue and be sued, see *Montana Band v. R.* (1997), (sub nom. *Montana Band v. Canada*), [1998] 2 F.C. 3 (Fed. T.D.) and *Clow Darling Ltd. v. Big Trout Lake Band of Indians*, (1989), [1990] 4 C.N.L.R. 7 (Ont. Dist. Ct.)

11 On the subject of a First Nation's liability for criminal and provincial offences, see *Paul Band (Indian Reserve No. 133) v. R.* (1983), (sub nom. *R. v. Paul Indian Band*), [1984] 1 C.N.L.R. 87 (Alta. C.A.).

12 The Federal Court has found that a Band Council is a federal board, commission or other tribunal; *Gabriel v. Canatonquin* (1980), [1981] 4 C.N.L.R. 61 (Fed. C.A.)

13 Band Councils are subject to the *Canada Labour Code*. See *Francis v. Canada (Labour Relations Board)*, [1982] 4 C.N.L.R. 94. In *Florence v. Shackelly*, [1999] B.C.J. No. 163 (B.C.S.C.), an employee of the Band was in an accident. As the Band owned the vehicle, the Band was found to be vicariously liable under the provincial *Motor Vehicle Act*.

14 For an account of some of the politics around relations between elected council and traditional councils see, Brian Maracle, *Back on the Rez: Finding the Way Home* (Toronto: Viking, 1996) and Gerald Alfred, *Heeding the Voices of Our Ancestors* (Toronto: Oxford University Press 1995).

15 Courts have held that Band Council Resolutions are necessary to formally bind the Band in contracts. See *Basque v. Woodstock Indian Band* (1996), 175 N.B.R. (2d) 241 (N.B. C.A.) and *Heron Seismic Services Ltd. v. Peepeekisis Indian Band* (1990), (sub nom. *Heron Seismic Services Ltd. v. Muscowpetung Indian Band*), [1991] 2 C.N.L.R. 52 (Sask. Q.B.), affirmed (1991), (sub nom. *Heron Seismic Services Ltd. v. Muscowpetung Indian Band*) [1992] 4 C.N.L.R. 32 (Sask. C.A.)

16 The procedure for Band Council resolutions is found in section 2(3)(b) of the *Indian Act* which provides:

2.(3) Unless the context otherwise requires or this Act otherwise provides,

. . .

(b) a power conferred on the council of a band shall be deemed not to be exercised unless it is exercised pursuant to the consent of a majority of the councillors of the band present at a meeting of the council duly convened.

R.S.C., 1985, c. 32 (1st Supp.), s. 1 R.S.C. 1985, c. 17 (4th Supp.), s. 1. See *Leonard v. Gottfriedson* (1980), [1982] 1 C.N.L.R. 60 (B.C. S.C.)

17 *Sheard v. Chippewas of Rama First Nation Band Council* (1996) [1997] 2 C.N.L.R. 182 (Fed. T.D.) is a case where the court found that the Band Council should follow the rules of natural justice.

18 On the subject of *Indian Act* elections procedures, see *Indian Band Council Procedure Regulations*, C.R.C. 1978, c. 950. These are a set of outdated regulations which are probably universally ignored. For example, they contemplate that an official from Indian Affairs will attend all Chief and Council meetings.

19 Because Band custom elections are held pursuant to the inherent authority of the Band, not pursuant to the *Indian Act*, the procedural requirements in section 2(3) do not apply. See *Bone v. Sioux Valley Indian Band No. 290*, [1996] 3 C.N.L.R. 54 (Fed. T.D.)

20 The fiduciary duty of the Chief to the Band is explained in *Williams Lake Indian Band v. Abbey*, (sub nom. *Gilbert v. Abbey*) [1992] 4 C.N.L.R. 21, (B.C. S.C.) For other cases, see *Leonard v. Gottfriedson* (1980) [1982] 1 C.N.L.R. 60 (B.C. S.C.) and *Barry v. Garden River Ojibway Nation #14*, (sub nom. *Barry v. Garden River Band of Ojibways*) [1997] 4 C.N.L.R. 28 (Ont. C.A.)

21 In *Wewayakai Indian Band v. Chickite* (1998), (sub nom. *Assu v. Chickite*) [1999] 1 C.N.L.R. 14 (B.C. S.C.) the British Columbia Supreme Court noted that "it would be impossible for Band Councils to operate if courts applied strict rules regarding conflicts of interest" [at 28].

22 On the subject of by-laws excluding provincial law, section 88 of the *Indian Act* makes all provincial law "of general application" applicable, unless it is inconsistent with the Act "or any order, rule, regulation or by-law made thereunder."

23 On the subject of by-laws superceding federal law, see endnote 30 below.

24 On the subject of making by-laws, see section 2(3)(b) of the *Indian Act*.

25 On the subject of making by-laws, see s. 82(1) of the *Indian Act*.

26 On the subject of making by-laws, see s. 82(2) of the *Indian Act*.

27 On the subject of by-law registration, all First Nation by-laws are considered by the federal government to be subject to the *Statutory Instru-*

ments Act. This means that the government will treat the by-law the same way it treats regulations which are made under any statute. The by-law may therefore be subject to further scrutiny by federal clerks. A problem is unlikely as long as the by-law is properly authorized by the *Indian Act*, there is nothing unusual about it, "it does not trespass on existing rights and freedoms," and it is properly drafted. In the usual course of events, the by-law is then registered.

28 On the subject of dependent children of members of a First Nation, section 18.1 of the *Indian Act* extends rights to dependent children or children in the custody of the member of the First Nation.

29 In *Six Nations of the Grand River Band v. Henderson* (1996), [1997] 1 C.N.L.R. 202 (Ont. Gen. Div.) the court held that the by-law violated section 15 of the *Charter* but that the violation was justified because of the economic circumstances of the Band, and the overcrowding on the reserve. See also *Jacobs v. Mohawk Council of Kahnawake*, [1998] C.H.R.C. No. 2 (C.H.R.T.); *Canada (Human Rights Commission) v. Gordon Band Council*, (sub nom. *Canadian Human Rights Commission v. Gordon Indian Band Council*) (1997), 140 F.T.R. 230 (Fed. T.D.) and *MacNutt v. Shubenacadie Indian Band* (1997), (sub nom. *Shubenacadie Indian Band v. Canadian Human Rights Commission*) [1998] 2 C.N.L.R. 212 (Fed. T.D.) which deal with the application of the *Canadian Human Rights Act* in cases of discrimination against a non-Indian spouse. In *Sheard, supra* note 17, the court held that Band Councils must follow the rules of natural justice in a case involving residence on reserve for a non-Indian spouse.

30 On the subject of fishing by-laws, see *R. v. Ward* (1988), [1989] 2 C.N.L.R. 142 (N.B. C.A.), leave to appeal refused (1989), 92 N.B.R. (2d) 360n (S.C.C.). In this case, the Eel Ground First Nation had passed a by-law which regulated on-reserve fishing, based on s. 81(o) of the *Indian Act*. That section gives bands authority to make fishing by-laws, but only for "the preservation, protection and management of fish". Section 6 of this particular by-law, however, allowed band members to fish "at any time and by any means" except by the use of explosives. This conflicted with the stricter regulations made under the federal *Fisheries Act*. The question of the section's validity arose when a member of the First Nation who was fishing in violation of the Fisheries Regulation, but in compliance with the First Nation by-law, was charged under the Fisheries Regulation.

A lower court decided that, although the by-law as a whole was valid, s. 6 could be separated from the rest of the by-law and struck down. The lower court decided that the section was so broad that it could no longer be considered "for the purpose of the preservation, protection and management of fish".

The Court of Appeal held that the lower court was mistaken in focussing on one section of the by-law in isolation from its context. Since the rest of the by-law had various conservation measures, the by-law as a whole fell within the First Nation's powers.

Although the federal government attempted to appeal this decision to the Supreme Court of Canada, the Supreme Court refused to hear the case.

See also *R. v. Vidulich*, [1988] 2 C.N.L.R. 145 (B.C. Co. Ct.), reversed on other grounds, [1989] 3 C.N.L.R. 167 (B.C. C.A.) which stated that a band by-law might be able to allow the sale of fish to non-Indians and *R. v. Jimmy*, [1987] 3 C.N.L.R. 77 (B.C. C.A.) which determined that a by-law approved by the Minister may regulate fishing on a reserve and offer a defence to an Indian charged under the *Fisheries Act*.

31 *R. v. Lewis*, [1996] 3 C.N.L.R. 131 (S.C.C.)

32 The Federal Court of Appeal upheld the Minister's rejection of a by-law made on gambling under section 81(1)(m) of the *Indian Act*. See *St. Mary's Indian Band v. Canada (Minister of Indian Affairs & Northern Development)* (1995), [1996] 2 C.N.L.R. 214 (Fed. T.D.), affirmed (1996), [1997] 1 C.N.L.R. 206 (Fed. C.A.), leave to appeal refused [1997] 1 C.N.L.R. iv (S.C.C.)

33 On the subject of tax and finance by-laws, it should be noted that regulations may be made under the *Indian Act* that will override by-laws made under section 83 (section 83(5)).

34 The ITAB Chairperson can be contacted at (250) 828-9857/fax: (205) 828-9858/web address: http://itab.cactuscom.com.

35 *Canadian Pacific Ltd. v. Matsqui Indian Band*, (sub nom. *Matsqui Indian Band v. Canadian Pacific Ltd.*) [1995] 2 C.N.L.R. 92 (S.C.C.) for a case that discusses appeal mechanisms under a First Nation taxation scheme.

36 See *Matsqui, supra* note 35 and *Westbank First Nation v. British Columbia Hydro Power Authority* (1997), [1998] 2 C.N.L.R. 284 (B.C. C.A.), affirmed (June 21, 1999), Doc. 26450 (S.C.C.), additional reasons at (September 10, 1999), Doc. 26450 (S.C.C.), which hold that First Nation taxation cannot be imposed on land which is no longer part of the reserve because of surrender or expropriation.

37 The *Budget Implementation Act*, 1997 (S.C. 1997, c. 26, ss. 36, 44, 52) and the *Budget Implementation Act*, 1998 (S.C. 1998, c. 21, ss. 59, 70) have resulted in providing new taxing powers to three First Nations in British Columbia. The Kamloops Band can tax its members on alcohol, tobacco and fuel; the Westbank Band can tax tobacco and alcohol; and the Cowichan Tribes can tax tobacco. The statutes provide that the tax exemp-

tion under s. 87 of the *Indian Act* does not apply to the members of these Bands when they are being taxed for these items. The Cowichan Tribes taxing power was upheld in *Large v. Canada (Minister of Justice)*, (1997) (sub nom. *Large (c.o.b. Cowichan Native Tobacco Co.) v. Canada (Minister of Justice)*) [1998] 3 C.N.L.R. 109 (B.C. S.C.)

38 See *Tsawwassen Indian Band v. Delta (City)* (1997), [1998] 1 C.N.L.R. 290 (B.C. C.A.), leave to appeal refused (S.C.C.).

39 On the subject of making by-laws, see section 2(3)(b) of the *Indian Act*.

40 On the subject of alcohol by-laws, this section of the *Indian Act* became law in 1985, after the Manitoba Court of Appeal struck down the former section 97(b) which prohibited a person from being intoxicated on a reserve (*R. v. Hayden* (1983), [1984] 1 C.N.L.R. 148 (Man. C.A.), leave to appeal refused [1984] 2 C.N.L.R. 190, 36 C.R. (3d) xxiv, 32 N.R. 386, 8 C.C.C. (3d) 33n, 3 D.L.R. (4th) 361n, 26 Man. R. (2d) 318 (S.C.C.)). In *R. v. Campbell* (1996), [1997] 1 C.N.L.R. 120 (Man. C.A.) the by-law was upheld and applied to someone who lived off-reserve, but was intoxicated on-reserve.

41 On the subject of penalties, see s. 85.1(4) of the *Indian Act*.

42 Department of Indian and Northern Affairs, *Indian Band By-Law Handbook* (Ottawa: Minister of Supply and Services, 1993) at 21, para. 14.6 [hereinafter, *Indian Band By-Law Handbook*].

43 For an outline on the law of entitlement to Indian status and membership codes see Larry Gilbert, *Entitlement to Indian Status and Membership Codes in Canada* (Toronto: Carswell, 1996).

44 See the *Indian Band By-Law Handbook*, *supra* note 42 at 13, para. 8.2.

45 For greater detail, see the *Indian Band By-Law Handbook*, *supra* note 40 at 13-17, paras. 8.1 to 8.8.

46 See the *Indian Band By-Law Handbook*, *supra* note 42 at 20-21, para. 14.2.

47 See the *Indian Band By-Law Handbook*, *supra* note 42 at 19, para. 12.1-12.4.

48 On the subject of by-law enforcement, see B. Morse, "By-law enforcement options: a brief survey", [1980] 2 C.N.L.R. 61. In Ontario, the *Police Services Act, 1990*, R.S.O. 1990 SC. P15 provides in section 54 for the appointment of First Nations Constables.

49 *R. v. Jones*, (sub nom. *R. v. Pamajewon*) [1996] 4 C.N.L.R. 164 (S.C.C.).

50 *Manychief v. Poffenroth* (1994), [1995] 2 C.N.L.R. 67 (Alta. Q.B.) concerned a common law wife claiming benefits as a spouse. The court held that there was such a thing as Blood customary marriage, although in this case it was held that such a marriage had not taken place.

It should be noted that the Royal Commission on Aboriginal Peoples has stated that the inherent right of self-government cannot be exercised by individual Bands. They must be exercised by larger nations. See Royal Commission on Aboriginal Peoples, *Restructuring the Relationship*, Volume 2 — Part One (Ottawa: Supply and Services, 1996) at 234-236 [hereinafter RCAP, Vol. 2 — Part One].

51 *Alexander v. Maxime* (1995), [1996] 1 C.N.L.R. 1 (B.C. C.A.). The Spallumcheen First Nation, pursuant to its child welfare by-law, changed custody of a child from his grandmother, to his mother. The grandmother, who lived in Vancouver, refused to give up custody of the child. She challenged the validity of the First Nation by-law. The Court of Appeal did not decide on whether the by-law was authorized under the *Indian Act*. However, the court upheld the exercise of *parens patriae* jurisdiction by the court below to stay the Spallumcheen custody in order to determine the best interests of the child. In *S. (E.G.) v. Spallumcheen Band Council* (1998), [1999] 2 C.N.L.R. 318 (B.C. S.C.), non-Aboriginal foster parents of a child who was a member of the Spallumcheen First Nation asked the court to exercise its *parens patriae* jurisdiction. The foster parents disagreed with the decision of the First Nation to place the child with the child's maternal aunt. The court upheld the decision made under the First Nation's by-law, and dismissed the application of the foster parents.

See Royal Commission on Aboriginal Peoples, *Gathering Strength*, Volume 3 (Ottawa: Supply and Services, 1996) at 24 [hereinafter RCAP, Vol. 3]

52 *Cree-Naskapi (of Quebec) Act*, S.C. 1984, c. 18. The eight Bands identified in the Act are Whapmagoostui Aeyouch (Whapmagoostui Band), Chisasibi Eeyouch (Chisasibi Band), Wemindgi Eeyou (Wemindji Band), Wapanoutauw Eeyou (Eastmain Band), Waskaganish Eeyou (Waskaganish Band), Nemaskauw Eenouch (Nemaska Band), Waswanipi Eenouch (Waswanipi Band) and Mistasini Eenouch (Mistassini Band).

53 *Sechelt Indian Band Self-Government Act*, S.C. 1986, c. 27.

54 *First Nations Land Management Act*, S.C. 1999, c. 24 (Bill C-49). The Act received Royal Assent June 17, 1999. At the present time, only the following First Nations will be affected by the legislation:

1. Westbank
2. Musqueam
3. Fort George (also known as Lheit-Lit'en and Lheidli T'enneh)
4. Anderson Lake (also known as N'Quatqua)
5. Squamish
6. Siksika Nation
7. John Smith (also known as Muskoday)
8. Cowessess
9. The Pas (also known as Opaskwayak Cree)
10. Nipissing Band of Ojibways (also known as Nippissing)
11. Scugog (also known as Mississauga of Scugog Island)
12. Chippewas of Rama (also known as Chippewas of Mnjikaning)
13. Chippewas of Georgina Island
14. Saint Mary's

55 *Yukon First Nations Self-Government Act*, S.C. 1994 c. 35. Seven First Nations have signed the agreements: Teslin Tlingit Council; Champagne & Aishihik First Nation's; Vuntut Gwichin First Nation; Nacho Nyak Dun First Nation; Selkirk First Nation; Little Salmon/Carmack First Nation; Tr'on Dek Hwech'in First Nation. All have passed some laws.

56 Section 2(1) of The *Indian Act* provides that:

"reserve"

(a) means a tract of land, the legal title to which is vested in Her Majesty, that has been set apart by Her Majesty for the use and benefit of a band, and

R.S.C. 1985, c. 32 (1st Supp.), s. 1 and c. 17 (4th Supp.), s. 1.

57 See *Ross River Dena Band v. Canada*, [1998] 3 C.N.L.R. 284 (Y.T. S.C.) for a description of the situation in the Yukon. In that case, the Band was arguing that land set aside by the federal government should be considered a reserve.

58 These figures are based on Statistics Canada, Aboriginal Peoples Survey (1991). For an explanation see Royal Commission on Aboriginal Peoples, *Restructuring the Relationship*, Volume 2, Part Two (Ottawa: Supply and Services, 1996) at 801 and 803 [hereinafter RCAP, Vol. 2 — Part Two].

59 RCAP, Vol. 2 — Part Two, *supra* note 58 at 966.

60 These figures are based on Statistics Canada, Aboriginal Peoples Survey (1991). For further explanation see Royal Commission on Aboriginal Peoples, *Gathering Strength*, Volume 3 (Ottawa: Ministry of Supply and Services Canada, 1996) at 121 [hereinafter RCAP, Vol. 3].

61 RCAP, Vol. 3, *supra* note 58 at 368.

62 *Birth Registration No. 67-09-022272, Re* (1975), (sub nom. *Natural Parents v. Superintendent of Child Welfare)* [1976] 2 S.C.R. 751 (S.C.C.)

63 *Derrickson v. Derrickson,* [1986] 2 C.N.L.R. 45 (S.C.C.)

64 *R. v. Francis,* [1988] 4 C.N.L.R. 98 (S.C.C.)

65 *Four B Manufacturing Ltd. v. U.G.W.,* [1979] 4 C.N.L.R. 21 (S.C.C.)

66 See Chapter 3, "Hunting, Fishing and Trapping" for more details.

67 For cases on the tobacco quota system, see *Tseshaht Indian Band v. British Columbia,* (sub nom. *Tseshaht Band v. British Columbia)* [1992] 4 C.N.L.R. 171 (B.C. C.A.), leave to appeal allowed (1993), 98 D.L.R. (4th) vii (S.C.C.). The appeal has been discontinued; *R. v. Murdock* (1996), [1997] 2 C.N.L.R. 103 (N.S. C.A.); *Bomberry v. Ontario (Minister of Revenue)* [1989] 3 C.N.L.R. 27 (Ont. Div. Ct.), leave to appeal refused (1993), [1994] 2 C.N.L.R. vi (note) (Ont. C.A.) For cases upholding the gasoline quota system, see *Laforme v. Canada (Minister of Finance)* (1998), (sub nom. *Laforme v. Canada (Minister of Finance))* [1999] 1 C.N.L.R. 84 (Ont. Gen. Div.); *Chehalis Indian Band v. British Columbia,* [1987] 3 C.N.L.R. 44 (B.C. S.C.); affirmed (1988), [1989] 1 C.N.L.R. 62 (B.C. C.A.)

68 See *Surrey v. Peace Arch Enterprises Ltd. (District)* (1970), 74 W.W.R. 380 (B.C. C.A.) where the court determined a surrender under the *Indian Act* is not a surrender in the conveyancing sense. Indians are forbidden from leasing or conveying reserve lands, and this function must be performed by a government official. A surrender for the purpose of leasing land is a conditional surrender. Such land is still within the category of lands described in s. 91(24) of the *Constitution Act, 1867* as "lands reserved for Indians". Where land was reserved for Indians in 1887, and they still maintain a reversionary interest in it, the exclusive legislative jurisdiction remains with the federal Parliament and provincial or municipal zoning, building, water service and sewage disposal by-laws, cannot be enforced against the non-Indian Lessee.

69 For cases on the application of landlord and tenant law on reserve see *Park Mobile Home Sales Ltd v. Le Greely* (1978), 85 D.L.R. (3d) 618 (B.C. C.A.); *Matsqui Indian Band v. Bird* (1992), [1993] 3 C.N.L.R. 80 (B.C. S.C.); *Millbrook Indian Band v. Nova Scotia (Northern Counties Residential Tenancies Board)* (1978), 84 D.L.R. (3d) 174 (N.S. T.D.), affirmed [without reference to this point] (1978), [1979] 4 C.N.L.R. 59 (N.S. C.A.).

70 See sections 87, 89 and 90 of the *Indian Act* for provisions exempting property situated on a reserve from seizure.

71 See Chapter 16, "Wills and Estates".

9

Indian Act Registration, Band Membership and First Nation Citizenship

POINTS TO REMEMBER

1. Marriage does not affect the status of spouses. A registered Indian who marries a non-Indian will retain his or her registration and the non-Indian spouse will not gain registration.

2. In the future, children will be registered as Indians by the federal government if they have two grandparents who were registered.

3. First Nations wishing to take control of their own membership criteria may do so by obtaining the consent of the majority of their electors.

1. INTRODUCTION

Individuals first became registered under the *Indian Act* by belonging to certain Bands. Many were signed up when lists were made at treaty time. Others were signed up when their Band was established. There were many inconsistencies in the making up of these lists. In some cases Métis were added to treaty lists, and in some cases they were excluded. In other cases, families, or even whole Bands were missed, so that individuals were not registered at all.

Who was registered became more complicated by the two policies behind the statute. The federal government has used the *Indian Act* to encourage assimilation. But the Act also "protected" Indians until they were "ready" to be treated like other Canadians.[1] This dual policy of paternalism and assimilation, lead to a mishmash of nonsensical, ethnocentric, and sexist rules. For example, Eurocentric patrilineal (father's line) rules on family lineage were imposed on all First

Nations, even on those First Nations, such as the Mohawks and the Nisga'a, which were matrilineal (mother's line). The most infamous of these rules provided that when an Indian man married a non-Indian woman, the woman became registered as an Indian. On the other hand, when an Indian woman married a non-Indian man, she and her minor children were taken off the registration books and treated as whites.

To encourage assimilation, individual Indians were told that they would be allowed to vote if they "enfranchised". The catch was, in order to vote, they would have to give up their Indian status. Voluntary enfranchisement was never very popular, and during one period government tried to increase the pace by forcing Indians who became lawyers, doctors, Christian clergymen, or university graduates to enfranchise.[2] It was not until 1960, that Indians were allowed to vote in federal, and most provincial elections without enfranchising.

2. *INDIAN ACT* REGISTRATION AND BAND MEMBERSHIP

Changes to the *Indian Act* made by Bill C-31 in 1985 have removed the discrimination based on sex, and given registration back to most people who had lost it. The federal government has retained control, however, of who is registered as an Indian, and the rights which flow from registration. The *Indian Act* also defines who are Band members. The rules for registration and *Indian Act* Band membership are described in this section. What happens when the First Nation decides to take control of its own membership list is described in the next section, "Membership or Citizenship Codes".

(a) Who Has Indian Status?

The rules for federal registration are complicated, and the details cannot all be explained simply. Some of the highlights are listed below.[3]

(i) *People who were registered before April 17, 1985*

People who were on First Nations' lists or the general list held by Indian Affairs all keep their Indian status.

(ii) *People who recovered Indian status in 1985 because of Bill C-31*

Women who married someone other than a registered Indian lost their Indian status under the old law. They recovered their status automatically under Bill C-31 if they applied for reinstatement.[4] Their children could also recover their status. Men who voluntarily enfranchised also got back their status.

Children who have at least one parent and two grandparents who are registered under the *Indian Act* also recovered their status.

An Indian child who is adopted by non-Indian parents retains his or her entitlement to registration.[5] A non-Indian child adopted by registered Indians is entitled to registration.[6]

Because marriage to a registered Indian no longer affects status, the only registrants in the future will be children who are born into status. The general rule is that a child must have at least two grandparents who are entitled to be registered. The grandparents need not be from the same side of the family.[7] This provision is causing some controversy: it is feared that it will lead to a decline of the Indian population, especially in areas where there is a high rate of inter-marriage.

(b) Continuing Control of Membership by Indian Affairs

Over half the Bands in Canada still have their membership codes controlled by the Department of Indian Affairs. In this case, the Band membership will be the same as the rules for registration as an Indian.

On marriage, each spouse remains on the membership list of his or her own Band unless the Band Council agrees to a transfer of membership. Where the parents belong to different Bands, the children may be registered with either, but not both, Bands.[8]

(c) Disputes about Registration or Band Membership

The *Indian Act* provides for a protest about registration as an Indian or about inclusion on a Band's membership list which is controlled by Indian Affairs. A person can protest against the refusal to register by writing to the Registrar in Ottawa within three years of the refusal. There is an appeal from the decision of the Registrar.[9]

3. MEMBERSHIP OR CITIZENSHIP CODES

The *Indian Act* now recognizes that First Nations can decide who will belong to that nation in the future. First Nation "membership codes" will take the place of the Band membership rules under the *Indian Act*. Some First Nations prefer to call these "Citizenship Codes" in order to emphasize the fact that they belong to nations. I will also call them Citizenship Codes for the same reason and to distinguish them from Band membership rules set out in the *Indian Act*.

Although the first citizens will be those included on the Indian Affairs list, the First Nation can decide about the admission of new members.[10] For example, First Nations could provide for non-Indians to become citizens or require that citizens have sixty per cent "Indian blood".

It is important to note that First Nation citizenship is different from registration under the *Indian Act*. Therefore, while the First Nation may set up its own Code, not all citizens will necessarily be registered under the *Indian Act*. For example, the children of women who had married men who were not registered Indians, or men who voluntarily enfranchised, might be excluded from Band membership by a Band-enacted citizenship code. In that case, the person would have Indian status but would not be a member of a particular Band.

The situation is very complicated then. An individual may be registered, but not belong to a Band, or a person who is not a registered Indian could be the citizen of a First Nation. The differences are described below in the section on "Benefits of Indian Status".

(a) Disputes about membership or citizenship

A Citizenship Code will indicate whether there is a right of appeal from a decision about citizenship. In general, it appears that Codes which have an initial decision made by a citizenship committee will allow an appeal to Chief and Council. Where Chief and Council make the initial decision, no appeal is provided. Another option is for Codes to provide for appeals to an outside body. This body could be, for example, the courts or an Aboriginal review tribunal made up of individuals drawn from a number of First Nations.

Some Codes provide that the final decision on membership is to be made by a vote of members of the First Nation.[11]

(b) How to pass a Membership or Citizenship Code

The Minister of Indian Affairs has no right to refuse to recognize a Citizenship Code as long as it is enacted according to the procedures set out in the *Indian Act*:[12]

1. The First Nation Council must draft a citizenship code

    Most First Nations strike a membership committee and hold community meetings to discuss the issues before coming up with a draft.

2. Appropriate notice must be given about a vote on the Code

    A First Nation Council could post notices around the First Nation's public premises and make announcements on community radio or TV, put ads in local newspapers and inform off-reserve organizations such as Friendship Centres.

3. Who can vote on the Code

    As a general rule, electors who can vote for Chief and Council are allowed to vote.[13] Over one half of all the people who are entitled to vote must accept the Code for it to pass; it is not enough to have a majority of people who actually vote.[14]

4. What must the people vote on?

    The *Indian Act* requires that the people consent to two things: first, they must agree to take over the membership list from Indian Affairs, and secondly, they must consent to the actual membership or citizenship code proposed. Both questions can be put on a single ballot.

5. Notice to Minister

    A copy of the Code is sent to the Minister "forthwith". If the procedures have been followed, the Minister must recognize the Code.

(c) What are the rights and benefits of a citizen under a Citizenship Code?

If a citizen under a Code is also registered as an Indian under the *Indian Act*, all the rights and benefits will be available. However, if the citizen is not registered, he or she will not get some of the benefits of registration, such as exemptions from tax. More details are provided in the next section.

4. BENEFITS OF INDIAN STATUS

The benefits of Indian status are difficult to list completely. This is because some of the benefits are dependent on government policy, and others are dependent on Band membership, residence or *Indian Act* registration. Some highlights are listed below:

1. Registered Indians who are members of a Band and live on the reserve:
   - can vote in Band elections and run for office (See Chapter 10, "Elections and Referenda")
   - can enjoy Aboriginal and treaty rights (See Chapter 2, "Aboriginal and Treaty Rights")
   - are entitled to tax exemptions (See Chapter 20, " Taxation")
   - can enjoy rights, such as residence, granted by the Band
   - are eligible to receive health, educational and economic development benefits provided by Indian Affairs

2. Registered Indians who are members of a Band and live off the reserve:[15]
   - may not be able to vote in Band elections or run for office
   - can enjoy Aboriginal and treaty rights
   - are entitled to partial tax exemptions — but may not be exempt from provincial sales tax
   - have the potential to exercise rights granted by the Band
   - are eligible to receive some health, educational and economic development benefits provided by various provincial or federal agencies

3. Registered Indians who live on the reserve but are not members of that Band:
   - cannot participate in the political affairs of the Band
   - may not be able to enjoy Aboriginal and treaty rights (not clear)
   - are entitled to full tax exemptions

- may exercise some privileges of membership as extended by the Band, such as permission to reside on reserve[16]
- are eligible to receive some health, educational and economic development benefits provided by various provincial or federal agencies

4. People without Indian registration who are members of a First Nation which has its own Citizenship Code:[17]
   - can participate in the political affairs of the First Nation
   - may enjoy only partial Aboriginal and treaty rights (still not clear)
   - are not entitled to tax exemptions
   - can enjoy rights granted by the First Nation such as residence, housing, etc.
   - are eligible for some health, educational and economic development benefits provided by various provincial and federal agencies.

ENDNOTES

1 For more information on the history of the *Indian Act* status provisions and a description of the law before 1985, see Shin Imai and Katherine Laird, "The Indian Status Question: A Problem of Definitions", in *Native People and Justice in Canada*, (1982), 5 Canadian Legal Aid Bulletin (No.1) 113. For an analysis on the *Indian Act* and its historical civilization and assimilation policies see Royal Commission on Aboriginal Peoples, *Looking Forward, Looking Back*, Volume 1 (Ottawa: Minister of Supply and Services, 1996) at 255-332 [hereinafter RCAP, Vol. 1].

2 *The Indian Act, 1876*, S.C. 1876, c. 18, s. 86(1). This provision was repealed in 1880.

3 For a full description of the rules for registration, see Larry Gilbert, *Entitlement to Indian Status and Membership Codes in Canada* (Toronto: Carswell,1996). Indian and Northern Affairs Canada has published an annotated guide called "The Indian Act, Past and Present: A Manual for Registration and Entitlement Legislation" (1991, #QS-5283-000-BB-A1).

4 The requirement that women be reinstated to the Band lists is being challenged by the oil-rich Sawridge Band of former Conservative Senator Walter Twinn. See *Sawridge Band v. R.* (sub nom. *Sawridge Band v. Canada*) [1997] 3 F.C. 580, (Fed. C.A.), leave to appeal refused (December 1, 1997), Doc. 26169 (S.C.C.)

5 On the subject of adoption and status, the leading case is *Birth Registration No. 67-09-022272, Re* (1975), (sub nom. *Natural Parents v. Superintendent of Child Welfare*) [1976] 2 S.C.R. 75 (S.C.C.). In this case, an Indian child who had been adopted by non-Indian parents under provincial adoption legislation did not lose Indian status.

6 A case under the old law which suggested that a non-Indian child adopted by registered Indians will not be granted Indian status is *Sahanatien v. Smith* (1982), [1983] 1 C.N.L.R. 151 (Fed. T.D.). After 1985, non-Indian children adopted by registered Indians will be registered. See Larry Gilbert, *supra*, endnote 3, at pages 48-49.

7 On the subject of children's eligibility for registration, see section 6 of the *Indian Act*.

8 On the subject of registering children of parents from different First Nations, see sections 11, 12 and 13 of the *Indian Act*.

9 For rules on protesting registration, see sections 14.2 and 14.3 of the *Indian Act*.

10 In *Omeasoo v. Canada (Minister of Indian Affairs & Northern Development)* (1988), [1989] 1 C.N.L.R. 110 (Fed. T.D.) an application was made by the Band requiring the Minister of Indian Affairs to give notice that the Band membership code was in force. The Minister had previously rejected the Band membership code because it did not meet the requirements of s.10 of the *Indian* Act. The Band passed a BCR amending the membership code. The court held that this was not within the Band's authority. In *Martel v. Omeasoo* (1992), [1994] 1 C.N.L.R. 102 (Fed. T.D.) the applicants were reinstated to the Band list under Bill C-31. The Band maintained that it retained authority to establish membership criteria and did not accept the applicants as Band members. The court dismissed the application and sent the issue of Band membership to trial.

11 For examples of Codes, see Gilbert, *supra*, endnote 3.

12 On the subject of membership codes, see section 10 of the *Indian Act*.

13 On the subject of electors who can vote on membership codes, if the First Nation has *Indian Act* elections, then those "ordinarily resident" on the reserve may vote. If the First Nation wants to extend voting to those living off-reserve, it may do so by passing a by-law under section 10(3).

14 For example, if a Band has 300 voters, at least 151 must vote in favour. Even if only 200 people vote, but 151 vote in favour, that is sufficient. However, if 200 people vote and 101 of those are in favour, the Code will not be approved.

15 The Supreme Court of Canada in *Corbiere v. Canada (Minister of Indian Northern Affairs)*, [1999] 3 C.N.L.R. 19 (S.C.C.) has held that rules which restrict participation by off-reserve members, such as the right to vote in Band elections, violates section 15 of the *Charter*. The federal government has to pass new legislation by early 2001.

16 On the subject of First Nation services, see *Courtois v. Canada (Department of Indian Affairs & Northern Development)* (1990)[1991] 1 C.N.L.R. 40 (Can. Human Rights Trib.)

17 Section 4.1 of the *Indian Act* states that certain sections will apply to those whose names are entered in a Band List.

10

Elections and Referenda

POINTS TO REMEMBER

1. The majority of Bands have elections under the *Indian Act* every two years to elect a chief and council.

2. Bands may also have elections following Band custom. In these elections, the Band can decide who will vote, and when to end the term of office of the chief and council.

3. An election held under the *Indian Act* can be overturned by the federal cabinet, but no rules are in place for contesting elections held according to Band custom.

4. Aboriginal organizations incorporated under federal or provincial laws may make by-laws and have elections for boards of directors in accordance with those by-laws and federal or provincial corporate law.

1. INTRODUCTION

This chapter will discuss elections of chief and council on reserves, as well as elections to other types of Aboriginal organizations. Elections of chief and council are covered under the *Indian Act*. Elections to other political organizations, such as Tribal Councils, Friendship Centres, Native Women's Associations, and Métis organizations are usually governed by legislation dealing with corporations.

2. ELECTION OF BAND COUNCILS

First Nations had many different types of political organizations at the time of first contact with Europeans, but it is unlikely that any First Nation structured its society in the way prescribed by the *Indian Act*. The *Indian Act* imposed the European system for elections by secret ballot on Aboriginal communities. It was fiercely resisted by some First Nations, particularly those belonging to the Six Nations, and traditional councils continue to exist on some reserves. Adherents to traditional councils continue to refuse to recognize chiefs elected under the *Indian Act*. Canadian courts, however, do not recognize traditional councils as having governing authority.[1]

The *Indian Act* recognizes two methods for choosing the chief and councillors. The first method is a procedure set out in the *Indian Act* itself. The second method is by "custom", and recognizes selection processes developed by the First Nation.

It is important to note that there can be confusion between traditional councils, and *Indian Act* Band Councils elected by Band custom. The traditional councils operate outside of the *Indian Act* altogether, and, in the case of the Haudensaunee, refuse to participate in the electoral process. On the other hand, Band Councils chosen by custom are recognized under the *Indian Act* as governing authorities.

(a) *Indian Act* — section 74

Many First Nations have a chief and council which is elected according to the rules set out in the *Indian Act*. The Minister can make a declaration that the *Indian Act* applies, even if the First Nation does not consent.[2] The Act and regulations made under the Act provide a complete code for Band elections:[3]

(i) *Who may vote*

According to the *Indian Act*, only members of the Band who are eighteen and "ordinarily resident on the reserve" may vote in an *Indian Act* election.[4] This means that members who live off-reserve may not vote.[5] The restriction on the voting rights of members of the First Nation who live off reserve was struck down by the Supreme Court of Canada in 1999. The federal government was given eighteen months to draft a section which provided better balance between the rights of reserve residents and off-reserve residents.[6]

(ii) *Who can run for chief*

In most cases, chiefs are elected directly by the members of the Band, but it is also possible for the chief to be chosen from among the elected councillors.[7] There is no requirement that the chief be a member of the Band. There are cases where the elected chief has been a member of another Band, and the Federal Court of Appeal has held that a non-Aboriginal person married to a Band member could be elected Chief.[8]

(iii) *Who can run for council*

According to the *Indian Act*, only members of the Band who reside on the reserve may run for council,[9] but this rule has often been ignored.

(iv) *Who can nominate*

A person must be eligible to run for chief or council in order to nominate another person to run for chief or council. A candidate for chief or council requires a nominator and a seconder.[10]

(v) *How an election is called*

At least six days before the nomination meeting, and at least twelve days before the election, an "electoral officer" must post a notice calling for a nomination meeting. An electoral officer is a neutral person, usually appointed by the Band Council. After nominations, the electoral officer must prepare a voters' list, and post it.

(vi) *Elections by secret ballot*

Elections should be conducted from 9 a.m. to 6 p.m., although the electoral officer has the option of keeping the ballot boxes open until 8 p.m. If there is a tie, the electoral officer may cast the deciding vote; otherwise he or she does not vote.

(vii) *Election results may be contested*

Within thirty days after an election, a candidate or an elector may lodge an appeal with Indian Affairs. There must be reasonable grounds to believe that there was a corrupt practice, a violation of the *Indian Act*, or the candidate was ineligible to run for office. The Minister may investigate and make a report to Cabinet, which can set aside the election.

(viii) *Term of office*

The chief and council hold office for two years. An earlier election may be called if the position of chief or councillor becomes vacant. In practice, elections are sometimes called later than the two year term, but it is not clear if this practice is legal.

(ix) *Removal from office*

A person automatically loses his or her position as chief or councillor upon conviction of an indictable offence, death, or resignation. In other cases, the Minister may declare that the person is unfit to continue because of a summary conviction or provincial offence, absence for three consecutive meetings without authorization, or being guilty of a corrupt practice with respect to the election. In practice, communities sometimes exert great pressure on their chiefs and councillors, forcing them to resign.[11]

(b) *Indian Act* — Band Custom

In the majority of Bands, the chief and council are chosen "according to the custom of the Band."[12] The First Nation determines who may vote, how the voting is carried out, and when elections are held. Electoral rules may be traditions which have been passed from previous generations. For example, some First Nations in the James Bay area used to elect their chief by having the members of the First Nation line up behind the candidate of their choice. At another reserve, a First Nation elects by secret ballot, but elections are not called until the community feels that the time is appropriate, which may run four or five years.

The custom elections are recognized by the *Indian Act* but are not created by the *Indian Act*. This important distinction was made by the Federal Court in *Bone v. Sioux Valley Indian Band*.[13]

> I do not think that the power of the Band to choose its council in a customary manner is a "power conferred on the Band" as is contemplated [under] the *Indian Act*. Rather it is an inherent power of the Band; it is a power the Band has always had, which the *Indian Act* only interferes with in limited circumstances, as provided for under s. 74 of the Act. Thus, in my view the Band may exercise this inherent power unrestrained by ss. 2(3)(a) of the *Indian Act*." (at 65)

In another case, the court held that chiefs would not necessarily have to be elected — they could be hereditary.[14] However, whatever system is chosen, there must be broad consensus in the community for the method of choosing the Chief and Council.[15] The *Indian Act* rules on length of time in office and voting procedures do not apply when there are custom elections. The rules are determined by the First Nation code on elections.[16]

A dispute about a custom election can be taken to the Federal Court of Canada.[17] Two Mohawk communities have had court cases dealing with their band custom elections. In Akwesasne, the Mohawk Council decided to change from an *Indian Act* election to a band custom election. The court found that such a change could be made, and that no declaration from the Minister of Indian Affairs was necessary.[18] At Kanestake, the situation was reversed: the chief was appointed by clan mothers, but many in the community felt that there should be *Indian Act* elections. At their request, the federal government held a referendum. The court held that the referendum was appropriate, although the federal government could have changed to an *Indian Act* election system even without a referendum.[19]

The Department of Indian Affairs does have a policy,[20] however, for First Nations to follow if they want to convert back to Band custom. The requirements for the code are that the request:

- be in writing
- allow for election appeals and amendments
- follow the principles of natural justice
- conform to the *Charter of Rights and Freedoms*
- is "found it to be satisfactory" by the Department of Indian Affairs

A vote of 50 per cent plus 1 of the electors must approve the election code. In the alternative, a method of "community approval" can be employed with the approval of Indian Affairs.

3. WHEN TO HOLD A REFERENDUM

Certain decisions require the participation of members of the First Nation:

- surrender of land[21] (see Chapter 17, "Commercial Relations")
- designation of land (see Chapter 17, "Commercial Relations")

- membership or citizenship codes (see Chapter 9, "Indian Act Registration and First Nation Citizenship")
- alcohol by-laws (see Chapter 8, "Bands, Band Councils and Reserves")

The Band may hold referenda on other issues, but is not required by law to do so.

4. ELECTIONS FOR OTHER ABORIGINAL ORGANIZATIONS AND ASSOCIATIONS

Unlike Band councils under the *Indian Act* or Métis Settlements under the *Métis Settlements Act*, most Aboriginal organizations are not established by statute. Therefore, they are generally incorporated as non-profit corporations under provincial or federal laws.

Outlined below are some of the major provisions in federal and provincial legislation for non-profit corporations. It is important to refer to the constitution and by-laws of the organization as well, since some of them may differ from the general rules outlined in the statutes. Each province and territory has laws that may be slightly different. While this section provides a general discussion of the major issues, the specific laws in each region must be consulted for the details. Special reference is made to the laws of Canada, Ontario, British Columbia and Alberta for purposes of illustration.

(a) Who are the members of the corporation?

The constitution and by-laws of the corporation determine membership. For a community-based corporation such as a Friendship Centre or an Education Authority, the members may be interested local individuals. For regional or provincial organizations, members may be representatives from local chapters or First Nations within the region. Membership in Tribal councils, for example, may be structured in a number of ways. All members of First Nations who belong to the Tribal council may be members of the corporation, or alternatively, all chiefs and council members of First Nations who belong to the Tribal council may be members of the corporation. Another possibility is for only the chiefs of the member First Nations to be members of the corporation. (For more information on how to structure a corporation, see Chapter 12, "Community Corporations.")

(b) Meetings

An annual general meeting of the membership must be held at least once a year.[22] At these meetings, by-laws may be discussed, directors may be elected and the report of the auditor delivered. An annual general meeting or other general meeting of members can be called by the directors. A meeting can also be called by a requisition by at least 10% of the members who are entitled to vote at the meeting.[23] The by-laws will usually specify how much notice of a meeting must be given, but there may also be requirements for the number of days in the legislation.[24]

(c) Who may vote

Members of corporations are allowed to vote. As a general rule each member has one vote. However, the by-laws can create different classes of membership, so that associate members might have no vote; while others can have more than one vote.[25] The federal legislation contains no similar details, only requiring that the by-laws include provisions regulating rights of voting.[26]

(d) Who can run for Board of Directors

Only people who are members of the corporation (or who become members within ten days of becoming a director) and are at least 18 years old may be on the Board of Directors in Ontario.[27] In British Columbia and Alberta, it appears that Board members may be younger than 18. There is no similar provision in the federal legislation, although the people who initially apply for incorporation must be at least 18.[28] The legislation may provide for a minimum number of directors.[29]

The President and other officers of an Ontario corporation may be elected directly by the members or may be chosen from among the elected Board members according to what the by-laws or letters patent say. If these do not refer to election of officials, the directors elect the president from among themselves.[30]

A change in the directors or officers of a corporation must be reported to the government. In Ontario, the report must be within 14 days, in Alberta within 30 days, and in British Columbia "without delay".[31] For federally registered corporations, a change in the directors or officers will be filed as part of the Annual Summary which is required by the Department of Consumer and Corporate Affairs.[32]

(e) How to call an election

Directors are elected at a general meeting called for that purpose.[33] The by-laws and constitution of the corporation should outline how many days' notice is needed to call an election. If they do not, the provision from the legislation will apply (see Meetings section above). Procedures for voting by proxy are contained in the Ontario legislation and can be addressed in the by-laws in British Columbia.[34] Again, the federal legislation is much less detailed, and simply requires that the by-laws provide for the appointment and removal of directors.[35]

(f) Term of office

The general rule for directors of an Ontario corporation is a one year term. This may be extended up to five years by the letters patent or supplementary letters patent.[36] Staggered elections which will change part of the Board each year may also be provided for in the letters patent.[37] There are no parallel provisions in the federal, Alberta or B.C. legislation.

Removal from office by death or resignation are two obvious reasons for a position to become vacant. Ontario law also provides that a director must resign if he or she becomes a bankrupt.[38] The by-laws may provide other reasons for removal as well. A director of a provincial corporation can be removed at a general meeting called specially for the purpose if 2/3 of the votes at the meeting vote to remove him or her.[39] There are no parallel provisions in the federal legislation, so these matters should be addressed in the by-laws.

(g) Disputes

Where there is a dispute about the by-laws or the elections, the matter can be taken to court.[40] In practice, organizations have generally dealt with disputes internally, and avoided court actions.

ENDNOTES

1 On the subject of traditional councils, see *Isaac v. Davey*, [1977] 2 S.C.R. 897 (S.C.C.) On January 14, 1793, Governor Simcoe provided a patent of the Grand River lands to the Six Nations. Until 1924, the Six Nations were governed by a hereditary council. In 1924, the federal government declared that the Band should have *Indian Act* elections pursuant to Orders in Council in 1924 and 1951.

The traditional people, who wanted to return to the hereditary system, blocked the council elected under the *Indian Act* from entering the Council House. The court found that the Orders in Council were valid, and observed that the declaration itself may bring the Six Nations under the definition of "Band" found in section 2 of the *Indian Act*.

See also Jack Woodward, *Native Law*, (Toronto: Carswell, 1998) at 165-168. An excellent account of the interaction of elected Band Councils, traditional councils and the community of Kahnawake is Gerald R. Alfred, *Heeding the Voices of our Ancestors: Kahnawake Mohawk Politics and the Rise of Native Nationalism*, (New York: Oxford, 1995).

2 On the subject of imposing *Indian Act* elections, section 74(1) of the *Indian Act* provides:

> Whenever he deems it advisable for the good government of a band, the Minister may declare by order that after a day to be named therein the council of the band, consisting of a chief and councillors, shall be selected by elections to be held in accordance with this Act.

The Bands that are subject to a declaration are listed in the *Indian Bands Council Elections Order*, SOR/97-138. This Order is updated from time to time. These updates are tracked in the annual volumes of the *Annotated Indian Act and Aboriginal Constitutional Provisions*, (Carswell).

3 On the subject of Band elections procedures, sections 74 to 80 of the *Indian Act* establish the system for elections. There also exist several regulations setting out specific procedures. See *Indian Band Election Regulations*, C.R.C. 1978, c. 952, as am.

4 On the subject of voting rights, First Nations with their own membership or citizenship codes may allow a person registered under the code to vote, even if they are not registered under the *Indian Act*.

The definition of "ordinarily resident" in the *Indian Band Election Regulations*, s. 3(b) attempts to explain the self-explanatory, with humorous results:

> generally, that place which has always been, or which he has adopted as, the place of his habitation or home, whereto, when away therefrom, he intends to return . . .

5 Members resident off-reserve may vote only if the Band is under "band custom" elections and the custom is to allow off-reserve members to vote.

6 *Corbiere v. Canada (Minister of Indian & Northern Affairs)*, [1999] 3 C.N.L.R. 19 (S.C.C.). The Batchewana Band in Ontario had almost 70% of its membership living off-reserve, most of whom had been re-registered after the changes to the *Indian Act* made by Bill C-31. The off-reserve members of the Band challenged the voting restriction to those ordinarily living on-reserve. They claimed that there was a violation of the equality rights guaranteed by section 15 of the *Charter of Rights and Freedoms*.

The decision of the Supreme Court in *Corbiere* is quite sophisticated, attempting to balance the interests of the Band members off-reserve against the interests of Band members who live in the reserve community. The court found that there was discrimination against the off-reserve members, so that there was an infringement of section 15 of the *Charter of Rights and Freedoms*. However, the infringement was *partially* justified under section 1 of the *Charter* because people living off-reserve would have different interests and concerns from those who were actually living in the reserve community. The discrimination was not *completely* justified because the equality rights of the off-reserve members were infringed more than was necessary. In the end, the court declared that the voting restriction in section 77 of the *Indian Act* was unconstitutional, but suspended the implementation for 18 months to allow the government to enact new legislation.

This year and a half is provided "to enable Parliament to consult with the affected groups, and to redesign the voting provisions of the *Indian Act* in a nuanced way that respects equality rights and all affected interests" [at 69]. L'Heureux-Dubé, J. describes some ways to achieve the desired balance.

> Recognizing non-residents' right to substantive equality in accordance with the principle of respect for human dignity, therefore, does not require that non-residents have identical voting rights to residents. Rather, what is necessary is a system that recognizes non-residents' important place in the band community. It is possible to think of many ways this might be done, while recognizing, respecting, and valuing the different positions, needs, and interests of on-reserve and off-reserve band members. One might be to divide the "local" functions which relate purely to residents from those that affect all band members and have different voting regimes for these functions. A requirement of a double majority, or a right of veto for each group might also respect the full participation and belonging of non-residents. There might be special seats on a band council for non-residents, which give them meaningful, but not identical, rights of participation. The solu-

tion may be found in the customary practices of Aboriginal bands. There may be a separate solution for each band. Many other possibilities can be imagined, which would respect non-residents' rights to meaningful and effective participation in the voting regime of the community, but would also recognize the somewhat different interests of residents and non-residents. However, without violating s. 15(1), the voting regime cannot, as it presently does, completely deny non-resident band members participation in the electoral system of representation. Nor can that participation be minimal, insignificant, or merely token [at 61].

7 On the subject of a chief being elected or chosen from among the councillors, see the Election Order under section 74 of the *Indian Act* which states which method is to be used.

8 On the subject of eligibility for chief, section 75(2) of the *Indian Act* says only that:

75(2) No person may be a candidate for election as chief or councillor of a band unless his nomination is moved and seconded by persons who are themselves eligible to be nominated.

In *Goodswimmer v. Canada (Minister of Indian Affairs & Northern Development)*, [1995] 3 C.N.L.R. 72, set aside/quashed (sub nom. *Goodswimmer v. Attorney General of Canada*) [1997] 1 C.N.L.R. iv (S.C.C.) (Fed. C.A.) the members of the Sturgeon Lake Indian Band elected a chief who was not registered under the *Indian Act*, but who was married to a member of the Band. The court found that the chief need not be an "elector" in order to be chief, although it was clear that councillors must be "electors". The Supreme Court of Canada decided not to hear the case after the issue became moot.

9 On the subject of the residence restriction on eligibility for council, see section 75(1) of the *Indian Act*. This restriction may be modified following the decision in *Corbiere v. Canada, supra*, endnote 6.

10 The eligibility of nominators for chief and council is in section 75 of the *Indian Act*.

11 For a case holding that a Band Councillor can only be suspended in accordance with section 78 of the Indian Act, see *Sault v. LaForme* (1989), (sub nom. *Sault v. Mississaugas of the New Credit Indian Band Council*) [1990] 1 C.N.L.R. 140 (T.D.)

12 For the definition of band custom, see the *Indian Act*, section 2(i), "council of the band". See *Bigstone v. Eagle* (1992), [1993] 1 C.N.L.R. 25 (Fed. T.D.) for an election when two new Bands were created.

13 In *Bone v. Sioux Valley Indian Band No. 290*, [1996] 3 C.N.L.R. 54 (Fed. T.D.). The court observed that custom elections arose out of the inherent power of the Band, not from a delegation under the *Indian Act.*

14 See *Crow v. Blood Band* (1996), (sub nom. *Crow v. Blood Indian Band Council*) [1997] 3 C.N.L.R. 76, (Fed. T.D.) for a discussion of the Blood Tribe Custom Election By-law, and the observation that band custom need not be secret ballot elections. One system that was based on family representation in the Saulteau First Nation is discussed in *Saulteau Indian Band #542 v. Garbitt*, [1997] B.C.J. No. 1250 (B.C. S.C.)

15 The "broad consensus" needed to support a band custom system has been discussed in a number of cases. See *Bigstone v. Big Eagle* (1992), [1993] 1 C.N.L.R. 25 (Fed. T.D.) ; *Bone v. Sioux Valley Indian Band No. 290*, [1996] 3 C.N.L.R. 54 (Fed. T.D.) and *Lac des Mille Lacs First Nation v. Chapman*, [1998] 4 C.N.L.R. 57 (Fed. T.D.).

16 See *Crow v. Blood Band* (1996), (sub nom. *Crow v. Blood Indian Band Council*) [1997] 3 C.N.L.R. 76 (Fed. T.D.)

17 On the subject of taking disputes about customary elections to court, see *Whitefish v. Canada (Dept. of Northern Affairs & Northern Dev.)* (1985), [1986] 1 C.N.L.R. 180 (Sask. Q.B.) in which the Saskatchewan court held that the dispute should be addressed in Federal Court, and *Joe v. John* (1990), [1991] 3 C.N.L.R. 63 (Fed. T.D.) in which Marilyn John, a chief elected according to custom, was challenged by Michael Joe, the former chief who was a traditional life chief of the First Nation. See also *Baptiste v. Goodstoney Indian Band* (1989), [1991] 1 C.L.N.R. 34 (Fed. T.D.)

18 On the subject of changing from an *Indian Act* election to a band custom election, see *Jock v. R.* (1991), [1992] (sub nom. *Jock v. Canada (Minister of Indian & Northern Affairs)*) 1 C.N.L.R. 103 (Fed. T.D.)

19 On changing from a "band custom" election to an *Indian Act* election, see *Six Nations Traditional Hereditary Chiefs v. Canada (Minister of Indian & Northern Affairs* (1991), [1992] 3 C.N.L.R. 156 (Fed. T.D.), and *Badger v. R.* (1990), (sub nom. *Badger v. Canada*) [1991] 2 C.N.L.R. 17, affirmed (1992), (sub nom. *Badger v. Canada*) 57 F.T.R. 311 (note) (Fed. C.A.)

20 The two page "Conversion to Community Election System Policy" was in force in December, 1996. Letter from John Barg, Elections Analyst, Registration, Revenues and Band Governance, Indian and Northern Affairs Canada, January 20, 1998.

21 On the subject of First Nation referenda, the *Indian Referendum Regulations*, C.R.C. 1978, c. 957, as am., apply to surrenders, but do not appear to apply to any other situation where members must vote.

22 For annual general meetings, see *Canada Corporations Act*, R.S.C. 1970, c. C-32, s. 102 [hereinafter *Canada Corporations Act*]; Ontario *Corporations Act* [hereinafter *Ontario Corporations Act*], R.S.O. 1990, c. C.38, s. 293; *Society Act*, R.S.B.C. 1996. c.433, s.56(1) [hereinafter B.C. *Society Act*]; and *Societies Act*, R.S.A. 1980, c. S-18, s.21 [hereinafter Alta. *Societies Act*]

23 If 10% of the members want, they can call a general meeting of members under *Ontario Corporations Act*, *supra* note 22, s. 294 and 295(1); and B.C. *Society Act*, *supra* note 22, s.58(2). No such provision is in the federal or Alberta Acts, although they could presumably provide for this in the by-laws.

24 Fourteen days notice is required under the *Ontario Corporations Act*, *supra* note 22, s. 93. The B.C. *Society Act*, *supra* note 22, s. 60 specifies ten days.

25 In Ontario, some members can have no votes, or some can have more than one vote, in *Ontario Corporations Act*, *supra* note 22, s. 125. In the B.C. *Society Act*, *supra* note 22, s. 7, voting members can only have one vote, and voting members must outnumber non-voting members.

26 *Canada Corporations Act*, *supra*, note 22, s. 155.

27 The age and membership requirements for the Board of Directors are found in *Ontario Corporations Act*, *supra* note 22, s. 286;

28 For age requirements, see B.C. *Society Act*, *supra* note 22, s. 7; Alta. *Societies Act*, *supra* note 22, s. 16, and *Canada Corporations Act*, *supra*, note 22, s. 154 and 155

29 At least three directors are required by the *Ontario Corporations Act*, *supra* note 22, s. 283 and the B.C. *Society Act*, *supra* note 22, s. 24(4). In Alberta, five is the minimum under the Alta. *Societies Act*, *supra*, note 22, s.3(1) .

30 *Ontario Corporations Act*, *supra* note 22, s. 289.

31 For reporting change in directors, see *Ontario Corporations Act*, *supra* note 22, s. 285; B.C. *Society Act*, *supra* note 22, s. 24(7); and Alta. *Societies Act*, *supra* note 22, s.22(3).

32 For annual reports to the federal government, see *Canada Corporations Act*, *supra*, note 22, s. 133.

33 For elections, see *Ontario Corporations Act*, *supra* note 22, s. 287; and B.C. *Society Act*, *supra* note 22, s. 24.

34 For proxy voting, see *Ontario Corporations Act*, *supra* note 22, s. 84; B.C. *Society Act*, *supra* note 22, s. 6(1)(d).

35 For proxy voting for federal corporations, see *Canada Corporations Act, supra*, note 22, s. 155. The Alberta *Societies Act* does not address this issue.

36 For term of office of director, see *Ontario Corporations Act, supra* note 22, s. 287(2).

37 For staggered elections, see *Ontario Corporations Act, supra* note 22, s. 287(5).

38 For vacating position of director, see *Ontario Corporations Act, supra* note 22, s. 286(5).

39 For provisions on removal of director by a vote of the members, see *Ontario Corporations Act, supra*, note 13, s. 67; and B.C. *Society Act, supra* note 22, s. 31.

40 Examples of cases where disputes within organizations have been addressed through legislation on non-profit corporations are *Hammersmith v. Métis Society of Saskatchewan Inc.* (1995), 126 Sask. R. 106 (Sask. Q.B.); *Northern Lake Superior Aboriginal Assn. v. Ontario Métis Aboriginal Assn.*, [1997] O.J. No. 4888 (Ont. Gen. Div.) and see *Card v. Western Region 2A Regional Council Inc.* (1997), 156 Sask. R. 213 (Sask. Q.B.) where the court resolved a dispute within a Saskatchewan Métis organization by referring to the Constitution of the Métis Nation of Saskatchewan and the provincial *Non-Profit Corporations Act*, 1995, S.S. 1995, c. N-4.2. *Parisien v. Sasknative Economic Development Corp.*, [1999] S.J. No. 417 (Sask.Q.B.) was a case in which the court disapproved of the interference of the political leadership in the management of the corporation. The court dealt with the dispute between a provincial Métis association and one of its locals in *North Cariboo Métis Assn. v. Métis Provincial Council of British Columbia*, [1999] B.C.J. No. 2038 (B.C.S.C.).

The Community

A second disadvantage is that time and effort will be expended on administering the existing program rather than identifying the needs of the community, and opportunities for working toward a community-developed program may be lost. In the welfare example, a trapper may need supplements from welfare, but the welfare rules may prohibit the trapper from receiving assistance while on the trapline because he or she is not "looking for employment". So the First Nation may get embroiled in an argument with the trapper about whether the rules allow the payment to the trapper when what is really needed is a different program that takes the trapper's situation into account.[1]

Third, the existing program may just fail: alien, cumbersome and unresponsive, its problems may combine to defeat efforts to deliver the service. As people become discouraged and governments become distrustful, the chances for other attempts to develop programs will be affected negatively as well.

Finally, governments may use the fact that administration of the program has been transferred to the First Nation to divest itself of responsibility. It may underfund the program, provide no training or fail to arrange for support services.

This litany of disadvantages sounds bleak, but not all of them apply to a given set of circumstances. Careful preparation will help a community decide if its needs can be met by an existing program. Below we suggest some steps for a community to create its own program. These steps can also be used to see how an existing program compares to what the community would like to develop.

The steps outlined below are meant to assist people in the communities. The information should also help funding sources understand and support the process in the communities.

Step 1 — Identify the need

It is important for the Aboriginal community to identify what service is needed, what form it should take, and how it should be delivered, before starting to look for funding. As discussed, even though a ready-made government program may be offered, it is a mistake to accept it without first giving serious thought to whether the program will fit the needs of the community.

Step 2 — Find out what the community's priorities are

It is impossible to take over all programs at once. In small communities in particular, there will not be enough people who can develop proposals, lobby, and carry out the work. The community must therefore establish priorities for its work.

Step 3 — Expect a lot of time to pass between getting an idea and getting the service in place

Getting the program approved and funded is a time-consuming process. Developing the program, writing the proposal, and identifying sources of funding can take years. The community should be sure the project is important enough to warrant their time and energy.

Step 4 — Encourage and organize community involvement

Nearly every program will require participation by community members through a committee or board of directors. On reserve the board or committee may be a combination of volunteers and representatives of Council. Off reserve, interested members of the community can volunteer their time.

Step 5 — Set the project up properly

A program that is set up properly in the first place can get on with the business it was meant to do. Paying proper attention to details such as incorporation, office administration, and employment policies puts the project on a solid footing from the outset.

Step 6 — Keep the project running well

The work involved in keeping the project running needs to be considered. The community may not have the resources to run everything. Good organization is essential if a community is to be responsible for some of its services. Buying services from neighbouring communities may prove to be a wiser course.

In urban areas, most services are free-standing, in that they are not run through a central agency. There have been attempts in Toronto, Vancouver, Winnipeg and other urban centres to increase co-ordination among service agencies, but these attempts have met with mixed success. It is up to community volunteers to ensure that other members of the Aboriginal community in their area know about their program, and that new volunteers are identified to help manage the project.

On small reserves the Chief and Council may be able to run the programs. In some cases, councillors may be given specific portfolios, so that they are responsible for certain activities. Another structure, for larger reserves, might be to divide the programs into major activity areas: First Nation administration, social services, First Nation capital projects, and economic development, for example. Management groups could consist of representatives from the programs in the activity area, and be co-ordinated by a councillor. The social services group, for example, could include the child welfare representative, the alcohol and drug abuse counsellor, the community health worker and welfare administrator. The members of the group could meet regularly to ensure that the programs in their area fit together.

3. EXAMPLES OF SPECIFIC PROGRAMS FOR FIRST NATIONS ON-RESERVE

Outlined below are some of the services with actual or potential First Nation involvement which have been funded. This list is not complete, and the commentary is not comprehensive, but it illustrates what is available now.

(a) Child Welfare Services

First Nation children in need of protection have traditionally been cared for by Children's Aid Societies. A Children's Aid Society is an independent organization run by an elected board of directors. Each Children's Aid Society receives money from the provincial government, and its activities are governed by provincial laws.

(See Chapter 15, "Welfare of Children" for options for increasing Aboriginal control over child welfare.)

(b) Welfare

Twenty years ago, welfare payments for members of First Nations were paid out of Department of Indian Affairs District Offices. Since that time, District Offices have disappeared, and more First

Nations have begun distributing welfare assistance. In some cases, welfare assistance is delivered under provincial statute, and in others, it is delivered according to rules set by the Department of Indian Affairs.

(c) Alcohol and Drug Rehabilitation and Counselling

The federal government funds alcohol and drug rehabilitation counselling on reserve.

(d) Community Health Worker

Many of the northern reserves have community people who serve as public health workers. They provide information, and act as a liaison between the First Nation and fly-in medical services.

(e) Aboriginal justice system

Aboriginal communities may increase their control over the justice system in a number of ways. Participation in the courts, control over policing and influence over sentencing are discussed in the Chapter 24, "Aboriginal Justice".

(f) Education

All schools located on reserve used to be run by the Department of Indian Affairs out of their District Offices. Some children were sent to off-reserve, non-Indian schools. In the last fifteen years, Indian Affairs has begun to transfer administrative responsibility to First Nations for on-reserve schools. Although some First Nations have created Education Authorities, the perception in some cases is that less funding is available than when the schools were controlled by Indian Affairs.

Other education activities funded include daycare centres, management training programs and technical institutes. Federal government funding programs change regularly, making it difficult and time-consuming to maintain a program.

4. OFF-RESERVE SERVICES

Aboriginal people are now beginning to take control of an increasing number of institutions to serve Aboriginal people off-reserve. By providing services directly through Aboriginal institutions, Aboriginal people hope to provide more relevant, and more appropriate, services.

(a) Friendship Centres

The most significant off-reserve institution for Aboriginal people is the Friendship Centre.[2] Located in many cities and towns across Canada, they provide a number of programs aimed at supporting Aboriginal people in an urban setting. These include programs for children, adult upgrading programs, Aboriginal court workers and other community centre services.

(b) Child Welfare

Although there are a number of Aboriginal children's aid societies which serve First Nation reserves, there are none which serve urban Aboriginal people. At the time of writing, a child welfare agency for Aboriginal people in Toronto is being developed.

(c) Health Services

Anishnawbe Health is a clinic in downtown Toronto providing medical services and counselling to Aboriginal people.

(d) Justice

In most provinces, the federal and provincial governments fund Native Courtworkers who act as a buffer between the court system and Aboriginal people who become involved with the courts. Some provinces and territories have programs for appointed Native Justices of the Peace.

There are several community legal aid clinics which provide services to Aboriginal people. In Ontario, they include those in Toronto, Moosonee, Thunder Bay, Manitoulin Island, Fort Frances and Sioux Lookout. Aboriginal Legal Services of Toronto has developed a pilot project in which minor criminal matters are dealt with by a community panel.

(e) Housing

Many urban centres have housing projects aimed at Aboriginal people, including seniors' residences, non-profit housing projects, men's residences, and women's shelters.

(f) Other services

Other services include special libraries, cultural centres, an alcohol treatment centre, schools and colleges.

5. CONCLUSION

Increasing Aboriginal involvement in, and control over, services is an important part of self-governance. Aboriginal people must create their own organizations based on communities' own needs, to choose their own directions and, inevitably, to make their own mistakes. At the same time as control over services shifts hands, Aboriginal political leaders must ensure that proper funding and accountability mechanisms are in place to guarantee the long-term existence of the service.

ENDNOTES

1 To address the problems around providing welfare payments to trappers, the James Bay and Northern Quebec Agreement provides for the creation of a special trappers' assistance program.

2 Friendship Centres are community-based, non-political organizations run by a volunteer board of directors.

12

Community Corporations

POINTS TO REMEMBER

1. Incorporation protects individuals involved in organizing community projects. Without incorporation, individuals may have to pay out of their own pockets if the community project runs into financial difficulties.

2. Although a corporation may be located on reserve and owned by Indians, it does not receive the tax exemptions available to individual registered Indians.

3. Some organizations register with the federal government as charities in order to raise money from foundations and other non-governmental sources. However, there are restrictions on the activities of charities.

1. INTRODUCTION

Whether one wants to create a Friendship Centre, take over responsibility for child welfare, create an Education Authority or promote economic development, sooner or later the question of whether to incorporate will arise. Sometimes a government agency will require incorporation before providing funding. Banks may also require incorporation before lending money. The people involved in an organization must decide if incorporation is a necessary step.

The corporations discussed in this chapter are created in accordance with federal and provincial laws relating to "non-profit" or "non-share capital" corporations. Their objects must be charitable, educational, social or "of any other useful nature." These types of corporations do not issue shares or make a profit for individuals. Individuals or groups wanting to set up a business for personal gain should refer to Chapter 17, "Commercial Relations".[1]

If the corporation makes money, that money must be spent on community projects. Upon dissolution of the corporation any remaining property or assets will be distributed to other charitable or community concerns. The members of the corporation will not make any personal profit.

2. ADVANTAGES OF INCORPORATION

(a) Limited Liability

If an organization owes money or is sued for doing something wrong, the directors of an unincorporated organization may be personally responsible. This means they would have to pay out of their own pockets.

If the organization is incorporated, the directors are generally not personally responsible.[2] This means that all money which the corporation owes will be paid only by the corporation. If the corporation does not have enough money to pay, the directors will generally not have to make up the difference.[3]

The limited liability aspect of a corporation is especially useful for special projects, such as construction projects, where the directors may want the corporation to exist for a specific purpose, and then be dissolved.

(b) On-Going Structure

A corporation is a body which has by-laws and regular elections. It continues to exist even if the individuals who control it change. Funding agencies often require that an organization be incorporated for this reason.

(c) Protection for the Community Interest

In some cases, the corporation may be working for the community as a whole. For example, a co-operative store on reserve, a Friendship Centre or an Inuit economic development venture is established to benefit the community as a whole and not just the individuals who have established it. It is possible for all members of the community to be granted certain rights in an incorporated organization. Incorporation thereby reduces the danger of individuals diverting a community enterprise for personal gain.

3. DISADVANTAGES OF INCORPORATION

(a) A Corporation Might Have to Pay Tax

As noted in the chapter on taxation, registered Indians have income tax and sales tax exemptions, but the courts have held that a corporation does not have the same exemptions as an individual registered Indian.[4] A corporation must therefore pay retail sales tax and all other taxes like non-Indians.[5] A corporation must also file income tax returns although it may not have to pay tax on its profits. (For further information see Chapter 20, "Taxation".)

(b) More Paper Work

A corporation is incorporated under federal or provincial law and is then governed by those laws. Once incorporated, there are requirements for certain types of elections, audits and other procedures which an organization may find unacceptable or too onerous.

(c) Permit to Locate on Reserve

Since a corporation is not an Indian it must get permission to be located on a reserve. Like any other non-Indian, a corporation requires a permit from the Minister, a certificate of occupation, or license. (Chapter 17, "Commercial Relations" has more information on the use of reserve lands.)

4. FEDERAL OR PROVINCIAL INCORPORATION?

In many cases, there is little difference between the two types of corporations. In some cases, Aboriginal people may prefer a federal incorporation to show a link to the federal Crown. Corporations which deal with issues within the province will usually incorporate provincially while an organization representing people across the country might incorporate federally. There may be differences in filing fees and paperwork required, but that will depend on the province or territory involved.

5. SHOULD THE ORGANIZATION REGISTER AS A CHARITY?

A corporation can apply for charitable status if the members and directors believe it will be beneficial to do so. Charitable registration provides some advantages: people can make contributions to the corporation and their own income taxes will be reduced accordingly. Charitable foundations, a valuable source of funding, will also be able to contribute to the corporation. On the other hand, being granted charitable status also means that the organization will be subject to close financial examination, and there are restrictions on any activity which is considered "political."

A charitable corporation must engage primarily in one of the following charitable purposes:[6]

- the relief of poverty;
- the advancement of education;
- the advancement of religion;
- the advancement of other charitable purposes which benefit the community as a whole.

It appears that some activities of Aboriginal organizations such as a native communications society will qualify as a charity.[7] Economic development activities or political organizations such as Tribal Councils, however, may not qualify for charitable status.

A charitable organization may make a profit, even on a business, but the activity must be secondary to, and a result of carrying out the objects for which the corporation was created.

Whether the organization is provincially or federally incorporated, charitable registration is under federal jurisdiction.

6. HOW IS A COMMUNITY CORPORATION ORGANIZED?

A corporation is established by filing certain documents (application, letters patent, and by-laws) with the appropriate provincial office, or the Department of Consumer and Corporate Affairs (federal). These documents set out the objects of the corporation, its directors and its members. The corporation is run by a board of directors, generally elected by the membership. The directors establish the by-laws of the corporation, which determine such things as how people become members, how meetings are conducted and when elections of directors are held. The by-laws can be considered a guidebook for the operation of the corporation.

Members of the Board should be accountable to the community, and decisions should be made for the benefit of the community as a whole. The members of the corporation are able to control what the board of directors can do because all by-laws and changes must be confirmed by a vote at a members' meeting. There must be at least one members' meeting a year. Some corporations will have a limited number of members while others may include an entire community.

The major decisions of the corporation are decided by the elected board of directors, but the day-to-day management of the corporation is usually conducted by hired staff. Boards meet regularly to go over financial statements, review the work of the organization and the work of the staff. Directors may receive "reasonable remuneration and expenses" if the corporation is non-profit, but may not receive remuneration if the corporation also has charitable status. More information on the election and removal of board members is provided in Chapter 10, "Elections and Referenda."

It is important to note that corporations are controlled by federal or provincial laws. They must follow some strict rules to remain in good standing: for example, they should have audits every year, keep orderly financial books, and report changes in the board of directors to the government.

7. WHICH TAXES DOES THE COMMUNITY CORPORATION HAVE TO PAY?

As noted above, the corporation is not treated as a registered Indian, even if all its members are Indians and the office is located on reserve. The corporation must therefore pay federal and provincial sales tax on its purchases. One way to reduce tax is for the corporation to lease the equipment from a First Nation Council or some other body which does not have to pay sales tax. Usually corporations must pay tax on profits. A non-profit corporation, however, will not have to pay tax, but must still file income tax returns each year. The corporation can contact the local District Taxation Office to establish its non-profit status and exemption from income tax. (See Chapter 20, "Taxation", for more details.)

8. WHAT IF THE PEOPLE CANNOT AFFORD TO SET UP A CORPORATION?

The government fees, and lawyers fees associated with forming a corporation could easily run over a thousand dollars. Groups considering incorporation may wish to contact a local community legal aid clinic, which may be able to provide the legal service for free. Even in that case, the organization will still have to pay the government registration fees.

Some organizations may never need to be incorporated. A local drum group, for example, or a social club would not usually run into any situations where incorporation would be necessary. Every organization must consider its own circumstances in light of the factors discussed in this chapter, and determine whether incorporation is a tool which will help it to meet its objectives.

ENDNOTES

1 On the subject of incorporating, non-profit organizations are incorporated in Ontario under the *Corporations Act*, R.S.O. 1990, c. C.38 and federally under the *Canada Corporations Act*, R.S.C. 1970, c. C-32. Profit-making business corporations are incorporated under separate statutes, either the Ontario *Business Corporations Act*, R.S.O. 1990, c. B.16 or the *Canada Business Corporations Act*, R.S.C. 1985, c. C-44.

2 On the subject of directors' protection from personal liability, this statement assumes that the directors have not been negligent and have not otherwise incurred personal liability (by acting in bad faith, for example). If they have, then they may be liable even if the organization is incorporated.

3 There are exceptions to the rule of a director's protection from personal liability. For example, directors are personally liable for up to six months' wages and up to twelve months' vacation pay for employees of the company (See section 81(1) of the Ontario *Corporations Act, supra*, note 1, and section 204 of the *Canada Corporations Act, supra*, note 1; section 91 of the Alberta *Companies Act*, R.S.A. 1980, c. C-20.

4 On the subject of taxation of Indian-owned corporations, see *Kinookimaw Beach Ass. v. R. in Right of Saskatchewan*, [1979] 4 C.N.L.R. 101, (Sask. C.A.) refused (1979) leave to appeal 1 Sask. R. 179n (S.C.C.). In this case, seven First Nations incorporated a company to operate a resort on reserve lands. The company purchased capital equipment for use on the land. The province levied an education and hospital tax upon the purchases,

stating that the corporate entity was not entitled to the exemption pursuant to s. 87 of the *Indian Act*.

The Saskatchewan Court of Appeal refused to lift the "corporate veil" and look to see who the owners were. It held that the separate legal existence of the corporation could not be disregarded, and that to grant the exemption would destroy the legal obligations of the corporate entity.

5 On the subject of tax and corporations, the fact that the corporation must pay tax does not necessarily mean that Indian employees of the corporation must pay income tax. The two are separate issues. See Chapter 20, "Taxation".

6 On the subject of charities, the activities which define a charitable corporation derive from common law. A list of charitable activities was first discussed in *Commissioners for Special Purposes of the Income Tax Act v. Pemsel*, [1891] A.C. 531 (U.K. H.L.). For requirements for registration of a charitable association in Alberta see section 200(1) of the *Companies Act*, R.S.A. 1980, c.C-20 as am.; in British Columbia see section 2 of the *Society Act*, R.S.B.C. 1996, c. 433, as am.

7 On the subject of activities eligible for charitable status, see *Native Communications Society of British Columbia v. Minister of National Revenue*, [1986] 4 C.N.L.R. 79 (Fed. C.A.).

13

Housing

1. INTRODUCTION

Getting housing both on and off-reserve can be a nightmare. On-reserve there are long waiting lists, the houses are often substandard (the number of deaths by fire is seven times the national average), and the rules governing right of possession are unclear. Off-reserve, rents are high, buildings are often poorly maintained, and enforcing legal rights is slow and costly. This chapter discusses living on-reserve, housing construction, and the landlord and tenant relationship off-reserve.

2. LIVING ON-RESERVE

Reserves are tracts of land set aside by law for the use and benefit of Indians. Title to a First Nation reserve is held by the Crown and matters relating to the allocation and use of reserve lands are regulated by the *Indian Act* and by-laws passed by the band.[1]

(a) Certificate of Possession

The certificate of possession[2] was one of the methods used by the federal government to assimilate Indians by encouraging private ownership of land. Although this concept was foreign to First Nations, the *Indian Act* said that a band council could, with the approval of the Minister of Indian Affairs, give a certificate of possession to an individual member of the band. This meant that individual band members could own property, which could not be reassigned by the band council.

In a family, a certificate of possession might be in the husband's name. This would mean the husband could keep the house if the husband and wife separate, even if the wife and children have nowhere else to live. (For more information on this situation, see Chapter 14, "Marriage, Separation, Divorce".)

(b) Custom Land Allocation

According to the *Indian Act*, no one is lawfully in possession of reserve lands unless they have a certificate of possession. Most First Nations have not made a practice of issuing certificates of possession and so, legally speaking, hardly anyone on reserves is "lawfully in possession" of reserve lands. Rather, housing is usually allocated through the First Nation council or through housing committees, without any accompanying written formalities.

First Nations have different ways of dealing with First Nation-owned housing when a family no longer wishes to live together or when residents have abandoned a house. Often it is up to the chief and council or the housing committee to decide what to do.

(c) Housing Relationships on-Reserve

Bands or individual members of a band can own housing on reserve. It is important to remember the unique nature of reserve land allocation however. Unlike home ownership off-reserve, entitlement to possession of the land, and title to the building on it, may be two different things. If there is a certificate of possession for a house lot on reserve, the owner of the certificate owns[3] the land the house is built on. Assuming the owner of the land also owns the house on the land, the owner can keep the house empty, rent it, or even sell it to someone else.[4]

This introduces the possibility for a number of landlord and tenant combinations on reserve. A band may rent to an Indian or to a non-Indian,[5] an Indian may rent to another Indian, a non-Indian renting from an Indian may in turn rent to another non-Indian or to an Indian. Although the courts have not dealt definitively with the matter, it is likely that provincial landlord and tenant or residential tenancy laws do not apply to rental relationships on reserve.[6]

3. FUNDING FOR NEW HOUSING ON-RESERVE

Members of a First Nation are entitled to reside on-reserve. The reality, however, is that often there is insufficient housing for the large numbers of people desiring to live on-reserve. The crisis in housing availability has been fuelled by two major factors. One is the recent pattern of First Nation population growth which means that over half of all Aboriginal people in Canada are currently under the age of 25.[7] The second is the return of more women and children whose registered Indian status was reinstated after the 1985 changes to the *Indian Act*. (On the subject of reinstatement, see Chapter 9, "Indian Act Registration and First Nation Citizenship".)

Most often, it is the First Nation itself which builds housing on-reserve. Until recently, First Nations received funding only from Indian Affairs to build a small number of houses each year. Then a First Nation would have to decide how to deal with the fact that it could not build enough houses for all the people who need one. Each First Nation has developed its own way of dealing with this. In some cases, a first-come-first-served approach might be used. In other cases, priority might be given to large families or people having close family ties on reserve.

(a) Funding from Indian Affairs

For on-reserve housing under Capital Projects, individual First Nations submit proposals for a five-year capital program. The First Nations administer their own housing programs.

(b) Innovative Housing Fund

In 1996, Indian Affairs introduced a new housing program for First Nations. It was designed to put more emphasis on future planning and community control of reserve housing decisions and to gradually relieve the reserve housing crisis. The new program now gives a First Nation the ability to plan its housing strategy for more than one year at a time, as well as to incorporate a broader range of housing possibilities.[8] Also, a First Nation will be able to integrate other community initiatives such as training and social assistance programs with housing. The new program is voluntary, which means that the First Nation may choose to continue with the existing program or switch to the new one.

DIAND will contribute $2 million to the Fund which will be distributed equally to all nine regional offices and is accessible to First Nations within these regions. The project was developed in consultation with the Assembly of First Nations. The money will be used to fund two to three projects per region designed to develop innovative housing ideas such as new house building techniques and alternative designs (i.e., log homes that use local building materials and skills) and energy sources. Funding criteria require that projects be cost-shared with the private sector and/or First Nations organizations and/or other government organizations.

(c) Canada Mortgage and Housing Corporation (CMHC)

Indian Affairs' capital subsidies for housing construction and major renovations have become the main source of First Nation housing funding. Approximately 24 per cent of on-reserve housing has been built with subsidies or loan assistance from the Canada Mortgage and Housing Corporation (CMHC), a federal agency providing funding assistance to First Nations.[9] Through the Non-Profit Housing Program that CMHC administers, debt financing costs are reduced through the provision of ongoing subsidies. However, CMHC requires income testing of the members who will be the housing recipients, before granting the First Nation this subsidy. CMHC will probably also want to review the First Nation's financial books before entering into this agreement.

On the basis of a guarantee by the Minister, an agreement is signed with a financial institution, such as a bank or credit union, to provide the funds for construction of the housing. Under this type of agreement, the First Nation is fully responsible for the loan, as well as the upkeep of the housing until the loan is paid off. Normally, a First Nation will also want to enter into a legal agreement with the participant band members to formalize rental payments to the First Nation until the loan is paid off, and to control title to the house and right to possession of the land it is located on, during the repayment period. It should also address what happens if the Band member fails to make the rent payments, as well as what happens when the loan is fully repaid.

CMHC also administers a loan program,[10] which provides funds for repairing houses five years old or more.

(d) Loans to individual Band members

Indian Act restrictions on the seizure of property on-reserve mean that it is very difficult to borrow money from a bank. Because the bank wants to be able to take the land and the house if the borrower fails to pay, the bank will not lend money for reserve land because it is not allowed to seize reserve lands. Lenders will in some instances loan money directly to a band member, but a guarantee from the Minister of Indian Affairs will be required. Usually, the lender will also insist on some additional security, in the form of a Band Council Resolution guaranteeing the loan.

(e) Defaulting on a loan

If the First Nation or a member defaults on a loan provided under the Non-Profit Housing Program, the financial institution will turn either to CMHC or the Minister for repayment. Either CMHC or the Minister will pay off the outstanding loan. Eventually the claim will work its way to the First Nation. The lender cannot take possession of a house and sell it, as mentioned previously, because of the legal restrictions on seizure of property on reserve. However, the Minister can reclaim the amount of the outstanding loan from the First Nation's funds. Defaulting on a housing loan can therefore mean that the Minister will withhold funds which would otherwise have been used to deliver programs to the members.

The practical effect of the guarantee which a lender requires when lending directly to a member of the First Nation is that the First Nation becomes responsible for the loan on default. If the member defaults, the Minister will pay it off and then attempt to reclaim the outstanding amount from the First Nation. The First Nation will have to pay off the outstanding loan and then determine whether it will evict the member from the house. These situations are obviously difficult and present a clear reason for considering all the potential consequences before a First Nation should agree to guarantee a member's loan. If the member whose loan is being guaranteed holds a certificate of possession, the First Nation will want to be sure that the member agrees to the cancellation of the certificate of possession in the event that he or she defaults on a loan.

4. OFF-RESERVE RENTAL HOUSING

(a) Legislation

Off-reserve rental housing[11] is governed by provincial or territorial housing laws.[12] These laws establish minimal housing standards and are designed to provide tenants with some protection from eviction. It is important for both tenants and landlords to know that no matter what conditions or agreements the parties make between themselves, in most cases, the minimum standards provided by law will still apply. In other words, clauses in accommodation agreements which deliver less than the minimal standards will not be enforceable.[13]

(b) Rent and rent increases

The rules regarding rent and allowable rent increases are addressed in the residential tenancy and rent control laws. Rent is generally payable in advance and is normally due on the first day of the rental period which it covers. Usually, this is the first of the month for monthly-paid rents.

In some provinces, a housing official called a rentalsman oversees a rent registry and review board which decides applications by tenants for freezing or reduction of rents, as well as complaints about lack of maintenance or loss of services. For a rent increase in some provinces, landlords must apply to the rentalsman, while in others, tenants must apply if they believe the increase to be illegal.

Everywhere in Canada, housing laws require that a landlord give prior notification of a rent increase to tenants. This must be done in writing, and there may be a prescribed form which must be used for the notice. Generally, a landlord is limited to one rent increase in twelve months.[14]

(c) Security deposits

With the exception of Quebec,[15] all provinces and territories of Canada authorize landlords to request a security deposit from tenants. Nonetheless, the amount which can be collected as a security deposit is restricted by law. The authorized range varies from the lesser of $125.00 or one-half of one month's rent in Saskatchewan, up to one month's rent in Alberta, New Brunswick, N.W.T., Ontario, P.E.I. and the Yukon. Refer to Appendix II of this chapter to see what amount applies in your province or territory.

The deposit a tenant pays at the start of his or her tenancy is held throughout the rental term by the landlord or the rentalsman. This amount may later be applied to pay for claims against the tenant for damage to the premises or nonpayment of rent, for example.

Tenants do not automatically lose their right to return of the deposit amount however. Holding a deposit does not automatically entitle the landlord to claim some or all of the security deposit at the end of the tenancy. The landlord will have to follow steps such as notifying the tenant of the cause for claiming part or all of the deposit, respecting time limits for tenants to respond or correct the problem, and perhaps applying to the rentalsman for an order against the tenant, with permission to withhold the deposit. The particular procedures and the associated time frames for these processes are laid out in the law.

When a tenant leaves the premises at the end of a lease term, the security deposit must be returned. In some provinces there is a maximum time for a landlord to return the security deposit plus any interest which has accumulated to the end of the tenancy. Tenants continuing with a new lease term or on a periodic rental by the month or week will not get their deposit back. Instead, it will be applied to the next rental term. In that case, the tenant may be required to add to the deposit to keep it current with any new rental rates taking effect.

Most provincial laws require that a security deposit be kept in a separate trust account. Generally, interest must be paid at a rate predetermined by regulation.

(d) Repairs

The landlord is responsible for keeping the rented housing in a state of good repair, fit for habitation, and in compliance with any local housing standards by-laws. Examples of this obligation include keeping the heating working, fixing the roof and plumbing, and having kitchen appliances repaired. For their part, tenants are obliged to keep the rental premises maintained to a reasonable standard. Thus, careless, deliberate or wilful damage by the tenant, or by someone permitted on the premises by the tenant, must be remedied by the tenant.

Since disputes about responsibility for extraordinary repairs often take place at the end of a tenancy, return of the tenant's security deposit, as mentioned above, may become an issue. Landlords are usually required to provide tenants with the option of completing the actual repair themselves. Tenants who choose not to complete the required repairs themselves within the specified time limit will have to pay the repair cost to the landlord.

Tenants will not ordinarily be responsible for normal wear and tear, such as carpets becoming threadbare, or an old appliance breaking down, unless caused by extraordinary use and circumstances not expected of a tenant making usual use of the rental residence.

Terms of the applicable law, as well as the terms of any accommodation agreement or lease between the parties, control the ways in which maintenance and repair problems are resolved. When agreement cannot be reached between the parties by themselves, disputes about repairs are taken to an administrative review process overseen by the rentalsman, in provinces where there is one. In other provinces, the parties must resort to the courts or to a housing tribunal for a decision.

(e) Termination

One of the main reasons that governments passed housing laws was to provide tenants with increased protection from unjustified eviction. To do that, it was necessary to anticipate a broad range of situations in which a landlord might try to terminate a tenant's residency. Consequently, detailed provisions were created in the housing laws which deal with termination by either the landlord or the tenant at the expiry of a rental term as well as early termination for cause by either party.[16]

(i) At the end of the Tenancy Term by the Landlord or the Tenant

A lease, sometimes referred to as a tenancy or rental agreement, is a contract between the landlord and tenant. The lease formalizes the exchange of rent in return for the possession and use of a residential property for a specified length of time called the tenancy or rental term.

Notice by either the landlord or the tenant to the other party is generally required when one party does not want to renew the lease at the end of its term. In most provinces, a landlord must give longer notice of not renewing the lease than the tenant has to give to the landlord. For example, for a lease with rent paid monthly, a landlord in Nova Scotia must give the tenant three months' termination notice before the end of the tenancy term that the lease will not be renewed. The tenant in the same situation is only obliged to give the landlord one month's notice that he or she does not intend to renew the lease.[17]

The ability of a landlord to end a tenancy is usually restricted to certain situations or criteria. Valid reasons for a landlord not renewing the rental relationship might include, for example, requiring the premises for the landlord's own or immediate family's occupation, major renovations, or conversion to a condominium or non-residential uses. As will be seen below, several of these reasons may also allow a landlord to terminate the tenancy before its term has expired.

A tenant does not have to leave just because the lease has expired, and neither can he or she just walk out. What happens at the end of the tenancy term specified in the lease varies according to the province or territory, and tenants should find out well ahead of time what applies where they live. For example, a tenant in the Northwest Territories with a lease or rental agreement which contains an expiry date is required to give notice in writing of an intention to move. This must be done at least 30 days prior to the expiry date. Without such notice, the tenancy is automatically renewed. The rights and obligations for both landlord and tenant under the previous agreement will apply to the new term, with the exception that the landlord has a right to change the amount of rent.

In contrast to that situation is the one in British Columbia and Ontario. If no notice of moving has been given and no new lease has been signed to take effect at the end of the old one, the tenant automatically becomes a monthly tenant. A monthly tenant is one who does not have a lease and pays rent from month to month.

(ii) Early Termination for Cause by the Tenant

In certain circumstances, the tenant may be able to end the tenancy early, before the expiration of the rental term agreed upon or specified in the lease.

Landlords, as we have noted previously, are required to comply with their legal obligations. They must also abide by the terms of a rental agreement or lease with the tenant. If, for example then, the heating in a rental residence breaks down in February, and the landlord refuses to acknowledge the problem or does not have it fixed in a timely fashion, the tenant probably has grounds for ending the tenancy, even though the rental term has not expired.

In some provinces, the tenant with valid cause will be entitled to move out immediately. In others, the tenant will be obliged to apply to the court, housing tribunal or rentalsman for an order declaring the tenancy agreement terminated. Naturally, in this type of situation, the usual notice periods for moving do not apply.

Tenants should deal openly and directly with their landlord to try and resolve problems which arise in the course of a tenancy. Not all disputes will give rise to an automatic right to terminate early, and an important first step before considering moving is to make the landlord aware of what needs to be resolved, repaired, changed, etc. If difficulties persist, valid cause combined with attempts in good faith to have resolved the problems will assist a tenant in successfully defending against a landlord who goes to a court or tribunal to force the former tenant to pay for the outstanding rent to the end of the lease term.

(iii) *Early Termination for Cause by the Landlord*

While landlords are prohibited from evicting for no reason, there are certain grounds, such as harmful, disturbing, illegal or destructive behaviour by tenants, which allow a landlord to cut a rental agreement or lease short. Many of the grounds are common to most provinces and territories, and a number of the more usual ones are mentioned here.

(A) For tenant's non-payment of rent

In most provinces and territories, residential tenancy laws allow a landlord to take action quickly for non-payment of rent on the due date. However, a variety of procedures and remedies are provided across Canada. Ontario law is different from Saskatchewan's, New Brunswick's from Newfoundland law, and so on.

(B) Because of the tenant's conduct

Damage to the individual rental premises or common areas by a tenant or by anyone whom the tenant allows on the premises will normally result in the landlord's delivering a notice to repair to the tenant. If the tenant does not make the necessary repairs, the landlord may make an application to the rental authority, or the court, as applicable, to end the tenancy and regain possession of the premises. Some provinces permit orders to be made for the tenant to pay the costs of both the repairs and the termination order, although it is more usual for the landlord to have to go to court again to recover those amounts.

Almost all of the twelve provinces and territories include provisions in their residential tenancy laws which allow the landlord to end a tenancy when tenants interfere with the reasonable use and enjoyment of rental premises by other tenants or the landlord. An example might be playing a stereo at excessive volume on a daily basis. Repetition of the interference after requests to stop it will constitute cause for early termination.

A number of provinces specifically provide that carrying on an illegal trade, business, occupation, or committing other illegal acts is cause for termination with notice. Furthermore, a tenant must not permit someone else to do any of those things on the rental premises.

Similarly, impairing the safety of other tenants, having an excessive number of occupants, subletting without permission, and persistent late payment of the rent are other grounds for early termination in some provinces.

(C) When the landlord requires the premises

If a landlord wants to live in the premises, or wants possession so that a family member can live there, he or she is permitted to give notice to the tenant. The genuine intention of the landlord must be to occupy the premises, and most laws provide procedures and remedies in the event a former tenant challenges the early termination and successfully proves bad faith on the part of the landlord.

Cause for termination by the landlord may also stem from the need for vacant possession of the premises to complete major renovation work or repairs, or conversion to condominium or commercial uses. However, from time to time provinces have enacted restrictions on conversion in order to maintain a supply of affordable housing.

In most provinces, a landlord is entitled to end the lease of an employee when the employment relationship ends. For example, a landlord may terminate the tenancy of a building superintendent who benefits from an apartment on the premises, who resigns to go to a different job.

APPENDIX A
Security Deposits

	Security Deposit Limit	Interest Payable?	Period for Return of Security Deposit at End of Tenancy
Alberta	1 month's rent	Yes	10 days
British Columbia	1/2 of 1 month's rent	Yes	15 days
Manitoba	1/2 of 1st month's rent	Yes	14 days
New Brunswick	1 month's rent	No	On application to rentalsman will be returned or transferred to new tenancy.
Newfoundland & Labrador	1/2 of 1 month's rent	Yes	30 days
Northwest Territories	1 month's rent; 1/2 payable at start of tenancy, balance within 3 months	Yes	10 days
Nova Scotia	1/2 of 1 month's rent	Yes	10 days
Ontario	1 month — If rent increases after initial deposit; deposit may be increased to new rent amount	6 percent per year	Must be applied in payment of rent for last month of tenancy which is not continuing.
Prince Edward Island	1 month's rent	Yes	10 days
Quebec	Collection of deposit prohibited	Not applicable	Not applicable
Saskatchewan	Lesser of $125.00 or 1/2 of 1 month's rent	Yes	10 days
Yukon	1 month's rent	Yes	15 days

APPENDIX B

Legislation Governing Residential Tenancies

Alberta
Residential Tenancies Act, R.S.A. 1980, c. R-15.3.
Mobile Home Sites Tenancies Act, S.A. 1982, c. M-18.5.
Landlord's Rights on Bankruptcy Act, R.S.A. 1980, c. L-7

British Columbia
Residential Tenancy Act, R.S.B.C. 1996, c. 406
Manufactured Home Act, R.S.B.C. 1996, c. 280

Manitoba
The Residential Tenancies Act, S.M. 1990-91, c. 11.

New Brunswick
Landlord and Tenant Act, R.S.N.B. 1973, c. L-1.†
Residential Tenancies Act, S.N.B. 1975, c. R-10.2.

Newfoundland
Residential Tenancies Act, R.S.N. 1990, c. R-14.

Northwest Territories
Residential Tenancies Act, R.S.N.W.T. 1988, c. R-5

Nova Scotia
Residential Tenancies Act, R.S.N.S. 1989, c. 401.
Rent Review Act, R.S.N.S. 1989, c. 398.

Ontario
Tenant Protection Act, S.O. 1997, c. 24

Prince Edward Island
Rental of Residential Property Act, S.P.E.I. 1988, c. 58.

Quebec
Act Respecting the Régie du logement, R.S.Q., c. R-8.1 [in S.Q. 1979, c. 48].

---

† When provisions of the *Landlord and Tenant Act* conflict with provisions of the *Residential Tenancies Act*, the *Residential Tenancies Act* provisions apply.

Saskatchewan
Residential Tenancies Act, R.S.S. 1978, c. R-22.

Yukon
Landlord and Tenant Act, R.S.Y.T. 1986, c. 98.†

ENDNOTES

1 Sections 18, 60 and 81 of the *Indian Act*, R.S.C. 1985, c. I-5, are relevant. These provisions govern the definition of reserve lands, their use for the benefit for Indians, the withdrawal of Indian Affairs control over lands and the powers of council to enact by-laws for the purposes of managing the survey and allotment of reserve lands among band members.

In the move toward granting First Nations more authority and autonomy to administer and control reserve lands fourteen First Nations will be opting into the *First Nations Land Management Act* S.C. 1999, c. 24. The Act received Royal Assent June 17, 1999. This statute establishes the basis for the development of individual land codes whose implementation would remove the First Nations from the *Indian Act* with respect to most of its provisions affecting the management, use and development of reserve lands.

2 On the subject of certificates of possession, the *Indian Act*, R.S.C. 1985, c. I-5, s. 20 says:

(1) No Indian is lawfully in possession of land in a reserve unless, with the approval of the Minister, possession of the land has been allotted to him by the council of the band.

(2) The Minister may issue to an Indian who is lawfully in possession of land in a reserve a certificate, to be called a Certificate of Possession, as evidence of his right to possession of the land described therein.

3 Ownership of reserve land is different from ownership of land off-reserve. On-reserve the person with a certificate of possession has exclusive possession of the land, but the land will always remain part of the reserve and can only be transferred to another Band member. See *Indian Act*, section 28(2) and section 24.

---

† Part IV applies solely to residential tenancies. Provisions in other parts of the Act which conflict with the provisions of Part IV are inoperative with respect to residential tenancies.

4 On the subject of certificates of possession, if a house on the land was built by the First Nation there may be questions about ownership of the house, although the land would continue to belong to the individual.

5 It should be noted that in the case of rentals to non-Indians of reserve lands, either customary law or council by-laws might prohibit such a practice. While First Nations may informally establish their own rules about this type of matter, section 28 of the *Indian Act* requires that the Minister's written authorization be obtained for any agreements made with non-members affecting use of reserve lands.

The *Indian Act* reads as follows:

28. (1) Subject to subsection (2), any deed, lease, contract, instrument, document or agreement of any kind, whether written or oral, by which a band or a member of a band purports to permit a person other than a member of that band to occupy or use a reserve or to reside or otherwise exercise any rights on a reserve is void.

(2) The Minister may by permit in writing authorize any person for a period not exceeding one year, or with the consent of the council of the band for any longer period, to occupy or use a reserve or to reside or otherwise exercise rights on a reserve.

6 On the application of the provincial landlord and tenant legislation on-reserve, see *Park Mobile Home Sales Ltd. v. Le Greely* (1978) 85 D.L.R. (3d) 618 (B.C. C.A.), *Matsqui Indian Band v. Bird* (1992), [1993] 3 C.N.L.R. 80 (B.C. S.C.), and *Millbrook Indian Band v. Nova Scotia (Northern Counties Residential Tenancies Board)*, (1978) 84 D.L.R. (3d) 174 (N.S. T.D.), affirmed without reference to this point [1978], [1979] 4 C.N.L.R. 59 (N.S. C.A.)

7 Approximately 53 percent of on-reserve Registered Indians are under the age of 25 years. See Department of Indian Affairs and Northern Development, *Backgrounder: Demographics* (Ottawa: Indian and Northern Affairs Canada, 1997).

8 The new program requires that a First Nation establish a set of housing policies, programs and a multi-year plan detailing a work plan, a resource plan and training, job creation and business development issues. More detail can be obtained by consulting the Indian Affairs publication entitled "Guidelines for the Development of First Nations Housing Proposals" which also includes a working guide for the preparation of proposals.

9 See Royal Commission on Aboriginal People, *Gathering Strength*, Volume 3 (Ottawa: Supply and Service, 1996) at 369.

10 CMHC's Emergency Repair Program assists rural homeowners (many of whom are Aboriginal) to carry out emergency repairs to make

their homes safe. CMHC covers the cost of materials and labour. Among the repairs classified as emergency are those to heating systems, chimneys, doors and windows, foundations, plumbing and electrical systems. This program is accessible to all Canadians.

The Homeowner Residential Rehabilitation Assistance Program (RRAP) federal component/on-reserve component assists Aboriginal homeowners who have substandard housing. Through the program, Aboriginal households can carry out repairs to bring their dwellings up to a minimum level of health and safety. The program also provides some financial support to alleviate overcrowding. Eligibility for this program depends on household income. A portion of the funding may be forgiven, based on household income.

CMHC provides mortgage insurance for high risk borrowers under s. 10 of the *National Housing Act*. This is a straight loan and therefore there is no funding limit. It is available to on-reserve, off-reserve and other Canadians.

For details contact CMHC at (613) 748-2000.

11 Note that this chapter focuses on housing, and does not discuss commercial tenancies (such as offices or stores).

12 In many of the provinces, several statutes work together to regulate the rental housing market. Most of the provinces have rent control legislation, which may be a separate statute. For example, in Nova Scotia, the *Residential Tenancies Act* and the *Rent Review Act* must both be consulted to determine the full range of housing law. In other cases, such as the Yukon, the *Landlord and Tenant Act* sets the minimal standards for housing, deals with rent and generally regulates the relationship between landlords and tenants in residential accommodation.

See Appendix I for a list of relevant legislation.

13 Minimal standards for residential housing and the governance of landlord-tenant relationships are guaranteed in most legislation through clauses which explicitly prevent either party contracting out of the statutory standards.

14 This restriction applies to all provinces and territories, with the exception of Alberta, which does not specify any restriction on rent increases. However, the relevant statute must be consulted to determine the interpretation and calculation of the twelve-month period for the applicable jurisdiction.

15 Anyone entering into a residential lease or other accommodation agreement in Quebec should be aware that civil code laws governing residential tenancies may vary markedly from the other Canadian jurisdictions.

16 In the matter of termination of tenancies, it is to be noted that there is greater and more frequent variation between the jurisdictions here than in many of the other housing matters. As always, to be properly informed, the statute of the relevant jurisdiction must be consulted.

17 Notice periods must usually run so that the last day of the month is the final day of the notice period. For example, if a monthly tenant in Ontario decides on June 20th that she wants to move out, the applicable 60 days' notice period would take her to August 19th. However, because the final day of the notice period has to be the end of the month, she would not be able to give notice for a date earlier than August 31st. Simply put, she would count 60 days and then round up to the end of that month.

The Family

14

Marriage, Separation, Divorce

POINTS TO REMEMBER

1. Marriages
   Customary marriages are recognized in some circumstances by courts, but most Aboriginal people get married in a church or by a justice of the peace.

2. Separation
   In most provinces, couples do not have to sign any papers or do anything special to separate.

3. Divorce
   The legal justifications for divorce are the following:
   — living separate and apart for one year
   — adultery
   — physical or mental cruelty.

4. Support Payments
   A husband and wife both have an obligation to support themselves and each other. A court can order one spouse to support the other if the other spouse cannot support himself or herself . A common situation is a spouse who has been out of the workforce for several years caring for the family.

5. Division of Property on Separation or Divorce
   The property which a couple accumulates during a marriage will be divided between the spouses, including business property that a husband or wife operated alone. In off-reserve cases, the court can decide who should continue to live in the house. The court cannot decide who lives in an on-reserve house, though, because possession of reserve land is governed by the *Indian Act*.

1. INTRODUCTION

Family law is a complex area of law, especially for Aboriginal people. Federal laws, provincial laws, and customary laws can all apply to a case. For first Nations, the *Indian Act*, and *Indian Act* by-laws may also be relevant. This chapter will discuss how these laws apply to Aboriginal people both on and off reserve.[1]

As a rule, family laws apply in the same way to all Aboriginal people. There are a few exceptions for registered Indians, and they are noted below.

2. MARRIAGE

Even something so apparently simple as deciding to join as a family is complicated in law. Marriage is governed by federal laws, provincial laws and, in some cases, Aboriginal customary law.

The federal law prohibits certain marriages. For example, it prohibits marriages between brother and sister.[2]

The provincial law defines what constitutes a marriage: a couple is married if they go to a justice of the peace or a judge or get married at a church.[3]

Customary Aboriginal marriages have been recognized by Canadian courts in a number of cases.[4] The issue has never been considered directly in a case by itself, however, but only when it has come up in relation to another question. For example, the customary wife of a man accused of a crime may have refused to testify, or the child of a customary marriage may be seeking to inherit. In these cases, some courts have recognized the customary marriage.

3. SEPARATION AND DIVORCE

There is no requirement to go to court for a separation. A couple may simply decide to live separately. The decision might be mutual or the result of one spouse deciding not to go on with the marriage. If the spouses want to set out the terms of their separation, they may go to lawyers or mediators to arrange a separation agreement, or they may make an agreement between themselves.

Divorce in Canada is governed by the *Divorce Act*[5] a federal statute. It is simple for married people to obtain a divorce as long as both spouses want to get divorced. In such a case, if there are no issues of child custody or financial support to resolve, the couple can probably obtain a divorce simply by filing papers in court. The couple may even proceed without a lawyer, although it is advisable to retain a lawyer simply to avoid errors in the preparation and filing of documents. If children are involved, if there is any property to divide, or if one spouse claims support, a lawyer should be retained. Most divorces are completed through negotiation.

Where there is a disagreement about the divorce, the splitting of the property, or the custody of children, it may be necessary to go to court for a trial. These trials can cause a lot of bitterness, and cost a great deal of money in lawyers' fees.

The grounds for divorce in Canada are that there has been a breakdown of the marriage. The usual and easiest way of proving marriage breakdown is if the spouses have lived "separate and apart" for at least one year. If not, a spouse can obtain a divorce by proving that the other spouse has committed adultery during the marriage or has treated the spouse requesting the divorce with "physical or mental cruelty of such a kind as to render intolerable the continued cohabitation of the spouses."[6]

A spouse may file for divorce immediately after separation from the other spouse. For example, a person may move out of the house, file for divorce the next day, and obtain the divorce one year later.

(a) Support Payments — General

Provincial laws generally impose a legal obligation upon spouses to support themselves and to support the other spouse in accordance with his or her need and ability to pay. "Spouses" now include same-sex spouses.[7]

In Ontario, for example, the law imposes an obligation upon both parents to support their children. When a couple separates, one spouse may therefore be required to provide support payments to the other spouse for his or her own use and for child support. In order for a spouse to receive support upon separation, the couple must have:

(i)   been married, or
(ii) been living together continuously for at least three years, or
(iii) been "in a relationship of some permanence", if they have had a natural or adopted child together.

In other words, a "common law spouse" as well as a legally married person can claim support for himself or herself and for children of the relationship.[8]

When married people separate, the consequences are different from the separation of people living together as if they were married (i.e., "common-law" relationships). For example, married couples can apply for support under the *Divorce Act* or the provincial family law, but non-married couples can apply under the provincial family law only. The factors which a judge will consider in making a decision about support and the decision itself will be similar under both statutes. One important distinction between the two situations may be the time frame for going to court for support. In Ontario, for example, the application to court must take place within two years from the date of separation if the couple was not married. If they were married, the application can be made at any time.

(b) Federal Child Support Guidelines[9]

If support payments are made in a divorce proceeding after April 30, 1997, the Federal Child Support Guidelines will apply. If the support payments are made pursuant to a separation, then the provincial law will apply.

The Federal Child Support Guidelines were enacted to provide some consistency in the awarding of support orders for children. They take into account the average costs of raising a child and include rules for calculating child support payments. The calculation is based on the support-paying parent's income, the number of children and the province or territory where the supporting-paying parent lives. Under these guidelines, child support payments can be adjusted to recognize a child's special expenses or to prevent financial hardship for a parent or child in extraordinary circumstances.

Agreements on support payments made before 1997, which do not comply with the Guidelines can be re-opened.

(c) Enforcement

When a couple separates, whether married or not, they may negotiate between themselves over the issues of spousal and child support. They can also decide on child custody and access (allowing the parent who does not have custody some regular time with the child). The results of their negotiations can then be written up in a separation agreement. If they cannot agree on some issues, either person may go to court and have a judge resolve the dispute, or they may go to a mediator.

In many provinces a Family Support Plan provides for regular support payments to be deducted automatically from the pay cheques of employees with support obligations. So, for example, a man working for a First Nation may find that the First Nation is deducting money from his cheque. This money goes to meet his support obligations to his wife and children.[10]

Enforcement of orders under the Federal Child Support Guidelines has been increased. Now, parents who owe money can be traced through their income tax returns, and it is possible to have passports and federal licenses suspended for those in arrears.

The *Indian Act* also provides that a husband's treaty payments could be redirected to his wife. Given that treaty payments are only a few dollars per person per year, they are not a significant source of support.[11]

4. DIVISION OF PROPERTY

Provincial family law provides details on how to divide family property on separation or divorce. The *Family Law Act*[12] in Ontario, for example, treats legally married persons as if they were in a business partnership. Consequently, on separation, the two parties should split the "profit" which they accumulated during the relationship. The idea that one spouse is "at fault" does not matter. Judges do not have much power to give less than a fifty-fifty split of this profit, which is called the "net family property."

"Net family property" is the total value of all property (including land, savings, assets, and anything else of value) accumulated by both persons during the marriage, after deducting all debts. Some property is not included, such as gifts and inheritances. The value of assets owned at the date of marriage is also not included. One exception to that rule is if either spouse owned a house before marriage and that house is used as the "matrimonial" (family) home on the date of separation. When the spouses separate, the value of the house must be included in the calculation. This division of property may mean, for example, that the profits arising out of a major business transaction must be split between the two spouses. This calculation tries to ensure that the spouses share equally in the economic consequences of the marriage.

There is one limit on the application of provincial law. Some First Nations allocate certificates of possession of reserve land. If a certificate of possession was issued to the husband only, then the court cannot take away the husband's possession and give posession to the wife. The court can, however, order that the husband pay cash to the wife instead, which may amount to forcing the husband to sell the property.[13]

5. MEDIATION OR COURT?

We have said that a couple could go to a mediator to try to sort out their disagreements. Mediation can save the time and expense of going to court, and may be preferable to having deep and personal disagreements judged by a stranger.

On the other hand, mediation is not the best way to handle every case. The mediator cannot force the parties to agree, so if one or both spouses are fixed in their positions, they will have to go to court. As well, mediation works best when both spouses can deal with each other as equals. Courts may be better if the couple cannot relate to each other as equals. For example, if the husband beats the wife or otherwise behaves as though she is not worthy of respect, he is unlikely to deal with her fairly during mediation. She may be reluctant to insist on what she needs and is entitled to. She should have legal advice and formal representation.

ENDNOTES

1 On the subject of laws affecting Aboriginal families in Ontario, for example see:

Child and Family Services Act, R.S.O. 1990, c. C.11, as am. S.O. 1992, c. 32, s. 3; 1993, c. 27, Sched.; 1994, c. 27, s. 43; 1996, c. 2, s. 62; 1999, c. 2 [Not in force at date of publication.]

Children's Law Reform Act, R.S.O. 1990, c. C.12, as am. S.O. 1992, c. 32, s. 4; 1993, c. 27, Sched.; 1996, c. 2, s. 63; 1996, c. 25, s. 3; 1998, c. 26, s. 101.

Constitution Act, 1867 (U.K.), 30 & 31 Victoria, c. 3.

Divorce Act, R.S.C. 1985, c. 3 (2nd Supp.), as am. R.S.C. 1985, c. 27 (2nd Supp.); S.C. 1990, 18.

Family Law Act, R.S.O. 1990, c. F.3, as am. S.O. 1992, c. 32, s. 12; 1993, c. 27, Sched.; 1997, c. 20; 1997, c. 25, Sched. E, s. 1; 1998, c. 26, s. 102.

Family Orders and Agreements Enforcement Assistance Act, R.S.C. 1985, c. 4 (2nd Supp.), as am.

Marriage Act, R.S.O. 1990, c. M.3, as am. O. Reg. 726/91 S.O. 1993, c. 27; 1994, c. 27 Sched./, s. 89; 1998, c. 18, Sched. E, ss. 179-182 [ss.1980-182 not in force at date of publication].

Marriage (Prohibited Degrees) Act S.C. 1990, c. 46, s. 5.

Regulations Establishing Federal Child Support Guidelines, SOR/97-175, as am. SOR/97-563.

Support and Custody Order Enforcement Act, R.S.O. 1990, c. S.28, now called the *Family Support Plan Act*, R.S.O. 1990, c. S.28, as am. S.O. 1991, c. 5 (Supp.), ss. 1-12; Repealed.

2 *Marriage (Prohibited Degrees) Act*, R.S.C. 1990, c. 46, s. 5.

3 All provinces have laws which determine such things as licensing, people authorized to perform ceremonies, etc.

Legally, marriage in Ontario is commenced by a ceremony either under the authority of a licence or the publication of banns (*Marriage Act*, R.S.O. 1990, c. M.3, s. 4). If they wish to marry under the authority of the publication of banns, "the intention to marry shall be proclaimed openly in an audible voice during divine service", in the church where each of them attends (s. 17).

Other provinces have similar legislation: See *Marriage Act*, R.S.A. 1980, c. M-6, as am. S.A. 1983, c. 86; 1984, c. C-8.1; 1988, c. 15; 1988, c. 30; 1990, c. M-14.3; 1994, c. G.-8.5; 1996, c. 32. *Marriage Act*, R.S.B.C. 1996, c. 282, as am. R.S.B.C. 1996 (Supp.), c. 282, [to come into force February 28, 2000.] *Solemnization of Marriage Act*, R.S.N. 1990, c. S-19, as am. S.N. 1993, c. 53, 1997, c. 13. *Solemnization of Marriage Act*, R.S.N.S. 1989, c. 436, as am. S.N.S. 1992, c. 16; 1996, c. 23. *Marriage Act*, R.S.O. 1990, c. M.3, as am. O. Reg. 726/91 S.O. 1993, c. 27; 1994, c. 27; 1998, c. 18. *Marriage Act*, S.S. 1995, c. M-4.1. *Marriage Act*, R.S.M. 1987, c. M50, as am. S.M. 1989-90, Man. Reg. 255/91; c. 90; 1993, c. 48; 1994, c. 20; 1997, c. 42 [Not in force at date of publication.]; 1998, c. 36, s. 131 [Not in force at date of publication.] *Marriage Act*, R.S.N.B. 1973, c. M-3, as am. S.N.B. 1979, c. 39; 1980, c. 32; 1980, c. C-2.1; 1983, c. 50; 1985, c. 33; 1986, c. 8; 1986, c. 52; 1990, c. 61; 1991, c. 9; 1992, c. 54; 1995, c. 10; 1996, c. 73; 1998, c. 17; 1999, c. 2. *Marriage Act*, R.S.P.E.I. 1988, c. M-3, as am. S.P.E.I. 1990, c. 34; 1991, c. 26; 1993, c. 16; 1994, c. 58. *Civil Code of*

Quebec, S.Q. 1991, c. 64, as am. S.Q. 1992, c. 57; 1995, c. 33; 1995, c. 61; 1996, c. 21; 1996, c. 28; 1996, c. 68; 1997, c. 75; 1997, c. 80; 1998, c. 5; 1998, c. 32; 1998, c. 51. *Marriage Act*, R.S.N.W.T. 1988, c. M-4, as. am. R.S.N.W.T. 1988, c. 104 (Supp.); S.N.W.T., 1995, c. 11; 1998, c. 17. *Marriage Act*, R.S.Y. 1986, c. 110.

See also *Casimel v. Insurance Corp. of British Columbia* (1993), [1994] 2 C.N.L.R. 22 (B.C. C.A.) where the British Columbia Court of Appeal recognized customary adoption for the purpose of motor vehicle insurance.

4 On the subject of customary marriages, see Norman Zlotkin, "Judicial Recognition of Aboriginal Customary Law in Canada: Selected Marriage and Adoption Cases," [1984] 4 C.N.L.R. 1. According to Zlotkin, customary marriages have been recognized by the Canadian courts where the marriage meets the criteria of English common law marriages: it must have been voluntary; it must have been intended by the parties to last for life; and it must not have been polygamous. A more recent case is *Manychief v. Poffenroth* (1994), [1995] 2 C.N.L.R. 67 (Alta. Q.B.) in which a common law wife claimed benefits as a spouse. The court held that there was such a thing as Blood customary marriage, but in this case, there was no such marriage.

5 See the *Divorce Act*, R.S.C. 1985, c. 3 (2nd Supp.) [hereinafter *Divorce Act*].

6 The three grounds for divorce are provided in section 8 of the *Divorce Act, supra* note 5.

7 See *M. v. H.*, 171 D.L.R. (4th) 577, 238 N.R. 179, 43 O.R. (3d) 254 [1999] 2 S.C.R. 3 (S.C.C.).

8 See the *Family Law Act*, R.S.O. 1990, c. F.3 ss. 29, 31; as am. S.O. 1997, c. 20, s. 2.

9 Note that some provinces, such as Ontario, have adopted the federal guideline for provincial proceedings. Information packages on the Federal Child Support Guidelines and enforcement measures, are available by calling 1-888-373-2222 and in the National Capital Region, by calling 946-2222. Information is also available on the Internet. View the Department of Justice's site at http://canada.justice.gc.ca. For information on the new tax rules, call Revenue Canada at 1-800-959-8281.

10 On the subject of garnishing wages, see *Potts v. Potts*, [1992] 1 C.N.L.R. 182 (Alta. C.A.) and *Ontario (Director of Support & Custody Order Enforcement) v. Nowegejick*, [1989] 2 C.N.L.R. 27 (Ont. Prov. Ct). Registered Indians are exempt from garnishment by non-Indians, but not when the dispute is between two registered Indians. In cases where the spouse is a registered Indian, then, garnishment is valid. In cases where the

spouse is not a registered Indian, the registered Indian may be exempt for property located on a reserve.

11 On the subject of redirecting treaty payments, see s. 68 of the *Indian Act*, which provides:

68. Where the Minister is satisfied that an Indian

(*a*) has deserted his spouse or family without sufficient cause,

(*b*) has conducted himself in such a manner as to justify the refusal of his spouse or family to live with him, or

(*c*) has been separated by imprisonment from his spouse and family,

the Minister may order that payments of any annuity or interest money to which that Indian is entitled shall be applied to the support of the spouse or family or both the spouse and family of that Indian.

R.S.C. 1985, c. 32 (1st Supp.), s. 13.

In *British Columbia v. Minister of National Revenue*, [1980] 1 C.N.L.R. 41 (Alta. Q.B.) it was argued that provincial support laws do not apply because there was already a federal provision in the *Indian Act*. The father contended that section 68(3) of the *Indian Act* occupied the field and that the provincial legislation was invalid. The court held that the Alberta *Maintenance and Recovery Act* was not incompatible with the *Indian Act*, except where it related to "annuities or interest moneys, pursuant to s. 68(3) of the *Indian Act*." Therefore, there was no conflict between the federal and the provincial laws, and that the provincial law was valid.

12 *Matrimonial Property Act*, R.S.A. 1980, c. M-9, as am. S.A. 1983, c. C-7.1; 1988, c. 27; 1988, c. P-4.05; 1991, c. 21; 1992, c. 21 [Not in force at date of publication.] 1995, c. 24; 1996, c. 28; 1996, c. 32. *Marital Property Act*, R.S.M. 1987, c. M45, as am. 1989–90, c. 45; 1992, c. 46; 1993, c. 48; 1998, c. 41 [Not in force at date of publication.]. *Family Relations Act*, R.S.B.C. 1996, c. 128, as. am. R.S.B.C. 1996 (Supp.), c. 128; 1997, c. 15; 1997, c. 20; 1998, c. 28; 1999, c. 15; 1999, c. 2 [Not in force at date of publication.]; 1999, c. 25 [Note in force at date of publication.]. *Family Law Act*, R.S.N. 1990, c. F-2, as am. S.N. 1994, c. 42; 1997 c. 33. *Matrimonial Property Act*, R.S.N.S. 1989, c. 275 as am., S.N.S. 1995-96, c. 13. *Family Law Act*, R.S.O. 1990, c. F.3, as am. S.O. 1992, c. 32; 1993, c. 27; 1997, c. 20; 1997, c. 25, Sched. E; 1998, c. 26. *Matrimonial Property Act*, S.S. 1997, c. M-6.11, as am. S.S. 1998, c. 48. *Marital Property Act*, R.S.N.B. 1980, c. M-1.1, as am. S.N.B. 1985, c. 4; 1987, c. 6; 1991, c. 62; 1994, c. 50; 1994, c. 63. *Family Law Act*, S.N.W.T. 1997, c. 18, as am. 1998, c. 17 (Fri); 1999, c. 5, Sched. c. *Family Property and Support Act*, R.S.Y. 1986, c. 63, as. am. S.Y. 1991, c. 11; 1998, c. 8 [Not in force at date

of publication]. *Civil Code of Quebec*, S.Q. 1991, c. 64, as am. S.Q. 1992, c. 57; 1995, c. 33; 1995, c. 61; 1996, c. 21; 1996, c. 28; 1996, c. 68; 1997, c. 75; 1997, c. 80; 1998, c. 5; 1998, c. 32; 1998, c. 51.

13 On the subject of on-reserve matrimonial homes or land, in *Derrickson v. Derrickson*, [1986] 2 C.N.L.R. 45 (S.C.C.), the Supreme Court of Canada held that provincial legislation about division of matrimonial property or the matrimonial home does not apply since the *Indian Act* is paramount on possession of reserve land. There is no conflict with the *Indian Act*, however, if a compensation order is made adjusting the division of assets to ensure that the woman receives an equal share of the property accumulated during marriage.

15

Welfare of Children

POINTS TO REMEMBER

1. Adoption
   Provincial child adoption law applies to Aboriginal people on- and off-reserve. Adoptions under Aboriginal customary law have been recognized by Canadian courts. Adoption does not deprive a child of registered Indian status.

2. Custody of Children
   Courts will decide what is in the best interests of the child in determining custody. A child's cultural heritage will be considered.

3. Children's Aid Societies
   If a child needs to be protected or taken away from the parents, the local Children's Aid Society has responsibility. Before the Society can remove a child from the parents' care, it must prove in court that the child is "in need of protection." There are now several Children's' Aid Societies which are run by Aboriginal people for Aboriginal people.

4. Right of participation in child welfare hearings
   In some provinces, representatives of Aboriginal communities are entitled to a say in what happens to the children from their community.

5. Recognition of Aboriginal culture, traditions and heritage
   In some provinces, the law requires that priority be given to placing an Aboriginal child in an Aboriginal home, and that any placement must consider the importance of Aboriginal culture, traditions and heritage.

1. INTRODUCTION

The raising of children in the family is of central importance to any culture, because it is through the children that culture is transmitted. It is no coincidence, then, that colonial authorities focussed their efforts on assimilating children. From the late 1800s to the latter half of the 1900s, children were taken out of their parent's care and forced into residential "schools".[1] Some schools were rife with physical, psychological and sexual abuse. Others were staffed by well meaning missionaries. In either case, the goal was the same — to stamp out the child's Aboriginal identity.[2]

This was followed by the "Sixties Scoop" — an awful decade when child welfare authorities removed thousands of children from struggling Aboriginal homes for adoption outside of the communities, and even outside of Canada.[3]

The federal government has now acknowledged the horror of these events. On January 7, 1998, it offered a Statement of Reconciliation which acknowledged its role in the development and administration of the residential school system, and apologized to victims who were physically and sexually abused within these institutions. As a first step in addressing the legacy of physical and sexual abuse at residential schools the federal government has committed $350 million for community-based healing. These funds will be paid out over a ten-year period.

The money will be used to establish holistic and community based healing initiatives, but will not be used as compensation to residential school victims. The fund will be administered by the Aboriginal Healing Foundation, a non-profit corporation run by Aboriginal people, which is independent of both government and the representative Aboriginal organizations. The Foundation has already established four main program themes: healing projects, restoring balance, developing and enhancing Aboriginal capacities and honour and history.[4]

2. ADOPTION

Customary adoptions in Aboriginal communities may not look like "adoptions" as understood in Anglo-Canadian law. The arrangements may look informal, and not be in the nature of a permanent transfer of family allegiance.

Courts in Canada have recognized such adoptions for many years. Courts have looked at four criteria for recognizing such an adoption:[5]

- there must be evidence that the custom extended back in time as far as living memory;

WELFARE OF CHILDREN   229

- the custom must be reasonable;
- the custom "must be certain in respect of its nature generally, as well as in respect of the locality where it is alleged to obtain and the persons whom it is alleged to affect;" and
- the custom must have continued without interruption until the present.

In British Columbia, the *Adoption Act* provides:

On application, the court may recognize that an adoption of a person effected by the custom of an Indian band or aboriginal community has the effect of an adoption under this Act.[6]

A procedure for recognizing custom adoptions, and issuing certificates was developed in the Northwest Territories under the the *Aboriginal Custom Adoption Recognition Act*. The consequences of these adoptions are determined by customary law, not by the territorial *Adoption Act*.[7]

It is important to note that if a registered Indian child is adopted by non-Indians, the child does not lose his or her registered Indian status. The adoption papers should indicate that the child is a registered Indian. If a child who is not a registered Indian is adopted by registered Indians, that child may also be registered as an Indian.[8]

3. CUSTODY OF CHILDREN

The custody of children usually becomes an issue when spouses are separating. They must decide where the children should live, and how often the other parent will be able to spend time with them. (For information on obligations to provide support, see Chapter 14, "Marriage, Separation and Divorce")

In many First Nations, family members, a counsellor, an Elder, or the Chief will help couples make their own arrangements for the children. This method allows people in the community to decide what is best for the children.

Where these arrangements are not possible, and the courts get involved, they will generally apply provincial law. A court might order that the children live with one parent, and that the other parent be able to visit regularly. Or the court might order "joint custody", in which case both parents would have an equal say in deciding the course of the children's lives. Other people, such as grandparents or step-parents, can also claim custody or "access" to the children. Whether or not the legislation says anything about the importance of Aboriginal culture, courts should take it into consideration in deciding on the best interests of the child.[9]

Custody of, and access to, children is an issue which is often very difficult to resolve. In some cases, rather than have a judge decide who should have custody, people use a mediator. A mediator will help people to reach their own agreement.[10]

4. CHILDREN IN NEED OF PROTECTION

(a) The Children's Aid Society

For a variety of reasons, parents may not be able to take care of their children properly, and relatives or friends may not be able to help. In those cases, a Children's Aid Society can intervene. In general, the Children's Aid Society must prove that a child is in need of protection before it can remove a child from the parents' custody without their permission. The standard for proving that a child is in need of protection includes situations where a child has suffered physical harm at the hands of the care-giver, where a parent refuses to provide the child with necessary medical treatment, or where there is a risk that the child will suffer some kind of emotional or physical harm while in the parent's care. Where there are grounds for believing such a situation exists, an application may be brought to court, usually by a Children's Aid Society, to determine if a child is indeed in need of protection. Then a hearing will be held.

In some cases, the child is so seriously at risk that she or he must be apprehended right away. When that happens, the Children's Aid Society must go to court in a matter of days to justify the apprehension in front of a judge.

Where a child is found to be in need of protection, the court may make different types of orders. It may order that the child is to be left in the home, but with Children's Aid Society supervision of the parent and child. It can order that the child is to be placed with a foster parent or in a group home. After that, a number of stages can occur which will result in the child being put up for adoption, and the parents could permanently lose all contact with the child.

A judge's decision in a child protection hearing must be made in the "best interests of the child." Many factors will be considered in determining the child's best interests, such as stability in the child's life and the child's blood ties. Generally, the test for making this decision involves finding the least restrictive alternative for the child.

In response to demands by Aboriginal people for greater Aboriginal involvement, there have been a number of initiatives to modify the child welfare system.

(b) Aboriginal participation in child welfare proceedings

The Ontario *Child and Family Services Act* (CFSA) provides an extensive role for Aboriginal community representatives in hearings.[11] In an application to have a child made a ward of the Children's Aid Society, for example, the child's First Nation Council must be informed of the court case. A representative of the First Nation can then go to the hearing, and observe the proceedings, or participate. In some cases, the First Nation representative will have a proposal for a new arrangement for the child. The judge can take the views of the First Nation representative into account, but the judge must make an independent decision on what is best for the child.

If a First Nation intends to be involved, it should participate in the process as early as possible. Since a full trial of the issues may not be held for more than a year, there will be an interim hearing to decide where a child should live until trial. Any party interested in the child's situation should take part at this stage.

The CFSA also provides for consideration of Aboriginal culture whenever the interests of the child are being considered. The judge must consider the importance of the uniqueness of Aboriginal culture, heritage and traditions, and of preserving the child's cultural identity.[12] In placing an Aboriginal child, priority must be given to placement with the family, with the community or with another Aboriginal family.[13]

"Customary care" is also recognized. When a child is in "customary care" the caregivers may be given an allowance by the Children's Aid Society.[14] It is not clear how the term "customary care" is defined, and there has been some controversy over its application. It appears, however, that informal arrangements for care of children are meant to be covered by this section.

In British Columbia, under the *Adoption Act*,[15] the director or adoption agency must make reasonable efforts to discuss the child's placement with the child's band or Aboriginal community before the adoption of an Aboriginal child. The *Child, Family and Community Service Act*[16] provides for Aboriginal participation much in the same way the Ontario legislation does.

The British Columbia legislation was considered by the Supreme Court of Canada in *H. (D.) v. M. (H.)*.[17] The custody dispute was between the grandparents of a child, "I". The grandfather of I. lived on the Sagkeeng First Nation reserve, and was the father of I's mother. I's mother had been adopted as a child however, and brought up in the United States by Americans. The American grandparents also wanted custody of I. The trial court had found that grandparents on both sides were capable of providing a loving environment for the child. The proceedings were pursuant to provisions in British Columbia's *Child, Family and Community Service Act*, which provides that: "If the child is an aboriginal child, the importance of preserving the child's cultural identity must be considered in determining the child's best interests".[18] The trial judge considered this provision, but also considered the fact that I's father was African — American, and decided to give custody to the American grandparents. The court also gave I's mother and the Canadian grandfather the right to spend time with I. The British Columbia Court of Appeal overturned the trial decision, finding that the trial judge had not given enough emphasis to the Aboriginal cultural heritage. The Supreme Court of Canada restored the decision of the trial judge. In a unanimous decision, the Supreme Court noted that the child was of mixed heritage, and that Aboriginal culture was an important, but not exclusive consideration.

(c) Aboriginal CAS

In most Aboriginal communities, the local Children's Aid Society has jurisdiction, and will come onto the reserve to make arrangements for the children. There are a growing number of Aboriginal-run services which have boards made up of representatives of local Aboriginal communities. The advantage of an Aboriginal-run Children's Aid Society is that it provides for Aboriginal involvement in an area where the exercise of judgment and cultural sensitivity is vitally important. However, this type of Children's Aid Society operates under the authority of provincial legislation.[19]

(d) Tripartite Agreements

A tripartite agreement is one that is signed by three parties — the federal government, the provincial government and the Aboriginal group. These agreements are administrative vehicles for providing funding to Aboriginal organizations for child welfare. The provincial law continues to operate.

(e) By-laws under the Indian Act

A child welfare by-law offers a way of dealing with the matter in the short term. The Spallumcheen First Nation in British Columbia has enacted a child welfare by-law which has not been disallowed by the Minister under the *Indian Act*, and which has been recognized by the provincial government. Unfortunately, the federal government has refused to allow any more such by-laws, and the *Indian Act* itself does not explicitly authorize them.[20] The Spallumcheen solution will only become available again when the *Indian Act* is amended to authorize such by-laws and take away the disallowance power of the Minister.

(f) Federal enabling legislation

In the United States, the *Indian Child Welfare Act* recognizes and encourages tribal jurisdiction over child welfare.[21] In many tribes, decisions on children in need of protection are made by the tribal courts. A Canadian court recently recognized an American tribal court decision.[22]

Canadian legislation similar to that in the United States has been advocated for many years. Such legislation would set the stage for federal and provincial recognition of First Nation laws on child care. Unfortunately, the federal government has so far refused to introduce such legislation.[23]

(g) Self-government agreements

Control over family and children is passing to First Nations control in self-government agreements. For example in the Yukon self-government agreements, the First Nations have the power to pass laws regarding adoption, social and welfare services.[24] The Nisga'a

Final Agreement provides that Nisga'a laws on "child and family services" will be paramount over provincial laws.[25]

(h) Declaration of First Nation law

A First Nation could enact its own child welfare law, declare that it is in force, and declare that it overrides the provincial law. It is not certain what response the courts would have to such a declaration, or what response can be expected from the provincial and federal governments. The Royal Commission on Aboriginal Peoples identifies "family matters" as part of the core jurisdiction of Aboriginal nations, so that those nations with inherent rights of self-government could make such a declaration.[26] It is clear, however, that recognition of such a First Nation law would come more easily if the First Nation offered a clearly developed alternative to the provincial child welfare laws.[27]

ENDNOTES

1 There are now many lawsuits arising out of the abuse. Two important British Columbia decisions have found that both the church which ran the residential school, and the Crown are vicariously liable for the abusive behaviour of the people who worked at the schools. See *B. (W.R.) v. Plint*, [1998] 4 C.N.L.R. 13 (B.C. S.C.) and *F.S.M. v. Clarke*, [1999] B.C.J. No. 1973 (B.C. S.C.).

2 For an overview of the effect of the residential schools on its survivors see the Royal Commission on Aboriginal Peoples, *Looking Forward, Looking Back*, Volume 1 (Ottawa: Supply and Services, 1996) at 337 [hereinafter RCAP, Vol. 1] and the Royal Commission on Aboriginal Peoples, *Gathering Strength*, Volume 3 (Ottawa: Supply and Services, 1996) at 36 [hereinafter RCAP, Vol. 3].

3 The Sixties Scoop has been characterized as a continuation of the residential school legacy. See RCAP, Vol. 3, *supra* note 2 at 26.

4 To contact the Aboriginal Healing Foundation, 75 Albert St., Ste. 400, Ottawa, On K1P 5E7/ph: (613) 237-4441 or 1-888-725-8886/web: www.ahf.ca

5 On customary adoption, see *Deborah E4-789, Re*, [1972] 5 W.W.R. 203 (N.W. C.A.). In *Tagnornak, Re* (1983), [1984] 1 C.N.L.R. 185 (N.W.T. S.C), Marshall, J. suggested that customary adoptions are also recognized and affirmed by section 35 of the *Constitution Act, 1982*.

There is, however, an indication that when there is a conflict between a customary adoption and federal law, federal law will prevail. *K. (C.) v. E. (C)* (1985), [1986] 2 C.N.L.R. 38 (N.W.T. S.C.) deals with an application by Inuit maternal grandparents for custody of a child they adopted by customary law.

6 See the *Adoption Act*, R.S.B.C. 1996, c. 5, s. 46(1). In *Re: B.C. Birth Registration No. 1994-09-040399* [1998] 4 C.N.L.R. 7 (B.C.S.C.), the adoptive parents of a child asked for a declaration under s.46 of British Columbia's *Adoption Act, 1996* that the Aboriginal custom adoption had the effect of an adoption under the *Adoption Act*. Both the birth mother and the adopting parents were Carrier people, although they were from different Bands. The court found that the four criteria set out in *Re Tagornak Adoption Petition*, were met. In addition, the court held that the Aboriginal adoption met a fifth important criterium that "the relationship created by custom must be understood to create fundamentally the same relationship as that resulting from an adoption order" [at para. 15].

7 See *Aboriginal Custom Adoption Recognition Act*, S.N.W.T. 1995, c. 26. For an application by Inuit parents, see *S.K.K. v. J.S.*, [1999] N.W.T.J. No. 94 (N.W.T.S.C.).

8 "Adoption and the Indian Child", Canada: Minister of Government Services, 1993 (QS-5117-000-EE-A4).

9 On the subject of heritage in custody decisions, in *S. (D.) v. N. (D.)*, [1989] 3 C.N.L.R. 190 (Ont. Fam. Ct.), Sandy, a registered Indian living in Toronto, had, with the consent of the child's mother and father, looked after a 15-month-old registered Indian child almost since birth. When the child's mother died, Sandy applied for custody of the child. Her application was opposed by Nootchtai, the child's maternal aunt, who also wanted custody of the child. Nootchtai, was living in Sudbury and planning to move back to her reserve 20 miles away where a number of the child's relatives also lived. The child's father did not seek custody, only access to the child.

The court stated that the decision had to be made in the best interests of the child. The *Children's Law Reform Act* makes no specific reference to Aboriginal children, so the court looked to other provincial law for guidance, specifically to s. 3(4) of the *Child and Family Services Act*, R.S.O. 1990, c. C.11, which refers to the importance of the child's Aboriginal cultural identity. The court said at p. 194: "In a custodial dispute affecting an Indian child, the child's native culture, heritage and tradition is of some importance."

The court also said that extended family members should have a meaningful role in the child's upbringing when possible (although the blood relationship does not overcome all considerations). Custody of the child was given to his aunt, Nootchtai. Sandy and the father were given visiting rights.

10 For example, in Ontario, Section 31 of the *Children's Law Reform Act*, R.S.O. 1990 c. C.12 provides:

(1) Upon an application for custody of or access to a child, the court, at the request of the parties, by order may appoint a person selected by the parties to mediate any matter specified in the order.

11 "A representative chosen by the child's band or native community" is entitled to receive notice, commence an application or take part in:

* any proceeding in relation to child protection (s. 39(1));

* any hearing, to "make, vary or terminate an order respecting a person's access to the child or the child's access to a person . . ." (s. 58(1) and (2)(b));

* a review hearing with regard to the status of a child under a supervision order or who was made a society or Crown ward (s. 64(4)(d) and (6)(e));

The representative may appeal any child protection order, other than an order for assessment, to Ontario Court (General Division) (s. 69(1)(e)). Where a restraining order "restraining or prohibiting a person's access to or contact with the child" was made, the representative may apply to extend, vary or terminate such an order (s. 80(4)(f)). The representative is entitled to receive a copy of the report on the assessment (medical, emotional, developmental, psychological, educational or social) of a child (s. 54(3)(f)). Where an assessment of a child is performed to determine if a child with a mental disorder should be placed in a "secure treatment program", the representative shall receive a copy of the report (s. 116(4)(g)).

Notice to the First Nation (band) in cases of wardship and adoption are mandatory, and cannot be avoided by the consent of the parties to a proceeding: *Children's Aid Society of Nipissing (District) v. M. (R.)*, (1987) [1989] 2 C.N.L.R. 21 (Ont. Fam. Ct.)

12 Section 47(2)(c) of the *Child and Family Services Act* states that where a child protection hearing takes place, the court must determine if a child is Indian or native and to which band or community the child belongs. Section 37(4) states that:

Where a person is directed in this Part to make an order or determination in the best interests of a child and the child is an Indian or native person, the person shall take into consideration the importance, in recognition of the uniqueness of Indian and native culture, heritage and traditions, of preserving the child's cultural identity.

13 Where an Indian or native child is found to be in need of protection and is to be removed from his or her parents' care, the child shall, "unless there is a substantial reason for placing the child elsewhere", be placed with either "(a) a member of the child's extended family; (b) a member of the child's band or native community; or (c) another Indian or native family" (s. 57(5) or s. 61(2)(d) of the *Child and Family Services Act* if the child is made a society or Crown ward).

14 See *Child and Family Services Act*, Part X, s. 212. For a case in which the Court rejected the customary care arrangement, see *Weechi-it-te-win Ch. H & Family Services v. M. (A)*, (1992) [1993] 1 C.N.L.R. 169 (Ont. Prov. Div.)

15 See the *Adoption Act*, R.S.B.C. 1996, c. 5, s. 7.

16 See the *Child, Family and Community Services Act*, R.S.B.C. 1996, c. 46.

17 *H. (D.) v. M. (H.)*, [1999] 2 C.N.L.R. iv (note) (S.C.C.)

18 See *Child, Family and Community Services Act*, R.S.B.C. 1996, c. 46, s. 4(2).

19 Increased Aboriginal control over child welfare administration has resulted in the development of Aboriginal child welfare agencies. Among such organizations are the Native Child and Family Services of Toronto, the Métis Child and Family Services of Edmonton, Mi'kmaw Family and Children's Service of Nova Scotia and Nuu-chah-nulth Community and Human Services in British Columbia. For a summary of developments in child welfare in Aboriginal communities see RCAP, Vol. 3 at 30, *supra* note 1. Aboriginal child welfare agencies capabilities were scrutinized in the inquiry respecting the death of Lester Desjarlais, a child who committed suicide while in the care of the Manitoba Aboriginal Child Welfare Agency. Specifically, the inquiry recommended that the provincial director of child welfare take an active role in monitoring Aboriginal agencies. For a brief discussion, see RCAP, Vol. 3 at 52, *supra* note 2.

20 The by-law was considered in *Alexander v. Maxime* (1995), [1996] 1 C.N.L.R. 1 (B.C. C.A.) The Spallumcheen First Nation, pursuant to its child welfare by-law, changed custody of a child from his grandmother, to his mother. The grandmother, who lived in Vancouver, refused to give up custody of the child. She challenged the validity of the First Nation by-law. The Court of Appeal did not decide on whether the by-law was authorized under the *Indian Act*. However, the court upheld the exercise of *parens patriae* jurisdiction by the court below to stay the Spallumcheen custody in order to determine the best interests of the child. In *S.(E.G.) v. Spallumcheen Band Council* (1998), [1999] 2 C.N.L.R. 318 (B.C. S.C.), non-Aboriginal foster parents of a child who was a member of the Spallumcheen

First Nation asked the court to exercise its *parens patriae* jurisdiction. The foster parents disagreed with the decision of the First Nation to place the child with the child's maternal aunt. The court upheld the decision made under the First Nation's by-law, and dismissed the application of the foster parents.

21 *Indian Child Welfare Act*, 25 U.S.C.A. §1901 (1978)

22 In *V. (T.K.) v. V. (R.C.)* [1993] 1 C.N.L.R. 165 (Alta. Prov. Ct.) a child custody order from Blackfeet Tribal Court in Montana was recognized under Alberta's *Extra-Provincial Enforcement of Custody Orders Act*, R.S.A. 1980, c. E-17.

23 In negotiating child welfare agreements, the federal government has continued to require that Aboriginal child welfare services provided under such agreements adhere to provincial regulations. For a discussion on this issue see RCAP, Vol. 3, *supra* note 2 at 36.

24 See the *Yukon Umbrella Final Agreement*, 1993, under s. 13 of the agreements.

25 The *Nisga'a Final Agreement Act*, R.S.B.C. 1999, c. 2, Sched., Chapter 11, para. 89–93 concern Child and Family Services. The relevant sections provide:

89. Nisga'a Lisims Government may make laws in respect of child and family services on Nisga'a Lands, provided that those laws include standards comparable to provincial standards intended to ensure the safety and well-being of children and families.

90. Notwithstanding any laws made under paragraph 89, if there is an emergency in which a child on Nisga'a Lands is at risk, British Columbia may act to protect the child and, in those circumstances, unless British Columbia and Nisga'a Lisims Government otherwise agree, British Columbia will refer the matter back to Nisga'a Lisims Government after the emergency.

91. In the event of an inconsistency or conflict between a Nisga'a law under paragraph 89 and a federal or provincial law, the Nisga'a law prevails to the extent of the inconsistency or conflict.

93. Laws of general application in respect of reporting child abuse apply on Nisga'a Lands.

26 Aboriginal agencies have increasingly become involved in the development, design and implementation of child welfare services. However, the agencies continue to be affected by external control issues. See RCAP, Vol. 3 at 36, *supra* note 2.

See also Recommendation 3.2.2 of RCAP, Vol. 3 at 53, *supra* note 2:

Aboriginal, provincial, territorial and federal governments promptly acknowledge that child welfare is a core area of self-government in which Aboriginal nations can undertake self-starting initiatives.

27 On the subject of the inclusion of child welfare as an inherent right under s. 35(1) of the *Constitution Act, 1982*, a Provincial Court judge in British Columbia has found that the provincial law on apprehension of children is not prevented from applying on reserve by s. 35(1). In this case, there was no countervailing Aboriginal law put forward: *Family & Child Service Act (British Columbia), Re*, [1990] 4 C.N.L.R. 14 (B.C. Prov. Ct.).

16
Wills and Estates

POINTS TO REMEMBER

1. By making a will, people can direct what happens to their property after their death.

2. Reserve land cannot be left in a will to a person who is not a Band member.

3. If a person dies without a will, federal or provincial law determines what happens to that person's property. (It goes to certain members of the person's family.)

4. All provinces and territories have rules which ensure that some money from the estate is left for spouses or dependent children.

1. INTRODUCTION

A person's "estate" includes all property and debts which that person possesses at the time of his or her death. Estates law is concerned with the distribution of a person's estate after death.

The estates of registered Indians who are not ordinarily resident on a reserve[1] and the estates of Aboriginal people who are not registered Indians are treated the same as the estates of non-Aboriginal people. Their estates are governed by provincial laws. In the event of the death of a registered Indian who is ordinarily resident on a reserve, the *Indian Act* and the Indian Estates Regulations provisions related to the making of wills and the distribution of estates will apply.[2]

2. PREPARING A WILL

(a) Wills in General

To ensure that a person's property will be distributed after that person's death as he or she would wish, the person must prepare a will. A will should include the following information:

- The will should name the "testator". The testator is the person whose will it is.
- The will should name an "executor." The executor is the person who will be responsible for carrying out the terms of the will after the death of the testator. There can be more than one executor.
- The will should state who the "beneficiary" is to be. The beneficiary is the person who inherits under a will. There can be more than one beneficiary, in which case the will should state how the estate is to be divided among the beneficiaries. Note that reserve land can be willed only to another band member. A term in a will which gives reserve land to a non-member will not be valid.
- The will should deal with the possibility of change. Between the time when a person draws up a will and the time when he or she dies, many things can happen. For example, the person might buy or sell a piece of property, or a beneficiary might die. When the will is drafted, it should cover as many possibilities as can be thought of. The will should be updated as soon as a change which the will does not cover occurs.
- The will should be signed, dated and witnessed. The signature should be the testator's usual signature.

It is not necessary to have a lawyer draft the will. On the other hand, a lawyer's assistance will help you ensure that the will achieves what the testator wants it to and nothing important is left out.

A will can be changed as often as the testator likes. Only the most recent will is carried out. To avoid confusion, it is a good idea to destroy the old will when a new one is made. It is also a good idea to keep the will in a safe place and let someone (the executor, for example) know where it is.

Provincial and territorial laws make provisions for surviving spouses and dependent children. For example, under the *Family Law*

Act in Ontario a surviving spouse is entitled to one half of the "net family property". If someone leaves his or her spouse less than this in a will, the court will make an adjustment so the surviving spouse receives the share the law entitles him or her to.

(b) Indian wills

"Indian" here means "registered Indian ordinarily resident on a reserve". The *Indian Act* states that "The Minister may accept any written instrument signed by an Indian in which he indicates his wishes or intention with respect to the disposition of his property on his death".[3] "Instrument" in this context does not mean anything special: a letter, a will, a note, are all "instruments".

(c) Other Aboriginal wills

The requirements for an effective will are more stringent for people who are living off-reserve because provincial laws will apply. The will must be in writing, and the testator must sign the will at the end. This signing must be done in the presence of two witnesses who also sign the will in the presence of the testator. Neither of the witnesses should be a beneficiary or the spouse of a beneficiary. Having a beneficiary or spouse of a beneficiary witness the will may invalidate the gift to that beneficiary.

In some areas of the country it is possible for a will to be hand-written by the testator. Such a will is called a "holograph" will. It must be completely in the testator's handwriting (no typed parts or parts written by someone else) and signed by the testator. A holograph will does not need to be witnessed.

3. INTESTACY

If a person dies without a will, that person is said to die "intestate". If a registered Indian living on reserve dies intestate, or if his or her will is not clear or not valid, the Department of Indian Affairs will apply the rules set out in the *Indian Act* and the Indian Estates Regulations.[4]

If the person lived off-reserve the provincial law sets out how the estate is distributed.

4. DISTRIBUTION OF ESTATE

When a registered Indian living on-reserve dies, his or her First Nation should advise an Estates Officer at the Department of Indian Affairs. A search should also be conducted for a will. A will may be on file with Indian Affairs.

The Minister of Indian Affairs has exclusive jurisdiction over the estate of a registered Indian who lived on reserve. The Minister has the power to decide whether the will is valid, and whether the named executor is competent to act; the Minister also has the power to administer the estate or to appoint or authorize an executor to do so. The Minister can transfer this jurisdiction to the courts, but retains full decision-making power over the estate if he or she does not do so.

The executor named in the will usually work with the estates officer to administer the estate. The will must be probated (i.e., its validity must be determined) within the Department. An inventory of assets and liabilities must be prepared and beneficiaries notified. If there are no problems with the will, and the terms of the will are not challenged, the estate will then be distributed to the beneficiaries.

In the event of the death of someone who was not a registered Indian living on-reserve, it would be best to contact a lawyer for assistance with the formalities of probate where there is a will and the requirements of the *Succession Law Reform Act* where there is not.

ENDNOTES

1 Section 4(3) of the *Indian Act* makes the estates provisions of the *Act* inapplicable to Indians living off-reserve. The Supreme Court of Canada has upheld the jurisdiction of the federal government to override provincial laws in *Canada (Attorney General) v. Canard* (1975), [1976] 1 S.C.R. 170 (S.C.C.).

2 For details of the law of Indian estates see sections 45 to 52.5 of the *Indian Act* and the *Indian Estates Regulations*, C.R.C. 1978, c. 954.

3 On Indian wills, see *Indian Act*, s. 45(2).

4 Sections 48 to 50 of the *Indian Act* set out the rules for distributing an estate where there is no will. Generally, these rules provide for the distribution of the estate to the deceased person's family. All assets up to a value of $75,000 go to the deceased person's spouse. If any assets are left after that, they are divided among the spouse and the deceased person's

children, if any. If there is neither spouse nor children, the estate goes to the deceased person's parents. If there are no parents surviving, the estate goes to the deceased person's brothers and sisters, and so on.

Economic Activity

17

Commercial Relations on Reserves

POINTS TO REMEMBER

1. There are several sections in the *Indian Act* which affect commercial relations on reserves.

2. Non-Indian businesses should be aware of the distinct status of Indian organizations, Indian lands and Indian property on reserve when entering into commercial relations.

3. When using reserve land for development, the First Nation should consider using "designation" for assigning the land to a non-traditional use, rather than the surrender mechanisms.

4. A corporation can offer significant legal and financial protection to people conducting business. On the other hand, there are formalities and administrative requirements to be met if the corporation is to work.

5. A joint venture can be a good way to get a project done. It provides a framework for business relations when a number of individuals or corporations want to work as partners on a particular project.

1. INTRODUCTION — COMMERCIAL RELATIONS BETWEEN NON-INDIAN BUSINESS AND RESERVE-BASED INDIANS

The *Indian Act* creates a special legal regime for Indian communities on reserves. More and more Bands are becoming directly involved in commercial enterprises. It is therefore important to recognize that the business environment changes when one of the parties is Indian, or when reserve lands are affected.

(a) Contracting parties

Occasionally there is a misunderstanding about the identity of the contracting parties. Because of the extensive involvement of the federal Department of Indian Affairs, which may in some cases be providing the funding for a project, the parties may assume that the federal government is providing a guarantee for the project. This may not be the case at all. If the contracting party is the First Nation Council, then, unless there are clear contractual responsibilities on the federal government, only the First Nation Council is responsible for the contract. The Department of Indian Affairs will not automatically guarantee a First Nation's financial obligations.

This means that there must be a proper agreement with the First Nation. The Band is capable of entering into contracts. It usually acts through Band Council Resolutions, and it is wise to require a Resolution approving an agreement.[1]

(b) Seizure of Goods and Money Situated on a Reserve

Under the *Indian Act*[2] the personal property of an Indian or band cannot be taken by non-Indians. For example, if an Indian owes money to a non-Indian, the non-Indian cannot go onto a reserve and take goods belonging to the Indian.

There are some exceptions to this rule. If an item is purchased on a conditional sale contract (on time payments, for example), then the non-Indian can take the item back for failure to make payments.[3] Corporations are not Indians so a corporation's property can be taken. Indians can seize property of other Indians.[4]

Off-reserve property is generally subject to seizure.[5] However, if the property is usually used on reserve, such as a school bus, it cannot be seized when it goes off reserve.[6] Off-reserve bank accounts can be seized.[7] However, if the account holds money provided by the Crown, that money cannot be seized.[8]

(c) Indian reserve lands

The land regime in the *Indian Act* makes conventional mortgages and use of reserve land as collateral very difficult. The next section of this chapter discusses this issue in more detail.

2. USE OF RESERVE LANDS FOR ECONOMIC DEVELOPMENT

Reserves have been very important to First Nations, and provisions in the *Indian Act* have protected many reserves from being sold off by individuals or the Department of Indian Affairs. These very protections have sometimes caused problems, however, when First Nations decide to use parts of the reserve for economic development. Recent changes to the *Indian Act* have provided ways to avoid some of the old problems.

(a) Surrenders

Under the *Indian Act* a First Nation could surrender[9] part of its reserve.[10] To do this, the *Indian Act* required that the majority of the electors of the First Nation agree to the surrender at a meeting or in a referendum.[11]

Until 1988, surrendering reserve land was the only way for First Nations to use land for economic development, and there were serious problems with this procedure. In one case, the First Nation instructed the federal government to sell the land, but the government never did. In that case, the courts held that the federal government did not have to return the land; upon surrender the land had become provincial land.[12] In other cases, disputes arose about the price the government obtained for the land on behalf of the First Nation.

Often the surrender was not an absolute surrender for the purpose of selling the land. A surrender could be conditional, dealing with the sale of timber rights only, for example, or a limited-term lease. Problems have arisen where the federal government did not act properly on the First Nation's behalf after this type of surrender. The federal government is now the subject of many lawsuits for failing to follow the directions of the First Nation or to get fair market value for these transactions. In one major case a First Nation obtained a $10 million judgment against the federal government.[13]

There were other problems associated with the surrender of lands. For example, it was not clear whether surrendered lands were to be considered reserve lands, and whether First Nation by-laws applied on those lands.

(b) Designated lands

A new provision in the *Indian Act* allows First Nations the advantages of surrender without some of the drawbacks. Instead of surrendering part of the reserve, First Nations can "designate" it for development.[14] The 1988 *Indian Act* amendments allowing for the designation of reserve land are commonly referred to as the "Kamloops Amendment" after the First Nation which pushed for them.[15]

In Kamloops the First Nation had surrendered some of its reserve to lease the land for an industrial park. The First Nation then discovered that, once the land was surrendered it was no longer considered part of the reserve. This had three consequences: members of the First Nation had to pay provincial sales tax on purchases made on the surrendered land; the Town of Kamloops imposed a tax on non-Indians on the land, though the Town provided no services; and the application of First Nation by-laws on the land was not clear.

To correct these problems, the federal government created the "designated land" category. This is a cross between a surrender and a certificate of occupation. To designate part of a reserve, the First Nation must follow the same procedures as for a surrender. Once the land is designated, however, it is still considered to be part of the reserve for many significant purposes. For example, members of the First Nation will not have to pay sales tax, and First Nation by-laws will clearly apply to non-Indians.

It is not clear whether the First Nation's new ability to impose taxes on designated land means that municipalities must discontinue taxing non-Indians on that land. This issue will have to be decided by the courts. In Ontario the issue is not significant because the province has not permitted municipalities to impose a tax on conditionally surrendered lands.[16] In British Columbia, the *Indian Self-Government Enabling Act*[17] prevents municipalities from taxing reserve land once the Band has decided to exercise its power to tax.[18]

The designated lands category will be helpful for First Nations which have decided to use part of a reserve for development by non-Aboriginal companies or persons (such as cottagers). It will clarify the First Nation's jurisdiction over the designated land and the people who occupy it.

(c) Permits for use of reserve lands

The Minister may grant possession of lands on reserve or author-ize their use[19] for a number of purposes including "the general welfare of the band".[20] Unfortunately the manner in which such permits are granted has raised difficulties in a number of cases. The Minister's authority has not been subject to the First Nation's consent, and sometimes permits have been issued contrary to the interests or wishes of the First Nation.[21]

3. CORPORATIONS

Corporations are the most common vehicle for commercial ac-tivities. Corporations protect the owners from being personally re-sponsible if the corporation owes money. For example, if the owners of a business are short of cash and fail to pay their bills, the creditors may attempt to seize business assets including money in a bank account. If the business is not incorporated, the members of the board of directors or the owners may have to pay the creditors out of their own pockets. Incorporation means that the business becomes a sepa-rate legal entity. It is unlikely that the owners or board members will be personally financially responsible for the business losses, even if the business cannot pay all creditors.[22]

Corporations may be formed for profit-making ventures or for a non-profit purpose. Generally, the provincial or territorial legislation which applies to non-profit and charitable corporations is different from business corporations. Non-profits and charities are discussed in Chapter 12, "Community Corporations".

Aboriginal people can use the advantages and protections of corporate status in their dealings both within the community and in joint ventures and other business arrangements with non-Aboriginal individuals and companies.

To create a corporation and keep it running properly, a document called Articles of Incorporation must be prepared and filed with payment at the appropriate provincial or federal office. The Articles of Incorporation are not difficult to prepare and the people involved may be able to do so themselves. On the other hand, they may want to have a lawyer prepare the documents or at least look them over to be sure they are prepared properly. The process of incorporating is usually quite simple and should not take long. The one delay which may occur is in finding an acceptable name that is not already in use.

Even if everyone involved in the corporation is a registered Indian, the corporation is not considered a registered Indian. It will therefore have to pay taxes on the goods it purchases. It must also file an income tax return each year and pay taxes on its profits. More information on this is provided in Chapter 20, "Taxation". Working out the financial details and reports with an accountant will help to make sure the business takes advantage of all the tax breaks to which it is entitled.

Once a corporation is formed, there are requirements for keeping it in order: certain procedures must take place and certain records must be kept and filed regularly. People considering corporate status should weigh the burden of the administrative work against the benefits of incorporation. This is important; if a corporation does not comply with the legal administrative requirements, it may be dissolved and the objectives for which it was established in the first place will not be met.

4. JOINT VENTURES

Many reserves and Aboriginal communities want to participate in business projects that affect them. In cases where they also want to take advantage of the expertise of a non-Aboriginal company, joint ventures and partnerships are useful for organizing the relationship.

For example, a First Nation Council may want to build houses on a reserve, and it may know of a company with expertise in housing construction. The First Nation or particular members of the First Nation may want to learn about project management. Another member of the First Nation may want to provide employment or equipment to the project. By entering into a joint venture, the First Nation can share in profits which the enterprise will earn. This also means that the First Nation must bear some of the financial risks of the project. Non-Aboriginal companies may be interested in an on-reserve joint venture because of the tax advantages they may gain.

Each joint venture is different, and there are several forms the relationship could take: partnerships, limited partnerships, corporations and subcontracting. The joint venture should accomplish the following goals:

- protect against personal liability
- minimize payment of sales tax
- avoid payment of tax on income from the project
- ensure that the First Nation benefits through local employment and involvement, and through "profits" which accrue to the benefit of the First Nation as a whole
- ensure that the non-Indian partner receives a fair return on its investment
- ensure that the structure of the joint venture is acceptable to the funding source
- ensure that the project is carried on in a business-like manner

It would be best to get professional advice on the most effective way to structure a joint venture to meet the project's goals.

ENDNOTES

1 On the importance of a Band Council Resolution approving a contract with a Band, see *Heron Seismic Services Ltd. v. Peepeekisis Indian Band* (1990), (sub nom. *Heron Seismic Services Ltd. v. Muscowpetung Indian Band*) [1992] 4 C.N.L.R. 32 (Sask. C.A.). For the technical requirements for a Band Council Resolution, see section 2(3) of the *Indian Act*, and *Basque v. Woodstock Indian Band* (1996), 175 N.B.R. (2d) 241 (N.B.C.A.) and *Leonard v. Gottfriedson* (1982), 1 C.N.L.R. 60 (B.C.S.C.).

2 On the subject of seizure of the personal property of an Indian, see section 89(1) of the *Indian Act*.

3 On the subject of seizure and conditional sale contracts, see *Chrysler Credit Corp. v. Penagin*, (1981), [1982] 1 C.N.L.R. 19 (Ont. Dist. Ct.). In that case, an Indian on a reserve bought a truck from a dealer under a conditional sales contract. The vendor of the truck assigned the conditional sales contract to the plaintiff. The plaintiff attempted to repossess the truck when payments were not made.

The court held that an assignee has the right to enforce a conditional sales contract on a reserve, just as the original vendor. The reference in section 89(2) includes an assignee of the contract, and the assignee can also exercise rights under the general laws of the province. The general law of assignment does not "terminate or destroy any rights or status that an Indian may have under the Indian Act." To hold otherwise would provide Indians with a remedy never considered by the framers of the Act.

4 On the subject of seizure for debts between Indians, in *Potts v. Potts*, [1989] 2 C.N.L.R. 96 (Alta. Q.B.), affirmed (1991), [1992] 1 C.N.L.R. 182

(Alta. C.A.), the court held that the Director of Maintenance Enforcement could attach moneys payable to a band council when the garnishment is "in favour or at the instance of an Indian." The plaintiff was thus entitled to garnishee maintenance payments.

In *Ontario (Director of Support & Custody Enforcement) v. Nowegijick*, [1989] 2 C.N.L.R. 27 (Ont. Prov. Ct.), the court held that a treaty (in this case, the Robinson-Superior Treaty) cannot impair the operation of the *Indian Act* sections 88 and 89 and exempt the debtor from garnishment of his wages to pay support to his Indian wife.

5 On the subject of seizure of off-reserve property, see *Geoffries v. Williams* (1958), 26 W.W.R. 323 (B.C. Co. Ct.).

6 On the subject of seizure of a Band vehicle when it was off-reserve, see *Kingsclear Indian Band v. J.E. Brooks & Associates Ltd.* (1991), [1992] 2 C.N.L.R. 46 (N.B. C.A.).

7 On the subject of seizure of off-reserve bank accounts, see *Avery v. Cayuga* (1913), 28 O.L.R. 517 (Ont. C.A.). See also *Houston v. Standingready* (1990), [1991] 2 C.N.L.R. 65 (Sask. C.A.)

8 On the subject of seizure of moneys from the Crown, in the case of *Mitchell v. Sandy Bay Indian Band*, [1990] 3 C.N.L.R. 46 (S.C.C.) the court held that moneys payable under an agreement between the government of Manitoba and the band could not be attached. Mitchell assisted the band in negotiating for a rebate of sales tax from Manitoba Hydro on a 20% contingency fee. The negotiations were successful and the funds to be rebated were placed in a trust account. When Mitchell was not paid, he obtained a garnishment order, and the proceeds were paid into court by the Manitoba government. The First Nation attempted to have the garnishment order set aside. The Supreme Court of Canada considered the case, and concluded that the garnishment should be set aside, and the money paid back to the First Nation. The reasoning is not clear because there were three judgments. Dickson, C.J. felt that s. 90(1) protected money from a provincial Crown as well as the federal Crown. However, the six other members of the court felt that only money from the federal Crown was protected. In spite of this finding, the six members of the court found in favour of the Peguis Band for different reasons.

See also: *Fayerman Brothers Ltd. v. Peter Ballantyne Indian Band* (1984), (sub nom. *Fayerman Bros. Ltd. v. Peter Ballantyne Indian Band*) [1986] 1 C.N.L.R. 6 (Sask. Q.B.) and *Fricke v. Michell* (1985), (sub nom. *Fricke v. Moricetown Indian Band*) [1986] 1 C.N.L.R. 11 (B.C. S.C.).

9 For more information on surrenders, see Jack Woodward, *Native Law* (Scarborough: Carswell, 1998) at Chapter 9.5 [hereinafter *Woodward*].

10 On the subject of surrenders, the *Indian Act*, R.S.C. 1985, c. I-5, s. 37, as am. R.S.C. 1985, C.17 (4th Supp.), s. 2, provides:

(1) Lands in a reserve shall not be sold nor title to them conveyed until they have been absolutely surrendered to Her Majesty pursuant to subsection 38(1) by the band for whose use and benefit in common the reserve was set apart.

(2) Except where this Act otherwise provides, lands in a reserve shall not be leased nor an interest in them granted until they have been surrendered to Her Majesty pursuant to subsection 38(2) by the band for whose use and benefit in common the reserve was set apart.

Section 38 provides:

(1) A band may absolutely surrender to Her Majesty, conditionally or unconditionally, all of the rights and interests of the band and its members in all or part of a reserve.

(2) A band may, conditionally or unconditionally, designate, by way of surrender to Her Majesty that is not absolute, any right or interest of the band and its members in all or part of a reserve, for the purpose of its being leased or a right or interest therein being granted.

11 On the subject of proper surrender procedure, section 39(1) of the *Indian Act* provides:

(1) An absolute surrender or a designation is void unless

(a) it is made to Her Majesty;

(b) it is assented to by a majority of the electors of the band

(i) at a general meeting of the band called by the council of the band,

(ii) at a special meeting of the band called by the Minister for the purpose of considering a proposed absolute surrender or designation, or

(iii) by a referendum as provided in the regulations; and

(c) it is accepted by the Governor in Council.

Unless these steps are followed, there is no conveyance of reserve land (see *Easterbrook v. R.* (1930), [1931] S.C.R. 210 *Hopton v. Pamajewon* (1993), (sub nom. *Skerryvore Ratepayers Assn. v. Shawanaga Indian Band*) [1994] 2 C.N.L.R. 61 (Ont. C.A.), leave to appeal refused (sub nom. *Ontario (Attorney General) v. Pamajewon*) [1994] 3 C.N.L.R. vi (S.C.C.).

However, the presence of an unfair bargain, economic duress or unconscionability do not invalidate a surrender (see *Chippewas of Kettle & Stony Point v. Canada (Attorney General)*, [1998] 3 C.N.L.R. iv (S.C.C.)

Also see Paul Salembeir, "How Many Sheep Make a Flock? An analysis of the Surrender Provisions of the *Indian Act*", [1992] 1 C.N.L.R. 14.

12 On the subject of land after surrender, see, for example, *R. v. Smith* [1983] 1 S.C.R. 554 (S.C.C.). In that case, the Red Bank First Nation from New Brunswick gave a surrender of reserve lands to the federal Crown in 1895 so that the land could be sold on their behalf. The land was not sold by the federal government. Nonetheless, the Supreme Court of Canada held that neither the federal government nor the First Nation had any interest remaining in the land. All federal and Indian interest disappeared at the moment of surrender.

13 On the subject of the Crown's fiduciary obligations respecting surrendered land, in *Guerin v. R.* (1984), [1985] 1 C.N.L.R. 120 (S.C.C.), the Musqueam First Nation surrendered part of its reserve to the Crown in 1957 on the understanding that the Crown would lease the land according to terms agreed upon by the First Nation Council. The Crown leased the land, but on terms less favourable than those agreed to. The Department of Indian Affairs refused to deliver a copy of the lease to the First Nation until 1970. The Supreme Court of Canada held that the Crown was in breach of its fiduciary obligation to the Musqueam First Nation by inducing the First Nation to surrender land on certain terms and then failing to meet those terms during leasing negotiations. This obligation arises out of the concept of Aboriginal title to land, and is confirmed by section 18(1) of the *Indian Act*. Damages were determined by analogy with the principles of trust law, and were fixed at $10 million. See also *Apsassin v. Canada (Department of Indian Affairs & Northern Development)* (1995), (sub nom. *Blueberry River Indian Band v. Canada (Department of Indian Affairs & Northern Development)*) [1996] 2 C.N.L.R. 25 (S.C.C.) and *Semiahmoo Indian Band v. Canada* (1997), [1998] 1 C.N.L.R. 250 (Fed. C.A.).

14 For more information on designated lands see Woodward, *supra* note 9 at Chapter 9.6.

15 On the subject of the Kamloops Amendment, see *Act to Amend the Indian Act*, S.C. 1988, c. 23.

16 For provincial taxation of conditionally surrendered lands, see *Assessment Act*, R.S.O. 1990, c. A16, s. 3.

17 See *Indian Self-Government Enabling Act*, S.B.C 1990, c.52,

18 *Tsawwassen Indian Band v. Delta City* (1997), [1998] 1 C.N.L.R. 290 (B.C. C.A.), leave to appeal refused [1998] 2 C.N.L.R. iv (S.C.C.).

19 For more information on permits, see Woodward, *supra* note 9 at Chapter 9.4.

20 On the subject of the Minister's authority to grant permits, section 18 of the *Indian Act* provides:

(1) Subject to this Act, reserves are held by Her Majesty for the use and benefit of the respective bands for which they were set apart; and subject to this Act and to the terms of any treaty or surrender, the Governor in Council may determine whether any purpose for which lands in a reserve are used or are to be used is for the use and benefit of the band.

(2) The Minister may authorize the use of lands in a reserve for the purpose of Indian schools, the administration of Indian affairs, Indian burial grounds, Indian health projects or, with the consent of the council of the band, for any other purpose for the general welfare of the band, and may take any lands in a reserve required for such purposes, but where an individual Indian, immediately prior to such taking, was entitled to the possession of such lands, compensation for such use shall be paid to the Indian, in such amount as may be agreed between the Indian and the Minister, or, failing agreement, as may be determined in such manner as the Minister may direct.

Section 20 provides that an Indian is entitled to possess land on a reserve with the approval of the Band Council and the Minister. If the Minister withholds permission, the Indian is entitled to occupy the land under a Certificate of Occupation. An Indian can reside on land in accordance with a Certificate of Occupation for a period of up to four years. After that period the Minister must either approve possession or declare that the land is available for the Band Council to re-allot the land.

Section 28(2) provides that the Minister may grant a permit to non-Indians to occupy or use land on a reserve for up to one year, or longer if approved by the Band Council. In *Opetchesaht Indian Band v. Canada* (1997), [1998] 1 C.N.L.R. 134 (S.C.C.) the Supreme Court of Canada upheld an indefinite right of way for B.C. Hydro.

Section 58 provides that the Minister may, with Band approval, "improve or cultivate" reserve lands which are uncultivated or unused, by employing people to do so, by leasing the land or by granting permits to remove sand, gravel and other non-metallic substances from the land. If the lands affected are covered by a Certificate of Possession, the Minister shall pay the individual in possession an amount for rent, the remainder of the proceeds going to the Band.

21 On the subject of permit problems, in one case, *Boyer v. Canada*, [1986] 4 C.N.L.R. 53 (Fed. C.A.), leave to appeal refused (1986), 72 N.R. 365 (note) (S.C.C.), a former chief of the Batchewana had a certificate of occupation approved by the First Nation Council and the Minister. He then

decided to lease the land for development to a corporation of which he and his wife were sole shareholders. The Chief and Council had initially approved in principle the leasing of the land to the corporation. However, Council objected to the final lease provisions and argued that the Minister did not have authority to approve the lease without consent. The Federal Court of Appeal held that the lease was legal and that section 58(3) of the *Indian Act* did not require the Minister to obtain the First Nation's consent before agreeing to the lease.

22 On the subject of personal responsibility for business losses, there are some exceptions to the general rule that the people behind the business are not personally responsible for its debts. For example, under section 131(1) of the *Ontario Business Corporations Act* the directors of a corporation are liable for up to six months' wages and twelve months' vacation pay for the business's employees.

It should be noted that if the lending institution requires a personal guarantee from a shareholder, incorporation will not assist in protecting the shareholder from personal liability.

18

Economic Development

1. INTRODUCTION — SUSTAINABLE DEVELOPMENT

The economic development of reserve lands and traditional territories is important for Aboriginal communities seeking greater financial independence. By reducing dependence on government, the theory goes, Aboriginal people will have more control over their lives.[1]

Economic development can take many forms. According to statistics from the Department of Indian Affairs, there are approximately 20,000 Aboriginal-owned or operated businesses in Canada:[2]

25% business & personal services sector
15.1% are in construction and related industries
16.9% are in the primary or natural resources
18.8% retail/wholesale trade

But, unless Aboriginal communities determine their own needs and priorities for resource development, "economic development" may do more harm than good. The development and sale of natural resources can be a significant source of wealth, but the resources which the land and waters provide are also essential to the survival of Aboriginal peoples. If the traditional sources of wealth are sacrificed for temporary jobs and a share of royalties, communities will end up with little to give future generations. Historically, resource development companies have moved away as resources become depleted, leaving ghost towns behind them. Aboriginal communities can learn from this bleak pattern.

One way to preserve resources for the future is to promote "sustainable development"[3] which will balance needs of the present against the needs of future generations. Canada committed itself to the principles of sustainable development when it signed the *Convention on Biological Diversity* and participated in an international action plan to achieve sustainable development (Agenda 21).[4]

According to Agenda 21, Canada should pursue sustainable development initiatives that accommodate, promote, and strengthen the role of indigenous peoples and their communities by:

- establishing a process which empowers indigenous peoples
- strengthening the role of indigenous people in the national formulation of policies, laws and programs relating to resource management and other development processes which affect them
- facilitating participation of indigenous peoples at local levels in resource management and conservation strategies and other relevant programs established to support and review sustainable development strategies.[5]

2. ECONOMIC DEVELOPMENT ON WHAT LANDS?

It is very important to be aware of the status of the lands which are to be used for resource development because different laws will apply. On Indian reserve lands, there are federal laws which provide for forestry, mining and oil and gas. A very different set of rules applies on lands which are identified under land claims agreements such as the James Bay and Northern Quebec Agreement, or in Nunavut.

3. RESERVE LANDS

Lands identified as Indian reserves under the *Indian Act* are subject to rules under the *Indian Act* and other federal legislation. Reserve lands cannot be bought and sold like non-reserve lands. There are restrictions on uses which usually mean the involvement of the Band Council and the Department of Indian Affairs. (See Chapter 17, "Commercial Relations", for a description of surrender and designation.)

The *Canadian Environmental Assessment Act*[6] sets out requirements for determining the impact that development will have on the land. Before funding is provided for certain projects, the Band Council is required to conduct an assessment.[7] Projects which require assessment include schools, disposal of gravel, operation of a garbage dump, exploration of gas and minerals and burial grounds.[8]

(a) Leasing Land on Reserves

Reserves near urban centres can lease land for residential housing, business parks and malls. Reserves in more rural areas can lease land for cottages.

The terms of the leases range from 20 years to 99 years, although some old leases are for 999 years. The lease will usually provide for a renegotiation of the annual rent every few years. Sometimes, this renegotiation will result in a large increase in the rent because the land has increased in value. This has caused controversy because the non-Aboriginal people renting the land object to the higher rent. If the higher rent is justified by a clause in the lease which ties the rent to the fair market value of comparable land, the court will enforce the higher rent.[9]

In some cases, the First Nation provides a certificate of possession to a member of the First Nation for a large parcel of reserve land. That member can then lease the land to others. For example, he or she can work with an off-reserve developer to set up cottage lots, and sell the leases to non-Indian cottagers. While these projects benefit individual members of the First Nation, they have less benefit to the community as a whole than projects which are run by the First Nation itself.

(b) Natural Resources on-Reserve

Although reserves are generally very small, there is some possibility for selling the natural resources on those reserves.One potential area is forestry. There are 240 First Nations with more than 1000 hectares of forest on reserve. The 1992 Report of the Auditor General of Canada estimates that with improved timber management, timber on reserve land could yield $200 million annually with employment for 10,000 people. The legal requirements for timber management on reserve are set out in the *Indian Timber Regulations.*[10]

Apparently, there are 854 reserves that have potential for sand and gravel development. These activities are authorized through a permit or lease from the Department of Indian Affairs with the consent of the Band Council.[11]

Some Bands in Alberta, for example, become very wealthy due to the revenues from the sale of oil and gas. The exploitation of oil and gas is addressed in the *Indian Oil and Gas Act.*[12] Mineral exploitation on-reserve is regulated by the *Indian Mining Regulations.*[13]

(c) Gaming on-Reserve

Some First Nations try to raise revenue through bingos or gambling. This activity is attractive because it promises a source of funding for community projects. However, gambling, especially high stakes gambling has its drawbacks because of detrimental effects on the community members. Many communities have refused to allow gaming operations on their reserves.

At the present time, it is against the *Criminal Code* to hold any bingos unless the sponsor of the bingo has a licence for charitable gaming from a provincial government. Casino operations that involve slot machines are treated differently. The *Criminal Code* requires that slot machines be operated directly by the province. The province is not permitted to issue a licence to another body to operate slot machines.[14]

In an attempt to challenge the law, Shawanaga First Nation in Ontario enacted its own laws for licensing community bingos, and ran bingos without a provincial licence. The Chief and Councillors were charged under the *Criminal Code* and convicted. The conviction was upheld in the Supreme Court of Canada.[15] Attempts by Bands to enact by-laws on gaming have been rejected by the federal government.[16]

Various provinces have reached arrangements with First Nations concerning gaming. In Ontario, for example, there are two initiatives. First, some reserves have been approved for permanent charitable gaming activities. These reserves do not have VLT's or slot machines, and there are small betting limits. Second, an agreement was reached with all First Nations to locate one full service casino on the Rama reserve, with no betting limits. Proceeds from the casino will be shared among all of the First Nations in Ontario.[17]

In Alberta, the Native Gaming Report recommended that four casinos be licensed on-reserve with 10 per cent of revenues directed to a First Nations trust fund for the benefit of all.[18]

4. NON-RESERVE LANDS

Lands that are either subject to Aboriginal title, or are covered by a treaty provide opportunities for Aboriginal involvement. The *Canadian Environmental Assessment Act*[19] applies to lands where there is a federal interest. Before projects are undertaken, whether by Aboriginal people, or by non-Aboriginal corporations, a study on the environmental impact is necessary. These lands include lands described in land claims agreements and "lands in respect of which Indians have interests."[20]

(a) Aboriginal Title Land

Lands which lie outside *Indian Act* reserves, and which are not covered by a treaty, may be subject to Aboriginal title. (See Chapter 4, "Land") In 1997, the Supreme Court of Canada made a very important decision with respect to lands which are under Aboriginal title for the Gitskan and Wet'suwet'en nations of British Columbia. In *Delgamuukw v. British Columbia*[21] the court made three significant findings:

- First, if Aboriginal title is established, then the Aboriginal nation has exclusive use and occupation of that land. It appears that the uses are not restricted to traditional uses, and could include mining or oil extraction.
- Second, there is a limitation on the use that the Aboriginal nation could make of those lands, in that the nation could not use the land in a way which breaks the special bond the nation has with the land. For example, if hunting is important to that nation, the forests could not be cut so that hunting would be impossible.
- Third, there are some types of developments including settlement, forestry and mining, which could be authorized by the Crown. In these cases, there must be consultation with the Aboriginal nation and appropriate compensation would have to be paid.

As a practical matter, it is not clear how these different elements will interact in a real situation. There has yet to be a case where Aboriginal title has been established under the new rules, and until that happens, the provincial governments appear to be largely ignoring the ruling. Many First Nations are, however, bringing cases to court in relation to their traditional lands.[22]

(b) Treaty Lands

Many treaties provide for the surrender of large tracts of land in return for small reserves. However, the First Nation often has hunting, fishing, and other rights over the land surrendered. The exact nature of the rights depends on the wording of the treaty, but it seems clear that the Aboriginal nation has interests in its traditional lands which cannot be ignored.

For example, the Tsawout First Nation had entered into a treaty in 1852 which recognized their right to a fishery. The First Nation successfully opposed the construction of a marina in Saanichton Bay which would have interfered with their fishery.[23]

While the exact nature of the rights is not clear, the practical result is that there has been an increase in co-management agreements and other mechanisms which facilitate Aboriginal participation in decision-making and resource sharing. An example of such an agreement is the 1993 *Gwaii Haanas Agreement between the Government of*

Canada and the Council of the Haida Nation. The Royal Commission on Aboriginal Peoples described the agreement as follows:

> This agreement is unique in that it contains parallel statements on sovereignty, title and ownership to the archipelago and affirms the parties' willingness to work together, without placing the Haida under the authority of the *National Parks Act.* The agreement also recognizes continued traditional harvesting rights of the Haida and their identification of significant spiritual and cultural sites within the region. All other resource extraction activities are prohibited except for 'essential activities' in support of fishing in adjacent waters. The objective of the agreement is to protect and preserve the archipelago's natural environment and Haida culture for the benefit and education of future generations."[24]

(c) Lands Subject to Land Claims Agreements

Land claims agreements contain detailed provisions for the use of land, both on the reserve and off the reserve. These provisions may cover participation in decision-making for resource projects, revenue sharing, priority for certain types of enterprises and compensation for lost land.

For example, the Gwich'in Comprehensive Land Claim Agreement and the Sahtu Dene and Métis Comprehensive Land Claim Agreement establish the Mackenzie Valley Environmental Impact Assessment and Review Board which will make recommendations to the Minister on development applications. Half the Board members are to be nominated by the Aboriginal parties, and half are to be nominated by the Crown governments.[25] (See Chapter 6, "Inuit", for examples of other co-management boards).

5. ECONOMIC DEVELOPMENT OFF-RESERVE

The discussion above shows that the legal status of the land, and the political power of the Aboriginal communities, will determine the extent to which those communities can participate in the use of their traditional lands. The Department of Indian Affairs has a funding program called Resource Access Negotiations (RAN) which can assist communities access business and employment opportunities and attract investments in the natural resources and tourism sectors.[26]

What initiatives can result is only limited by the imagination. The program has been used to support projects relating to resource co-management, forestry, major off-reserve resource developments and mineral development, agriculture, fisheries, hydro-electric development, oil and gas development, real estate and tourism.[27] For general information on business opportunities, a good place to start is Aboriginal Business Canada. This federal agency provides support, information, and some funding to promote the development of Aboriginal businesses.[28]

6. FISHERIES

The management scheme for fisheries is mixed in Canada with the federal, provincial and First Nation governments playing different roles. Access to fisheries and integration into the management of the fishery resource for First Nations are important components of most land claim settlements.

The Aboriginal Fisheries Strategy (AFS) was created in 1992 to ensure stable fishery management.[29] The AFS seeks to provide for the effective management and regulation of the aboriginal fishery and ensure that the Aboriginal right to fish is respected, through negotiations of mutually acceptable, and time-limited Fisheries Agreements between the Department of Fisheries (DFO) and Aboriginal groups. Where an agreement cannot be reached, the DFO will issue a communal fishing license to the groups allowing them to fish for food, social and ceremonial purposes. Since its implementation, 211 commercial licenses have been issued annually to Aboriginal groups.

Under the AFS, the Aboriginal Allocation Transfer Program (ATP) was created to provide public funds for the retirement of commercial fishing licences and vessels so that the commercial fishing opportunities represented by the licences can be transferred to the Aboriginal people as an economically viable opportunity to participate in the existing commercial fishery. This is accomplished through the issuance of a commercial fishing licence as a communal holding by an Aboriginal group. The ATP provides compensation to commercial licence holders who retire their licences, which are than reissued to Aboriginal groups. There is no restriction on what Aboriginal groups can benefit, but the AFS primarily provides opportunities to Aboriginal groups in the coastal areas of Canada.

With the depletion of the fishery stocks, the development of aquaculture programs has become pressing. Aquaculture is a general term describing the husbandry of aquatic animals or plants. Commercial aquaculture is the culture of aquatic animals or plants for profits. Fish culture (or fish farming) is an example of aquaculture. The annual revenues of aquaculture exceed $220 million and provide more than 5200 jobs. There are a number of government-sponsored programs and DFO has the role of encouraging private-sector development in the aquaculture sector and regional aquaculture coordinators serve as contacts for industry, the provincial government, and the academic community.

ENDNOTES

1 For a full discussion of economic development issues, see the Royal Commission on Aboriginal Peoples, Volume 2, Part 2, *Restructuring the Relationship*, Chapter 5. (Ottawa: Canada Communications Group, 1996) See also Claudia Notzke, *Aboriginal Peoples and Natural Resources in Canada* (North York: Captus University Publications, 1994)

2 *Backgrounder: Economic Development* (Ottawa: DIAND, 1998).

3 *Auditor General Act*, R.S.C. 1985, A-17, as am. 1995, c. 43, s. 1, in force December 15, 1995 (R.A.) interpretation section provides "sustainable development" means development that meets the needs of the present without compromising the ability of future generations to meet their own needs.

4 The Convention on Biological Diversity, 31 I.L.M. 818 (1992) was held in Brazil June 5, 1992 and attended by more than 170 countries. Agenda 21 provides a broad framework for global sustainable development. It was entered into force September 29, 1993. As of December 1995, 137 parties were signatories, including Canada.

5 Chapter 26 "Recognizing and Strengthening the Role of Indigenous People and their Communities" Agenda 21 A/CONF. 151/26 (Vol. III) 14 August 1992.

6 See the *Canadian Environmental Assessment Act*, S.C. 1992, c. 37.

7 s. 10. (1) Before a person or body receives financial assistance provided by a federal authority for the purpose of enabling a project to be carried out in whole or in part on a reserve that is set apart for the use and benefit of a band and that is subject to the *Indian Act*, the council of the band for whose use and benefit the reserve has been set apart shall ensure that an assessment of

> the environmental effects of the project is conducted in accord-
> ance with any regulations made for that purpose under paragraph
> 59(1) as early as is practicable in the planning stages of the project
> and before irrevocable decisions are made.

Canadian Environmental Assessment Act, S.C. 1992, c. 37, s. 10(1).

8 See *Inclusion List Regulations*, SOR/94-637 Part IX.

9 The leading case dealing with the interpretation of leases is *Musqueam Indian Band v. Glass*, [1999] 2 F.C. 138 (Fed. C.A.), additional reasons at (1999), 241 N.R. 194 (Fed. C.A.). This case overturned previous cases which gave a lower value to First Nation land. In the *Musqueam* case, the land had been surrendered for a 99-year lease, with periodic increases in the rent. The land was in "one of the most attractive and desirable locations in Vancouver", and the value of comparable fee simple land in the vicinity was $600,000. The people leasing the reserve land had been paying a very modest rent, which had gone up from $298 per year to $375 per year over a period of 30 years. The lease required that the rent be calculated at "six percent (6%) of the current land value". The Band's attempt to raise the rent to reflect the fair market value of the land was opposed by the lessees.

The court held that the proper interpretation of the words in the lease, were that, in calculating rent, the "current land value" was the value of compa-rable fee simple land. This was consistent with the common law in this area.

> [a] landlord, who puts land out for long-term lease, is entitled to a return on the fee simple value of the land. No distinction can be made for the case of Aboriginal lands and I am of the opinion that the principle enunciated in these cases should govern.

> The view that it should be the land itself that is valued, rather than the tenant's interest, is consistent with case law that suggests that in general a landlord's rent should not be affected by the value of the land to the tenant. For instance, if the tenant does not put the land to its highest and best use, the valuation of the land is not reduced to reflect the tenant's choice [at 158].

10 See *Building a Future: An overview of Resource Development, The Management of Forests on Reserve* (Ottawa: DIAND, 1995) and *Indian Timber Regulations*, C.R.C. 1978, c. 961, as am. SOR/93-244; SOR/94-690; SOR/95-531.

11 For more information on the process, see *Building A Future: An Overview of Resource Development Sand & Gravel* (Ottawa: DIAND, 1993).

12 *Indian Oil and Gas Act*, R.S.C. 1985, c. I-7.

13 *See Indian Mining Regulations*, C.R.C. 1978, c. 956, as am. SOR/90-468 s. 6(1) for process for mineral development on reserve, and *Building a Future: An Overview of Resource Development Metallic Mineral Explorations and Development on Reserves* (Ottawa: DIAND, 1993), also *Report on Aboriginal Participation in Mining* (Ottawa: DIAND, 1997).

14 For the provisions on gaming, see the *Criminal Code*, R.S.C. 1985, c. C-46, s. 207.

15 On the subject of bingos, see *R. v. Jones*, (sub nom. *R. v. Pamajewon*) [1996] 4 C.N.L.R. 164 (S.C.C.) and *R. v. Nelson*, [1999] M.J. No. 382 (Man. C.A.) which held that the sponsoring of gambling was not an Aboriginal right. In *R. v. Bob*, [1991] 2 C.N.L.R. 104 (Sask. C.A.) the defendants were charged with holding a bingo without a licence. Their bingo event met the requirements to qualify for a licence from the province, but they refused to get one on the basis that the licence fee was a tax from which they were exempt. The court agreed, saying that in refusing them a licence unless they paid the fee the province was attempting to collect an unconstitutional tax. The defendants were therefore not at fault in having no licence, and were acquitted.

16 The Federal Court of Appeal upheld the Minister's rejection of a by-law made on gambling under section 81(1)(m) of the *Indian Act*. See *St. Mary's Indian Band v. Canada (Minister of Indian Affairs & Northern Development) (1995)*, [1996] 2 C.N.L.R. 214 (Fed. T.D.), affirmed (1996), [1997] 1 C.N.L.R. 206 (Fed. C.A.), leave to appeal refused [1997] 1 C.N.L.R. iv (S.C.C.).

17 See Chiefs of Ontario, *Revenue Sharing Information Package* (Chiefs of Ontario: 1997) [unpublished].

18 See *Native Gaming Committee Report and Recommendations on Native Gaming* (Government of Alberta, Alberta: April 1996).

19 See the *Canadian Environmental Assessment Act*, S.C. 1992, c. 37.

20 See the *Canadian Environmental Assessment Act*, S.C. 1992, c. 37, s. 48.

21 See *Delgamuukw v. British Columbia* (1997), [1998] 1 C.N.L.R. 14 (S.C.C.)

22 For examples of First Nation opposition to development on their traditional lands, see Chapter 26, "Injunctions and Blockades".

23 In *Claxton v. Saanichton Marina Ltd.*, [1989] 3 C.N.L.R. 114, 13 C.C.C. (3d) 488, 12 D.L.R. (4th) 73 (B.C.C.A.) the First Nation successfully opposed the establishment of a marina which would have interfered with off-reserve treaty rights. In *Halfway River First Nation v. British Columbia (Ministry of Forests)*, [1997] 4 C.N.L.R. 45 (B.C. S.C.), affirmed

(August 12, 1999), Doc. Vancouver CA023526, CA023539 (B.C. C.A.) the British Columbia Supreme Court found that granting a forestry permit without consultation was a breach of rights in Treaty No. 8. In *TransCanada Pipline Ltd. v. Beardmore (Township)* (1997), [1998] 2 C.N.L.R. 240 (Ont. Div. Ct.), leave to appeal allowed (May 25, 1998), Doc. CA M21842 (Ont. C.A.), leave to appeal refused (May 25, 1998), Doc. CA M21857 (Ont. C.A.) the court held that an attempt to expand the boundaries of a municipality without consulting the First Nations affected was not permissible. For a more detailed discussion of First Nation interests in treaty lands, and the possible application of *Delgamuukw v. British Columbia*, see Shin Imai, "Preliminary Thoughts on *Delgamuukw and Treaty Rights*" (1998) 6: 4, 5 & 6 Canada Watch 74 and Patrick Macklem, "The Impact of Treaty 9 on Natural Resource Development in Northern Ontario" in Michael Asch, ed. *Aboriginal and Treaty Rights in Canada: Essays on Law, Equity, and Respect for Difference* Vancouver: UBC Press, 1997, p. 97-134.

24 For a description of the agreement between the Government of Canada and the Council of Haida nation see the Royal Commission on Aboriginal Peoples, *Restructuring the Relationship*, Volume 2, Part 2 (Ottawa: Minister of Supply and Services, 1996) at 751.

25 The *Mackenzie Valley Resource Management Act*, S.C. 1998, c. 25 provides for the implementation of the land claims agreements of the Gwichi'in and the Sahtu Dene and Métis by establishing land use planning boards, land and water boards, and an environmental impact review board. For an examination of current co-management models, see Report of the Royal Commission on Aboriginal Peoples, *Restructuring the Relationship*, Volume 2, Part 2 (Ottawa: Ministry of Supplies and Services Canada, 1996) at 666-680 [hereinafter RCAP, Vol. 2, Part 2).

26 See *Building a Future: Resource Access Negotiations (RAN) Program* (Ottawa: DIAND, 1997); For more information on tourism development see *Building a Future: An Overview of Resource Development, Tourism* (Ottawa: DIAND, 1993).

27 RAN is administered by the Environment and Natural Resources Directorate in the Lands and Trusts Service sector of DIAND. Some examples of Resource co-management: the development by the Opaskwayak Cree Nation in Manitoba of an aquaculture industry to supplement its commercial fishing operation, including the stocking of lakes using young fish produced in the First Nation nursery; the development of a forest fire suppression agreement by the Prince Albert Grand Council and the Province of Saskatchewan which allows Saskatchewan First Nations to supply stand-by fire crew; the negotiation of an agreement relating to a

forest company operating adjacent to the reserve by the Confederation of Mainland Micmacs with Nova Scotia and private sector businesses.

28 Aboriginal Business Canada, Industry Canada, 1st Floor West, 235 Queen Street, Ottawa, Ontario K1A 0H5, telephone (613) 957-7010, fax (613) 957-7010, internet http://abc.gc.ca, email abc.ottawa@ic.gc.ca

29 For more information on DFO's Aboriginal Fisheries Strategy, contact: Aboriginal Fisheries Strategy, Fisheries & Oceans Canada, 200 Kent Street, Station 13194, Ottawa, Ontario K1A 0E6, Tel: (613) 990-6898, Fax: (613) 993-7651

19

Construction Contracts

1. INTRODUCTION

Many First Nations and Aboriginal communities are entering into construction contracts. These projects range from housing to multi-million dollar complexes. To have more Aboriginal involvement on projects, while also having access to the expertise non-Aboriginal construction contractors can offer, Aboriginal groups are looking at innovative ways to structure their projects. These ways include joint ventures, partnerships and sub-contracts. For more information on joint ventures and incorporation, see Chapter 17, "Commercial Relations".

Often Aboriginal groups do not have the legal and financial protections built into non-Aboriginal construction projects. This is partly because some funding sources are not aware of the types of protection which are necessary for carrying out projects, and so cannot communicate the information to the Aboriginal groups.

2. CONTROLLING COSTS

One of the most significant issues in construction is the project's cost. Runaway construction costs have become a major cause of deficits in First Nations' finances. Runaway costs may lead to projects being left uncompleted, or money being taken out of future programs to cover the deficit.

The easiest way to control costs is to hire a general contractor to do the project for a *fixed price*. This means that the contractor will agree to do the whole project for a guaranteed price before the project begins. To get a fixed price contract, the First Nation or Aboriginal organization will have to give the contractor every detail of the project. If something is forgotten at the beginning, or if something has to be added to the work, the contractor may increase the price to cover the extra work.

A fixed price contract may not always be possible or desirable. For example, there may not be any general contractors in the area who want to enter into a fixed price contract for a particular project. In other cases, the First Nation or organization may prefer to run the project itself to have more control.

A second way to organize the project is the "*cost plus*" contract. In this type of contract, a general contractor will charge for a percentage of the cost of materials and labour. For example, if the total cost of materials and labour is $100,000, the contractor may add 15 per cent, making the final price $115,000. Under this type of contract there is no guarantee of price. It is sometimes preferred over the fixed price contract, however, because there is no incentive to inflate initial estimates. As well, it does not encourage contractors to cut corners.

Project management is the third possible arrangement. The First Nation or Aboriginal organization hires a project manager who will organize the project. The project manager will hire the various trades and contractors. If done properly, this method should provide the best price. However, there is no guarantee on the price, and this approach is also the most vulnerable to runaway costs.

3. ORGANIZING THE PROJECT: WHO ARE ALL THESE PEOPLE AND WHAT ARE THEY DOING?

Most construction projects involve a wide range of people doing very different tasks. Knowing the different roles can help the people work together, and increase the chances of the project running smoothly.

The *owner* of the project is the First Nation, Friendship Centre, or community corporation which is organizing the project. The owner may be getting funding from the federal or provincial governments to build. The ultimate responsibility for the project rests with the owner, and the owner will get the benefit of owning the constructed building.

The *owner's representative* is usually the person responsible for monitoring the project for the owner. In the case of an Inuit community corporation, for example, the representative will monitor the project, go to job site meetings, and keep the community council informed of the progress of the project.

The *consultant* is the architect or engineer who assists the owner with the design of the project. This person will help the owner prepare the tenders for the contractors and may also work with the owner throughout the project to ensure the specifications are being met.

The *contractor* is the company responsible for the actual construction. If a general contractor is hired, the contractor will be responsible for all aspects of the project.

The *sub-contractor* is hired by the general contractor to perform specific parts of the contract. For example, a general contractor may hire a sub-contractor to put in the electricity. The sub-contractor works for the contractor, not for the owner.

Some projects will have a *project manager* instead of a general contractor. The project manager is responsible for co-ordinating all aspects of the construction, and monitors the work on the site.

The *employees* will be doing the actual construction. Generally these people will be employed by the contractors. If a project management approach is used, they may be employed directly by the owners.

The *lawyer* is responsible for reviewing all the contracts involved in the project. In a typical project, there may be a contract between the funding source and the owner, a contract between the owner and the consultant, and a contract between the owner and the contractor. The lawyer would also draft any partnership or joint venture agreements. The lawyer may be involved during the project if problems occur with performance of the contracts.

Because of the number of players involved in a project, it is important for the owner to ensure that each one is kept informed of what the others are doing. At the very least, the owner should organize a meeting of the consultant, the contractor, the lawyer, and government representatives before construction starts. What is better is to establish a *steering committee* or *project team* consisting of representatives of the owner and representatives of the Department of Indian Affairs or Public Works. The consultant and the contractor may be part of this project team. This group will be responsible for co-ordinating the project and ensuring that things run smoothly.

4. BONDS AND INSURANCE

Many things can go wrong in a construction project. The contractor may go bankrupt or refuse to complete the work. Someone may get injured, and sue the owner and the contractors; or a half-completed building may burn down. To protect the owners of the projects against these events, it is common to have performance bonds and insurance held by the contractors.[1]

General contractors should carry *general liability insurance*. This type of insurance will cover injuries on the construction site. For example, if a hole is left in the road and someone is injured, both the contractor and the First Nation or Aboriginal group could be sued. The general liability insurance policy is to protect the First Nation or Aboriginal group and the contractor in such a situation. That is why it is important for the policy to include the name of the contractor and the owner of the project.

The contractor should also carry *automobile liability insurance*. If someone gets injured by one of the contractor's vehicles, the insurance can pay the damages.

If a building is going up, it is important to find out who has the *insurance on the building* until the building is completed. If, for example, the building burns down when it is half built and no one has insurance on it, then no one may have the money to build it up again. Usually the owner's insurance policy does not come into force until completion, so it is a good idea to require the contractor to have insurance on the building while it is being put up.

If the contractor also has equipment, the owner might want the contractor to carry *equipment insurance.* Although the loss of the equipment would not be the owner's responsibility, if the contractor goes bankrupt because it does not have money to replace the equipment, the owner is left with a half-completed project.

It is common to require *performance bonds or letters of credit* from contractors. Bonds and letters of credit are moneys set aside by the contractors which the owner can use if the contractor does not finish the project. Suppose a Métis Society is building a $200,000 building and the contractor has a $100,000 performance bond. Half way through the project, the contractor goes bankrupt. In that case, the Métis Society has a right to claim the $100,000 to complete the project. Contribution Agreements from Health and Welfare Canada and Indian Affairs require that owners of the project get performance bonds or letters of credit from their contractors.

Bonds and insurance are not required when the federal or provincial government is carrying out the project itself because the government will arrange the necessary protections. However, when a First Nation, Friendship Centre or Aboriginal corporation decides to do a project itself, insurance and bonds are important. Bonds and insurance add to the cost of contracts. The contractors must be informed in advance, in the tender documents, so that they may consider the cost of these when giving their price for the project.

ENDNOTES

1 For suggested bonds and insurance clauses in construction contracts, see the standard contracts prepared by The Canadian Construction Documents Committee (CCDC). To contact the Committee: Tel. (613) 236-9455 (Ext. 406) Fax: (613) 236-9526 Web address: www.ccdc.org or write the Canadian Construction Association, 400-75 Albert Street, Ottawa, On., K1P 5E7.

20

Taxation

POINTS TO REMEMBER

1. The tax benefits in the *Indian Act* apply only to registered Indians.

2. Registered Indians working on a reserve do not have to pay income tax. Registered Indians in other circumstances may be tax exempt, depending how clearly the income is connected to work on a reserve.

3. Aboriginal people who live off-reserve generally do not have any tax exemptions.

4. Generally, the tax benefits available to registered Indians are also available to Bands.

5. Corporations are not "Indians" even if they are owned by Indians, so corporations generally must pay tax. Corporations owned by Bands may get some tax breaks. Nonprofit corporations get some tax benefits, not because they are "Indian", but because they are not for profit.

1. INTRODUCTION

The tax exemption for registered Indians originated before Confederation. The historic status of the First Nations as independent, self-governing communities is the most likely rationale for the exemption.[1]

Some non-Aboriginal people express resentment at the "special" tax treatment of registered Indians. However, only a minority of Aboriginal people qualify for tax exemption. As well, the widespread poverty of Aboriginal people is such that few would pay much tax even if they were not exempt. On the other hand, most First Nations receive almost no benefits from the economic development which occurs on their traditional territories. It is probably fair to say that they would be glad to pay taxes and royalties if their land was returned to them. Indeed this is the case with the Nisga'a in British Columbia who will be giving up their tax exempt status as part of their land claims treaty.[2]

Under the *Indian Act*, First Nations may tax on-reserve individuals and businesses. More information on this power is provided in the chapter on Band Powers under the *Indian Act*.

This chapter will summarize the taxes imposed by federal and provincial governments and the effect of Aboriginal status on the taxpayers liability.[3] Many of the tax benefits described below apply only on-reserve. There are two types of taxes. The first type of tax is tax on any money coming to the individual such as wages, income from employment insurance, or income from investments. Some are exempt from tax, while others are not. The second type of tax is tax on goods purchased or services received. The exemptions from these types of taxes are only available in very limited circumstances.

2. INDIVIDUALS

Section 87 of the *Indian Act* states that the "personal property of an Indian situated on a reserve" is exempt from tax. Note first that this section is restricted to "Indians." This means that this section cannot apply to Aboriginal people who are not registered even if they live on-reserve. Second, note that the property must be "situated on a reserve" so that it will not help registered Indians off-reserve, unless they have property on a reserve.

(a) Income tax on wages

Whether a registered Indian has to pay income tax on his or her wage depends on whether the income could be considered "the personal property of an Indian . . . on a reserve."[4] If income is taxable, then the employer must make deductions from the employee's paycheque. If the income is tax exempt, deductions for income tax are not necessary.

In 1992, the Supreme Court of Canada decision of *Williams v. Canada*[5] dealt with tax exemption of unemployment insurance benefits. Revenue Canada interpreted this decision as determining income tax exemption as well, and has developed guidelines on when exemption from income tax is available.

The *Williams* case held that several factors must be examined:

- the location of the head office[6]
- the residence of the employee
- the place where the work is performed
- the place where the wages are paid.

If, considering all factors, income is connected to a reserve, then wages paid to a registered Indian would be exempt from income tax. Employers would not deduct income tax from pay cheques.

These guidelines, published in 1994, are not law, nor binding. However, they generally provide an accurate picture of Revenue Canada's position in a given situation.[7] The following is a summary:

1. When at least 90 per cent of the duties of an employment are performed on a reserve, all of the income of an Indian from that employment will usually be exempt from income tax. When less than 90 per cent of the duties of an employment are performed on a reserve and the employment income is not exempted by another guideline, the exemption is prorated. The exemption will apply to the portion of the income related to the duties performed on the reserve.

2. When the employer is resident on a reserve and the Indian lives on a reserve, all of the income of an Indian from an employment will usually be exempt from Income Tax.

3. When more than 50 per cent of the duties of an employment are performed on a reserve and the employee is resident on a reserve, or the Indian lives on a reserve, all of the income of an Indian from an employment will usually be exempt from income tax.

4. When the employer is resident on a reserve and the employer is: an Indian band which has a reserve, or a tribal council representing one or more Indian bands which have reserves, or an Indian organization controlled by one or more such bands or tribal councils, if the organization is dedicated exclusively to the social, cultural, educational or economic development of Indians who for the most part live on reserves; and the duties of the employment are in connection with the employer's noncommercial activities carried on exclusively for the benefit of Indians who for the most part live on reserves; all of the income of an Indian from an employment will usually be exempt from income tax.

It is difficult to predict how courts will decide certain situations. Here are some case examples.

(i) *Majority of logging work off-reserve*

Southwind was a member of the Sagamok First Nation and resided on-reserve. He had a business which involved logging activity for an off-reserve logging company. He was away from the reserve for forty weeks per year, but administered his business from his home. The court held that his income was taxable because his business was not integral to the life of the reserve.[8]

(ii) *Work in a hospital or school close to the reserve*

Two members of Norway House First Nation who lived on-reserve did not have to pay tax on income. The school and the hospital were both located off-reserve, but were adjacent to the reserve, and both institutions primarily served Indians.[9]

(iii) *Work off-reserve for an Indian organization*

The courts have gone both ways on this issue. In an early case, the courts held that employees of the National Indian Brotherhood (forerunner to the Assembly of First Nations) were required to pay tax because their main office was located off-reserve.[10] Recently, the Tax Court of Canada has held that the Executive Director of the Manitoba Indian Education Association, located in Winnipeg, was required to pay tax. However, another member of the Tax Court of Canada held that an employee of the Saskatchewan Treaty Indian Women's Council did not have to pay tax even though most of her work was off-reserve.[11]

(b) Tax on income from an unincorporated business

Income from an unincorporated business is treated as if it is the personal income of the person operating the business. If the permanent establishment of an unincorporated business is located on-reserve, then the profit of a registered Indian operation the business would be tax exempt.

(c) Income tax on scholarships

A registered Indian who lives on-reserve does not have to pay income tax on a scholarship to attend an off-reserve university.[12]

(d) Income tax on employment insurance payments and Canada Pension Plan (CPP)

Everyone has employment insurance premiums taken off his or her pay cheques. When a person stops working, he or she may qualify for employment insurance payments.

The 1992 *Williams* decision decided the issue of whether employment insurance benefits for registered Indians are taxable. The Supreme Court of Canada decided that two factors have to be examined: (1) the location of the income earned giving rise to the unemployment insurance benefit; and (2) the residence of the person claiming unemployment insurance.

If the income giving rise to the employment insurance benefit was tax exempt, then the employment insurance benefits will be tax exempt, too. Since Canada Pension Plan payments are also related to employment, the same rules apply.[13]

(e) Income tax on income from investments[14]

There are many types of investments that will provide income including interest from bank deposits, dividends from shares and rental income. There is no simple answer to deciding whether there will be tax on the income, because the "connecting factors" in each case are different.

Two examples with strong connecting factors to the reserve are the following:

1. An Indian earning income on the reserve deposits money in a bank account on reserve and earns interest on that account.

2. An Indian rents property on the reserve to another Indian.

Two examples where tax may have to be paid are the following:

1. An Indian lives off-reserve, earns income not connected with being an Indian, and deposits money through a bank machine connected to a bank branch located on-reserve.

2. An Indian buys securities from a bank located on a reserve, but the income from the securities is generated outside the reserve in the commercial mainstream.[15]

(f) Income tax on withdrawals from RRSP's and RRIF's

The Tax Court of Canada has found that money withdrawn from a registered retirement savings plan (RRSP) and from a registered retirement income fund (RRIF) were taxable.

The taxpayer was a member of the Mistawasis band in Saskatchewan, but she did not live on-reserve. She was employed as a lawyer in Vancouver. She opened an RRSP and RRIF at a branch of a bank on the Squamish Reserve, and then withdrew amounts from those accounts. She challenged the tax charged on the amounts withdrawn. The court considered a number of connecting factors and decided, among other things, that:

> It cannot be said that the income earned is integral to the life of the reserve. In fact it had nothing to do with the reserve. There is no factor connecting the income to the reserve apart from the fact that the RRSP and the RRIF were opened at the CIBC branch on the reserve (at 2151).[16]

(g) Provincial sales tax on goods purchased

The imposition of provincial sales tax on registered Indians was considered in *Union of New Brunswick Indians v. New Brunswick (Minister of Finance)*. Until 1993, in New Brunswick, and in many other provinces, registered Indians did not have to pay provincial sales tax on goods which were purchased off-reserve for use on-reserve. In 1993, the provincial sales tax legislation was changed to require that sales tax be paid on goods purchased off-reserve, even if the goods were to be used on-reserve. The change in the provincial law in 1993 resulted in protests and road blockades. A test case was brought by the Union of New Brunswick Indians to challenge the provincial decision.

Madam Justice McLachlin, writing for the majority of the Supreme Court of Canada, finds that the sales tax exemption "catches only property physically located on a reserve". As the sales tax was imposed while the property was located physically off the reserve, the goods were not exempt. She rejects the argument that goods, which are destined for future use on the reserve, should be considered to be situated on the reserve.[17]

However, Justice McLachlin makes it clear that when the "point of sale" is on-reserve, registered Indians do not have to pay sales tax, whether they plan to use the goods on or off-reserve. The "point of sale" could be on-reserve, either because there is an on-reserve retailer, or because the goods are delivered to the reserve. For example, she says that a car delivered to the reserve, and sold on the reserve could be tax free.[18]

Justice McLachlin feels that this scheme will provide two benefits to First Nations. First, it will give a competitive edge to on-reserve businesses and encourage on-reserve economies. Second, it will provide a source of revenue for Band taxation. She points out that the Cowichan Tribes in British Columbia have taken advantage of taxing powers granted under the *Budget Implementation Act* to impose tobacco taxes on members of the reserve.[19]

A person who is not a registered Indian must pay sales tax, even for goods bought on reserve.

Here are three examples of how the rules operate:

1. A registered Indian who lives on-reserve buys a table at an off-reserve store to use at his or her house. The table is delivered to the house on the reserve. The Indian will not have to pay provincial sales tax because the table was delivered to the reserve, and will be used on-reserve.

2. A registered Indian who lives on-reserve buys a meal at a restaurant in town. Provincial tax must be paid because the meal is consumed off-reserve.

3. A non-Indian buying something from a craft shop on-reserve has to pay provincial sales tax because the exemption applies to registered Indians only.

(h) Tobacco

Registered Indians living on-reserve do not have to pay provincial tax on cigarettes. In order to limit the illegal sale of cigarettes to non-Aboriginal people, many of the provinces have set quotas on cigarettes for each reserve. This quota system used in Ontario was struck down by an Ontario court in 1989. A different type of quota system was upheld by the British Columbia Court of Appeal and by the Nova Scotia Court of Appeal.[20]

If it is the Band which charges tobacco tax, however, that tax must be paid, even by members of the Band.[21]

(i) Gasoline

Registered Indians on-reserve do not have to pay tax on gasoline which is provided on-reserve.[22] A Nova Scotia court has held that this allows vehicles to use the gasoline off the reserve as well. Peter Paul was a member of the Eskasoni Mi'kmaq Band and lived on the reserve. He bought tax-exempt diesel fuel from a gas station on-reserve and loaded his truck with logs to sell to an off-reserve store in Sydney, Nova Scotia. The province charged him under the provincial *Revenue Act* arguing that he should have to pay tax on the diesel because he was using the truck for commercial purposes off-reserve. The court followed *Union of New Brunswick Indians v. New Brunswick (Minister of Finance)* and held that the "point of sale" was on the reserve, and therefore was tax exempt even if the fuel was used off-reserve.[23]

(j) Other provincial taxes

Registered Indians are exempt from other provincial taxes which might otherwise attach to goods or services located on-reserve. For example, a British Columbia case held that a provincial tax attached to an electricity bill was illegal.[24]

(k) Federal goods and services tax (G.S.T.)

G.S.T. is not payable in the following circumstances:[25]

- on-reserve purchases of goods (e.g. clothing) by registered Indians
- on-reserve purchases of services (eg. small engine repairs) by registered Indians where the benefit will be realized mainly on-reserve
- off-reserve purchases by registered Indians of goods delivered to the reserve by the vendor.

It is important to note that people living on reserves with road access will usually have to pay G.S.T. if they want to bring the goods to the reserve in their own vehicle. There is an exception for remote locations. In a predominantly Aboriginal community such as Moosonee, Ontario, a store located near the reserve and doing 90 per cent of its business with Indians does not have to deliver to the reserve for the purchase to be exempt from G.S.T.

Unincorporated Indian-owned businesses are treated the same way as Indian individuals. In addition, like non-Indian businesses, they can also claim input tax credits for purchases on which they paid G.S.T. (eg. an off-reserve purchase that they did not have delivered).

Incorporated Indian-owned businesses are discussed in the section on "Business corporations owned by private individuals" later in this chapter.

(i) Harmonized Sales Tax (H.S.T.)

The Harmonized Sales Tax (H.S.T.) began on April 1, 1997 in Nova Scotia, New Brunswick & Newfoundland. The H.S.T. replaced the federal G.S.T. and the provincial sales tax in these provinces. The harmonized rate is 15%. Revenue Canada's guidelines state that the H.S.T. applies the same way the G.S.T. did. Good and services sold to Indians, Indian bands, and band-empowered entities that were relieved of tax under the G.S.T. are also relieved under the H.S.T. Likewise, goods and services which were taxable under the GST, remain taxable under the H.S.T.[26]

(ii) Customs duties

Indians claimed that the Jay Treaty, signed in 1794, said that they would not be charged a duty when crossing the border. The Supreme Court of Canada has held, however, that the Jay Treaty has not been adopted into Canadian law, so that the Jay Treaty cannot be used to avoid customs duties.[27] Therefore, the federal government takes the position that most Aboriginal peoples have to pay custom duties when crossing into Canada. However, the Mohawks of Akwesasne in Ontario have proved to the court that they have an Aboriginal right to bring in goods for personal consumption and for "noncommercial scale trade" with other First Nations in Ontario or Quebec.[28] This decision does not apply to *all* First Nations. Each Aboriginal group will have to establish its own Aboriginal right to trade.

(iii) *Other federal taxes*

Indians might not get a reduced price if the producer or manufacturer has already paid federal tax on the goods.[29]

3. BANDS, BAND-CONTROLLED INSTITUTIONS AND TRIBAL COUNCILS

The general rule is that Bands organizations are treated, for tax purposes, like registered Indians, and get the tax breaks provided by the *Indian Act*. Bands and Band-owned corporations may get additional tax advantages because they are treated as municipalities under the *Income Tax Act*.

(a) Tax on income earned

In Canada, municipalities are exempt from taxes for all sources of income. In the *Otineka* case, the Pas Indian Band owned two companies located off-reserve. The Tax Court of Canada stated that the Pas Indian Band should have the same benefits as municipal corporations, and be free from tax on the income earned by the two corporations.[30]

(b) Provincial sales tax

A Band is exempt from provincial sales tax, the same as registered Indians living on-reserve.[31] However, Band Council-controlled corporations must pay provincial sales tax. Again, this is because a corporation is a separate entity, and whether a registered Indian owns or controls it is not taken into consideration for tax purposes.

(c) Federal goods and services tax (G.S.T.)

Bands, Tribal Councils, Band-owned or Band-controlled schools, hospitals and social services are treated in the same way as registered Indians living on-reserve. These tax exemptions are available even if the entities are incorporated.[32] According to G.S.T. guidelines,

"G.S.T. will not apply to services such as legal or accounting services when purchased by an Indian band for band management, or in connection with real property located on-reserve."[33]

(d) Other Federal taxes

Although registered Indians and Bands are not subject to other federal taxes, they may not get a rebate if the price of goods includes taxes already paid during the production and sale process.[34]

4. COMMUNITY NONPROFIT CORPORATIONS

All nonprofit corporations get some tax benefits. These tax benefits have nothing to do with being an Aboriginal organization. They apply to all such organizations both on and off-reserve.

(a) Tax on profits

The general rule is that nonprofit corporations do not have to pay tax on their profits, as long as their profits are used for community purposes.[35] These corporations must still file income tax returns each year. In order to get an exemption from payment of tax on their profits, they should write to a Revenue Canada District Taxation Office, and enclose a copy of the corporation's letters patent.

(b) Provincial sales tax

All provincial sales taxes must be paid, even if the corporation has its head office on a reserve. Again, this is because a corporation is a separate entity. Who owns or controls the corporation is not taken into consideration for tax purposes.[36]

(c) Federal G.S.T. and the Harmonized Sales Tax (H.S.T.)

The G.S.T. must be paid, although there are some exemptions for Band controlled corporations. In Nova Scotia, New Brunswick and Newfoundland, the 15% H.S.T. must be paid in the same way as G.S.T.

5. BUSINESS CORPORATIONS OWNED BY PRIVATE INDIVIDUALS

As a general rule, business corporations owned by private individuals are not eligible for *Indian Act* tax benefits.

Individuals or First Nations may decide to become shareholders in business corporations. These corporations operate like non-Aboriginal businesses. Any profits go into the pockets of the shareholders. There is no requirement that the profits be used for community purposes.

(a) Tax on profits

Corporations pay corporate tax on profits. An accountant's advice will help the corporation minimize its liability to taxes. Because corporations are treated as non-Aboriginal entities, there are no special tax provisions for corporations owned by Aboriginal people.

(b) Provincial sales tax

Because corporations are treated as non-Aboriginal entities, provincial taxes must be paid.

(c) Federal sales tax

Again, because corporations are treated as non-Aboriginal entities, G.S.T. and other federal taxes must be paid.[37]

(d) Harmonized Sales Tax (H.S.T.)

In Nova Scotia, New Brunswick and Newfoundland, the 15% H.S.T. must be paid in the same way as G.S.T.[38]

6. TAXATION BY FIRST NATIONS

Bands have power to impose tax on-reserve, and have attempted to impose tax on non-Aboriginal users of the reserve.[39] (See Chapter 8, "Bands, Band Councils and Reserves", for more information.) Three First Nations in British Columbia have imposed taxes on their own members. The Kamloops Band can tax its members on alcohol, tobacco and fuel; the Westbank Band can tax tobacco and alcohol; and the Cowichan Tribes can tax tobacco. The statutes provide that the tax exemption under section 87 of the *Indian Act* does not apply to the members of these Bands when they are being taxed for these items.[40]

7. ABORIGINAL ORGANIZATIONS LOCATED OFF-RESERVE

There are no special tax provisions for Friendship Centres, locals of the Ontario Métis and Aboriginal Association, and other off-reserve institutions. Such institutions may, however, take advantage of benefits available to nonprofit corporations and charities, which are described above in the section on "Community Non-Profit Corporations".

APPENDIX A

Tax and Corporations		
Corporation: Tax:	Community nonprofit corporation	Business Corporation
Tax on Profits	Exempt if profits are used for community purposes	Tax payable
Provincial Sales Tax	Tax payable	Tax payable
Federal Sales Tax	Tax payable (possible rebate on G.S.T.)	Tax payable

APPENDIX B

Other Taxes			
Taxpayer: **Tax:**	**Registered Indian or unincorporated business of a registered Indian**	**Band**	**Band-controlled institution**
Provincial sales tax on goods purchased on-reserve	Exempt	Exempt	Tax payable if incorporated
Provincial sales tax on goods purchased off-reserve	Tax payable unless goods are delivered on-reserve	Tax payable unless goods are delivered on-reserve	Tax payable if incorporated
Other provincial taxes	Tax payable unless goods are purchased on-reserve or delivered on-reserve	Tax payable unless goods are purchased on-reserve or delivered on-reserve	Tax payable if incorporated
G.S.T. and H.S.T. on goods and services purchased on-reserve	Exempt	Exempt	Exempt
G.S.T. and H.S.T. on goods and services purchased off-reserve	Tax payable unless goods are delivered to reserve by vendor or service is to be supplied on-reserve	Tax payable unless goods are delivered to reserve by vendor or serve is to be supplied on-reserve	Tax payable unless goods are delivered to reserve by vendor or service is to be supplied on-reserve

Other Taxes			
Taxpayer: **Tax:**	**Registered Indian or unincorporated business of a registered Indian**	**Band**	**Band-controlled institution**
Customs duties	Tax payable unless an Aboriginal right to cross-border trade is established	Tax payable unless an Aboriginal right to cross-border trade is established	Tax payable if incorporated
Gasoline tax	Exempt if gasoline is purchased on-reserve	Exempt if gasoline is purchased on-reserve	Tax payable if incorporated
Tax on profits			May be exempt if Band considered a municipality
Income tax	See guidelines on work connected to the reserve		

ENDNOTES

1 In *Mitchell v. Sandy Bay Indian Band*, [1990] 3 C.N.L.R. 46 (S.C.C.), Mr. Justice LaForest stated the reason for the tax exemption:

> I noted above that the Crown, as part of the consideration for the cession of Indian lands, often committed itself to giving goods and services to the natives concerned. . . . The exemptions from taxation and distraint have historically protected the ability of Indians to benefit from this property in two ways. First they guard against the possibility that one branch of government, through the imposition of taxes, could erode the full measure of the benefits given by that branch of government entrusted with the supervision of Indian affairs. Secondly, the protection against attachment ensures that the enforcement of civil

judgments by non-natives will not be allowed to hinder Indians in the untrammelled enjoyment of such advantages as they had retained or might acquire pursuant to the fulfilment by the Crown of its treaty obligations (at 57).

2 The *Nisga'a Final Agreement Act*, S.B.C. 1999, c. 2, Sched., Chapter 16, s. 6 provides that the *Indian Act*, s.87 in respect of transaction taxes will have no application to the Nisga'a citizens eight years from the effective date of the agreement. In respect of all other taxes, the *Indian Act*, s. 87 will have no application 12 years from the effective date of the agreement. As a result, in twenty years, the Nisga'a will no longer be subject to the taxation provisions under s. 87 of the *Indian Act* and the Nisga'a Lisims government may make laws of direct taxation of Nisga'a citizens on Nisga'a Lands.

3 For more information on taxation, see R. H. Bartlett, *Indians and Taxation in Canada*, 3rd ed. (Saskatoon: Native Law Centre, 1992); J. Woodward, *Native Law*, (Toronto: Carswell, 1998), Chapter 12; R.A. Reiter, *The Fundamental Principles of Indian Law*, ch. VII, p. 34-42; and KPMG, *First Nations and Canadian Taxation*, 2nd ed. (Prince George: KPMG, 1997) [hereinafter KPMG].

4 These words are quoted from Section 87 of the *Indian Act*.

5 For an analysis of the tax implications of *Williams v. R.*, [1992] 3 C.N.L.R. 181 (S.C.C.) within an historical context, see Richard H. Bartlett, *Indians and Taxation in Canada*, 3rd ed., (Saskatoon: Native Law Centre, 1992), Chapter 8.

6 The following criteria have been established by Revenue Canada for determining whether business is considered on-reserve:

- the location of the head office
- the location where business transactions are made
- the location where employees work and are paid
- the location where the physical activities are carried out
- the location of where the product/efforts of business are carried out
- the location of where contracts are executed and maintained
- the nature of the product delivered/provided by the business
- who the customer is (i.e. Aboriginal vs. non-Aboriginal)
- the location where repairs and maintenance are carried out
- the location of physical assets

See KPMG, *supra* note 3 at 33-34.

7 See Interpretation Bulletin IT-397RSR S.R.(July 15, 1995) and *Indian Act Exemption For Employment Income Guidelines* (June 1994)

8 Tax must be paid because work was off-reserve : *Southwind v. R.*, [1998] 2 C.N.L.R. 233 (Fed. C.A.). See also *Walkus v. R.*, [1998] 4 C.T.C. 2526 (T.C.C.); *Amos v. R.* (1998), (sub nom. *Amos v. Canada*) [1999] 1 C.N.L.R. 7 (T.C.C.), reversed [1999] 4 C.T.C. 1 (Fed. C.A.); *Wavey v. Minister of National Revenue*, (sub nom. *Kirkness v. Minister of National Revenue*) [1991] 2 C.T.C. 2028 (T.C.C.)

9 Tax not paid because work was connected to the reserve: *Clarke v. Minister of National Revenue* (1997), (sub nom. *Clarke v. M.N.R.*) 148 D.L.R. (4th) 314 (Fed. C.A.); and *Clarke v. Minister of National Revenue* (1994), (sub nom. *Poker v. Canada (Minister of National Revenue)*) [1995] 1 C.N.L.R. 84, reversed in part (sub nom. *Canada v. Folster*) [1997] 3 F.C. 269 (Fed. C.A.) (Fed. T.D.)

10 *R. v. National Indian Brotherhood* (1978), [1979] 1 F.C. 103 (Fed. T.D.), leave to appeal refused (1986), 66 N.R. 78 (S.C.C.)

11 For contradictory cases on whether employees of Indian organizations located off-reserve have to pay tax, see *Desnomie v. R.*, [1998] 4 C.T.C. 2207 (T.C.C.); *McNab v. Canada*, [1992] 4 C.N.L.R. 52 (T.C.C.).

12 On the subject of scholarships held by registered Indians, see *Greyeyes v. R.*, [1978] 2 F.C. 385 (Fed. T.D.). In that case, Greyeyes attended the University of Calgary as a full-time student. Pursuant to a treaty between the federal government and the First Nation of which Greyeyes' was a member, the government provided her with a scholarship to assist her in pursuing her education. Greyeyes did not include the amount of the scholarship in filing her income tax return. The Minister reassessed her income and included the scholarship amount as income. Greyeyes appealed on the basis of the s. 87 exemption.

The court allowed her appeal, holding that the scholarship fell within the s. 87 exemption on the basis that otherwise Greyeyes would have been "subject to taxation in respect of personal property situated on the reserve."

13 See KPMG, *supra* note 3 at 84.

14 For a more thorough discussion on taxation of income from investments, see views of Revenue Canada in TN7-210296 Technical News No. 7 (February 21, 1996) and KPMG, *supra* note 3 at 41-46.

15 Recalma lived on the Qualicam Beach reserve in southern British Columbia. He made investments in securities at a bank branch located on the Squamish reserve. He attempted to claim an exemption from tax for the income from the investments. The court held that the income was from mainstream economic activity located and structured off-reserve. The court found that the income was taxable. See *Recalma v. R.*, (sub nom. *Recalma v. Canada*) [1998] 3 C.N.L.R. 279 (Fed. C.A.), leave to appeal refused

(1998), (sub nom. *Recalma v. Canada*) [1999] 1 C.N.L.R. iv (note) (S.C.C.).

16 For a case finding that withdrawals from RRSP's and RRIF's are taxable, see *Bennett v. R.*, [1999] 3 C.T.C. 2137 (T.C.C. [Informal Procedure]).

17 McLachlan, J. says in the *Union of New Brunswick Indians v. New Brunswick (Minister of Finance)*, [1998] 3 C.N.L.R. 295 (S.C.C.):

> The location of property after the sale and the imposition of tax is irrelevant. This means that goods purchased off-reserve attract tax, while goods purchased on-reserve are exempt, regardless of where the purchaser may intend to use them. To make taxation dependent on place of anticipated use of the article purchased would render the administration of the tax uncertain and unworkable (at 307).

18 In the decision of the British Columbia Court of Appeal in *Danes v. British Columbia*, [1985] 2 C.N.L.R. 18 (B.C. C.A.) a car was delivered to a reserve for sale, and was found to be exempt from provincial sales tax. See *R. v. Paul*, [1999] N.S.J. No. 152 (N.S. Prov. Ct.) at footnote 23 for a case which held that diesel fuel bought tax-free on-reserve could be used in a truck while it was travelling off-reserve.

19 It should be noted Justice McLachlan distinguishes the principles that apply to the imposition of tax on the purchase of goods, from the principles that apply to seizure or taxation of goods *after* they have been purchased. She cites with approval the cases which provide exemption from tax or seizure to goods which do not *always* stay physically situated on-reserve. In *Kingsclear Indian Band v. J.E. Brooks & Associates Ltd.* (1991), [1992] 2 C.N.L.R. 46 (N.B. C.A.) the New Brunswick Court of Appeal held that a reserve school bus was exempt from seizure even though it was used to take children to an off-reserve school. In *Leighton v. British Columbia*, [1989] 3 C.N.L.R. 136 (B.C. C.A.) the British Columbia Court of Appeal held that provincial taxes could not be imposed on a motor vehicle if its "paramount location" was on-reserve. Both of these cases are cited with approval, and distinguished in the majority decision.

Mr. Justice Binnie, wrote a dissenting judgment, concurred in by Mr. Justice Gonthier. Justice Binnie noted that, in reality, delivery would not be available for many ordinarily household items purchased off-reserve. He felt that the section 87 tax exemption should extend to such purchases, and added

> . . . the province seeks to benefit from its 11 per cent impost on on-reserve living expenses under the Social Services and Education Tax which, ironically, does not benefit Indian people on the reserve, who receive such education and services (if at all) from the federal government (at 315).

20 On the subject of tobacco quotas, the case of *Bomberry v. Ontario (Minister of Revenue)*, [1989] 3 C.N.L.R. 27 (Ont. Div. Ct.), leave to appeal refused (1993), [1994] 2 C.N.L.R. vi (note) (Ont. C.A.) held that tobacco quotas imposed on Indian on-reserve retailers are invalid. The Court ruled that the Ministry had no legal authority to impose quotas, and that to do so was tantamount to restricting an individual's freedom before he or she was proven guilty of an offence. For a contrary view, see *Tseshaht Indian Band v. British Columbia*, (sub nom. *Tseshaht Band v. British Columbia*) [1992] 4 C.N.L.R. 171 (B.C. C.A.), and *R. v. Murdock* (1996), [1997] 2 C.N.L.R. 103 (N.S. C.A.)

21 See note 39 for Band taxing powers.

22 On the subject of on-reserve gasoline, see *Chehalis Indian Band v. British Columbia* (1988), [1989] 1 C.N.L.R. 62 (B.C. C.A.).

23 In *R. v. Paul*, [1999] N.S.J. No. 152 (N.S. Prov. Ct.) the court said that diesel fuel bought on-reserve could be used in the truck off-reserve.

24 On the subject of taxing a reserve electricity bill, see *Brown v. R.* (1979), [1980] 3 W.W.R. 360 (B.C. C.A.). Brown was living on-reserve in British Columbia. A tax was levied on the electricity delivered to her home. The provincial *Social Services Tax Act* specifically included "electricity" in its definition of "personal property." Brown argued, pursuant to s. 87 of the *Indian Act*, that the electricity should therefore be exempt from tax. The court agreed that electricity is personal property within the meaning of s. 87 and as such is not taxable.

25 For more detailed information on G.S.T. and Indians see the G.S.T. Technical Information Bulletin (B-039R) issued November 25, 1993.

26 See Revenue Canada, News Release, March 1997 "H.S.T. and Indians" (6 April 1997) [hereinafter H.S.T. and Indians].

27 On the subject of customs duties, the Jay Treaty states the following:

It is agreed that it shall at all times be free of His Majesty's subjects, and to citizens of the United States, and also to the Indians dwelling on either side of the said boundary line freely to pass and repass by land or inland navigation, into the respective territories and countries of the two parties, on the continent of America . . . and to navigate all the lakes, rivers and waters thereof, and freely to carry on trade and commerce with each other . . .

"No duty of entry shall ever be levied by either party on peltries brought by land or inland navigation into the said territories, nor shall the Indians passing or repassing with their own proper goods and effects of whatever nature, pay for the same any impost or duty whatever. But goods in bales, or other large packages, unusual among

Indians, shall not be considered as goods belonging bona fide to Indians.

Francis v. R., [1956] S.C.R. 618 (S.C.C.) held that the Jay Treaty was not adopted by Parliament and thus did not become law. The Court held that the privileges which the treaty accorded Indians was required by the events of 1794 and were probably not meant to be perpetual:

> Appreciating fully the obligation of good faith toward these wards of the state, there can be no doubt that the conditions constituting the raison d'être of the clause were and have been considered such as would in foreseeable time disappear.

See also *R. c. Vincent*, [1993] 2 C.N.L.R. 165 (C.A. Ont.), authorisation de pourvoi refusée (sub nom. *Vincent v. R.*) [1993] 4 C.N.L.R. vi, (C.S.C.)

28 The Aboriginal right of the Mohawks of Akwesasne does not extend to bringing in tobacco and firearms. See *Mitchell v. Minister of National Revenue* (1998), (sub nom. *Mitchell v. Canada (Minister of National Revenue)*) [1999] 1 C.N.L.R. 112 (Fed. C.A.).

29 On the subject of prepaid federal taxes, see *Saugeen Indian Band v. R.* (1989), (sub nom. *Saugeen Indian Band v. Canada*) [1990] 2 C.N.L.R. 166 (Fed. C.A.), leave to appeal refused (sub nom. *Saugeen Indian Band v. Canada*) [1990] 3 C.N.L.R. v (S.C.C.). The Saugeen First Nation sought a refund for federal excise taxes paid on certain goods purchased by the First Nation for its use on the reserve. The First Nation claimed exemption pursuant to s. 87 of the *Indian Act*, in that the tax was on "property situated on a reserve" or, alternatively, the tax rendered the First Nation "otherwise subject to taxation in respect of such property."

The First Nation's claim was dismissed. When the taxes on the goods were paid by the producer and manufacturer, the goods had not yet become the First Nation's property. Therefore the taxes were not paid on the personal property of an Indian or a First Nation situated on a reserve. When the First Nation bought the goods for the final price (which may well have included the price of the tax), it was not paying "tax".

30 For a case holding that a Band should receive the same exemption from taxation as a municipality, see *Otineka Development Corp. v. R.*, (sub nom. *Otineka Develoment Corp. v. Canada*) [1994] 2 C.N.L.R. 83 (T.C.C.) and KPMG, *supra* note 3 at 67-70.

31 Property used off-reserve may be tax exempt in situations described in section 980 of the *Retail Sales Tax Act*. For more information, see Woodward, *supra* note 1, at 305-306.

32 According to the G.S.T. Technical Information Bulletin (B-039R), a "Band-empowered school, hospital or social service entity", which is

exempt from the G.S.T., is a corporation, board, council, association, society, or other organization that is owned or controlled by a band, a tribal council, or a group of bands other than a tribal council."

33 For more information on the G.S.T. see Technical Information Bulletin (B-039R).

34 On the subject of prepaid taxes incorporated in a price, see *Saugeen Indian Band v. R, supra*, note 29.

35 On the subject of non-profit corporations, see *Gull Bay Development Corp. v. R.* (1983), [1984] 1 C.N.L.R. 74 (Fed. T.D.). Gull Bay was the employer in the *Nowegijick* case. In a separate and subsequent decision to *Nowegijick*, the court held that the corporation had been incorporated exclusively for social and welfare purposes, and was therefore exempt from taxation under s. 149(1) of the *Income Tax Act*.

36 On the subject of on-reserve corporations and provincial sales tax, see *Kinookimaw Beach Assn. v. Saskatchewan*, [1979] 4 C.N.L.R. 101 (Sask. C.A.), leave to appeal refused (1979), 1 Sask. R. 179. In this case, seven First Nations incorporated a company to operate a resort on-reserve lands. The company purchased capital equipment for use on the land. The province levied an education and hospital tax on the purchases, stating that the corporate entity was not entitled to the exemption pursuant to s. 87 of the *Indian Act*.

The Saskatchewan Court of Appeal refused to lift the "corporate veil" and look to see who the owners were. It held that the separate legal existence of the corporation could not be disregarded, and that to grant the exemption would destroy the legal obligations of the corporate entity.

In *Northwest/Prince Rupert Assessor, Area No. 25 v. N & V Johnson Services Ltd.* (1990), [1991] 1 C.L.N.R. 90 (B.C.C.A.) members of the Gitwangak Band had incorporated to operate a service station and restaurant on-reserve. They had a Certificate of Possession for the land their business occupied and they requested a lease from the Ministry of Indian Affairs so they could get financing from the Federal Business Development Bank. As a result of this lease from the Crown, the land became subject to tax under B.C. *Taxation (Rural Area) Act*, R.S.B.C. 1979, c. 400, and, because the lessee was not an Indian but a corporation the land was no longer exempt from taxation under section 87 of the *Indian Act*. The court reaffirmed that the corporation is a separate and distinct legal entity which "by its nature, . . . can have neither race nor religion or sex."

37 Revenue Canada's administrative policy states that businesses owned by Indians, bands, or band-empowered entities whose annual sales of property and services are more than $30,000, are required to register for the G.S.T. Like other businesses, once registered, they must collect tax on

their sales of property/services unless the sales are made to Indians on-reserve. In determining whether to register for the G.S.T. the business still must include all sales to Indians to determine whether they meet the $30,000 threshold. Vendors must keep evidence that the sales for which no G.S.T. was payable were made to Indians, Indian Bands or band-empowered entities.

Source: Revenue Canada, Policy B-039R — GST Administrative Policy: Application of GST to Indians — (updated 25 November 1993).

38 H.S.T. and Indians, *supra* note 26.

39 See Section 83 of the *Indian Act*, R.S.C. 1985, c. I-5, as am. R.S.C. 1985, c. 32 (1st Supp.); R.S.C. 1985, c. 27 (2nd Supp.), s. 10 (Sched.); R.S.C. 1985, c. 17 (4th Supp.); R.S.C. 1985, c. 43 (4th Supp.); R.S.C. 1985, c. 48 (4th Supp.); S.C. 1990, c. 16; 1990, c. 17; 1992, c. 51, s. 54; 1993, c. 28, s. 78 (Sched. III, items 73, 74); 1996, c. 23, s. 187(e); 1998, c. 30, s. 14(j); 1999, c. 3, s. 69.

40 *Budget Implementation Act, 1997*, S.C. 1997, c. 26, ss. 36, 44 52 and the *Budget Implementation Act, 1998*, S.C. 1998, c. 21, ss. 59, 70) have resulted in providing new taxing powers. The Cowichan Tribes taxing power was upheld in *Large v. Canada (Minister of Justice)* (1997), (B.C. S.C.) (sub nom. *Large (c.o.b. Cowichan Native Tobacco Co.) v. Canada (Minister of Justice)*) [1998] 3 C.N.L.R. 109.

21

Takeover of a Business

1. INTRODUCTION: WHY BUY A BUSINESS?

There are several reasons for deciding to take over an existing business rather than starting a business from scratch:

- the equipment, office location, licences and other things you need for the business are already there
- the people know the business, and there are already customers
- there may be employees and a management team who know how to run the business
- because the business is already up and running, it has probably experienced its first growing pains and corrected early mistakes
- the Aboriginal people can learn about the business and gain expertise in running it

However, in buying an existing business, it is important to be careful of the following things:

- Is the business financially sound? If the person is willing to sell, it may be because there are not enough customers or the business is badly run. The business' financial statements will reveal this information. It might be wise to consult an accountant. Information on who owned the business and who their contacts are will also be useful.
- What is included in the sale? The assets to be transferred should be clearly described and agreed upon before the sale. What condition are they in? Does the business own them outright, or does someone else own them? What contracts with other parties have the previous owners of the business made? Are there any outstanding lawsuits that the business is involved in? The purchaser would be wise to consult a lawyer and accountant about this.
- Is the business likely to meet the expectations of the purchaser? If one of the reasons behind an Aboriginal group's purchase of a business is to create employment, there should be Aboriginal people able and available to take the jobs. Buying a small airline, for example, won't create jobs if no community members have the skills to be pilots, mechanics or bookkeepers.

2. STEPS TO BUYING A BUSINESS

(a) Determine Community Needs

- Is there a service which could be better delivered by the community? For example, the community may be able to buy housing supplies directly, thereby saving the costs of an intermediary.
- Does the community need employment or skills training which an existing business could provide?

(b) Identify Community Human Resources

- Are there people who can run the business?
- Will there be enough customers?

(c) Determine Whether an Individual or the Community is Buying the Business

- Is the business to be run for profit by individual members of the community or is it to be run for the benefit of the community as a whole? This decision will affect how the company is set up.
- A business run for the community's benefit can be registered as a "non-profit corporation," and is eligible for tax advantages. (See Chapter 12, "Community Corporations" for more information.)

(d) Identify Funding Sources

- Several programs — federal, provincial and Aboriginal — can provide funding for economic ventures. Find out which ones have criteria suited to your proposal.
- Many programs will provide funding to conduct a feasibility study before they approve final funding for a takeover.

(e) Get the Team Together

- A project manager from the Aboriginal organization is needed to co-ordinate the whole project from beginning to end, and make sure that everyone is working together.
- Lawyers are needed to draw up contracts, check out the legal title to the property, and structure the corporation.
- Accountants are needed to check out the books and structure the transaction.

(f) Decide How to Carry on the Business After the Takeover

- Should everyone working for the business just carry on?
- If there is a union, there will have to be some negotiations with the union and the employees.
- Who will be in charge of the direction and management of the business?
- Will there be any changes in the way in which the business will be conducted?

22

Employment Relations

1. INTRODUCTION

When First Nations and Aboriginal organizations become employers, they assume a new set of responsibilities. Sometimes these responsibilities become an issue when a conflict emerges, and questions such as the following arise:

- How was the person hired for the job? Was the job advertised, or did someone with the right connections get the job?
- What benefits do the employees get? Are they entitled to vacation pay, sick benefits, or other benefits?
- How does an employer penalize or fire an employee? People who are fired often threaten to sue their employers. How can this be avoided?

- What special considerations apply when a First Nation takes over responsibility for matters formerly controlled by the federal government (education, for example)?

Employment law is a complex area. For First Nations, the problem is further complicated because federal law applies in some cases and provincial law applies in others.

2. FEDERAL OR PROVINCIAL LAW?

The first step in understanding the relationship of employer and employee and their respective rights is to determine whether federal or provincial law applies.

In general, employment relations arising out of the activities which relate to a First Nation or First Nation Council (Band Council) are covered by federal employment law. Federal laws governing employment relations have been held by courts to apply to the following:

- First Nation school teachers and other employees of a First Nation education authority[1]
- First Nation Council (Band Council) employees, and those working on projects of the First Nation, such as housing construction[2]
- An alcohol treatment centre[3]
- First Nation constables who are employed by the First Nation.[4]

On the other hand, provincial laws governing employment relations will apply when the activity is not related to Indian status, rights or privileges, or it is not an undertaking of the First Nation Council (Band Council). For example, in a case involving a business owned by Indians which manufactured shoes on a reserve, the court decided that the governing law was provincial.[5] The court reasoned that there was nothing specifically "Indian" about the business activity of manufacturing shoes, or about the industrial relations within the business. This reasoning would probably apply to most on-reserve businesses that are not related to a First Nation project or do not have specific links to Indian status, lands or rights.[6] Cases in which provincial law was applied include the following:

- An intermediate care facility owned by the Westbank First Nation, which had a majority of non-Aboriginal residents.[7]
- A commercial fishing company owned by the Musqueam First Nation.[8]

Métis organizations have also been found to be subject to provincial laws governing employment relations because they are not "Indians" recognized in the *Indian Act*.[9] As Inuit are not covered under the *Indian Act* either, in most cases, provincial laws will apply to them. In Nunavut, the territorial laws should apply.

Federal occupational health and safety laws will apply when federal employment law applies; likewise provincial occupational health and safety laws will apply when provincial employment law applies.

3. HIRING

A private business may, as a general rule, hire anyone it wishes to, as long as it does not discriminate on unacceptable grounds (see the section below on discrimination in hiring). For example, the owner of a private taxi service on reserve can hire his or her cousins and immediate family.

A community-based institution is different. A First Nation Council, an Inuit economic development corporation or an urban Friendship Centre, ought to operate for the benefit of the whole community. Job openings should therefore be made public, and hiring done by a neutral hiring committee. This does not mean that relatives or friends of the people in charge are disqualified from jobs.[10] It simply means that everyone should be given an equal chance at getting the jobs, and nobody is given special treatment. This is not a legal requirement, but it is recommended in order to keep the confidence of the community members.

Both private businesses and community-based organizations must be careful not to discriminate in ways which contravene the provincial law, such as the Ontario *Human Rights Code*[11] or the *Canadian Human Rights Act*.[12] Under both statutes it is illegal to discriminate on the basis of certain factors such as race, sex and disability.

For example, if an Aboriginal woman is denied employment because of her sex or race, she may file a complaint under the federal or provincial human rights laws. A possible result of the complaint is that she may be awarded the job or financial compensation from the employer.

What if an Aboriginal employer hires only Aboriginal people, and a non-Aboriginal person complains of discrimination? First, the question may be prevented altogether if the job description clearly states the qualifications, such as knowledge of an Aboriginal language or an Aboriginal culture, that are required for the job. Second, it is acceptable to give preference to Aboriginal people if it is part of an affirmative action program.[13]

4. WORKING CONDITIONS

It is good practice to have the employer and employee sign a contract which clearly sets out the working conditions, the procedure for dealing with unsatisfactory work, and the notice period for termination of employment. By doing so, both the employer and the employee will know what to expect from the agreement.

An alternative is to develop general written policies about these matters, and have the parties acknowledge in their contracts that the policies form part of the employment agreement.

Employers and employees forming such policies or entering into such agreements should be aware that there are many laws, both provincial and federal, that guarantee minimum working conditions to employees. These include health and safety regulations as well as laws setting minimum standards for things like wages, total hours of work, and vacations. Union contracts, or contracts of employment usually provide for better benefits than the minimum.

(a) Employment Standards

Standards which most commonly affect employees are briefly outlined in this section. While many standards are similar across the federal, provincial and territorial jurisdictions, they are not uniform. Easy-to-reference summary tables organized by jurisdiction are therefore included for the standards which are discussed. It is important to remember, however, that the text and tables in this chapter provide a summary and generalized information only. To determine a specific question, it is essential to refer to the appropriate statutes and regulations currently in force.

(b) Total Working Hours and Overtime Pay

The maximum number of working hours per week is specified by all jurisdictions, except New Brunswick. This does not mean that overtime is precluded. Most jurisdictions provide that overtime after a certain number of hours per day or total hours per week must be paid at a premium or higher rate than normal. For example, in Alberta, maximums are eight hours per day and 44 hours per week; overtime must be paid at the rate of 1-1/2 times the employee's regular rate any time the employee puts in more than eight hours in one day, or 44 hours in a week. In the federal jurisdiction, maximums are eight hours per day and 48 hours per week; overtime must be paid at the rate of 1-1/2 times the employee's regular rate any time the employee puts in more than eight hours in one day, or 40 hours in a week.

Most jurisdictions provide that payment must be made to an employee for a minimum of three hours. British Columbia provides for a specified time depending upon whether the employee was called in or already on the job. New Brunswick does not deal with minimum hours for payment.

A rest period of at least 24 hours in each week or seven-day period is most commonly provided for, and generally it should be on a Sunday. Some statutes state that the specified number of hours for the rest period is granted consecutively. Ontario offers perhaps the most comprehensive standard to ensure a genuine break from employment duties by setting a rest period of 24 consecutive hours for most employees. Retail employees in Ontario must be granted 36 consecutive hours of rest in every seven-day period.

(c) Statutory Holidays

All Canadian employment standards legislation specify certain days in the year which are annually granted as individual holidays for all employees. Generally these days are paid time off for an employee. This does not necessarily mean that an employee cannot be required to work, particularly for certain classes of employment such as the hospitality industry and essential services. However special conditions are usually linked to obligatory work on a statutory holiday. This can take the form of a replacement day off, or a substantial premium in addition to regular wages for the day.

The number of statutory holidays per year varies from five to nine across the federal, provincial and territorial jurisdictions.

(d) Vacation Entitlement

There are two principal questions about vacations. The first is about the length of service required to qualify for what quantity of time off. The second concerns pay for the vacation time.

In all jurisdictions in Canada, an employee qualifies for vacation time off after twelve months of employment. The specifics of the minimum length of vacation which must be granted vary. Most commonly, the statutes provide for two weeks of annual vacation after the initial twelve months of employment. Vacation usually increases after a certain number of years of service. For example, in the Northwest Territories, employees qualify for two weeks' vacation for each of their first five years, then get three weeks of vacation if they are with the same employer.

Many employers will provide that vacation days are earned at a certain rate per month. Consequently, some employees can take earned days off before the expiration of the full qualifying period given in the statute.

The pay rate for a vacation is linked to its length. Generally, a rate of 3 per cent of annual earnings applies to two-week vacations, and 6 per cent to three-week vacations. Vacation time which has not been taken must be paid when employment is terminated by either the employer or the employee. For part-year employment, the amount is prorated.

Most statutes provide that vacation time must be taken within a certain time period after qualifying for it. Generally the periods range from ten to twelve months.

(e) Child Care Leave

In certain circumstances, employment standards legislation gives women employees protection from job and seniority loss due to absence for pregnancy, childbirth and maternity. Male and female employees requiring leave for adoption or other child care such as a child's serious illness may be protected by standards legislation governing parental leave.

As previously noted, while the standards dealt with in this chapter are not uniform across all the jurisdictions, many of them are similar. The provisions dealing with pregnancy or maternity and parental leaves share some similarities too. The most common length of leave is 17 weeks and generally reinstatement after one of these leaves must be to the same or a comparable position with no loss of seniority or benefits accrued until the leave. In other respects, however, they create a strikingly diverse array of conditions and benefits.

An example of this variation between jurisdictions is the length of service required to qualify for these leaves, which varies from none (Québec), up to twelve months (Alta., Man., N.S., N.W.T., Yukon), or is not specified (B.C., N.B.). Also, the specifications for the notice period by an employee to the employer to take the leave, and to extend the length of leave, are markedly varied.

(f) Bereavement and Sick Leaves

Only federal and Newfoundland employment standards legislation deal specifically with sick leave. All other jurisdictions' legislation do not contain provisions dealing with sick leave.

Minimum standards for bereavement leave, or leave taken at the time of death and/or funeral of family members, are not provided for in Alberta, Manitoba, Nova Scotia and the Northwest Territories statutes. The remaining jurisdictions provide some time off, depending upon the employee's relationship to the deceased, and length of service. Generally, this type of leave is unpaid.

Residents of the Yukon should note that an employment standards provision unique to their territory provides that an employee designated as the funeral potlatch organizer by the family of a deceased member of a First Nation qualifies for up to one week's unpaid leave.

5. UNIONS

Most employees have a right to form a union. This is an important right for workers, and has helped to provide dignity in the work place, fair wages, and protection from arbitrary action by employers.

For employers, the best way to deal with a union is to develop a working arrangement with it. An employer who attempts to prevent the organization of a union may be faced with serious legal consequences.[14]

An employer should provide a fair wage and fair working conditions. If this is the case, having a union is unlikely to hurt the employer.

There are a number of reasons why employers fear unions, but many of the reasons are based upon wrong assumptions. There is, for example, a myth that an employer cannot fire anyone once a union enters the work place. This is not true. As noted below, there are ways to evaluate the work of the employees fairly, and there are ways to terminate employment. Whether a work place is unionized or not, an employer may run into difficulties if he or she does not abide by the law or its contract with employees, or if termination of an employee is not done fairly, for good reason.

Unions are also feared because of their power: a group of people acting together generally have more clout than a single individual. Unions do attempt to gain better conditions for their members, and do assist workers who may otherwise be faced with unsympathetic employers. Aboriginal people, especially those located off-reserve, often work in occupations with unsympathetic employers, and would clearly benefit from union representation.

6. TERMINATING AND DISCIPLINING THE EMPLOYEE WHEN THERE IS NO UNION

If there is a union, the collective agreement will provide for the method of termination and lay-offs.

In a non-unionized work place, the employer should establish an internal evaluation procedure so that the employer and the employee communicate regularly about expectations, performance and points of concern. The records of this on-going procedure will show whether the employer has good reasons to fire someone. Even better, such communication can improve working relations, and help to prevent problems before they arise. The evaluation procedure could be clearly set out in an Employee Agreement, and could provide steps that may be taken before or instead of firing someone, such as warnings or suspensions.

(a) Permanent Employees

A permanent employee may be terminated in two ways: termination for cause, and termination without cause.

(i) *Termination for cause*

First, the employee may be fired "for just cause". This will include such things as theft, dishonesty, neglect of duty, "misconduct" which affects the interests or reputation of the employer, committing a work-related crime, absence without proper permission or reasonable excuse, misrepresentation of skills and general "willful disobedience."

If the employee is guilty of such misconduct, the employer may fire the person right away without giving notice or termination pay. However, there may be a dispute about whether the allegations are true and whether there was in fact just cause for termination without notice. Such a dispute often results in the employee suing for "wrongful dismissal."

(ii) *Termination without cause*

The second way to terminate is by giving notice or pay instead of notice. If this is done, no reason is necessary for the termination. This would be the appropriate approach, if, for example, an employee is terminated because funding for the project has run out. However, there may be a dispute as to the amount of termination notice or pay which is appropriate. This may also be raised in a wrongful dismissal claim.

The time periods for notice for termination without cause under federal and provincial laws are included in the charts which follow. Note that these notice periods are only the minimum required by law. In some cases giving the minimum amount of notice might not be sufficient. An employee could be entitled to more than the minimum, depending on his or her particular circumstances. Relevant circumstances include length of service, type of work, and age, among others.

One way to promote certainty and avoid problems is to develop a fair, standardized policy about how much notice employees will be entitled to. This policy can then be included as part of the Employment Agreement the parties sign at the outset of the relationship.

(iii) *Examples of cases on dismissal*

Each fact situation is different, so that it is difficult to generalize. However, listed below are examples of cases associated with Aboriginal organizations.

- The Tribal Council was found to be justified in dismissing employees who criticized the Tribal Council.[15]
- A Band Council was not justified in dismissing an employee of six years with one month's notice. The court awarded six months' pay.[16]
- An employee of a Métis economic development corporation successfully sued for unjust dismissal when he was fired for failing to obey the head of a Métis political organization with whom he had no employment relationship.[17]
- A financial officer with the Ontario Native Women's Association successfully sued for unjust dismissal.[18]
- Three employees associated with the health programme on reserve were given their jobs back because the Adjudicator in this case found that the only reason they had been fired by the Band was because they practiced traditional Native spirituality.[19]

(b) Term Contract Employees

A person who is hired for a specific period of time (six months, for example) may, of course, be terminated at the end of the time period. He or she may also be terminated for just cause, as described above, at any point before the contract is completed.

7. WHAT RIGHTS DOES A TERMINATED EMPLOYEE HAVE WHEN THERE IS NO UNION?

An employee fired for just cause may claim that the firing was not justified, and an employee fired without cause may be able to claim that appropriate notice was not given.

Where the employer is covered by provincial law, the employee should contact the government department that handles the employment standards legislation.

The *Canada Labour Code* governs employers covered by federal law. A person who is fired may request a written statement from the employer providing the reasons for dismissal. This request must be complied with within 15 days after the request is made. A dismissed employee covered by federal law has 90 days to register a complaint with Labour Canada. An inspector will investigate, possibly accept the complaint and then make recommendations. The Minister will then appoint an adjudicator with all the powers of the Canada Labour Relations Board. Where the adjudicator finds that there has been "unjust dismissal", he or she may require the employer to reinstate the employee, pay compensation, or any other "like thing that it is equitable to require the employer to do."[20]

If the employee thinks he or she is entitled to more than the minimum amount which is provided by the provincial employment standards legislation or the Canada Labour Code, a lawyer may be retained to sue the employer for "wrongful dismissal".

Federal Employment Standards

Total Working Hours and Overtime Pay	Maximum 8 hours per day, 40 hours per week (s. 169). Payment for a minimum of 3 hours. One full day of rest per week, on Sunday when practicable (s. 173). Overtime pay of 1-1/2 times regular rate for more than 8 hours per day or 40 hours per week (s. 174).
Statutory Holidays	New Year's Day, Good Friday, Victoria Day, Canada Day, Labour Day, Thanksgiving Day, Remembrance Day, Christmas Day, Boxing Day (s. 192).
Vacation Entitlement	12-month qualifying period for 2 weeks to be taken within 10 months of entitlement, 3 weeks after 6 years (s. 183). Pay rate is 4% of annual earnings or 6% after 6 consecutive years (s. 183).
Termination/ Notice Periods	Notice period required of employer when employee's service is 3 months or more is 2 weeks (s. 230(1)(a)(b)). Wages are payable within 30 days of termination (s. 247). Employees are not bound by any notice requirements.
Pregnancy/ Maternity or Parental Leave	Pregnancy: 17 weeks (s. 206). Parental: 24 weeks (s. 206(1)). Qualifying period for either leave is 6 months' employment (s. 206). No length extension provisions specified. Employee must give employer 4 weeks' notice (s. 207). Employee is entitled to reinstatement to same or similar position with the same wages and benefits (s. 209(1)). Employment is deemed continuous (s. 209.2(4)).
Bereavement Leave	Up to 3 working days if they fall in the 3 days from date of death of an immediate family member (s. 210). Unpaid in first 3 months of employment, paid at regular wages after 3 months (s. 210(2)).
Sick Leave	At least 12 weeks' leave without pay after 3 months' employment (s. 239).

Alberta Employment Standards	
Total Working Hours and Overtime Pay	Maximum 8 hours per day, 44 hours per week (s. 20). Payment for a minimum of 3 hours. One day of rest per week; 2 days in each 14-day period; 3 days in each 21-day period; or 4 days in each 28-day period (s. 19). Overtime pay of 1-1/2 times regular rate for more than 8 hours per day or 44 hours per week (s. 22).
Statutory Holidays	New Year's Day, Family Day, Good Friday, Victoria Day, Canada Day, Labour Day, Thanksgiving Day, Remembrance Day, Christmas Day (s. 25).
Vacation Entitlement	12-month qualifying period for 2 weeks to be taken within 12 months of entitlement, 3 weeks after 5th and subsequent years (s. 34). Pay rate is 4% of annual earnings or 6% after 5th and subsequent years (s. 40).
Termination/ Notice Periods	Notice period required of employer when employee's service is more than 3 months but less than 2 years is 1 week; 2 or more but less than 4 years, 2 weeks; 4 or more but less than 6 years, 4 weeks; 6 or more but less than 8 years, 5 weeks; 8 or more but less than 10 years, 6 weeks; 10 years or more, 8 weeks (s. 56). Notice periods for employees to employer are 1 week for service over 3 months and under 2 years, or 2 weeks if employed 2 or more years (s. 58). Wages are payable within 3 days of termination with notice and 10 days without notice (s. 10).
Pregnancy/ Maternity or Parental Leave	Adoption: 8 weeks (s. 50). Pregnancy/parental: 18 weeks after 12 months employment. Extension of 3 weeks is possible (s. 45; s.46). Employee must give employer 2 weeks' notice (s. 47). Employee is entitled to reinstatement to same or comparable position with the same wages and 8 weeks benefits available at start of leave (s. 52).

Alberta Employment Standards	
Bereavement Leave	No statutory provision for bereavement leave.
Sick Leave	No statutory provision for sick leave.

British Columbia Employment Standards	
Total Working Hours and Overtime Pay	Maximum 8 hours per day, 40 hours per week (s. 35). Payment for a minimum of 2 hours if called in, or 4 if work already commenced (s. 34). 32 consecutive hours of rest per week are required (s. 36). Overtime pay of 1-1/2 times regular rate for more than 8 hours per day or 40 hours per week. 2 times regular rate is payable for more than 11 hours per day or 48 hours per week (s. 40).
Statutory Holidays	New Year's Day, Good Friday, Victoria Day, Canada Day, 1st Monday in August, Labour Day, Thanksgiving Day, Remembrance Day, Christmas Day (s. 44).
Vacation Entitlement	12-month qualifying period for 2 weeks to be taken within 12 months of entitlement, 3 weeks after 5th and subsequent years (s. 57). Pay rate is 4% of annual earnings or 6% after 5th and subsequent years (s. 58).
Termination/ Notice Periods	Notice period required of employer when employee's service is from 3 to 12 months is 1 week; from 12 months to 3 years, 2 weeks; 3 years, 3 weeks; 4 years or more, 1 additional week for each subsequent year to a maximum of 8 weeks (s. 63). Employees are not bound by any statutory notice requirements. Wages are payable immediately within 48 hours of termination (s. 18).

British Columbia Employment Standards

Maternity or Parental Leave	Pregnancy: 18 weeks; an extension of 6 weeks is possible (s. 50). Parental: 12 weeks; an extension of 5 weeks is possible (s. 51). No qualifying period specified for either leave. Employee must give employer 4 weeks' notice for either leave (s. 50). Employee is entitled to reinstatement to same or comparable position with all wage increases and benefits as though leave had not been taken (s. 54). Employment deemed continuous and employer obliged to continue its benefit plan contributions (s. 56).
Bereavement Leave	Up to 3 days unpaid for the death of an immediate family member (s. 53).
Sick Leave	No statutory provision for sick leave.

Manitoba Employment Standards

Total Working Hours and Overtime Pay	Maximum 8 hours per day, 40 hours per week (s. 10). Payment for a minimum of 3 hours (s. 51). 24 consecutive hours of rest in each 7-day period are required, on Sunday if possible (s. 45). Overtime pay of 1-1/2 times regular rate for more than 8 hours per day or 40 hours per week (s. 17).
Statutory Holidays	New Year's Day, Good Friday, Victoria Day, Canada Day, Labour Day, Thanksgiving Day, Remembrance Day (pay for this day not required unless required to work), Christmas Day (s. 21).
Vacation Entitlement	12-month qualifying period for 2 weeks to be taken within 10 months of entitlement, 3 weeks after 5th and subsequent years (s. 34; s.35). Pay rate 2% of annual earnings (s. 39(2)(a)). Pay rate on termination is 4% of annual earnings or 6% after 5th and subsequent years (s. 44(2)).

Manitoba Employment Standards

Termination/ Notice Periods	Notice period required of employer when employee's service is 30 days or longer: if pay period is monthly or more often, notice must be one pay period; if pay is received less frequently than once per month, then reasonable notice is necessary (s. 61; s.64). Employees are bound by the same statutory notice requirements. Wages are payable within 10 days of termination (s. 86).
Pregnancy/ Maternity or Parental Leave	Pregnancy/Parental: 17 weeks after 12 months employment (s. 53; s.54; s.58). No extension is specified. Employee must give employer 4 weeks' notice for either leave (s. 54). Employee is entitled to reinstatement to same or similar position (s. 60). Employment is deemed continuous (s. 59).
Bereavement Leave	No statutory provision for bereavement leave.
Sick Leave	No statutory provision for sick leave.

New Brunswick Employment Standards

Total Working Hours and Overtime Pay	The number of hours in any day, week or month is not limited by statute (s. 14), nor are the minimum hours for payment specified. 24 consecutive hours of rest per week are required, on Sunday if possible (s. 17). Overtime pay of 1-1/2 times minimum rate for more than 44 hours per week.
Statutory Holidays	New Year's Day, Good Friday, Canada Day, 1st Monday in August, Labour Day, Christmas Day (s. 2).
Vacation Entitlement	Generally a 12-month qualifying period for up to 2 weeks to be taken within 4 months of entitlement (s. 24); based upon 1 vacation day for each calendar month in which employee worked, to a maximum of 2 weeks. Pay rate is 4% of annual earnings (s. 25).

New Brunswick Employment Standards

Termination/ Notice Periods	Notice period required of employer when employee's service is 6 months to five years is 2 weeks; for five years or more employment notice is 4 weeks (s. 30). Employees are not bound by any statutory notice requirements. Wages are payable on date which employee would ordinarily be paid if continued in employment, to a maximum of 21 days after termination (s. 37).
Pregnancy/ Maternity or Parental Leave	Pregnancy: 17 weeks. Employee must give employer 4 months' notice of intent to take leave, and 2 weeks' notice of start date (s. 43). Child Care: 12 weeks. Employee must give employer 4 weeks' notice for a natural child and 4 months' notice for an adoptive child (s. 44.02). No qualifying or extension period specified for either leave. Employee is entitled to reinstatement to same or equivalent position. No loss of seniority, benefits and wages which had accrued to start of leave (s. 44).
Bereavement Leave	Up to 3 days unpaid for death of spouse, child, parent or guardian; 1 day unpaid for grandparents, siblings, parents-in-law and siblings-in-law on day of funeral (s. 44.03).
Sick Leave	No statutory provision for sick leave.

Newfoundland & Labrador Employment Standards

Total Working Hours and Overtime Pay	Maximum 40 hours per week (s. 21). Payment for a minimum of 3 hours (s. 23). 24 consecutive hours of rest per week are required, on Sunday if possible (s. 22). Overtime pay at prescribed hourly rate for each hour in excess of 40 hours per week (s. 25).
Statutory Holidays	New Year's Day, Good Friday, Memorial Day, Labour Day, Christmas Day (s. 14).

Newfoundland & Labrador Employment Standards

Vacation Entitlement	12-month qualifying period for 2 weeks to be taken within 10 months of entitlement (s. 8). Pay rate is 4% of annual earnings for service less than 15 years and 6% for service greater than 15 years (s. 9).
Termination/ Notice Periods	Notice period required of employer when employee's service is 1 month or more and less than 2 years is 1 week; for 2 years or more employment notice is 2 weeks (s. 55). Employees are bound by the same notice requirements as employers (s. 55). Wages are payable within 1 week of termination (s. 33(2)).
Pregnancy/ Maternity or Parental Leave	Pregnancy: 17 weeks after 20 weeks' employment (s. 40; s.43). Parental: 12 weeks after 20 weeks' employment (s. 43.3). No extension period is specified for either leave. Employee must give employer 2 weeks' notice for either leave (s. 40; s.43; s.43.3). Employee is entitled to reinstatement to duties, benefits, and position no less beneficial than prior to leave (s. 43.7). Employment deemed continuous. No accrual of benefits during leave except by agreement (s. 43.8).
Bereavement Leave	1 day paid + 2 days unpaid after 1 month's continuous employment for death of immediate family member (s. 43.10(1)).
Sick Leave	After 6 months' continuous employment and with a medical certificate, employer must grant 5 days of unpaid sick leave in a year (s. 43.10(2)).

Northwest Territories Employment Standards

Total Working Hours and Overtime Pay	Maximum 8 hours per day, 40 hours per week (s. 4). Payment for a minimum of 3 hours. 1 full day of rest per week, on Sunday if possible (s. 10). Overtime rate is 1-1/2 times regular rate for more than 8 hours per day or 40 hours per week (s. 11).
Statutory Holidays	New Year's Day, Good Friday, Victoria Day, Canada Day, 1st Monday in August, Labour Day, Thanksgiving Day, Remembrance Day, Christmas Day (s. 1).
Vacation Entitlement	12-month qualifying period for 2 weeks to be taken within 10 months of entitlement; 3 weeks after 6th and subsequent years (s. 16). Pay rate is 4% of annual earnings or 6% after 6th and subsequent years (s. 19).
Termination/ Notice Periods	Notice period required of employer when employee's service is 90 days or more but less than 3 years is 2 weeks; 3 years or more but less than 4 years, 3 weeks; 4 years or more but less than 5 years, 4 weeks; 5 years or more but less than 6 years, 5 weeks; 6 years or more but less than 7 years, 6 weeks; 7 years or more but less than 8 years, 7 weeks; 8 years or more, 8 weeks (s. 14.03). Wages are payable within 10 days of termination (s. 50(3)). Employees are not bound by any statutory notice requirements.
Pregnancy/ Maternity or Parental Leave	Pregnancy: 17 weeks; extension of 6 weeks is possible (s. 31(2)(3)). Parental: 12 weeks; extension of 5 weeks is possible (s. 34.3). Qualifying period for either leave is 12 months (s. 31; s.34). Employee must give employer 4 weeks' notice for either leave (s. 31(b); s. 34). Employee is entitled to reinstatement to same or comparable position with the same wages and benefits (s. 36). No loss of seniority accrued to commencement of leave. Wage and benefit increments accrue as though leave not taken (s. 36).

Northwest Territories Employment Standards	
Bereavement Leave	No statutory provision for bereavement leave.
Sick Leave	No statutory provision for sick leave.

Nova Scotia Employment Standards	
Total Working Hours and Overtime Pay	Maximum 48 hours per week. Payment for a minimum of 3 hours. 24 consecutive hours of rest in each 7-day period are required, on Sunday if possible (s. 66). Overtime pay at 1-1/2 times minimum rate for more than 48 hours per week.
Statutory Holidays	New Year's Day, Good Friday, Canada Day, Labour Day, Remembrance Day (pay for this day is not required unless required to work), Christmas Day (s. 1).
Vacation Entitlement	12-month qualifying period for 2 weeks to be taken within 10 months of entitlement (s. 32(1)(a)(b)). Pay rate is 4% of annual earnings (s. 32(c)).
Termination/ Notice Periods	Notice period required of employer when employee's service is three months or more and less than 2 years is 1 week; for 2 years or more but less than 5 years, 2 weeks; 5 years or more but less than 10 years, 4 weeks; 10 or more years, 8 weeks (s. 72(1)). Employees are required to give 1 week's notice for employment of more than 3 months but less than 2 years; 2 weeks' notice over 2 years (s. 73(1)). Wages are payable upon expiry of the termination notice period (s. 74).

Nova Scotia Employment Standards

Pregnancy/ Maternity or Parental Leave	Pregnancy/Parental: 17 weeks after 1 year (s. 59(1)). No extension period is specified for either leave. Employee must give employer 4 weeks' notice for either leave (s. 59D(1)(a)(b)). Employee is entitled to reinstatement to same or comparable position and the same wages and benefits. No loss of seniority or benefits accrued to start of leave (s. 59G).
Bereavement Leave	3 unpaid days for death of an immediate family member (s. 60A(a). 1 unpaid day for non-immediate family member (s. 60A(b).
Sick Leave	No statutory provision for sick leave.

Ontario Employment Standards

Working Hours and Overtime Pay	Maximum 8 hours per day, 48 hours per week (s. 17). Payment for a minimum of 3 hours. 24 consecutive hours of rest in every 7-day period are required for most employees, on Sunday if possible (shin: can't find this); 36 consecutive hours of rest in every 7-day period for retail employees (s. 50.1). Overtime pay at 1-1/2 times regular rate for more than 44 hours per week (s. 24).
Statutory Holidays	New Year's Day, Good Friday, Victoria Day, Canada Day, Labour Day, Thanksgiving Day, Christmas Day, Boxing Day (s. 1).
Vacation Entitlement	12-month qualifying period for 2 weeks to be taken within 10 months of entitlement (s. 28). Pay rate is 4% of annual earnings (s. 28(3)).

Ontario Employment Standards

Termination/ Notice Periods	Notice period required of employer when employee's service is three months or more and less than 1 year is 1 week; for 1 year or more but less than 3 years, 2 weeks; 3 years or more but less than 4 years, 3 weeks; 4 years or more but less than 5 years, 4 weeks; 5 years or more but less than 6 years, 5 weeks; 6 years or more but less than 7 years, 6 weeks; 7 years or more but less than 8 years, 7 weeks; 8 years or more, 8 weeks (s. 57). Employees are not bound by any statutory notice requirements. Wages are payable within 7 days of termination (s. 7(4)).
Pregnancy/ Maternity or Parental Leave	Pregnancy: 17 weeks; extension period of 6 weeks is possible (s. 37). Qualifying period is 13 weeks prior to estimated date of delivery (s. 35(1)). Parental: 18 weeks after 13 weeks' employment (s. 38; s.40). No extension period is specified. Employee must give employer 2 weeks' notice for either leave (s. 35). Employee is entitled to reinstatement to same or comparable work and the same wages as at commencement of leave. Seniority and benefits accrue during leave (s. 43).
Bereavement Leave	No statutory provision for bereavement leave.
Sick Leave	No statutory provision for sick leave.

Prince Edward Island Employment Standards

Total Working Hours and Overtime Pay	Maximum 48 hours per week (s. 15). Payment for a minimum of 3 hours. 24 consecutive hours of rest in each 7 days, on Sunday whenever possible (s. 16(1)). Overtime pay at 1-1/2 times minimum rate for more than 48 hours per week (s. 15(4)).
Statutory Holidays	New Year's Day, Good Friday, Canada Day, Labour Day, Christmas Day (s. 6).

Prince Edward Island Employment Standards	
Vacation Entitlement	12-month qualifying period for 2 weeks to be taken within 4 months of entitlement (s. 11). Pay rate is 4% of annual earnings (s. 11).
Termination/ Notice Periods	Notice period required of employer when employee's service is 6 months or more but less than 5 years is 2 weeks; 5 years or more, 4 weeks. Employees are bound by the same notice requirements as employers (s. 29). Wages are payable no later than the last day of the next pay period following termination (s. 30(5)).
Pregnancy/ Maternity or Parental Leave	Maternity/Parental: 17 weeks after 20 weeks' employment (s. 19; s.20). No extension period is specified for either leave. Employee must give employer 4 weeks' notice for either leave (s. 19). Employee is entitled to reinstatement to same or comparable work and the same wages and benefits as though the leave had not been taken (s. 21(1). No loss of seniority or benefits accrued to start of leave, however employer is not obliged to pay pension benefits during leave (s. 21(2)).
Bereavement Leave	Up to 3 consecutive days unpaid for death of an immediate family member, to start no later than the day of the funeral (s. 23).
Sick Leave	Sick leave with pay shall not be considered as vacation pay or pay in lieu of vacation (s. 11(4)).

Quebec Employment Standards	
Working Hours and Overtime Pay	Maximum 44 hours per week (s. 52). Payment for a minimum of 3 hours. 24 consecutive hours of rest per week (s. 78). Overtime premium of 50% of prevailing hourly wage for more than 44 hours per week (s. 55).

Quebec Employment Standards

Statutory Holidays	January 1st, Good Friday, Victoria Day or Dollard Day, National Holiday, Canada Day, Labour Day, Thanksgiving Day, December 25th (s. 60).
Vacation Entitlement	12-month qualifying period for 2 weeks to be taken within 12 months of entitlement; 3 weeks after 5 years' employment (s. 66; s.68; s.69). Pay rate is 4% of annual earnings; 6% after 5 years (s. 74).
Termination/ Notice Periods	Notice period required of employer when employee's service is 3 months or more but less than 1 year is 1 week; 1 year or more but less than 5 years, 2 weeks; 5 years or more but less than 10 years, 4 weeks; 10 years or more, 8 weeks (s. 82). Domestic employees, servants, labourers and journeymen, and their employers/masters are bound by civil code notice requirements of 1 week if hired by the week, 2 weeks if hired by the month, 1 month if hired by the year. Time frame for payment of wages upon termination is not statutorily specified.
Pregnancy/ Maternity or Parental Leave	Pregnancy: 18 weeks. Employee is entitled to reinstatement to same position (s. 81.4). Parental: 52 weeks. Employee is entitled to reinstatement to same or comparable position (s. 81.15). No qualifying period for either leave. Extension is not specified for either leave. Employee must give employer 3 weeks' notice for either leave (s. 81.6; s.81.12). Employee enjoys same rights and benefits as though no leave had been taken (s. 81.16; s.81.17).
Bereavement Leave	1 day paid + up to 3 additional days unpaid for death of married or common-law spouse or child, father, mother, brother or sister (s. 80). 1 day unpaid for death or funeral of other immediate family members (s. 80.1).
Sick Leave	No statutory provision for sick leave.

Saskatchewan Employment Standards

Total Working Hours and Overtime Pay	Maximum 8 hours per day, 40 hours per week (s. 9). Payment for a minimum of 3 hours. 1 day of rest in every 7 days if usually employed over 20 hours per week; 2 days in every 7 days, one of which is Sunday if possible for employers with more than 10 employees (s. 13). Overtime rate is 1-1/2 times regular rate for more than 8 hours per day or 40 hours per week (s. 6(2)).
Statutory Holidays	New Year's Day, Good Friday, Victoria Day, Canada Day, 1st Monday in August, Labour Day, Thanksgiving Day, Remembrance Day, Christmas Day (s. 38).
Vacation Entitlement	12-month qualifying period for 3 weeks to be taken within 12 months of entitlement; 4 weeks on 10th and subsequent anniversaries of employment (s. 30; s.31). Pay rate is 3/52 of annual earnings after one year's service; 4/52 of annual earnings on 10th and subsequent anniversaries (s. 33).
Termination/ Notice Periods	Notice period required of employer when employee's service is 3 months or more but less than 1 year is 1 week; 1 year or more but less than 3 years, 2 weeks; 3 years or more but less than 5 years, 4 weeks; 5 years or more but less than 10 years, 6 weeks; 10 years or more, 8 weeks (s. 43). Outstanding wages must be paid within 14 days of termination (s. 35). Employees are not bound by any statutory notice requirements.

Saskatchewan Employment Standards

Pregnancy/ Maternity or Parental Leave	Pregnancy: 18 weeks; extension of 6 weeks is possible (s. 23; s.24). Adoption: 18 weeks; extension not specified (s. 29(2)). Parental: 12 weeks; extension is not specified (s. 29(1)). Qualifying period for either leave is 20 weeks (s. 23(1)(a); s.29). Employee must give employer 4 weeks' notice for either leave (s. 23(1)(b); s.29(1)(b)(i)(ii). Employee is entitled to reinstatement to same or comparable position at not less than the same wages and benefits. No loss of seniority and pension benefits (s. 26).
Bereavement Leave	Up to 5 working days unpaid after 3 months' employment for death of an immediate family member (s. 29.3).
Sick Leave	No statutory provision for sick leave.

Yukon Employment Standards

Total Working Hours and Overtime Pay	Maximum 8 hours per day, 40 hours per week (s. 6). Payment for a minimum of 2 hours. 2 full days of rest per week, one on Sunday if possible (s. 11). Overtime rate is 1-1/2 times regular rate for more than 8 hours per day or 40 hours per week (s. 8).
Statutory Holidays	New Year's Day, Good Friday, Victoria Day, Canada Day, Labour Day, Thanksgiving Day, Remembrance Day, Christmas Day (s. 1).
Vacation Entitlement	12-month qualifying period for 2 weeks to be taken within 10 months of entitlement (s. 21). Pay rate is 4% of annual earnings (s. 18).

Yukon Employment Standards

Termination/ Notice Periods	Notice period required of employer when employee's service is 6 months or more but less than 1 year is 1 week; 1 year or more but less than 3 years, 2 weeks; 3 years or more but less than 4 years, 3 weeks; 4 years or more but less than 5 years, 4 weeks; 5 years or more but less than 6 years, 5 weeks; 6 years or more but less than 7 years, 6 weeks; 7 years or more but less than 8 years, 7 weeks; 8 years or more, 8 weeks (s. 48). Wages must be paid within 7 days of termination (s. 62(2). Employees with service less than 2 years are bound to give notice of 1 week; for 2 years or more but less than 4 years of service, 2 weeks; for 4 years or more but less than 6 years of service, 3 weeks; for service of 6 years or more, 4 weeks (s. 48(2)).
Pregnancy/ Maternity or Parental Leave	Pregnancy: 17 weeks (s. 36(2)). Parental: 12 weeks (s. 37(1)). Qualifying period for either leave is 12 months (s. 36(a)). Extension is not specified for either leave. Employee must give employer 4 weeks' notice for either leave (s. 36(b)). Employee is entitled to reinstatement to same or comparable position with the same wages and benefits as though leave not taken (s. 39). Employment is deemed continuous (s. 37.2).
Bereavement Leave	1 day unpaid for every month of employment to a maximum of 12 days; leave without pay up to 1 week, during which the funeral falls, for death in immediate family. Up to 1 week leave without pay if designated by the family of a deceased member of a First Nation as the funeral potlatch organizer (s. 58).
Sick Leave	No statutory provision for sick leave.

ENDNOTES

1 For a case applying the Canada Human Rights Code to a First Nations school, see *Qu'Appelle Indian Residential School v. Canada (Human Rights Commission)* (1987), (sub nom. *Qu'Appelle Indian Residential School Council v. Cdn. Human Rights Comm.*) [1989] 2 C.N.L.R. 99 (Fed. T.D.).

In this case the union brought a complaint of sex discrimination to the Canadian Human Rights Commission, alleging that women on staff at the school were not being paid equally for performing work of equal value. The school council brought an application to prevent the Commission from commencing an inquiry, on the grounds that the school's operations fell under provincial jurisdiction and were thus not subject to federal labour relations laws. This application was dismissed. The court stated that:

> [I]t can be concluded that in deciding the jurisdiction of labour relations in a particular case, the focus should not be on who the employer is, who the employees are, where the activity is taking place, or who is funding the activity. Instead at issue is the character or nature of the activity concerned (at 106).

The court decided that the function of the School Council could be "characterized as forming an integral part of the primary federal jurisdiction over Indians and Indian lands" (at 107). The School Council's by-laws and objects linked the school to Indian customs and education. The school was also run by the federal department for a period and had always been funded by and responsible to the federal government. The School Council had also previously accepted federal legislative jurisdiction when it bargained with the union. The result was that ". . . the Council's employees here are so directly involved in activities relating to Indian status, rights and privileges that their labour relations with the Council should be characterized as forming an integral part of the primary federal jurisdiction over Indians and Indian lands, under s. 91(24) of the *Constitution Act, 1867*" (at 109).

See also *M.T.S. v. Fort Alexander Indian Band, infra*, note 14.

2 There are two cases which hold that federal labour law applies to the First Nation Council (Band Council). In *Whitebear Band v. Carpenters Provincial Council (Saskatchewan)* [1982] 3 C.N.L.R. 181 (Sask. C.A.), the Saskatchewan Court of Appeal found that First Nation Council (Band Council) operations are "federal works, undertakings or businesses." Consequently, labour relations between the First Nation and people hired to build houses on a reserve involved First Nation Council operations and fell within federal jurisdiction.

In *Francis v. Canada (Labour Relations Board)*, [1982] 4 C.N.L.R. 94 (S.C.C.), employees of the First Nation Council (Band Council) applied to the Canada Labour Relations Board for certification as a union. The First Nation Council challenged the certification by arguing, among other things, that the Council was not an "employer" under the Canada Labour Code and thus was not subject to the jurisdiction of the Canada Labour Relations Board. The Supreme Court of Canada held that, since the *Indian Act* provides for the creation of the Band Council with the powers to pass by-laws, the enforcement of which requires the hiring of staff, then the Council is an employer for the purposes of the Code. The fact that the Council is not incorporated does not prevent it from having the same duties and liabilities as an individual would by law. To find otherwise would deprive the employees of their rights under the *Canada Labour Code*.

3 See *Sagkeeng Alcohol Rehab Centre Inc. v. Abraham* (1994), [1995] 1 C.N.L.R. 184 (Fed. T.D.) which held that an alcohol rehabilitation centre was designed for Indians.

4 For a case holding that First Nation constables hired by a First Nation Council come under federal labour law, see *Paul Band (Indian Reserve No. 133) v. R.* (1983), (sub nom. *R. v. Paul Indian Band*) [1984] 1 C.N.L.R. 87 (Alta. C.A.). To determine which authority has jurisdiction over labour relations, the court held that one must "look at the normal or habitual activities of the band council as a going concern and at the legislative authority over that operation rather than looking at the particular activities performed by some employees." In this case, the activities performed by local constables formed an integral part of the main operations of the First Nation Council (Band Council). The First Nation had the power to administer First Nation affairs on the reserve; a power derived from the *Indian Act*, and thus fell within exclusive federal jurisdiction under s. 91(24). The labour relations between the Council and the constables were therefore governed by federal legislation.

5 The leading case on the application of provincial labour law is *Four B Manufacturing Ltd. v. U.G.W.*, [1979] 4 C.N.L.R. 21 (S.C.C.).

6 On the subject of the "Indianness" of a business, an exception to the reasoning in this case would be if the business itself was a federally regulated business, such as a bank, in which case federal law would apply.

7 See *Westbank First Nation v. British Columbia (Labour Relations Board)* (1997), 39 C.L.R.B.R. (2d) 227 (B.C. S.C.)

8 See *Celtic Shipyards (1988) Ltd. v. Marine Workers' & Boilermakers' Industrial Union, Local 1* (1994), [1995] 3 C.N.L.R. 41, 94 C.L.L.C. 16,068 (B.C. L.R.B.)

9 A case holding that provincial labour law aplies to an off-reserve Aboriginal group is *O.P.S.E.U. v. Ontario Métis & Non-Status Indians Assn.*, [1980] 3 Can. L.R.B.R. 328 (Ont. L.R.B.)

10 Aboriginal communities are small, and everyone not only knows each other, many people are related in one way or another. In *Wewayakai Indian Band v. Chickite* (1998), (sub nom. *Assu v. Chickite*) [1999] 1 C.N.L.R. 14 (B.C. S.C.), the Band Council hired the common law spouse of one of the Councillors to be an interim Band Manager. That councillor had left the room during the discussions on hiring and salary, and did not vote. However, that councillor's sister and sister in law, who were also members of council, did stay to vote. The court felt that there was no breach of fiduciary duty in this case, and noted the difficulty of defining conflict of interest in a small community.

11 For example, the Ontario *Human Rights Code*, R.S.O. 1990, c. H.19 states in section 5:

(1) Every person has a right to equal treatment with respect to employment without discrimination because of race, ancestry, place of origin, colour, ethnic origin, citizenship, creed, sex, sexual orientation, age, record of offences, marital status, family status or handicap.

(2) Every person who is an employee has a right to freedom from harassment in the workplace by the employer or agent of the employer or by another employee because of race, ancestry, place of origin, colour, ethnic origin, citizenship, creed, age, record of offences, marital status, family status or handicap.

12 *Canadian Human Rights Act*, R.S.C. 1985, c. H-6 as amended. Section 3(1) of the Act states:

For all purposes of this Act, the prohibited grounds of discrimination are race, national or ethnic origin, colour, religion, age, sex, sexual orientation, marital status, family status, disability and conviction for which a pardon has been granted.

13 To discriminate in favour of a particular group over another may be acceptable if the goal of such discrimination is to work towards achieving equality or relieving some group of the disadvantages that it suffers. Section 16(1) of the *Canadian Human Rights Act* states:

It is not a discriminatory practice for a person to adopt or carry out a special program, plan or arrangement designed to prevent disadvantages that are likely to be suffered by, or to eliminate or reduce disadvantages that are suffered by, any group of individuals when those disadvantages would be based on or related to the prohibited grounds of discrimination, by improving opportunities respecting goods, services, facilities, accommodation or employment in relation to that group.

Section 16(2) states that the Commission will provide advice and assistance to individuals on how to implement such plans.

14 See *M.T.S. v. Fort Alexander Indian Band* (1984), [1985] 1 C.N.L.R. 163 (Can. L.R.B.), affirmed (1984), [1985] 1 C.N.L.R. 172 (Fed. T.D.) The teachers employed by the Fort Alexander First Nation, attempted to form a union. The teachers, including First Nation members, applied to the Canadian Labour Relations Board for certification. Three teachers were then banned from the reserve for engaging in union activity. They were later allowed back on the reserve but were fired when they refused to sign individual contracts with the school board. The school board refused to attend conciliation meetings.

The Labour Board held the Chief and Council responsible for the school board's decisions, and ordered the termination notices voided, reinstated the teachers and ordered the school board to refrain from continuing its illegal activities. The Labour Board then acted in place of the school board and settled the terms of a collective agreement with the union. The Labour Board's order was then filed with the Federal Court for enforcement. The school board did not comply with the order. As a result, the court imposed fines of $15,000 on the First Nation, $5,000 on the Chief, $1,000 on Council members, $500 on the school board and $50 for each school superintendent and school board member.

15 For a case where a court upheld the dismissal of employees who criticized the Tribal Council, see *Roseau River Tribal Council v. James*, [1989] 4 C.N.L.R. 149 (Can. Adj. L.R.B.).

16 For a case on wrongful dismissal see *Chadee v. Norway House First Nation* (1996), [1997] 2 C.N.L.R. 48 (Man. C.A.), leave to appeal refused (sub nom. *Norway House First Nation v. Chadee*) [1997] 3 C.N.L.R. iv (S.C.C.).

17 In *Parisien v. Sasknative Economic Development Corp.*, [1999] S.J. No. 417 (Sask.Q.B.), the court was so outraged with the behaviour of some of the Board of Directors that it ordered them to pay the wages personally, and ordered costs on a solicitor and client basis.

18 *Leonard v. Ontario Native Women's Assn.*, [1999] O.J. No. 1990 (O.S.C.).

19 *Charles v. Lac La Ronge Indian Band*, [1999] 2 C.N.L.R. 1 (Can. Labour Code Adj.).

20 See *Canada Labour Code*, R.S.C. 1985, c. L-2, ss. 241, 242, as am.

Justice

23

Criminal Law

POINTS TO REMEMBER

1. The *Criminal Code*, the *Young Offenders Act* and other federal laws dealing with drug offences apply on and off-reserve, whatever the Aboriginal status of the offender or victim. The only limitation is that federal legislation is subject to constitutionally-protected Aboriginal and treaty rights.

2. Provincial legislation generally applies to all Aboriginal people whether on or off-reserve, with a few exceptions. Provincial law, like federal law, is subject to Aboriginal and treaty rights. Provincial law may also be restricted in its application to Indians by federal laws such as the *Indian Act*.

3. *Indian Act* by-laws apply on reserve, and can exclude provincial laws that deal with the same subject matter.

4. Law enforcement is provided by the RCMP, provincial police, municipal police, and First Nations Constables. In addition, some First Nations also appoint their own "Band Constables" to enforce their by-laws.

5. Some First Nation people have their own justice initiatives, such as sentencing circles.

1. INTRODUCTION TO CRIMINAL LAW

Criminal law and Aboriginal people have a long unhappy history. One reason is that criminal laws have been used to prosecute Aboriginal people pursuing traditional activities such as hunting and fishing. Another reason that Aboriginal people, especially in urban centres, have been brought into the criminal justice system in disproportionate numbers. And a third reason is that rigid adherence to the mainstream criminal process has made it very difficult for Aboriginal people to design their own approaches to handling problems in their communities.

Many Aboriginal people argue that they have their own forms of criminal justice which ought to be recognized. The Royal Commission on Aboriginal Peoples agrees that Aboriginal nations have the power to make some of their own criminal laws.[1]

At the present time, however, federal laws, such as the *Criminal Code*, provincial laws, such as the *Highway Traffic Act* and *Indian Act* by-laws, such as alcohol prohibition, are enforced by the police and the provincial justice system.

This chapter describes the process for criminal trials. Aboriginal justice initiatives are described in Chapter 24.

2. THE CRIMINAL PROCESS IN A NUTSHELL

The criminal process usually begins when the police investigate an incident. When they identify an individual, that person is charged with an offence. Following that charge, there may be several appearances in court for a number of reasons including bail hearings, setting a date for the trial, and for pleading guilty or not guilty. If the person charged pleads guilty or takes responsibility for the crime, there may be an agreed punishment such as a fine, community service, or a shorter jail term.

If the person pleads not guilty, there will be a trial before a judge.

At the end of the trial, if the person is found guilty, there will be a hearing on sentencing. At this stage, there will be evidence presented by both the Crown and the defence lawyer about the most appropriate punishment for the crime. There are now many cases when judges will hold "sentencing circles" to get the advice of the victim and other community members on the appropriate sentence.

(a) Types of offences

The two major types of offences are summary conviction and indictable.

Summary conviction offences are less serious. A judge hears summary conviction cases in Provincial Court. There is no choice of court nor is there a right to a jury trial. The maximum punishment for a *Criminal Code* summary conviction offence is a fine of up to $2,000, a jail term of up to six months or both.[2] There is a six-month limitation period for summary conviction offences. No one may charge a person later than six months after the facts occurred.

Indictable offences are more serious crimes. There is more than one procedure for indictable offences. The procedure that applies depends on the seriousness of the offence. Some indictable offences must be tried by a judge in Provincial Court or in Nunavut, of a judge of the Nunavut Court of Justice.[3] No jury trial is available for these offences. Several very serious indictable offences, such as murder, must be tried by a judge and jury unless both the Attorney General and the accused person agree to a trial without a jury.[4] For all other indictable offences the Criminal Code gives the accused person a choice, called an election of the court.

(b) Appearance Notice or Summons

If the police have reason to believe a person has committed an offence, they will issue an appearance notice or a summons. The appearance notice or summons will state the person's name, the offence he or she is charged with, the time, place and date on which he or she is required to go to court or to attend at a police station to have fingerprints taken.

It is imperative that the accused attend at court or police station at the time and date of the notice. Failure to do so may result in another charge, "failure to appear."[5] It is important to arrive early at court and dress neatly.

(c) Arrest

If the police are unable to identify the person, believe the person will commit another offence, or believe the person might not show up for the court date, they might arrest the person. There may or may not be a warrant for the arrest, depending on the circumstances of the investigation. The police must advise anyone they arrest of a right to be represented by a lawyer. When an accused person indicates a desire to speak to a lawyer, the police are obligated to hold off from any efforts to have the accused participate in the police investigation, until the accused has had a reasonable opportunity to speak to the lawyer. The police have the power to release an accused person from custody without a bail hearing.[6] If the police do not release the person, they are obligated to bring the accused before a justice within 24 hours.[7]

Once the accused is brought before the justice, he or she will only be released if granted bail. Usually, release from detention will require "sureties." Employed Canadian citizens, especially family members who are willing to put up cash make ideal sureties. If released, it is important to abide by all the conditions of release.

(d) Charge Screening

At the first appearance, the accused is given "disclosure." This file will have the information surrounding the commission of the offence. It is important to read through this disclosure package as it will be used by the prosecution, and to give the disclosure to the defence lawyer. A Crown Charge Screening Form will also be provided, which explains the charge. The Crown may also suggest whether the offence is one which diversion is suitable.[8] There are diversion projects for adult and youth offenders (Aboriginal and non-Aboriginal) as well as for persons with psychiatric histories. Diversion requires the consent of the accused persons. There must be an acceptance of responsibility for the offence. Instead of a trial, the person may do community service, or take some other steps to correct the problem. Whether the Crown will consent to diversion, depends on a number of factors including the offender's criminal history and the gravity of the offence.

(e) Preliminary appearances

For a minor offence, when the accused person appears in court, he or she will be arraigned, that is, the charge will be read out to him or her. Then the judge will ask how the person pleads to the charge. The choices are guilty or not guilty. If the accused person pleads not guilty, the court will set a date for the trial. For more serious offences, a person may have a choice as to trial court, and may have the option of having a jury.

There may be several other appearances before a trial, including a pre-trial conference with a judge and the Crown Attorney.

A person should always have legal advice before deciding how to plead or deciding which option to choose for the trial.

(f) The Trial

At the trial, the accused person is presumed to be innocent of the charge. It is the Crown Attorney's task to prove beyond a reasonable doubt that the accused person is guilty. The Crown will try to do so by calling witnesses and bringing in physical objects. The accused person has the opportunity to refute the Crown's evidence by questioning the Crown witnesses and presenting evidence that shows his or her side of the story. The Crown also has the opportunity question the accused person's witnesses to reveal further information or discrepancies. The accused person does not have to testify, but if he or she chooses to do so, the Crown has the opportunity to question him or her.

Several Aboriginal accused have argued that they should be judged by juries that include Aboriginal people. Courts have not agreed, and have generally upheld existing procedures for selection juries.[9]

At the end of the trial, if the Crown has not proved the accused person's guilt, the presumption of innocence remains, and the person is free to go. If the Crown succeeds and the person is found guilty, then the court passes sentence.

(g) Sentencing

Before sentencing the guilty person, the court will listen to the lawyers for the accused and for the Crown about what sentence would be appropriate. If the guilty person has a criminal record, the Crown will bring it up. If the person has a good character, family, employment, community support, or unusual or special circumstances, the defence lawyer should tell the court about these factors. The court wants to know about the person's attitude toward the offence; does the person feel remorse or would he or she be willing to do it again?

An Aboriginal person may have special circumstances which are relevant to sentencing. For example, the fact that an Aboriginal person needed a gun to hunt has been taken into account on a weapons charge.[10] The fact that an Aboriginal person was thrown in jail merely for the inability to pay standard fines has led to the quashing of warrants for arrest.[11]

346 THE CRIMINAL PROCESS IN A NUTSHELL

Sentencing for *Criminal Code* offences must now take into account the circumstances of Aboriginal offenders. Under 718.2 (e) of the *Criminal Code,*

> "A court that imposes a sentence shall also take into consideration the following principles:
>
> . . .
>
> (*e*) all available sanctions other than imprisonment that are reasonable in the circumstances should be considered for all offenders, with particular attention to the circumstances of aboriginal offenders."

The Supreme Court of Canada said that this section should address the "tragic over representation" of aboriginal people in the prison system.[12]

There are a great number of possible sentences.

(i) *Jail*

Imprisonment is the most serious sentence under our law because it deprives a person of his or her freedom. The judge may order jail time for a person who is convicted of a serious offence or who is a repeat offender. A person goes to a provincial institution if his or her sentence is less than two years. A person sentenced to two years or more usually goes to a federal penitentiary. There is a range of ways to serve sentences in both the federal and the provincial correctional systems. For example, where a judge orders a sentence of imprisonment for 90 days or less the judge may order that the person serve the sentence[13] intermittently. This type of order allows a person to serve the sentence on weekends and holidays. At the same time, it allows a person to continue working, studying or looking after his or her family while serving a short sentence.

(ii) *Absolute discharge*

A discharge can be given when the person is found guilty or pleads guilty but the judge does not give him or her a sentence. No conviction is entered against the accused person. A person who receives a discharge has not been convicted of a criminal offence and does not need to apply for a pardon (see the section on pardons below).

(iii) *Conditional discharge, suspended sentence, probation, peace bond*

These sentences are all alternatives to jail terms, but they all involve the person having to fulfill certain conditions. For example, they must keep the peace, be of good behaviour, perform community service or pay back the victim for property damage.

(iv) *Fine*

A judge can order the person to pay a fine.[14] A fine is a set amount of money that the person pays to the court. Usually a judge gives a fine alone, but in some cases the judge may order imprisonment and a fine. If the person does not pay the fine, the judge may order the person to go to jail.

A person who cannot pay a fine immediately may be given time to pay. Depending on the amount of the fine, two or three months or more may be allowed to pay. If the whole fine cannot be paid in the time allowed, an extension may be allowed by asking the court office.[15]

(v) *Banishment*

A traditional punishment in many Aboriginal communities was banishment, and this, too, can be ordered by a court.[16] While generally, the courts are reluctant to order banishment, they will do so when banishment is related to the crime and where there may be a cultural background to the practice.

3. CRIMINAL RECORDS AND PARDONS

(a) How to Obtain a Criminal Record Check

A criminal record check may be required to adopt a child, for employment or volunteer work, for border crossing permits and visa applications. Applicants must obtain a form C-216C (fingerprint form) from the local police station and provide fingerprints. There may be a fee, depending on the police jurisdiction. All forms are to be forwarded to: RCMP, Box 8885, Ottawa, Ontario K1G 3M8 Att: CIVIL ENQUIRIES UNIT Telephone (613) 998-6362.

(b) Conditional and Absolute Discharges

All absolute discharges received after July 24 , 1992 are archived after a period one year from the date of the sentence, and purged after five years. Absolute discharges received before July 24, 1992 are purged upon a written request from the individual.

Conditional discharges after July 24, 1992, are archived three years following the date of the sentence, and purged after five years. Those registered before July 24, 1992, are purged upon written request from the individual.

A request to purge records for conditional or absolute discharges before July 24, 1992 are to be made in writing to: RCMP, Box 8885, Ottawa, Ontario K1G 3M8 Att: PURGE UNIT.

(c) How to Apply for a Pardon

After the mandatory waiting period, it is possible to apply for a pardon to erase a criminal record for federal offences. A booklet from the National Parole Board (1-800-874-2652) will explain the process, and the documentation necessary. A lawyer or other representative is not necessary.

The waiting period is calculated from the date the sentence is completed. For example, if the sentence was a fine, the waiting period begins on the date that the fine was paid off. If the sentence was jail or probation, the waiting period begins from the date that the sentence is served — including any part of the sentence served in the community.

For summary convictions, the waiting period is three years. For indictable convictions, the waiting period is five years.

A pardon is not necessary if charges were dismissed, stayed or withdrawn, or they did not result in a conviction.[17]

4. YOUNG OFFENDERS ACT

The *Young Offenders Act* is federal legislation which applies to all people who are over 12 and under 18 at the time they are said to have committed a crime or other federal offence. Young people are not processed through the regular criminal courts. Instead their cases are dealt with in a special Youth Court (although in very serious cases the Crown can apply to have the case transferred to the criminal courts). In either court, the trial process is similar.

Persons under 12 years old are not dealt with by the Youth Court as offenders. They are dealt with under provincial child welfare laws.

Section 4 of the *Young Offenders Act* permits the judge to make use of "alternative measures". An alternative measure could be a community-developed justice process. In appropriate cases the court could hand the young offender over to the community justice process instead of continuing its own process.

5. PROVINCIAL OFFENCES

Most provincial offences apply to Aboriginal people, whether they are on-reserve or off-reserve. The *Highway Traffic Act* is often given as an example of a provincial law that blankets the province.[18] There are some provincial laws that do not apply, however, such as those that infringe Aboriginal or treaty rights, or those that conflict with the *Indian Act*. For more information see Chapter 1, "Constitutional Framework" and see Chapter 3, "Hunting, Fishing and Trapping".

The usual steps for laying a charge are the same as for criminal charges. Provincial offence cases are heard in provincial offences court and can therefore be heard by a Justice of the Peace. All provincial offences are summary conviction offences, which means, in part, that there are never any jury trials.

6. *INDIAN ACT* BY-LAWS

These can be enforced by the RCMP, provincial police, First Nations Constables, or individuals appointed by the First Nation Council for that purpose.[19] Offences against *Indian Act* by-laws are tried in provincial courts or by Justices of the Peace appointed under the *Indian Act*.[20]

The proceedings take place in a summary conviction court which means that the charge must be laid within six months of the incident, and the accused person does not have the option of being heard by a jury.

If a person is found guilty he or she may be liable to a fine of not more than $1000 or to imprisonment for not more than thirty days, or both, depending on what the by-law says and the circumstances of the offence.

(For more information about the authority to make by-laws, see Chapter 8, "Bands, Band Councils and Reserves.")

7. WHAT LAWS APPLY OFF-RESERVE?

Indian Act by-laws only apply on-reserve.[21] Off reserve, all federal and provincial laws apply to Aboriginal people whatever their status. Offences committed off-reserve will usually be tried off-reserve.

The major exception to this rule is the protection provided by treaties or by existing Aboriginal rights. In these cases, federal and provincial laws which curtail these activities may not apply. (For more information on this point, see the Chapter 3, "Hunting, Fishing and Trapping.")

8. WHO ARE THE JUDGES?

Most trials are conducted in the courts of the province. There are three types of decision-makers: Justices of the Peace, judges of the provincial court, and judges of the superior court. A Justice of the Peace (JP) handles offences against provincial laws and *Indian Act* by-laws, and may deal with some pre-trial aspects of charges under the *Criminal Code*. A JP does not necessarily have a background in law. In Ontario, there exists a Native Justice of the Peace Program which recruits and trains Aboriginal people to become JPs. The provincial and *Indian Act* by-law offences on some reserves are handled by Aboriginal JPs.

For most Aboriginal people, the trials are in front of a judge of the provincial court. The province appoints these judges for life. They are required to be lawyers with at least ten years experience.

Trials before juries and the more serious non-jury trials are conducted by judges of the superior court, or court of Queen's Bench. These judges must have been lawyers for at least ten years, and are appointed by the federal government.

9. LEGAL ADVICE FOR THE PERSON CHARGED

When a person is arrested or detained by the police or other agent of government, that person has a right to know the reason why, and to get advice and representation from a lawyer. The person also has the right to be told of their right to legal counsel. There can be no delay in the person's access to these rights.[22]

If a person cannot afford a lawyer, he or she may be eligible for a legal aid from the province. This may be in the form of a legal aid certificate, or assistance from a staff lawyer at a legal aid office. In Ontario, assistance is also available from community legal clinics, five of which are established with particular emphasis on the needs of Aboriginal people.

In courts, duty counsel or a Native Court Worker is available to help unrepresented people with some aspects of their case, such as setting a date for trial or pleading guilty. They can also help with a legal aid application.

For more information on legal aid, community clinics, and community legal workers, see Chapter 25, "Getting Legal Advice".

10. VICTIMS OF CRIME

A person who is the victim of a crime should report it to the police. The police will investigate the crime. They will then lay charges if they conclude charges are warranted, and believe they know who did it. If the police need legal advice about whether to lay a charge, they contact the Crown Attorney.

(a) Laying an Information (Getting someone else charged with an offence)

In some cases, a private citizen can also lay a charge. This could happen if, for some reason, the victim decided not to call the police in the first place, or if the police had decided not to lay a charge and the victim disagreed with their decision. Then the victim can go to a Justice of the Peace (JP) and swear an information. If the JP believes there is substance to the allegations, the JP will issue a summons to court or a warrant for the accused person's arrest.

The accused person will then be tried for the offence. Usually, the trial is conducted by the Crown Attorney, and the person who laid the information will give evidence at the trial. Note that the Crown Attorney, and not the person who laid the information, has the power to decide whether to continue with the prosecution.

Women, especially, might take this route to try to get a peace bond. If the woman has been threatened, assaulted, or property damaged, a peace bond could result in a promise from the accused person to stay away.[23]

(b) Victim Impact Statements (VIS)

The VIS program provides victims of crime the opportunity to describe in writing the effect a crime has had on their lives. The statement is considered by the courts when determining the sentence of an offender.[24] It may be seen by the judge, defence lawyer and the accused. The VIS program is voluntary. Victims of crime choosing to participate in the program can obtain VIS forms and a descriptive brochure from police services, RCMP, or the Crown Attorney's office. Completed statements are retained by police until a charge is laid. After a charge has been laid, police file completed statements with the Court before sentencing. Where applicable, statements considered by the court are forwarded to provincial and federal correctional authorities to be used in pre-release and parole decisions.

(c) Victim Resources

Agencies for women such as helplines, transition houses and women's shelters now exist near most urban centres. Some of these have been established for Aboriginal people.

11. COMPENSATION

Most provinces and territories have established a fund to compensate victims of crime. The rules are different so it is important to check the legislation which applies. The following is a general description of some of the main provisions of this type of program.

There is generally a time limit to make a claim. For example, claims may have to be made within one year, although victims of incest may have an extended deadline. The victim must provide some evidence that a crime occurred. The fact that a matter was reported to the police will be helpful. However, if the crime was a sexual offence and was not reported, the claim will not necessarily fail, but there must be some evidence of the crime.

Costs which are typically covered include funeral expenses, lost wages or income, lost earning ability, damaged clothing, counselling, the cost of replacing glasses and other physical aids, childcare expenses and medication costs. Compensation may be limited for pain and suffering, or not available at all for money or stolen property.

An award may be made as a lump sum or as regular payments. Different provinces and territories have different procedures for awarding the compensation.[25]

12. COMPLAINTS AGAINST PEOPLE ASSOCIATED WITH THE JUSTICE SYSTEM

(a) Lawyers

Lawyers in all jurisdictions are governed by an organization of other lawyers, usually called a law society. Complaints should be made to this body, which has the power to discipline or take away a license to practice (called disbarment).

(b) Judges

Judges are governed by a council made up largely of other judges called a judicial council. Complaints about judges appointed by the province or territory should go to the provincial judicial council, which is usually chaired by the Chief Justice of the province.

A complaint against a federally appointed judge can be made to the Canadian Judicial Council, 112 Kent Street, room 450, Ottawa, K1A 0W8. Their telephone number is (613) 998-5182. The letter should name the judge and explain the complaint in detail. If the complainant has any documents, like a transcript of the proceedings, they should be included. The chairperson of the Judicial Conduct Committee will review the complaint and decide what action to take, and whether this is a matter which should involve the whole Judicial Committee. In the most serious cases of misconduct, the Committee can recommend that the judge be dismissed from office. The final decision on dismissal is up to the Minister of Justice. For less serious cases of misconduct, the judge might receive a reprimand. A letter detailing the results of the matter will be sent to the complainant.

Note that the Judicial Councils' powers are limited to investigating complaints about conduct incompatible with the execution of judicial office. They are not able to review actual decisions. Even if an investigation finds wrongdoing by a judge, the Judicial Councils do not have the power to change the decision. For review of a decision, the issue must be appealed to a higher court.

(c) Police officers

Municipal and provincial police officers are governed by police service boards which are made up of civilians. However, complaints must often be made to the police themselves, and independent investigation of complaints is not widespread.

A complaint against the R.C.M.P. can be made to the R.C.M.P Public Complaints Commission at P.O. Box 3423, Postal Station D, Ottawa K1P 6L4. This is an independent body and is not run by the police. Their telephone number is (613) 993-7267 or toll-free from outside the Ottawa area, 1-800-267-6637.

A complaint can also be made at any R.C.M.P. detachment. Complaints made at a detachment will be investigated by a senior R.C.M.P. officer. At the end of the investigation a letter will be sent to the complainant informing him or her of the findings and conclusions resulting from the investigation. If the complainant is not satisfied, he or she may ask the Public Complaints Commission to review the matter. The Commission has the power to conduct its own inquiry or to order a new one by the R.C.M.P. depending on what it believes is appropriate after examining the investigation documents.

Complaints about First Nation or Tribal Police can be made to the Chief and Council or the reserve's policing committee. There may also be a mechanism for complaints to be made to the affiliated police force, such as the RCMP or the Ontario Provincial Police.

ENDNOTES

1 On the subject of the right of Aboriginal nations to make their own criminal laws, see *Bridging the Cultural Divide: A Report on Aboriginal People and Criminal Justice in Canada*, (Minister of Supply and Services: Ottawa, 1996) at 219-232. On the subject of constitutional authority for Aboriginal systems of justice, see Patrick Macklem, "Aboriginal Peoples, Criminal Justice Initiatives, and the Constitution" (1992) U.B.C. Law

Review and P.A. Okanee and M.E. Turpel, "Aboriginal Peoples and Canadian Criminal Law: Rethinking Justice," (1992) UBC Law Review.

2 *Criminal Code*, s. 787(1) (1997 amendments).

3 *Ibid.*, s. 553.

4 *Ibid.*, s. 469.

5 *Ibid.*, s. 502.

6 *Ibid.*, ss. 496-99.

7 *Ibid.*, s. 503(a).

8 Diversion is an Alternative Measure. Under section 717 of the *Criminal Code* alternative measures may be used to avoid having a trial.

9 For cases discussing the composition of juries, see *R. v. Born With a Tooth* (1993), [1994] 2 C.N.L.R. 96 (Alta. Q.B.); *R. v. Bird*, [1984] 1 C.N.L.R. 122 (Sask. C.A.); *R. v. Kent*, [1986] 4 C.N.L.R. 93 (Man. C.A.); *R. v. Butler* (1984), [1985] 2 C.N.L.R. 107 (B.C. C.A.).

10 On special sentencing for Aboriginal people who need their rifles, see the case of *R. v. Chief* (1989), [1990] 1 C.N.L.R. 92 (Y.T. C.A.) in which a Yukon Indian was convicted of assault and possession of a weapon dangerous to public peace. According to the *Criminal Code*, a conviction for this offence provided that his gun should automatically be taken away for five years. Chief, however, was a trapper and needed his gun to trap and supply meat for his family. The Yukon Territorial Judge refused to apply the minimum five-year prohibition on weapons to Chief, saying that it was cruel and unusual punishment, in conflict with s. 12 of the *Charter*. This decision has been upheld by the Court of Appeal. The court held that the prohibition on guns would have a much more serious impact on Chief than on other people: "Some others may not even be inconvenienced by a five-year prohibition while the appellant is deprived of his livelihood and his lifestyle".

A similar decision has been made by the Ontario District Court. In *R. v. Cozy*, (13 May 1989), 1157/88 (Ont. Dist. Ct.). See also *R. v. McGillivary* (1991), 62 C.C.C. (3d) 407, 89 Sask. R. 289, [1991] 3 C.N.L.R. 113 (Sask. C.A.); *R. v. E.(P.)*, [1990] N.W.T.R. 246 (N.W.T. S.C.), and *R. c. Chabot* (1998), [1999] 1 C.N.L.R. 139 (C.Q.).

But other cases have found that, in the circumstances, a ban on weapons was justified. See *R. v. Tobac*, [1985] N.W.T.R. 201, [1985] 60 A.R. 253, 20 C.C.C. (3d) 49, 15 C.R.R. 356 (N.W.T. C.A.) and *R. v. Johnson* (1994), 31 C.R. (4th) 262, 48 B.C.A.C. 93, 91 C.C.C. (3d) 21 (Y.T.C.A.).

11 In the case of *Hill v. R.* (1990), (sub nom. *Hill v. Canada*) [1991] 2 C.N.L.R. 58 (Ont. Gen. Div.), Hill was an Indian who was poor and alcoholic. Over the years he was charged with and convicted of many

liquor-related offences. At the time of the case, Hill had been in jail for almost a year for a liquor-related break and enter. While he was in jail, more warrants for his imprisonment piled up, forty-four in total, and were tacked onto his sentence. These warrants were issued because Hill did not or could not pay his fines.

The court stated that the legislation intended incarceration for non-payment of fines to be used only as a last resort. The court noted that "a significant portion of our population is still being jailed for the "crime" of being a social nuisance and poor. That portion of our population being so treated is of Native ancestry. The Native community is no longer prepared to be subject to such a situation." The court found that the law was not being properly applied and quashed the outstanding warrants for Hill's committal.

   12 The Supreme Court of Canada interpreted the sentencing principle in *R. v. Gladue*, [1999] 2 C.N.L.R. 252 (S.C.C.).

Tanis Gladue was 19 when she stabbed her husband to death. Although she had been assaulted by him in the past, the trial judge did not find that she was a battered or fearful wife. At issue in this case was the proper application of sentencing principles provided in section 718.2 (e) of the *Criminal Code*.

The Supreme Court held that this provision should effect a change in the law:

> The remedial component of the provision consists not only in the fact that it codifies a principle of sentencing, but, far more importantly, in its direction to sentencing judges to undertake the process of sentencing aboriginal offenders differently, in order to endeavour to achieve a truly fit and proper sentence in the particular case [at para. 33].

The Crown argued that to treat Aboriginal offenders differently would amount to "reverse discrimination". The lawyers for the Aboriginal woman, on the other hand, argued that this provision was an affirmative action provision protected by section 15(2) of the *Charter of Rights and Freedoms*. The court felt that it did not have to address the constitutional validity of this section, but rejected the "reverse discrimination" argument:

> [t]he aim of s. 718.2(*e*) is to reduce the tragic overrepresentation of aboriginal people in prisons. It seeks to ameliorate the present situation and to deal with the particular offence and offender and community. The fact that a court is called upon to take into consideration the unique circumstances surrounding these different parties is not unfair to non-aboriginal people. Rather, the fundamental purpose of s. 718.2(*e*) is to treat aboriginal offenders fairly by taking into account their difference [at para. 87].

In the end, the Supreme Court felt the sentence served by the Aboriginal woman was fair, and no new trial was ordered.

R. v. Logan (1999), 45 M.V.R. (3d) 224 (Ont. C.A.). The principles in *Gladue* were applied in the context of a drinking and driving offence. A member of the Delaware Thames Band who lived on the Moravian Reserve was given a conditional sentence, as opposed to a period of incarceration.

13 *Ibid.*, s. 732(1).

14 *Ibid.*, s. 734(1).

15 *Ibid.*, s. 734(2) the court may consider the offender's ability to pay.

16 For a case on banishment, see *Saila v. R.* (1983), [1984] 1 C.N.L.R. 173 (N.W.T. S.C.), *R. v. Malboeuf*, [1982] 4 C.N.L.R. 116 (Sask. C.A.) and *R. v. Cardinal*, [1999] A.J. No. 482 (Alta. Q.B.)

17 To request a pardon application booklet or for additional information, write or call: Clemency and Pardons Division, National Parole Board, 340 Laurier Avenue West Ottawa, Ontario K1A 0R1 Telephone: 1-800-874-2652.

18 The application of provincial traffic laws on reserve was upheld in *R. v. Francis*, [1988] 4 C.N.L.R. 98 (S.C.C.)

19 People appointed by a First Nation Council to enforce by-laws are often called "Band Constables". Band Constables appointed this way are not the same as First Nations Constables appointed in accordance with the Ontario *Police Services Act*, R.S.O. 1990, c. P.15. In *R. v. Hatchard*, [1993] 1 C.N.L.R. 96 (Ont. Gen. Div.) the court held that a Band Constable was somewhere between a private citizen and a peace officer.

20 There are no only a few Justices of the Peace appointed under section 107 of the *Indian Act*.

21 In *R. v. Lewis*, [1996] 3 C.N.L.R. 131 (S.C.C.) the Supreme Court of Canada held that fishing by-laws did not apply to a river which ran adjacent to a reserve because the river was not part of the reserve.

22 *Canadian Charter of Rights and Freedoms*, s. 10.

23 *Criminal Code*, s. 810

24 *Ibid.*, s. 722 (1)

25 The following are contact addresses, accurate as of 1998.

Ontario:

Criminal Injuries Compensation Board, 439 University Avenue (4th Floor) Toronto, Ontario M5G 1Y8 (416) 326-2900 1-800-372-7463

Northwest Territories:

Criminal Injuries Compensation Officer, Office of the Public Trustee,

Department of Justice, Government of the Northwest Territories, Box 1320 Yellowknife, NT X1A 2L9 (403) 873-7464

Nova Scotia:
Victims Services Division, Nova Scotia Department of Justice, 5151 Terminal Road, 3rd Floor, PO Box 7, Halifax, NS B3J 2L6 Tel. 424-4858

Alberta:
Linda Unger, Secretary to the Crimes Compensation Board, 10365–97 Street, 7th Floor, J.E. Brownlee Building, Edmonton, Alberta T5J 3W7 Phone: 427-7217 Fax: 422-4213

Quebec:
Direction de l'indemnisation des victimes d'actes criminels (IVAC) [of the Commission de la santé et de la sécurité du travail] 1199, rue de Bleury, 9th floor, P.O. Box 6056, Station A, Montréal (Québec) H3C 4E1 Tel.: (514) 873-6019 (for the Montréal area) 1 800 561-IVAC (elsewhere in Québec)

Newfoundland:
Note that the criminal injuries compensation program was terminated in 1993, contact the victim services branch of the Attorney General's office.

British Columbia:
Criminal Injuries Compensation Program is administered by the Workers Compensation Board, call 1-800-563-0808 or visit any police station or Workers Compensation office for an application (see www.wcb.bc.ca/tour/offices.htm for a list of offices).

Saskatchewan
Victims services 787-3500

New Brunswick
Department of the Solicitor General, Victim Services Program, P.O. Box 6000, Fredericton, NB, E3B 5H1 telephone (506) 444 5267.

24

Aboriginal Justice

POINTS TO REMEMBER

"Aboriginal justice" refers to three types of conflict which affect Aboriginal people:

1. Internal community disputes concern members of the Aboriginal community only, and occur entirely within that community. Community-based solutions are the most appropriate for these types of disputes.

2. Reforms to the mainstream system are necessary for disputes which involve Aboriginal people and federal or provincial laws. Most of these disputes arise in the criminal and family law areas. In the past the quality of justice Aboriginal people have received in these disputes has often been poor.

3. Disputes which involve Aboriginal rights can arise when hunting, fishing or other charges are brought against Aboriginal individuals. They can also arise in the context of land claims and self-government negotiations. These disputes require the balancing of interests of Aboriginal and non-Aboriginal people. Therefore, decisions should be made by tribunals which include both.

---

1. INTRODUCTION

In the last decade, lawyers, judges, government policy analysts and Aboriginal people involved in the justice system, have all contributed enormous amounts of time cataloguing, analysing and making recommendations about Aboriginal justice. Major reports from the federal government and most of the provinces, have culminated in the recognition of serious flaws in the system by two major bodies — the Royal Commission on Aboriginal Peoples,[1] and by the Supreme Court of Canada.[2] Overt racism on the part of justice workers; innocent — but just as harmful — misconceptions,[3] cumbersome and expensive procedures; and culturally inappropriate laws have all contributed to the problems.

This chapter describes efforts to make the existing justice system more responsive to the needs of Aboriginal people, and to put more control over Aboriginal conflicts into Aboriginal hands. The chapter is organized into three main categories:

- Community disputes
- Reforms to the mainstream system
- Adjudicating Aboriginal rights claims

2. COMMUNITY DISPUTES

Disputes within Aboriginal communities should be the easiest to address. Yet the solutions are difficult to come by. This is partly because the people in the mainstream justice system define the issues only through concepts that exist within the mainstream system. Therefore, many of the studies on justice see problems with sentencing policies of judges, for example, but do not conceive of a system without judges.

The Report of the Manitoba Justice Inquiry illustrates this point. After a thoroughly researched, devastating condemnation of the existing system, the Inquiry recommends the establishment of a separate Aboriginal justice system. The "separate system", however, mirrors the existing justice system in nearly every respect, including the establishment of court houses, appropriately paid judges, legal aid and prosecutors.[4]

In my view, solutions for community disputes do not lie in justice system mega-projects. What is needed is implementation of justice initiatives which focus on the needs of the communities, and which allow the communities to develop their own approaches to problems. This takes time, patience, and leadership on the part of members of the community. Representatives of the mainstream system — government officials, lawyers and judges — should see their role, not as guardians of the mainstream system, but as facilitators for the implementation of Aboriginal community approaches.

This section will outline four issues which should be addressed when attempting to address issues around community disputes:

- Use a community approach, not a legalistic approach

- Define the community
- Identify priority disputes
- Make a plan for implementation

In Appendix B, there is a summary of the steps needed to implement restorative justice projects.

(a) Use a Community Approach, Not a Legalistic Approach

A community approach begins from the problem, and analyzes the solution from the perspective of general principles. These are the same principles which should apply to solutions in the mainstream justice system:

- does the enforcement mechanism address the problem?
- is the process quick and efficient?
- is the process fair to individuals involved?
- is the "punishment" appropriate for the "crime?"

A legalistic approach does not look at the problem itself, but at whether the mainstream process has been followed. Therefore, the questions are directed at the extent to which the situation strays from the *Criminal Code* and the requirements of the *Charter of Rights and Freedoms*. Legalistic questions include:

- whether the "accused" has the right to a lawyer
- whether a "neutral" judge is hearing the case
- whether the police have obtained warrants

A case involving search for, and seizure of, liquor illustrates the differences in these two approaches. Many northern reserves which are accessible only by air, enforce their liquor control by-laws by searching people and bags that come off the plane. Any liquor found is confiscated, and usually no further action is taken against the person who tried to bring it into the community. The reserves take this course because they consider it the most efficient and least intrusive one.

I was present in one case in northern Ontario. The community had been shocked into action after a youth had been found frozen to death in the bush after consuming alcohol. In response, the Council appointed two members of the reserve to be "Band Constables". These Band Constables got their authority from the Council, not from any provincial or federal legislation. The two Band Constables would go to the airport when a flight arrived, and search the passengers for drugs and liquor. One day, a member of the First Nation who was carrying liquor objected to the search, and a scuffle broke out. The liquor was seized and discarded. The member of the First Nation complained to the Ontario Provincial Police, who charged the two Band Constables with assault. The police argued that the charge was justified because the airport was located on provincial land off-reserve: therefore, the Band Constables had no authority to enforce the by-law there, and their attempt to search the passenger amounted to assault.[5]

Even if the search had taken place on the reserve, there might still have been some difficulty because of the constitutional right "to be secure against unreasonable search and seizure". This right embodies the principle that no police force should have the authority to search individuals randomly.[6]

Using a legalistic analysis, the police were right to charge the Band Constables. To comply with the *Criminal Code* the Band should have contacted the Ontario Provincial Police, who would have gotten a warrant from a court, entered the person's home to take the liquor, charged the person with an offence, and stored the liquor as evidence for court. The person charged would then have to make appearances, and retain a lawyer. As the court would fly in to the reserve every month or two, (at the same time as the defence lawyer) the trial would have taken place many months later. There are clearly problems with this approach to enforcement. Whether or not the accused person is found guilty, this process causes distress to the individual, makes enforcing the by-law cumbersome, and entails great expense to all parties. The costs are especially significant for the provincial government which must fly in a judge, a Crown Attorney, court reporters and defence lawyers to hold this trial.

The principle of limited police powers of search is a good one because it protects individuals from arbitrary state intrusion and disruption. The principle is based on assumptions, though, about the relationship of the individual and the state (or government or community) which may not be appropriate in some Aboriginal communities.[7] Furthermore, even in mainstream society there are cases when the police are empowered to randomly search for liquor.[8]

Using a community focussed approach, however, the actions of the First Nation appear to be logical and appropriate. The solution conforms with the general principles important for any justice system:

- it deals with the problem of liquor on the reserve
- it is quick and cost-effective
- the person is not put to a great deal of inconvenience, and
- there is no "punishment" such as a fine or jail term.

(b) Define the "community"

While "community" is an important term, unless it is used thoughtfully, it can lead to problems. There are many different types of communities. Some communities are geographic, and easily identified. A Métis settlement in Alberta or a First Nation reserve are self-contained, and defined in legislation. In some areas, such as the Yukon, or in Inuit territory, the communities are mixed, with no geographic boundaries between Aboriginal and non-Aboriginal residences. In urban areas, there may not be a geographic community at all, but rather a community of interest where Aboriginal individuals who share the same interests may undertake initiatives together. Within each of these communities, there may be another community with different interests. On Mohawk reserves, for example, there may be very different aspirations held by people who follow the traditional teachings of the Great Law of Peace, as opposed to those who participate in the *Indian Act* elections.

Since the particular approach to addressing disputes will involve development at the grassroots level, it is important to begin with those people who are committed to looking for solutions. That may mean, for example, that only disputes on-reserve are dealt with as opposed to disputes involving all members of the First Nation, whether on or off-reserve. It may mean looking at a mixed Aboriginal and non-Aboriginal community as a single community, or it may mean treating Aboriginal people in that mixed community separately. There is no right solution in the abstract — there can only be solutions which develop out of the "community" however defined. What is important, however, is that the entire community participate in the decision-making. Here, Aboriginal women have raised legitimate concerns about justice initiatives which have not included them in the design and implementation. The Royal Commission on Aboriginal Peoples recommends that Aboriginal women be involved in a formal way in all discussions.[9]

(c) Identify Priority Disputes

When one leaves the high level constitutional negotiating tables, to spend time in communities there is a different dialogue in justice. The discussions do not focus on lofty principles about the role of the judiciary in society, but on how to prevent break-ins, stop family violence or care for children. In this context, then it is important to begin by looking at what disputes are important for that community. If the major issue is break-ins, the community should decide who is involved, why they are involved, and what the community should do to address the issue. Should the youth be forced to confront representatives of the community in a circle, should they be forced to cut wood for the elders, or should the community provide radio time for the youth to begin their own program? The point here is to design what the community wants, and then give it an independent reference point in the community.

Unfortunately, the approach that is prevalent now is to begin with the existing justice system, and try to figure out what modifications could be made to that justice system. In other words, it is a legalistic approach which analyzes problems based on categories and concepts which exist in the mainstream system. In analyzing what to do about break-ins on reserve, for example, the issues become whether it is acceptable to have break-ins, which are indictable offences, dealt with outside of the mainstream justice system at all. If it is acceptable, what role should the Crown Attorney play in agreeing to "divert" those charges? How will the rights of the accused to remain silent be protected?

By using a community focused approach to identifying priority disputes, the task can be delineated and circumscribed. It should not be necessary to take on the entire justice structure in Canada to begin an initiative in a single community.

(d) Make a Plan For Implementation

One of the great failures in addressing community level justice concerns has been in implementation. The legalistic approach makes implementation practically impossible because every issue must be sorted out on paper before the community is allowed to begin its initiative. I have sat for hours, weeks, years, in heated discussions between government and First Nation lawyers about constitutional

principles embedded in the justice system, while the federal government has refused funding to hire a justice co-ordinator to begin a
justice project in the community.

In my view, the role of the Aboriginal nation is to identify the
community, identify the dispute, and explore ways of addressing the
problems. The role of government policy makers and players in the
mainstream justice system is to ensure that there is support from the
community, including Aboriginal women. To the extent that the
substance of the initiative is evaluated, it should be on the basis of the
general principles above, not on a narrow legalistic analysis. Unfortunately, the attitude from justice officials has too often been, "Show
me why you need to change what we are doing now". The time has
passed when there is any doubt that the existing process is not working
for Aboriginal people. The attitude should be "This is what I can do
to keep the mainstream system out of your hair." This is an opportunity for co-operation and partnership.

There are various ways of providing a framework for the justice
initiative:

(i) *Negotiations with the local Crown Attorney or the judges*

A surprising number of initiatives have no legislative or constitutional bases. They are arrangements which have been arrived at
through an understanding with the Crown Attorney or judges. Perhaps
the best example are sentencing circles. In these arrangements, the
accused usually acknowledges guilt for a crime. Members of the
community, the accused, the victim, lawyers and the judge sit in a
circle to discuss the wider context of the situation. They then arrive
at an appropriate sentence. While these arrangements increase involvement of the community, they are also highly dependent on the
individuals who come to the understanding. A change in the Crown
Attorney, or a new Chief could make the initiative collapse.[10]

(ii) *Band by-laws*

Although not many First Nations have used by-laws under the
Indian Act creatively, the Spallumcheen First Nation provides a role
model. They passed their own child welfare law, and enforced it.
Although there are legal questions as to the validity of the by-law, it

has withstood court challenges, and operates to this day.[11] Other First Nations are also making by-laws on alcohol, residence and taxation.

(iii) *Negotiated self-government agreements*

Self-government agreements can prepare the ground for justice initiatives. In the Yukon, for example, First Nations clearly have law-making power for the administration of justice. Under their agreement, if an agreement with the federal and territorial governments is not reached, the First Nation can take over the administration of justice.[12]

(iv) *Exercise of inherent right of self-government*

First Nations can assert their right to make laws on justice, and begin implementing those laws. Support for this approach is found in the report of the Royal Commission on Aboriginal Peoples, *Bridging the Cultural Divide*. They suggest that criminal law making power is an inherent right, although the power must be exercised in conformity with the *Charter of Rights and Freedoms*.[13]

(e) Examples of Justice Initiatives in Criminal Law

The unique nature of each community results in the establishment of unique solutions to justice-related issues. Some take place before the mainstream court system gets involved, while others occur at the end of a trial in the mainstream system. Some initiatives are based on healing and restoration while others look more like the adjudicatory model with fines and sentences. This section will briefly describe some of the initiatives. For a more thorough discussion, the best place to begin is *Bridging the Cultural Divide* by the Royal Commission on Aboriginal Peoples.[14]

Most of the justice initiatives deal with criminal law and they can leave the mainstream system at three points.

First, Aboriginal communities can deal with criminal matters before the courts get involved at all. For example, a First Nation constable, instead of laying a charge, could tell a young offender to appear before the First Nation's justice committee. The justice committee could address the youth in a variety of ways ranging from suggesting a treatment program, to providing restitution. In extreme cases, the committee could recommend banishment to Chief and Council.

Second, the Aboriginal community could take over the problem after charges have been laid, but before there has been a trial. In the mainstream system, this often referred to as "diversion". The Aboriginal community could address the offender in different ways. Many communities try to use a healing and restorative justice approach to the offender. An example is the Hollow Water project which deals with sexual abuse offenders by providing an intense program developed through healing circles.[15] In Toronto, the Aboriginal Legal Services provides a community council program. Individual accused meet with three members of the community in a "hearing". The community members suggest a course of action which is monitored by staff of the legal services clinic.[16] Two reserves in Ontario took a more adjudicatory approach with the appointment of "judges" by the Chief and Council who held hearings, and meted out fines and other sentences to offenders.[17]

The third stage for Aboriginal participation in the criminal proceeding is after the person has been found guilty and the person is about to receive his or her sentence.[18] In a typical case, a judge will sit with the accused, a victim, and members of the community to discuss the most appropriate sentence. The process was one of the first to formally recognize the importance of the community in addressing criminal problems, but it has also been riddled with problems. Because the sentencing circle is actually part of the proceedings in the mainstream system, appeal courts have become involved in controlling its use. And in Aboriginal communities themselves, concerns have been expressed about the process. A particularly serious concern has been raised by Pauktuutit, the Inuit Women's Association of Canada about the pressure put on women victims.[19]

(f)   Examples of Justice Initiatives That Are Not For Criminal Matters

Not all disputes are about criminal matters. There are a number of areas where Aboriginal peoples are already dealing with their own disputes and other areas where greater expansion is possible.

Many communities already have procedures for making decisions on membership, housing, taxation, and elections, and often have appeal procedures for those issues. Nonetheless, many of those disputes end up in the mainstream court system. An alternative, which has been talked about, but not implemented, is to establish an all Aboriginal body to make final appeal decisions on those community matters. While a national system may be difficult to implement, groups of communities, or tribal councils could appoint individuals to an appeal tribunal. When there was a disputed election, for example, the matter could be referred to the tribunal members who were not from the community in question.

For individual matters such as family disputes or disputes over money, it would be ideal to have Aboriginal laws in place. Until that happens, however, if the parties agree, it is possible to opt out of many of the federal and provincial laws on these matters by using arbitration or mediation.

The *Arbitration Act*[20] is an example of legislation which recognizes that the parties to a dispute may not want or need to bring their dispute before the courts. Under this Act people who have a dispute in the areas of family or civil law can choose to have an arbitrator listen to their problem and decide on a fair solution. The arbitrator does not have to be associated with the court at all. She or he just needs to be somebody the parties trust and respect. There is no set procedure that an arbitration has to follow. The legislation suggests some guidelines, but these guidelines do not have to be applied if the parties agree that they would not be helpful. As long as the parties are treated equally and fairly, and they both have the opportunity to present their version of the problem and respond to what the other person says, they can agree on the procedure that is most appropriate for their case. In some cases it is possible to appeal to the courts if a person disagrees with the arbitrator's decision, but generally speaking the arbitrator's decision is final. The decision of an arbitrator under the *Arbitration Act* is enforceable in the courts. If a community wants to set up its own dispute resolution process under the *Arbitration Act*, a lawyer's advice in setting up the process will help to get the maximum benefit for the community from the legislation.

Another way of resolving a dispute outside the courts is mediation. Mediation is different from arbitration because an arbitrator tells the parties what the resolution will be, whereas a mediator helps the parties to reach their own agreement. The parties need to agree on a mediator, and then they can begin to talk using whatever procedures they find most helpful. If an agreement is reached, it can be registered in the court as a settlement. It then becomes enforceable as an order of the court. If the parties can't reach an agreement, they can take their problem to arbitration or to court. There are some cases, particularly in family law, where mediation should be approached with caution, if at all. If a person has escaped or is escaping from an abusive relationship, mediation may well be useless or even harmful. Mediation may just give the abusive spouse an opportunity for more bullying. The problems of unequal power in the relationship must make any "agreement" suspect.

3. REFORMS TO THE MAINSTREAM SYSTEM

Donald Marshall, was a Mi'kmaq who spent eleven years in prison for a murder he did not commit. An inquiry into his case found clearly that he was a victim of racism in the Nova Scotia justice system.[21] Yet he would not have been helped by the existence of a First Nation court because the offence he was charged with took place in Halifax and involved non-Aboriginal people.

The need for change is beginning to be recognized in the federal and provincial justice systems, and there are a number of initiatives which address this issue.

(a) Legal Representation of Aboriginal People Going to Court

Aboriginal people have not been well represented in courts, either because they could not afford lawyers, or their lawyers were not familiar with Aboriginal people and Aboriginal rights.

One of the earliest programs to address this issue was the national Native Courtworker Program sponsored by the federal, provincial and territorial governments, and administered largely through Friendship Centres. Native courtworkers are available in court to help an Aboriginal defendant. They try to make sure the Aboriginal defendant has legal counsel, and, if not, perhaps get the case postponed. They explain what is going on, and act as a bridge between the Aboriginal defendant and the court process. They do not give legal advice or represent people in court.

Some jurisdictions have community legal clinics which provide services to Aboriginal people. The lawyers at these clinics develop expertise in Aboriginal law, and the clinics usually are run by a native

Board of Directors. There are a number of community legal clinics across Ontario. One clinic, Aboriginal Legal Services of Toronto, specializes in providing services to Toronto's Aboriginal residents (registered and non-registered). Clinics across northern Ontario include those at Thunder Bay, Kenora, Moosonee, Manitoulin Island, Fort Francis and Sioux Lookout. Other innovative ways of providing legal services have been explored. The Nishnawbe-Aski Legal Services Corporation was established in 1989 by the member nations in northern Ontario. The corporation employs lawyers and community legal workers to provide advice and assistance to people who have to go to court. They also issue Legal Aid certificates, provide interpretation services, conduct research and make recommendations about reforming the law.

Over the years, the Native Law Centre in Saskatoon, and law schools in many areas of Canada have attempted to address the shortage of Aboriginal lawyers in Canada. Their efforts have met with mixed results. However, there are now many more Aboriginal lawyers who are setting up practice in or near their communities. They can be contacted through the Indigenous Bar Association.[22]

(b) Judges And Justices of the Peace

If Aboriginal lawyers were scarce, Aboriginal members of the judiciary were almost non-existent. Their numbers are still small, but the attempts of some progressive governments to ensure diversity on the Bench have improved the situation.

Since 1984 the Ontario Native Justices of the Peace Program has sought to promote Aboriginal participation in the administration of justice by recruiting and appointing Aboriginal people as JP's.[23] Although the JP applies federal or provincial law, an Aboriginal JP can be expected to bring a different perspective to that law. An Aboriginal perspective in the judge's chair can lead to interpretations of the law which show an understanding of Aboriginal culture.

There is also a need for improvements to federal and provincial judicial councils so that they can deal more effectively with racist or sexist remarks and conduct. One important change would be to have an evaluation process. In the past, the importance of judicial independence has meant that judges have been largely immune from criticism. New ideas could be developed for on-going performance evaluation.

Judicial evaluation would need to be supported by continuing judicial education. One of the recommendations of the Royal Commission on the Donald Marshall, Jr. Prosecution was the development of courses and programs for law students, lawyers and judges. The courses would deal with legal issues facing visible minorities and encourage sensitivity to minority concerns. Continuing education would go further than simply telling judges what they were doing wrong. It would help them get it right.

(c) Policing

Many First Nations in remote locations or with significant populations have their own police force. This is due in large part to the federal First Nations Policing Policy (FNPP) This initiative gives First Nations communities the opportunity to participate with provincial and federal governments in the development of dedicated policing services in their communities.[24] First Nations communities may choose to develop and administer their own police service, or they may choose a police service delivered by a contingent of First Nations officers working within an existing police force.

The RCMP has traditionally policed First Nations communities pursuant to provincial policing agreements. Under the FNPP, the RCMP First Nations Community Policing Service will be governed by two separate agreements: a Framework Agreement between the province/territory and the federal government outlining funding and other managerial arrangements; and a Community Tripartite Agreement between the First Nation community, the provincial government and the federal government, outlining the specific details of the community policing service.

Communities interested in entering into a Community Tripartite Agreement for the delivery of RCMP services should inform the Attorney General of the provincial/territorial government and the federal Ministry of the Solicitor General, through a Band Council or community resolution, or some other formal declaration of support. The RCMP will then arrange to meet with the community to discuss policing models and the community's policing needs. The community

will work together to draft a policing proposal outlin-
)f the policing service.

cing proposal has been drafted, it should be submitted
ind negotiation with provincial/territorial and federal
all parties are satisfied with the proposal, the policing
arrangements will be formalized in a Tripartite Agreement.

The relationship between Fist Nation Police and the regular
police depends on whether it is the RCMP, the Ontario Provincial
Police or the Suréte de Québec.

In Ontario, for example, about 50 per cent of the reserves now
have First Nations Constables, which are assigned to, and reside, on
the reserve. They are appointed by the Commissioner of the Ontario
Provincial Police, and the appointments require the approval of the
First Nation Council or the reserve's police governing authority.[25]
First Nations Constables cannot be suspended or terminated without
the Commissioner first consulting with the body that approved the
appointment. These police have jurisdiction off-reserve as well.[26]

Some Bands have appointed Band Constables through a Band
Council Resolution. These Band Constables do not have official
police status, but they are empowered by Chief and Council to enforce
First Nation by-laws.[27]

4. ADJUDICATING ABORIGINAL RIGHTS CLAIMS

Land claims, hunting and fishing rights and taxation are not
individual disputes so much as constitutional issues involving the
determination of the powers of federal, provincial and Aboriginal
governments.

At the present time, most of these disputes are dealt with in the
existing court system. Although the courts have recently been more
balanced in their approach to Aboriginal claims, in the past the bias
against Aboriginal people was obvious. Certainly, there still persists
a perception of bias when rights of Aboriginal people are adjudicated
by non-Aboriginal people using non-Aboriginal procedure and non-
Aboriginal laws.

A variety of institutions have been used to address this problem.

The Waitangi Tribunal in New Zealand is an example of such a
body. The Tribunal combines negotiation and adjudication. It has no
power to make binding pronouncements, but it sets the stage for

productive negotiations by deciding and publishing what it considers to be the rights and wrongs of the cases that come before it. It is made up of Maori and non-Maori appointees, and has the authority to regulate its procedure "in such manner as it sees fit". The Tribunal conducts its proceedings in Maori and English often at the marae (long house) of the claimant tribe. The result is a forum in which the claimants can state their grievances in their own terms.

In Canada, there are three bodies which, like the Waitangi Tribunal, include both Aboriginal and non-Aboriginal representatives.

The Indian Claims Commission (ICC) was established in 1991. It is an independent body established jointly by the Assembly of First Nations (AFN) and Canada. The Commission consists of one Chief commissioner and six part time commissioners, nominated jointly by the AFN and Canada. Its mandate is to inquire into and report on disputes between First Nations and the Government of Canada relating to the specific claims process. The ICC focus is on research of relevant historical facts, mediation, and liaison between First Nations and government.[28]

The British Columbia Treaty Commission was established in 1992. It is an independent body established jointly by British Columbia First Nations Summit, Canada and British Columbia. The Commission is made up of five commissioners. Canada and British Columbia each nominate one commissioner, the Summit nominates two commissioners and all parties jointly nominate the Chief commissioner. The Commission's mandate is to assist the three parties in negotiating modern day treaties.

The Indian Commission of Ontario is an independent, neutral body with a mandate to identify, clarify, negotiate and resolve issues of concern to Canada, Ontario and First Nations in Ontario. Its governing body is composed of the federal Minister of Indian Affairs, the provincial Minister Responsible for Native Affairs, and representatives from the Chiefs of Ontario, Union of Ontario Indians, Grand Council Treaty No. 3, Nishnawbe-Aski Nation, Association of Iroquois and Allied Indians, and independent First Nations. The Commission provides professional services in a range of areas directed at resolving disputes. Issues addressed include land claim negotiations involving federal or provincial governments, resource management and land use, policing, education and other aspects of self-government.

The Royal Commission on Aboriginal Peoples recommended the establishment of an independent administrative tribunal, to be called the Aboriginal Lands and Treaties Tribunal. The mandate of the Tribunal would include resolving existing specific claims and overseeing the bargaining process. Where the parties cannot reach an agreement, the Tribunal should have the authority to adjudicate and make final and binding decisions. Judicial review of the Tribunal's decisions should be conducted in the Federal Court of Appeal and should be restricted to questions of constitutional law, jurisdiction and procedural fairness.[29]

APPENDIX A

SURVEY OF INQUIRIES INTO ABORIGINAL PEOPLE AND THE JUSTICE SYSTEM

There have been many inquiries and studies on Aboriginal justice. This list is not complete, but represents a representative sample from across Canada.

Inquiries covered by this survey:

- The Royal Commission on Aboriginal Peoples *Bridging the Cultural Divide*, 1996
- Report of the Saskatchewan Indian Justice Review Committee, January, 1992
- Report on Aboriginal Peoples and Criminal Justice: Equality, Respect and the Search for Justice, Law Reform Commission of Canada, Report 34, December, 1991
- Aboriginal People and Justice Administration: A Discussion Paper, Department of Justice, September, 1991
- The Justice System and Aboriginal People: Report of the Aboriginal Justice Inquiry of Manitoba, August, 1991
- Justice on Trial: Report of the Task Force on the Criminal Justice System and its Impact on the Indian and Métis People of Alberta, March, 1991
- Report of the Osnaburgh-Windigo Tribal Council Justice Review Committee, Ontario, July, 1990
- Royal Commission on the Donald Marshall, Jr., Prosecution, Nova Scotia, 1989

1. Exercising the Right of Self-government

The Royal Commission on Aboriginal Peoples in *Bridging the Cultural Divide*, came to the following conclusions on self-government in criminal justice.

- A renewed relationship between Aboriginal and non-Aboriginal peoples must recognize Aboriginal people's inherent right of self-government, which includes the right to establish Aboriginal justice systems.
- Aboriginal and federal jurisdiction over criminal law and procedure on Aboriginal territories is concurrent. In the event of a conflict arising between Aboriginal law and a federal law passed under section 91(24) of the *Constitution Act, 1867*, Aboriginal law will be paramount except where it can be shown that the need for federal action is compelling and substantial and the federal law is consistent with the Crown's basic trust responsibilities to Aboriginal peoples.
- The establishment of urban Aboriginal justice systems will require joint efforts between non-Aboriginal and Aboriginal justice systems. Urban Aboriginal governments will be involved with the delivery and administration of justice.

2. Court Administration

All the reports make suggestions for improving the existing system as it deals with Aboriginal people. Examples taken from Alberta's Report illustrate the sorts of changes which could make the courts more accessible and responsive to Aboriginal people:

- improving accessibility and responsiveness of legal aid to Aboriginal people
  - improving translation and interpretation services, and recognizing the right to be heard in the Aboriginal languages
  - holding of court sittings closer to Aboriginal communities
  - providing cross-cultural training for judges, police, legal aid administrators, corrections workers and other justice personnel
  - appointing Aboriginal justices of the peace, lay judges and probation officers

- improving bail provisions as they affect Aboriginal accused persons
- creating a position of Aboriginal Advocate who would facilitate and expedite complaints against any person or component of the criminal justice system

The Saskatchewan Report emphasizes the need to improve the administration of justice to young offenders.

3. Community Participation

Many of the reports make suggestions for increased Aboriginal participation in justice decision-making. The Law Reform Commission of Canada's Report, for example, puts forward the following options:

- Peacemaker Courts for mediation or arbitration of civil disputes
- permanent liaison mechanisms between local Crown prosecutors and Aboriginal communities and leaders
- statutory provision for sentencing advice from Elders or other respected members of the community
- a process for ongoing consultation between Aboriginal service providers and Corrections and Parole officials
- amendment to the Criminal Code to include a counterpart to the "alternative measures" provisions in the *Young Offenders Act*

The Osnaburgh-Windigo report recommends the creation of First Nation custodial facilities, which would offer programmes for education, work, counselling, spiritual support and recreation. The Osnaburgh report also calls for consultation with First Nations on all judicial appointments made in northern Ontario.

4. Aboriginal Courts

Many of the reports make reference to the possibility of community courts to handle a range of matters such as offences under community laws, pre-charge, pre-trial and pre-sentence diversion, bail hearings and summary offences. Generally, though, the reports do not focus on this option. The Manitoba Report is exceptional in this respect.

The Manitoba Report recommends the establishment of tribal courts as a first step in creating an Aboriginal justice system which would eventually include:

- a policing service
- prosecution branch
- a legal aid system
- a court system: youth court system, family court system, criminal court system, civil court system, and appellate court system
- a probation service
- mediation/counselling service
- a fine collection and maintenance enforcement system
- a community-based correctional system
- a parole system
- an Aboriginal constitution containing the principle of separation of the judicial from the executive and legislative arms of each Aboriginal government.

The report recommends a process of trilateral negotiations (rather than a community-based approach) as the means to establishing the framework for Aboriginal justice systems. The report states that every community is entitled to a justice system, but recommends that neighbouring communities share where logistics dictate and linguistic similarit is permit. A community's right to a justice system is not dependent on legal title to land: legal ownership of land is not the same as legal jurisdiction over an area. The report does envision, however, that the distinctness which entitles a community to a justice system will entail a distinct geographical area associated with the community.

The report envisions that the subject matter of Aboriginal justice systems will consist to a significant degree of laws passed by Aboriginal governments.

The report points out that the federal and provincial governments have two significant exits to the *Charter of Rights and Freedoms* in sections 1 and 33, and that to expect Aboriginal governments to operate on more stringent terms would be unreasonable. The report recommends that First Nation governments draft a charter of rights and freedoms which reflects Aboriginal customs and values.

5. Justice and Social Context

Many of the reports point out the social roots of the Aboriginal justice crisis. The Osnaburgh-Windigo report emphasizes the significance of these roots, addressing in its recommendations the land, economic and social issues which underlie the justice crisis.

The Osnaburgh-Windigo report recommends recognition of Aboriginal sovereignty and economically viable land bases, and the development of Aboriginal justice systems, whether traditional or otherwise. Among the report's specific recommendations are:

- Aboriginal representation in federal and provincial ridings where Aboriginal people constitute a majority, in addition to any self-government arrangements which are developed
- recognition of a First Nation right to representation in decision-making about natural resource use and economic development in areas surrounding community locations
- First Nation involvement in, or control of, conservation duties
- accommodation of existing laws to traditional economic pursuits
- an increase in the availability of decent housing, safe drinking water, sewage facilities, and the development of recreational facilities and programs
- establishment of a First Nation-operated, family-oriented alcohol, drug and solvent abuse rehabilitation programme, and the development of a co-ordinated program to address family violence
- provision of effective medical facilities
- improved educational standards and increased parental participation
- the full engagement of First Nations in devising solutions to "what has been rightly described as the domestic issue most noted to Canada's disadvantage on the international stage".

APPENDIX B

STEPS TO IMPLEMENTING A JUSTICE PROJECT

The summary which follows is based on, *Making it Work: Planning and Evaluating Community Corrections & Healing Projects in Aboriginal Communities* Series: Aboriginal Peoples Collection — Technical Series (Ottawa: Solicitor General Canada, Aboriginal Corrections Policy Unit, 1998) at 87-88 by R. Linden & D. Clairmont.

Aboriginal populations have been estranged from the justice system and from protecting their own communities. There is a movement towards restoring justice to the communities. In the literature, this is often referred to as "restorative justice." Restorative justice relies on reconciliation as opposed to incarceration. The focus is on repairing the harm caused to the victim and to the community through diversion programs; community based sentencing (eg., the sentencing or healing circle); and community corrections.

A suggested checklist for Aboriginal restorative justice initiatives:

1. Identify and describe problems and needs

    • gather information about your community's justice problems from various sources (social workers, police, courts, lawyers, schools, etc.)
    • prepare an inventory of justice/corrections agencies in your community
    • prepare a community needs assessment

2. Develop an action plan

    • define the boundaries which the project will serve
    • select the participants who will be involved in the planning
    • determine the type of program which will best meet your needs
    • specify the goals and objectives
    • prepare a work plan
    • complete a funding proposal

3. Implement your program

- obtain the support of community members and recruit volunteers
- public education campaign
- train program staff
- decide whether the program will be "phased in" or implemented at once
- establish operating procedures

4. Monitor and evaluate your program
- monitor the programs' implementations
- evaluate the programs' impact
- report the results

ENDNOTES

1 Royal Commission on Aboriginal Peoples, *Bridging the Cultural Divide: A Report on Aboriginal People and Criminal Justice in Canada* (Ottawa: Minister of Supply and Services, 1996) [hereinafter *Bridging the Cultural Divide*].

2 *R. v. Gladue*, [1999] 2 C.N.L.R. 252 (S.C.C.).

3 On the subject of misunderstanding, one culture may interpret refraining from looking someone in the eyes as a sign of respect, whereas another culture may interpret this as a sign of untrustworthiness. Reading the body language of a witness or accused person across a cultural gap can result in a wrong verdict. For a discussion of cultural assumptions in criminal court see Rupert Ross, *Dancing with a Ghost*, (Markham: Octopus Publishing Group, 1992).

4 See *The Justice System and Aboriginal People: Report of the Aboriginal Justice Inquiry of Manitoba*, August, 1991.

5 The First Nation Council was furious, and barred the circuit court from coming to the reserve for many months. The Attorney General refused to drop the charge, but, strangely, neither was the charge pursued. In another case, a member of the Fort Albany Band sued the provincial government after a First Nations Constable searched her bags for liquor when she got off the airplane. The search was conducted on provincial Crown land, just outside the reserve boundary. The case was dismissed in *Nakochee v. Linklater* (April 29, 1993), Whalen J. (Ont. Gen. Div.)

6 See *R. v. Hatchard* (1991), [1993] 1 C.N.L.R. 96 (Ont. Gen. Div.) for a discussion on the powers of "Band Constables".

7 An example of an imported assumption is that the individual exists separate and apart from the community or state, and that the state poses a threat to the individual.

8 To prevent drinking and driving, police can set up check points, and pull cars over randomly to question the drivers. See *R. v. Hufsky* [1988] 1 S.C.R. 621 (S.C.C.). People going to a concert may also have their bags searched for liquor or drugs at the entrance.

9 See Royal Commission on Aboriginal Peoples, *Bridging the Cultural Divide, supra* note 1 at 275.

Recommendation 8:

> The Commission recommends that all nations rely on the expertise of Aboriginal women and Aboriginal women's organizations to review initiatives in the justice area and ensure that the participation of women in the creation and design of justice systems is both meaningful and significant.

10 For a discussion on sentencing circles, see *Bridging the Cultural Divide, supra* note 1 at 109-116.

11 For a further discussion of this by-law see Chapter 8, "Bands, Band Councils and Reserves" and Royal Commission on Aboriginal Peoples, *Gathering Strength*, Volume 3 (Ottawa: Minister of Supply and Services, 1996) at 24.

12 The agreements provided for the negotiation of administration of justice between the First Nations and the Crown governments. In the event of failure to reach an agreement on this issue, the First Nations will administer justice. See, for example, the *Selkirk First Nation Self-Government Agreement*, 21 July 1997 at *The Champagne and Aishihik First Nations Self-Government Agreement*, 29 May 1993 at s. 13.1 and 13.3.17; s. 13.6.0-13.6.7.

13 For a detailed discussion of how the exercise of the inherent right would work, see chapter 4 of *Bridging the Cultural Divide, supra* note 1.

14 See *Bridging the Cultural Divide, supra* note 1.

The Aboriginal Justice Learning Network (AJLN) has information on sentencing circles and aboriginal justice projects: AJLN, 10th Floor 275 Sparks Street Ottawa, Ontario K1A 0H8. Information on Aboriginal Justice projects is also available from: Aboriginal Corrections Policy Unit Solicitor General Canada 340 Laurier Avenue West Ottawa, Ontario K1A 0P8 or online at http://www.sgc.gc.ca

15 This program is described in more detail in *Bridging the Cultural Divide, supra* note 1 at 159-167. However, it has been criticized for putting women in danger by not treating the offender seriously enough by Emma

LaRocque, "Re-examining Culturally Appropriate Models in Criminal Justice Application" in Michael Asch, ed., *Aboriginal and Treaty Rights in Canada: Essays on Law, Equity, and Respect for Difference* (Vancouver: UBC Press, 1997).

16 For a description of this project see *Bridging the Cultural Divide, supra* note 1 at 149-158.

17 For a description of these two projects see *Bridging the Cultural Divide, supra* note 1 at 169-172.

18 The first case to clearly document a sentencing circle was *R v. Moses*, [1992] 3 C.N.L.R. 116 (Y.T. Terr. Ct.) by Mr. Justice Stuart. Philip James Moses was a 26-year-old Aboriginal offender with 43 previous criminal convictions. Moses grew up amid alcohol abuse, poverty, and he was physically and sexually abused as a ward of the State. Moses pleaded guilty to assaulting an RCMP officer with a baseball bat. The sentencing circle attended by Justice Stuart, the defence and the prosecutor, Moses' family and community elders gave Moses a suspended sentence and two years probation. He had to live with his family, attend a residential program for native alcoholics and return to an alcohol-free home.

Since *Moses*, courts have developed criteria to determine the appropriateness of a sentencing circle:

1. The accused must agree to be referred to a sentencing circle.

2. The accused must have deep roots in the community in which the circle is held and from which the participants are drawn.

3. There must be elders or respected nonpolitical community leaders willing to participate.

4. The victim is willing to participate and has been subjected to no coercion or pressure in so agreeing.

5. The court should try to determine beforehand, as best it can, if the victim is subject to battered spouse syndrome. If she is, then she should have counselling made available to her and be accompanied by a support team in the circle.

6. Disputed facts should be resolved in advance.

7. The case is one in which a court would be willing to take a calculated risk and depart from the usual range of sentencing.

For leading cases, see the following: *R. v. Johnson* (1994), (Y.T. C.A.) [1995] 2 C.N.L.R. 158; *R. v. Johns* (1995), [1996] 1 C.N.L.R. 172 (Y.T. C.A.); *R. v. Morin*, [1995] 4 C.N.L.R. 37, (Sask. C.A.); *R. v. A.F.* (1994), Ontario Court of Justice, File No. 253/93.; *R. v. Cheekinew*, [1993] 3 C.N.L.R. 172 (Sask. Q.B.) where the accessed application for a sentencing circle was denied because the specifics of the cases did not fit the criteria;

R. v. Gingell (1996), 50 C.R. (4th) 326 (Y.T. Terr. Ct.); *R. v. Manyfingers* (1996), 191 A.R. 342 (Alta. Prov. Ct.).

The Native Law Centre at the University of Saskatchewan has put together an excellent bibliography of materials. It can be reached online at: http://www.usask.ca/nativelaw/jah_scircle.html

Articles include the following:

Barnett, Cunliffe (1995) "Circle Sentencing/Alternative Sentencing" 3 Canadian Native Law Reporter 3:1-7.

Crnkovich, Mary (1996) "A Sentencing Circle." Journal of Legal Pluralism and Unofficial Law, 36:159-181.

Henderson, James Youngblood (1995). "Exploring justice as healing." Justice as Healing: A newsletter on Aboriginal concepts of justice [on-line], Spring. Available on Internet: http://www.usask.ca/nativelaw/jah_henderson2.html

Huculak, Bria. "From the power to punish to the power to heal." Justice as healing: a newsletter on Aboriginal concepts of justice [on-line], Fall. Available Internet: http://www.usask.ca/nativelaw/jah_huculak.html

Janvier, Alphonse. (1994). "Sentencing Circles." In Continuing Poundmaker and Riel's Quest: Presentations Made at a Conference on Aboriginal Peoples and Justice. R. Grosse, J. Y. Henderson, and R. Carter, eds. pp. 301-302. Saskatoon, Saskatchewan: Purich Publishing.

LaPrairie, Carol. (1992). "Aboriginal crime and justice: Explaining the present, exploring the future." Canadian Journal of Criminology, 34(3-4): 281-298.

Quigley, Tom. (1994). "Some Issues in Sentencing of Aboriginal Offenders." In Continuing Poundmaker and Riel's Quest: Presentations Made at a Conference on Aboriginal Peoples and Justice. R. Grosse, J. Y. Henderson, and R. Carter, eds. Pp. 269-296. Saskatoon, Saskatchewan: Purich Publishing.

Restoule, Jean-Paul. (1997). "Moving Toward Native Justice: Intercultural Communication in Aboriginal Sentencing Circles in Canada." Media Development [on-line], 3. Available on the Internet: http://www.oneworld.org/wacc/media/restoule.html.

Royal Commission on Aboriginal Peoples. (1996). *Bridging the Cultural Divide: A Report on Aboriginal People and Criminal Justice in Canada.* Ottawa, Ontario: Canada Communication Group Publishing.

Sinclair, Murray. (1994). "Aboriginal Peoples, Justice and the Law." In Continuing Poundmaker and Riel's Quest: Presentations Made at a Conference on Aboriginal Peoples and Justice. R. Grosse, J. Y. Henderson, and R. Carter, eds. pp. 173-184. Saskatoon, Saskatchewan: Purich Publishing.

19 See *Bridging the Cultural Divide, supra* note 1 at 271-272. Pauktuutit made seven recommendations:

1. There must be full community discussion of the cases that should be eligible for such programs.

2. Where Circles are organized, there must be adequate preparation of the community for the Circle — people need to know what is expected of them.

3. Membership in the Circle cannot be decided unilaterally, the entire community must have full input into this process.

4. The victim must have a meaningful say in the deliberative process whether that be in person or through some type of impact statement.

5. Communities themselves must acquire greater awareness about wife abuse issues in general.

6. Sentencing alternatives must look beyond the needs of the offender.

7. Couples should not be required to attend counseling together. The needs of each party may be very different. Requiring both parties to attend counseling suggests that both parties are equally responsible for the assault.

20 Each jurisdiction has its own *Arbitration Act*. The overall thrust is the same, but there are some differences in details.

21 See Royal Commission on Donald Marshall, Jr., Prosecution (Halifax, Nova Scotia: 1989).

22 To contact the Indigenous Bar Association (IBA) call (613) 233-8686 or via internet at www.indigenousbar.ca.

23 The need for an Aboriginal JP in a particular area is determined through consultations with chiefs, councils, Aboriginal organizations and friendship societies as well as justice officials. There are nine full-time positions — in Cochrane, London, Brantford, Thunder Bay, Kenora, Sarnia, Toronto, Sault Ste. Marie, and Sudbury — and thirty to forty part-time positions across the province. In addition to word-of-mouth publication, vacancies are advertised in local newspapers, and the co-ordinators of the JP Program also visit the communities who would be served by the JP to meet and encourage likely people to come forward.

24 For more information, contact the Aboriginal Policing Directorate, Solicitor General Canada, 340 Laurier Avenue, West, Ottawa, Ontario K1A 0P8.

25 On the subject of appointing and removing First Nations Constables, see the *Police Services Act*, R.S.O. 1990, c. P.15, s. 54.

26 In *R. v. Stephens* (1995), [1996] 1 C.N.L.R. 200 (Ont. C.A.) the First Nation Constable stopped a Band member for a traffic offence outside of the reserve. The Court of Appeal held that the Constable had jurisdiction off reserve.

27 On the subject of Band Constables, see endnote 6 above.

28 *A Special Issue on Land Claims Reform*, Indian Claims Commission Proceedings [1995] 2 ICCP (Co-chairs: D.J. Bellegarde & P.E. James Prentice) at 9.

29 For the detailed description of the recommended Aboriginal Lands and Treaties Tribunal see Royal Commission on Aboriginal Peoples, *Restructuring the Relationship*, Volume 2, Part Two (Ottawa: Minister of Supply and Services, 1996) at 591-619 [hereinafter *RCAP, Vol. 2, Part Two*].

25

Getting Legal Advice

1. LAWYERS

(a) When to consult a lawyer

In general, it is wise to consult a lawyer when entering any new situation with legal implications. For example:

- signing an important contract
- setting up a joint venture, or other economic development scheme
- negotiating a self-government agreement with government
- passing by-laws
- upon receiving notification of a claim or requirement to appear in court

People do not need to consult a lawyer every time they turn around. On the other hand, involving a lawyer in a legal matter early can prevent problems later, or can prevent a small problem from getting bigger.

The law which affects Aboriginal people is often complex, often making professional advice necessary. In the past, the Department of Indian Affairs has not encouraged the use of lawyers by Aboriginal people, and has generally not provided money for legal consultation. This is astounding, considering that some First Nations run multi-million dollar operations. An enterprise of such magnitude would not be expected to exist in non-Aboriginal society without budgeting for legal advice.

Persons or organizations which have a regular lawyer, should be able to phone and ask whether a problem they are facing would benefit from legal advice. The lawyer should tell them whether and how he or she could help. If the problem is primarily political, such as deciding who should get priority for housing on a reserve, there will not be much a lawyer can contribute. This type of decision is one which the Aboriginal government must make on its own. If, however, the problem revolves around a question of law, such as knowing whether rent controls apply on reserve, a lawyer's advice will be helpful.

(b) Choosing a lawyer

A lawyer will not know everything. Most lawyers know very little about Aboriginal law. Until recently, law schools gave low priority to teaching this area of law. When it is taught, most students learn only about the theory of Aboriginal and treaty rights; they are not taught about practical issues which affect organizations and Aboriginal people on a day-to-day basis. The Aboriginal client may have to help educate the lawyer. The lawyer should be interested in learning Aboriginal law, and willing to consult an expert in Aboriginal law when he or she needs help.

For routine matters such as employment questions and incorporation, it is probably most convenient to choose a lawyer in the immediate vicinity. The consultation will be easier, and the costs will often be lower. For matters which are more complex or require specialized knowledge of Aboriginal law, the wisest course would be to consult an expert directly, or have a local lawyer do so.

It is important that the client feel comfortable with the lawyer he or she chooses and that the client have confidence in the lawyer. Asking the following questions may help the client decide:

- Does this lawyer have experience with Aboriginal communities?
- Does the lawyer have any experience in Aboriginal law?
- Does the lawyer know other lawyers who are experts in Aboriginal law?
- Does the lawyer listen to what the client has to say?
- Does the lawyer attempt to explain the legal situation in a way the client can understand?
- Does the lawyer consult the client before taking action?
- Has someone recommended this lawyer?
- What are the lawyer's rates? Can the client afford them?

(c) How much will a lawyer cost?

The answer depends, of course, on how much work the lawyer does. Almost everything, except the most routine jobs, is charged by the hour. Rates can range from less than $100 to over $400 per hour. The lawyer and client should discuss the rates and the estimate of cost for a project at the beginning. The client should tell the lawyer what he or she can afford. If the work has a public interest element or raises a new legal issue, sometimes a lawyer will offer to do the work for less than the usual fee.

Often a lawyer will ask for some money up front before beginning the work. This money, called "the retainer", must be placed in a trust account. The lawyer cannot take the money out of the trust account until he or she has earned it and sent a bill for it. The bill will typically include the following items:

- the cost for the professional services of the lawyer
- the cost for other lawyers or students who may have worked on the file
- the cost of photocopies, long distance charges, courier bills and travel expenses

If the client is paying a substantial amount of money up front, he or she can ask the lawyer to put it into an interest-bearing account, so that the client will be credited with interest on the money.

(d) What if the client cannot afford a lawyer?

(i) *Legal Aid Certificates*[1]

People who cannot afford a lawyer may be eligible for a legal aid certificate. The certificate means the person's legal fees will be paid by a provincial Legal Aid Plan. In theory, a person can then retain the lawyer of his or her choice. In practice, some lawyers' fees are more than legal aid will pay, so a potential client should check to make sure the lawyer he or she wants will accept payment under the legal aid certificate.

Legal aid is available to people of low income. If, for example, a person in need of legal services is on welfare, has debts, and has little or no money in the bank, he or she is probably financially eligible for legal aid. If the person's financial position is a little better, he or she may still be eligible for assistance, but may have to repay the Legal Aid Plan when he or she can. For example, let us say that a person is supporting a family on a low income, but owns the house the family lives in. Legal aid may give that person a certificate and take out a "lien" on the house. This means that when the house is sold, the Legal Aid Plan is entitled to be repaid out of the proceeds of the sale.

There are also some policy limits on the type of case that can be funded by legal aid. For example, in some cases, it must be "reasonable" for the client to try to resolve his or her problem through the legal process. The client may have a serious problem, but it may be one that the legal process is not well suited or able to handle. Or the legal aid assessor may think the client has no chance of winning. In such cases, it might not be possible to obtain a legal aid certificate.

A decision not to grant a legal aid certificate can be appealed. It is helpful to have legal advice for the appeal. This can put people in the unfortunate position of needing to hire a lawyer because they cannot afford to hire a lawyer! An inexpensive way to improve the chances of an appeal's success would be to pay a lawyer for enough time to learn what the strongest basis of appeal would be, and then do the appeal without the lawyer.

(ii) *Community Legal Aid Clinics*

Several provinces fund community legal aid clinics. These clinics are staffed by lawyers and their services are free for people who cannot afford to hire a lawyer. The clinics are governed by a Board of Directors drawn from the community.

The eligibility requirements for the clinics are not necessarily the same as for a legal aid certificate. Even if a person is turned down for a certificate, he or she may still be able to get help from a clinic. Some clinics are limited in the type of legal work they do. Calling the nearest clinic is the easiest way to find out if they can take a particular case.

In Manitoba, two Aboriginal paralegals work out of the Thompson Legal Aid office travel to the communities of Cross lake, God's Lake Narrows, Norway House, Shamattawa and Oxford House. Both speak English and Cree. In each of these communities the paralegals hold drop-in clinics to help residents understand and use Legal Aid services. They also assist community organizations in developing justice-related programs (such as crisis shelters or fine option programs) and dealing with larger legal problems affecting the entire community.

(iii) *Law Students at Law Schools*

Nearly every law school in Canada has a program which allows law students to represent people who cannot afford a lawyer. The students are supervised by a lawyer. The type of cases they handle vary from law school to law school.

(iv) *Nishnawbe-Aski Legal Services Corporation in Ontario*

The Nishnawbe-Aski Legal Services Corporation was established in 1989 by the member First Nations in northern Ontario to deliver a wide range of law-related services. The head office of the corporation is at the Fort William First Nation, but it employs community legal workers in all the member communities. The community legal workers are members of the Nishnawbe Aski Nation and speak the language of the community they serve as well as English. The Corporation also provides interpretation services, provides public legal education, conducts research, makes recommendations about reforming the law, and issues Legal Aid Certificates.

(v) *Small Claims Court*

In cases that are eligible for Small Claims Court a person may be able to handle the whole case him- or herself. Small Claims Court is set up so people can sue for a few thousand dollars, depending on the province, without needing a lawyer to represent them. The forms needed to start a claim are available from the court.

Because Small Claims Court is a forum mainly for people without lawyers, it is less formal than other courts, and the people involved in the case are not expected to know everything about the law. The important thing is to state the case clearly and concisely. Present any documents or witnesses that provide proof.

If a person who has to go to court can afford it, it might be helpful to get a bit of advice from a lawyer. The lawyer can explain where he or she stands with respect to the law and how best to put forward his or her case. This will not be nearly as expensive as hiring the lawyer to do the whole thing.

If a person is sued, he or she will receive a document called a Statement of Claim. The form will say how much time the defendant has to respond. The defendant should definitely respond: even if he or she knows he or she really does owe the other person what they are asking for, the court may give the defendant a bit of time to get the money, or let him or her pay in installments if needed. A document from court should never be ignored.

2. LITIGATION

Going to court can be expensive and time-consuming. In a typical case which is not a criminal case, the following steps take place. (The process in criminal cases is discussed in the chapter on criminal law.)

- one side (the Plaintiff) begins the court action and files a claim describing the situation
- the other side (the Defendant) files a defence outlining his or her side of the story
- in complex cases, there may be an Examination for Discovery, in which each side is entitled to question one witness from the other side. Often the additional information obtained makes it possible to settle the case at this point.

- there may be a pre-trial hearing in which the lawyers go before a judge to explain their case briefly, and see what the judge thinks about it. Often the case is settled at this point.
- there is a trial.
- there may be an appeal from the decision at the trial.

The loser at the trial will usually have to pay for his or her own lawyer and part of the other side's legal costs. The winner at the trial will usually have to pay some costs of his or her lawyer. So, even winning at trial means paying legal fees. Losing at trial means paying a lot. It is important, then, to assess the chances of success very carefully before going to trial. A lawyer's advice will be helpful on this point.

This is not to say that litigation should be avoided completely. In some cases, there is no other choice because the parties cannot agree on a settlement. In other cases, important matters of principle are at stake and require the decision of a judge for clarification.

3. NEGOTIATIONS

Many people who run into a problem think they have only two options: sue or give up. There is another option though: negotiation. A person who feels wronged should assess what he or she wants from the situation, and then approach the other side to see if they can come to an agreement. The other side probably has something they want as well, so the parties may be able to reach a compromise.

In some situations, if the two sides cannot come to an agreement, it may be helpful to have a neutral third person hear the problem and come up with a solution. This is especially true when the negotiations involve many parties, such as the federal and provincial governments. The Indian Commission of Ontario, the British Columbia Treaty Commission and the federal Indian Claims Commission, can provide a neutral facilitator for negotiations which involve the federal and provincial governments and a First Nation.

ENDNOTES

1 Below is information on legal aid plans in the provinces and territories.

PROVINCIAL LEGAL PLANS

Yukon — Legal Aid

For legal aid Administration, contact:
200–212 Main Street
Whitehorse, YT
Y1A 2A9 Fax: 667-8649
General Inquiries: 667-5210

CLARKE CAMPBELL COMMUNITY LAW CLINIC
102–2131 Second Avenue
Whitehorse, YT
Y1A 1C3
Fax: 393-6320
Phone: 667-3562

British Columbia — Legal Services Society

Matters Covered:

Criminal charges where the accused is likely to go to jail or you are charged under the *Young Offenders Act*;

Family problems including separation, custody, child support, restraining orders, and child removals;

Immigration problems where the person is at risk of being deported from Canada; and

Human rights problems if they are covered by the B.C. *Human Rights Act*.

Staff at legal aid offices can give you information and advice about welfare rights, tenants' rights, Employment Insurance (formerly known as Unemployment Insurance or UI).

For online information, see:
http://www.vcn.bc.ca/lssbc/LSS_LegalAid/LSS_ApplyLegalAid.html

Alberta — Alberta Legal Aid Society

Calgary: (403) 297-2260
Edmonton: (780) 427-7575
Fort McMurray: (780) 743-7356
Grande Prairie: (780) 538-5470
Hinton: (780) 865-8239

Lethbridge: (403) 381-5194
Medicine Hat: (403) 529-3553
Peace River: (780) 624-6250
Red Deer: (403) 340-5119
St. Paul: (780) 645-6205
Wetaskiwin: (780) 352-7011
Whitecourt: (780) 778-7178

Saskatchewan — Saskatchewan Legal Aid Commission.

Contact the office in your area for more information on eligibility and how to apply.

Central Office
#820–410 22nd Street East
SASKATOON, SK S7K 2H6
Phone: (306) 933-5300
Fax: (306) 933-6764
Toll Free: 1-800-667-3764
Northern Saskatchewan: 1-800-667-4095

Manitoba — Legal Aid in Manitoba

In Manitoba, there are three types of Legal Aid services:

1. Drop-in Advice and Information: Members of the public may meet with a lawyer or supervised paralegal to discuss any legal problem. No application is needed for this type of service — everyone qualifies. Legal Aid Manitoba operates a drop-in program which provides legal information, general advice and some basic assistance, general advice and some basic assistance. Lawyers or supervised paralegals provide free 15-30 minute consultations. Everyone is welcome to make use of this service — there are no financial eligibility criteria.

2. Duty Counsel: Lawyers are present in many criminal and youth and some child welfare courts to help and advise anyone who has to appear before a judge. An application is not needed for this type of service — everyone qualifies. Legal Aid Duty Counsel is available in the following Provincial Court locations:

3. Legal Aid Certificate/Formal Representation
Matters covered:
Criminal matters; if you are charged with an "indictable" offence;
Most family law matters, such as separations, divorces and child custody matters so as long as you will receive some benefit from going to court

Civil matters such as Workers Compensation Claims where the legal aid director determines that you have a reasonable chance of winning.

If more information is needed about the Legal Aid system call: (204) 985-8500

On-line information at http://www.mbnet.mb.ca/crm/law/legaid1.html#03

Ontario — Legal Aid Ontario

Unless you are on social assistance, there is a $25 application fee.

Case Eligibility: For criminal charges:any offense which could result in jail time (assault, murder, theft over $1,000, break and enter). In family courts: custody, restraining orders, child support, child protection. Immigration and refugee matters.

For other civil cases: workers compensation, social assistance review board, landlord and tenant, mental health, parole and prison matters.

For a list of legal aid offices see:
www.legalaid.on.ca/office.html

Ontario Legal Aid Plan
375 University Avenue
Toronto, Ontario M5G 2G1
(416) 979-1446
1-800-668-8258

Québec — La Commission des services juridiques (Legal Services Commission)

The Commission sets up community legal centres and local legal aid clinics. Its mandate is to help economically underprivileged persons by allowing them to obtain legal counsel from a lawyer or notary and to exercise their rights in court should it become necessary. Information is available from the Legal Aid office in the local municipality.

Nova Scotia — Nova Scotia Legal Aid

Office phone numbers are listed in the phone book under Nova Scotia Legal Aid. Metro Community Law Clinic is part of Legal Aid. Tel. 420-3450. Dalhousie Legal Aid serves Halifax/Dartmouth 423-8105.

Northwest Territories

Case eligibility: criminal (indictable) and some family matters (child custody, access, support; spousal support; restraining orders; child welfare).

For more information contact:
Legal Services Board (Legal Aid)
Box 1320
Yellowknife, NWT XlA 2L9
Phone: (403) 873-7450
Fax: (403) 873-5320

Prince Edward Island

For information, call the Legal Aid Office (902) 368-6015

New Brunswick — Legal Aid

For information, call: (506) 453-3693

Family Support Orders Service (506) 453-2015 (for the enforcement of child and spousal support).

Newfoundland

http://www.gov.nf.ca/just/other/legalaid.htm
Legal Aid Commission 21 Church Hill St. John's, NF A1C 3Z8
Telephone: (709) 753-7860
Facsimile: (709) 729-7851

26

Injunctions and Blockades

POINTS TO REMEMBER

1. Aboriginal communities may take actions such as blockades to enforce their claims, or to draw attention to a problem.

2. A court-ordered injunction could require people to end a blockade. A temporary injunction can be given by a court very quickly. The final decision on the injunction may require a full trial which could be years down the line.

3. Criminal charges arising out of a blockade may be addressed in various ways. Usually, there is a criminal trial. However, at various stages, the Attorney General, the Crown attorney, or the court may decide not to proceed with the charges.

4. Aboriginal people can try to use injunctions to stop development activity on their traditional lands.

1. INTRODUCTION

The way in which lands and resources are used has often lead to conflicts between Aboriginal communities and non-Aboriginal people. Some of these conflicts turn into confrontations on the ground in the form of blockades, and confrontations in court in the form of a request for an injunction.

This chapter will begin with a discussion of injunctions sought by federal and provincial governments, or by private parties to stop blockades. The next section will discuss how the courts treat the criminal charges which often arise from a blockade. Finally, there will be a discussion of how Aboriginal groups try to use injunctions to stop activity on their traditional territory.

(a) Blockades

Blockades and similar protests are used as a last resort by Aboriginal communities. Blockades can occur for a variety of reasons. In some cases, there is a dispute over the ownership of land or water. In other cases, there are collateral issues, such as the sympathy blockades that occurred all across Canada during the Oka Crisis, and the highway blockades in 1993 in New Brunswick over the imposition of the provincial sales tax. While blockades receive the most publicity, the most common action taken is in the form of information pickets and placards by the side of a public highway. Nevertheless, a simmering unresolved dispute over land can erupt into a violent situation. In 1990, an attempted expansion of a golf club into disputed territory led to the seventy-eight-day confrontation between the Canadian Army and Mohawk Warriors at Oka.[1]

(b) Injunctions

An injunction is a court order requiring someone to stop doing something. Federal and provincial governments often attempt to get injunctions to stop blockades and pickets by Aboriginal people. Aboriginal people may also attempt to get injunctions to stop development on their traditional lands or waters.

Injunctions are available in several types of circumstances. If there appears to be an emergency situation, the court may give an injunction after hearing only one side of the story (*ex parte* injunction). These injunctions are only temporary, and the court will, within a matter of days, hold a hearing with both sides. Eventually, there may be a full-blown trial on the issue related to the injunction. However, because it may be years before the trial occurs, there may be several hearings on the use of temporary injunctions (interim or interlocutory injunctions) until the issue if finally settled.[2]

Anyone ignoring an injunction can be found to be in contempt of court.[3] In blockade situations, injunctions are often granted by courts. Even if people have blockaded a road because they believe an injustice is taking place, they may face contempt of court charges or other charges under the Criminal Code.

(c) The case of the Teme-Augama Anishnabai

Clashes involving First Nations, environmentalists and Crown governments have occurred throughout Canada in such places as Clayoquot Sound and Old Man River. Examples follow of legal clashes over the construction of a logging road on the territory of the Teme-augama Anishnabai (Bear Island First Nation) in Temagami, Ontario that illustrate how injunctions, criminal charges and other court proceedings are related.

In 1973, the First Nation became involved in a court action relating to its title to the land. They lost their land claim in the trial court in 1987 and again in the Ontario Court of Appeal in 1989. In 1989, the provincial government decided to approve the building of the Red Squirrel logging road into the territory of the land claim. An environmental group, the Temagami Wilderness Society, applied for an injunction to stop construction of the logging road. When the court refused to grant an injunction, the Temagami Wilderness Society announced that on September 15, 1989, it would blockade the road. The day the blockade was supposed to go up, the provincial Attorney General applied for an injunction to prevent the blockade from occurring. The court turned down the application for the injunction. The court's view was that an injunction should not be granted before there was any illegal activity.

In October, the First Nation requested an injunction against the logging. This injunction was refused by the court. The First Nation began blockading the road, and called for support from First Nations across Ontario. This resulted in a request for an injunction by the Ontario government to stop the blockades. The court granted the injunction in favour of the Ontario government in November. Nevertheless, the blockades in support of the First Nation occurred off and on for the next few weeks. People chained themselves to machinery and in the words of the court, by "pretending to play beavers" they flooded portions of the road. Dozens of people were arrested, including New Democratic Party members of the provincial Legislature. Many charges arose out of these arrests, with some convictions and some acquittals.[4]

2. INJUNCTIONS AGAINST BLOCKADES

Not every protest will result in court proceedings. There are a number of activities which are legal and which will not result in injunctions or criminal charges.

One commonly used tactic is to provide information to passing motorists or to hold information pickets. Some of these activities will be protected by the *Canadian Charter of Rights and Freedoms* as legitimate forms of expression.[5]

The Serpent River First Nation in Ontario successfully brought attention to its problems without incurring criminal charges or injunctions through a series of escalating public demonstrations. This community had lived with one hundred acres of abandoned industrial waste on its reserve for more than two decades. The sulphur in the waste would occasionally ignite spontaneously, and there were persistent health complaints from the residents. After years of unproductive negotiations, the First Nation moved some of the sulphur-laden waste into a pile 8 metres high pile on the edge of the reserve, beside the Trans-Canada Highway. A member of the First Nation erected a 10-metre high sign beside the waste naming the federal government and the private sector companies involved in creating the waste.

When further negotiations produced no results, members of the First Nation lined the highways holding placards asking for support for removing the now smouldering pile of waste. The federal government finally provided funding for a $6 million clean up which removed the waste from the reserve and placed it in an environmentally sound waste disposal site.

Sometimes, it may not be clear whether a blockade is legal or illegal until after a court has decided on the request for an injunction. The whole point of many blockades is that a piece of land is in dispute. First Nations may claim a right to the land, while the federal or provincial government, or private interests, may claim that such right does not exist.

Courts in these situations must decide whether to grant an injunction. If the First Nation is successful, then they are not acting illegally. If the judge thinks that the First Nation is wrong, and the land is not theirs, then the First Nation could be acting illegally.[6]

In order to make a determination of which party is right, the court will usually want to hear evidence at a full trial. In the meantime, until a full trial can be held, the judge must decide whether to allow the blockade to continue. In these cases, the judge will make a temporary decision based on preliminary information and will consider three factors:[7]

1. Is there a serious legal question?

The courts have posed this question in different ways, but the basic purpose is for the judge to make a temporary decision to determine whether the proceeding is "frivolous or vexation." In other words, the judge should usually assume that the proceeding raises serious issues. The next stage is to look at questions two and three.

2. Will there be "irreparable harm?"

The court should consider whether one party will suffer the harm immediately, which cannot be made better later. For example, if money can compensate for a loss, there may be no irreparable harm.

3. What is the balance of convenience?

Each party may be inconvenienced, but the court will decide based on a consideration of the public interest.

The following three stories illustrate how courts may address these principles.

The Mount Currie First Nation in British Columbia blocked traffic on a road passing through its reserve, claiming that the road belonged to the First Nation. The province of British Columbia asked for an injunction, claiming that the road belonged to the province. The judge in this case first looked at the documents and decided that the province had a fair legal issue which could be argued at a full trial. Second, the judge looked at the balance of convenience and decided that he should try to maintain the status quo. Since the road through the reserve had been used as a public highway, and traffic had passed through it for years, the court held that the status quo required that the blockade be stopped.[8]

The Teme-Augama Anishnabai in the case referred to earlier, (Ontario) blockaded the construction of the Red Squirrel logging road through territory that was claimed by them. The provincial Attorney

General went to court to get an injunction. The court ruled that the Aboriginal people had no right to interfere with the construction of the road, and went on to say, "only at its peril will our society allow anyone to flout the law. . . . In such case, the Attorney-General does not have to show that irreparable harm will result if the injunction is not granted." However, the judge pointed out that peaceful demonstrations should not be prohibited, and that "[p]eaceful demonstrators can express their opposition without standing within a few feet of where the work is actually being performed."[9]

The Seton Lake First Nation blocked a B.C. Rail line on August 17, 1990, to support the Mohawks at Oka. The court issued several injunctions, which protesters ignored. One blockade of 25 protesters was cleared on August 19, but two days later another blockade was erected at another site. On August 23, a blockade went up again at the first site. Arrests followed, and protesters were transported to Vancouver to appear in court. The judge upheld the arrests and saying, "Defiance of the orders went to public injury. The public would have viewed the justice system with scorn if enforcement of the injunctions was not immediate and decisive." (at 392)[10]

3. ARREST AND CRIMINAL CHARGES

Criminal charges are often laid in the context of blockades. The charges vary, but are often for mischief, or contempt of court. The procedure for dealing with criminal charges is discussed in the chapter on Criminal Law. This section highlights some of the elements particular to blockades.

(a) Staying or withdrawing the charge

Even though charges are laid, the Crown Attorney, or the Attorney General may decide not to proceed with the charges. For example, in Moose Factory, Ontario, the RCMP charged members of the Moose Factory First Nation with goose hunting in the spring. The spring hunt was prohibited by the *Migratory Birds Convention Act*. However, when the Attorney General of Canada received information from the provincial Ministry of Natural Resources that the hunt did not pose a threat to conservation, and that the hunt had occurred informally in past years, the Attorney General decided to stay the charges.[11]

In Ontario, the Attorney General decided to withdraw charges against a number of the protesters involved in the blockades surrounding the Teme-Augama First Nation's claims. The Attorney General said that the prosecutions would be "contrary to the best interests of the administration of justice". In this case, the individuals charged were not the "leaders", and the Chief of the First Nation, the "principal architect of the blockade", had already been acquitted.[12]

Ontario did proceed with charges against the "leaders" of the Teme-Augama Anishnabai. However, the judge said that the distinction between the "leaders" and the followers was arbitrarily and unfairly applied. Therefore, the judge decided to stay the charges against the people who had been charged as the "leaders".[13]

(b) Refusal to recognize jurisdiction of the court

Some Aboriginal people refuse to recognize the jurisdiction of the provincial or federal courts, and refuse to enter a plea of guilty or not guilty. In such cases, the court will enter a plea of not guilty, and proceed with the trial.[14]

The issue came up in a case that arose out of a confrontation at Gustafson Lake in British Columbia in 1995. After 185 days of trial, the accused were convicted of a number of offences related to the confrontation. The accused appealed on the basis that the courts of British Columbia had no jurisdiction on the land that had been in dispute. The court rejected this ground, stating,

> It is well established that the courts of British Columbia have jurisdiction over aboriginal accused where an offence has allegedly been committed within the Province, regardless of whether or not the territory could be said to be "beyond the treaty frontier", or is "unsurrendered ground . . ."[15]

(c) Defence of colour of right

At the trial, the Crown must prove its case beyond a reasonable doubt. The accused person may also raise defences. One defence which is often raised is that the accused person had an honest belief that the land belonged to Aboriginal people. This was the defence raised by Chief Gary Potts of the Teme-Augama Anishnabai. In accepting that defence, the judge said,

When all is said and done, and all the pertinent facts are duly considered by this Court, having regard to the principles of law which govern it, this Court is of the view that Mr. Potts, Chief of the Teme-Augama Anishnabai People, could perhaps be very much mistaken in his reasoning processes as they involved very sensitive issues, and yet still be honest.[16]

The defence of "colour of right" has a limited application. First, it can only be used if there is some reason to believe that the land in question is Aboriginal land.[17]If the land is clearly not Aboriginal, the defence would not apply. For example, a blockade of a public highway to protest against the imposition of sales taxes would probably not qualify for a colour of right defence. Second, this defence can only be used once. After the court has informed the individual that there is no "colour of right", that individual probably could not convince a judge that he or she made the same mistake a second time.

(d) Sentencing

Because trials resulting from blockades are governed by the same rules as other court proceedings, the results vary from case to case. Charges may be dismissed for technical reasons, or individuals may "plea bargain". If there is a finding of guilt, the judge may consider the motives in passing the sentence.

4. INJUNCTIONS BY ABORIGINAL PEOPLE TO STOP DEVELOPMENT

Injunctions can be used by Aboriginal people to stop development on their lands.[18]

(a) James Bay Crees

One of the most significant injunctions in the past twenty years was the attempt by the James Bay Cree to stop hydro-electric development on their territories. Claiming that Quebec had not settled Indian rights to land in northern Quebec, the Cree succeeded in having a judge of the Quebec Superior Court grant an injunction against the James Bay Development Corporation on November 15, 1973.

However, a week later, on November 22, the Court of Appeal lifted the injunction temporarily and a year later confirmed its decision to lift the injunction.[19] While the dispute continued in the courts, the Quebec Cree were able to negotiate the James Bay and Northern Quebec Agreement.

(b) Meares Island

In British Columbia, there was a high profile dispute in 1985. It concerned logging on Meares Island, an area that was part of a land claim by the Nuu-Chah-Nulth Tribal Council on Vancouver Island. Non-Aboriginal and Aboriginal environmental protesters took a series of actions to prevent logging by MacMillan Bloedel, including removing survey marks and putting spikes in trees.

MacMillan Bloedel attempted to get an injunction to stop the protesters. At the same time, two First Nations in the area went to court to get an injunction to stop MacMillan Bloedel from logging.

The first trial judge said that the Indians had no prospect of success, so MacMillan Bloedel could continue logging. The British Columbia Court of Appeal heard the case, and came to a different decision from the first judge. The Court of Appeal granted an injunction against MacMillan Bloedel and stopped them from logging. The court also ordered the protesters to stop their activities.

Mr. Justice Seaton stated that there was a serious legal issue about Aboriginal rights in the forest, and that a full trial was necessary to address that very complex issue. If MacMillan Bloedel were allowed to cut down the forest before the trial, there would be no forest left if the First Nations won the case:

> Meares Island is of importance to MacMillan Bloedel, but it cannot be said that denying or postponing its right would cause irreparable harm. If an injunction prevents MacMillan Bloedel from logging pending the trial and it is decided that MacMillan Bloedel has the right to log, the timber will still be there.
>
> The position of the Indians is quite different. It appears that the area to be logged will be wholly logged. The forest that the Indians know and use will be permanently destroyed. The tree from which the bark was partially stripped in 1642 may be cut down, middens may be destroyed, fish traps damaged and canoe runs despoiled. Finally, the Island's symbolic value will be gone. The subject matter of the trial will have been destroyed before the rights are decided.[20]

(c) Tsawout First Nation

An injunction was successfully used to preserve a treaty fishing right. The Tsawout First Nation in British Columbia claimed a right to fish under the Saanich Treaty of 1852. A proposed marina on Saanich Bay would have interfered with the treaty fishing right. In 1989, the British Columbia Court of Appeal granted a permanent injunction against the establishment of a marina.[21]

(d) Tsay Keh Dene

The Tsay Keh Dene Band applied for an interim injunction to stop Kemess Mines from cutting timber on traditional lands which were part of a land claim. The court refused the injunction, partly because there would not be any irreparable harm. One of the reasons the court came to the conclusion, that there would be no irreparable harm to the Band, was the court's understanding that the Band only wanted monetary compensation.[22]

(e) Lower Fraser Fishing Authority

An application for an interlocutory injunction was brought by the Yale Indian Band to prevent other Indian bands from fishing pursuant to a communal license issued by the Crown. The band claimed that they had historically controlled the fishing in that part of the river. The application was refused.

The court found that the communal licence was part of a pilot project to help create a cooperative relationship between the federal government and Indian fishermen in an area where fishing rights had been disputed for years. There was no status quo to protect, the risk of irreparable harm to the respondents was substantial, and the injunction would threaten the cooperation between the federal government and the other First Nations.[23]

5. CONCLUSION

The longest, most significant confrontation in Canadian history occurred between the Canadian army and Mohawk Warriors in 1990 at Oka and Kahnawake. This is a description by journalist Geoffrey York of the interrogation of Mohawk Warrior Ronald "Lasagna"

Cross by the Quebec police (the "SQ") after the end of the standoff at Oka:

> Barely two hours after the end of the siege, Lasagna was in handcuffs at the SQ headquarters on Parthenais Street in Montreal. The police forced him to kneel in a corner of a room. "We're going to have a party with you", they told him. Then the beating began . . .
>
> By daybreak his face was badly bruised and swollen, his right cheek was black and blue, and his right eye was almost closed by a large bruise over the eye.[24]

Cross was eventually brought to trial and convicted of twenty charges by a jury and acquitted of another twenty. In his remarks accompanying sentencing of Cross, Mr. Justice Greenberg pointed out the reasons for Cross' actions at the barricades:

> I am satisfied that he was not motivated by greed or reasons of personal gain. He acted out of a deep anger, rage, desperation and a sense of hopelessness, all the result of the systematic discrimination and racism against his people over several centuries. For years, decades, even centuries, the aboriginal people of this country have endured, at best, indifference, neglect and unfairness and, at worst, open hostility, contempt, discrimination and racism . . . The aboriginal peoples occupy a special place in the firmament of Canadian society. They were the original inhabitants of this country; this continent. The white man, the European settlers, came here and, by dint of their superior numbers (and) state of technological development and, hence, by force of arms, took the land from the natives.[25]

ENDNOTES

1 For an excellent account of the Oka Crisis, see *People of the Pines* Geoffrey York and Loreen Pindera (Toronto: Little Brown and Company, 1992).

2 See Roger Townshend, "Interlocutory Injunctions in Aboriginal Rights Cases", [1991] 3 C.N.L.R. 1.

3 For a case on criminal contempt, see *B.C. Rail Ltd. v. Louie* (1990), (sub nom. *B.C. Rail Ltd. v. Seton Lake Indian Band*) 52 B.C.L.R. (2d) 373 (B.C. S.C.), where twenty-five Band members closed down the railway tracks in support of the Mohawks at Oka.

4 For reported court decisions on the logging road dispute of the Teme-Augama Anishnabai in Ontario, see the following cases: *Ontario*

(Attorney General) v. Temagami Wilderness Society (1989), 38 C.P.C. (2d) 296 (Ont. H.C.); *Bear Island Foundation v. Ontario* (1989), [1990] 4 C.N.L.R. 3 (Ont. H.C.); *Ontario (Attorney General) v. Bear Island Foundation* (1989), [1990] 4 C.N.L.R. 25 (Ont. H.C.); and *R. v. Drainville* (1991), [1992] 3 C.N.L.R. 44 (Ont. Prov. Div.).

5 For a case recognizing that blockading was a form of expression, see Fournier, J. in *R. v. Drainville* (1991), [1992] 3 C.N.L.R. 44 (Ont. Prov. Div.) at 49: "action taken by protesters and concerned citizens in sitting on a road, obstructing it — can be said to be an "expression" which, depending on the circumstances, might be afforded protection under the Charter. However, the courts have ruled that "violence" as a form of "expression" cannot receive such protection."

6 An example of different levels of courts coming to different decisions on rights to land, leading to different decisions on the granting of an injunction, is found in *Canadian Pacific Ltd. v. Paul* (1988), [1989] 1 C.N.L.R. 47 (S.C.C.)

7 See *RJR-MacDonald Inc. v. Canada (Attorney General)*, [1994] 1 S.C.R. 311 (S.C.C.) for the test. While this was a case dealing with tobacco advertising, it is now the accepted standard for cases dealing with interlocutory injunctions.

8 For a case on a blockade of a road passing through a reserve, see *British Columbia (Attorney General) v. Mount Currie Indian Band* (1990), (sub nom. *British Columbia (Attorney General) v. Andrew*) [1991] 1 C.N.L.R. 14 (B.C. S.C.), affirmed (November 2, 1990), Doc. Vancouver C906203 (B.C. S.C. [In Chambers]), affirmed (sub nom. *British Columbia (Attorney General) v. Andrew*) [1991] 4 C.N.L.R. 3 (B.C. C.A.)

9 For the Teme-Augama Anishnabai case on blockades, see *Ontario (Attorney General) v. Bear Island Foundation* (1989), [1990] 4 C.N.L.R. 25 (Ont. H.C.) at 27.

10 The case on arrest provisions contained in an injunction is *B.C. Rail Ltd. v. Louie* (1990), (sub nom. *B.C. Rail Ltd. v. Seton Lake Indian Band*) 52 B.C.L.R. (2d) 373 (B.C. S.C.).

11 For information on the James Bay goose hunt, see the Chapter on "Hunting, Fishing and Trapping".

12 For the full statement of the Attorney General of Ontario in withdrawing charges against protesters, see *R. v. Beardy*, (June 24, 1991) (Ont. Prov. Div.) [unreported].

13 For the reasons for staying the charges against participants in a blockade, see *R. v. Katt* (January 20, 1992) (Ont. Prov. Div.) [unreported].

14 Chief Gary Potts of the Teme-Augama Anishnabai refused to enter a plea in *R. v. Potts* (November 28, 1990) Fournier Prov. J (Ont. Prov. Div.) [unreported].

15 The court rejected the argument that it had no jurisdiction over Aboriginal people in *R. v. Pena* (1998), (sub nom. *R. v. Ignace*) 156 D.L.R. (4th) 713 (B.C. C.A.), leave to appeal refused (1998), (sub nom. *R. v. Ignace*) 228 N.R. 198 (note) (S.C.C.) at para. 717.

16 For the defence of colour of right, see *R. v. Potts, supra*, note 14 at 28. The defence was successful for the Labrador Innu in *R. v. Ashini*, [1989] 2 C.N.L.R. 119 (Nfld. Prov. Ct.), reversed (1989), 79 Nfld. & P.E.I.R. 318 (Nfld. C.A.). However, the defence was not successful when raised by an Anglican priest and MPP, Dennis Drainville, when he was charged in the same series of blockades as Gary Potts: *R. v. Drainville* (1991), [1992] 3 C.N.L.R. 44 (Ont. Prov. Div.).

17 For a case rejecting the colour of right defence, see *R. v. Pena* (1997), 148 D.L.R. (4th) 372 (B.C. S.C.).

18 For an excellent description of remedies available for violation of constitutional rights see Kent Roach, "Remedies for Violations of Aboriginal Rights", (1992) 1 Man.L.J. 498.

19 The cases chronicling the James Bay Cree dispute with Quebec are *Gros-Louis v. La Societe de Development de la Baie James et al* (1973), 8 C.N.L.C. 188; *James Bay Development Corporation v. Kanatewat*, (1973) 8 C.N.L.C. 414; and *La Societe de Development de la Baie James v. Kanatewat* (1974), 8 C.N.L.C. 373.

20 For the case in which the court orders an injunction against logging in an area disputed under a land claim, see *MacMillan Bloedel v. Mullin*, [1985] 2 C.N.L.R. 58 (B.C. C.A.). A similar issue arose in the case of *Grant v. British Columbia* (1989), [1990] 2 C.N.L.R. 21 (B.C.C.A.) where the issue of the injunction against transfer of land was settled when the City of Vancouver agreed to accept the land subject to any Aboriginal claims.

21 For a case in which an injunction against the construction of a marina was granted in order to protect a treaty fishing right, see *Saanichton Marina Ltd. v. Claxton*, [1989] 3 C.N.L.R. 46 (B.C. C.A.).

22 For a case refusing an injunction because the harm could be addressed through monetary compensation, see *Tsay Keh Dene Band v. British Columbia (Minister of Environment, Lands & Parks)* (1997), 24 C.E.L.R. (N.S.) 66 (B.C. S.C.).

23 For an attempted injunction against a fishing agreement see *Yale Indian Band v. Lower Fraser Fishing Authority* [1993] 1 C.N.L.R. 182 (B.C. S.C.).

24 Page 401. Ronald Cross died in November, 1999 while working as a steelworker. Two weeks before he died, the Quebec police ethics commission had finally gotten around to suspending the police officers who had beaten Cross. The officers had already left the force, so that the penalty was meaningless.

25 *Ibid.*, page 428.

Bibliography

Alfred, Gerald R. *Heeding the Voices of Our Ancestors: Kahnawake Mohawk Politics and the Rise of Native Nationalism.* New York: Oxford, 1995 146

Anaya, James. *Indigenous Peoples in International Law.* New York: Oxford University Press, 1996 129

Asch, Michael and Catherine Bell. "Definition and Interpretation of Fact in Canadian Aboriginal Title Litigation: An Analysis of *Delgamuukw*," (1994) 19 Queen's Law Journal 503 39

Barkwell, Peter A. "The Medicine Chest Clause in Treaty No. 6", [1981] 4 C.N.L.R. 1 44

Bartlett, R.H. *Indians and Taxation in Canada, 3rd edition.* Saskatoon: Native Law Centre, 1992 296

Bell, Catherine. *Alberta's Metis Settlements Legislation: An Overview of Ownership and Management of Settlement Lands.* Saskatchewan: Canadian Plains Research Centre, University of Regina, 1994 90

Bell, Catherine. *Contemporary Métis Justice: The Settlement Way.* Saskatoon: Native Law Centre, 1999 90

Boldt, Menno. *Surviving as Indians: The Challenge of Self-government.* Toronto, University of Toronto Press, 1993 . . . 127

Borrows, John. "A Geneology of Law: Inherent Sovereignty and First Nations Self-government", Osgoode Hall Law Journal 291, 1992 127

Borrows, John. "Frozen Rights in Canada: Constitutional Interpretation and Trickster." [1997] 22 American Indian Law Review 37. 63

Cassidy, F. and R. Bish. *Indian Government: Its Meaning in Practice.* Lantzville: Oolichan Books, 1989 129

Chartier, C. "'Indian': an analysis of the term as used in section 91 (24) of the BNA Act," (1978-79) 43 Sask. L. rev. 37 . . . . 23, 89

Department of Indian & Northern Affairs. "Comprehensive Claims Policy and Status of Claims" 9 September 1997 80

Department of Indian & Northern Affairs. "Comprehensive Claims (Modern Treaties) in Canada", March 1996 90

Department of Indian & Northern Affairs. *First Nations in Canada*. Ottawa: Minister of Public Works & Government Services Canada, 1997 80

Department of Indian Affairs & Northern Development. *Backgrounder: Demographics*. Ottawa: Indian & Northern Affairs, 1997 . . . . 212, 269

Dickason, Olive Patricia. *Canada's First Nations: A History of Founding Peoples from Earliest Times*. Toronto: McClelland & Stewart, 1992 20

Dupuis, Rene and Kent McNeil. *Canada's Fiduciary Obligation to Aboriginal Peoples in the Context of Accession to Sovereignty by Quebec*. Ottawa: Minister of Supply and Services, 1995 109

Flanagan, Thomas. "The Case Against Metis Aboriginal Rights", in Boldt and Long, *The Quest for Justice: Aboriginal Peoples and Aboriginal Rights*. Toronto: University of Toronto Press, 1985 91

Fleras, A. and J.L. Elliot. *The Nations Within: Aboriginal-State Relations in Canada, the United States and New Zealand*. Toronto: Oxford University Press, 1992 127

Gilbert, Larry. *Entitlement to Indian Status and Membership Codes in Canada*. Toronto: Carswell, 1996 . . . . 150, 161

Goddard, John. *Last Stand of the Lubicon Cree*. Vancouver: Douglas & McIntyre Ltd., 1991 145

Hardy, Richard. "Metis Rights in the Mackenzie River District of the Northwest Territories", [1980] 1 C.N.L.R. 1 91

Hogg, P.W. *Constitutional Law of Canada*. Loose-leaf ed., 4th ed. Scarborough: Carswell, 1997 21

Hylton, John, ed. *Aboriginal Self-government in Canada: Current Trends and Issues*. Saskatoon: Purich Publishing, 1994 127

Imai, Shin and Katherine Laird. "The Indian Status Question: A Problem of Definitions", in Native People and Justice in Canada, 5 Canadian Legal Aid Bulletin (No. 1), 1982 161

Imai, Shin. "Preliminary Thoughts on *Delgamuukw* and Treaty Rights", (October 1998) 6 Canada Watch 4, 5 &6 272

Imai, Shin. *Annotated Indian Act and Aboriginal Constitutional Provisions*. Scarborough: Carswell, 1999 21

Kapashesit, Randy and Murray Klippenstein. "Aboriginal Group Rights and Environmental Protection", (1991), 36 McGill Law Journal 926 . . . . 39, 127

LaRoque, Emma. "Re-examining Culturally Appropriate Models in Criminal Justice Application" in Michael Asch, ed., *Aboriginal and Treaty Rights in Canada: Essays on Law,*

Equity and Respect for Difference. Vancouver: U.B.C. Press,
1997 382
Little Bear, L. M. Boldt, J. Long (eds.), *Pathways to
Self-Determination.* Toronto: University of Toronto, 1986 . . . 78, 129
Macklem, Patrick. "Aboriginal Peoples, Criminal Justice
Initiatives and the Constitution", U.B.C. Law Review, 1992 354
Macklem, Patrick. "First Nations Self-Government and the
Borders of the Canadian Legal Imagination".[1991] 36 McGill
Law Journal 127
Macklem, Patrick. "The Impact of Treaty 9 on Natural Resources
and Development in Northern Ontario," in Michael Asch, ed.
Aboriginal and Treaty Rights in Canada: Essays on Law, Equity
and Respect for Difference. Vancouver: University of British
Columbia, 1997 . . . . 40, 42, 57, 272
Maracle, Brian. *Back on the Rez: Finding the Way Home.* Toronto:
Viking, 1996 146
McInnis, Edgar. *Canada.* Toronto: Holt Rinehart and Winston,
1969 20
McLeod, Clay. "The Oral Histories of Canada's Northern People,
Anglo-Canadian Evidence Law and Canada's Fiduciary Duty to
First Nations: Breaking Down the Barriers of the Past", (1992)
30 Alta. L. Rev. (No. 4) 1276 39
McNeil, Kent. "The High Cost of Accepting Benefits from the
Crown: A Comment on the Temagami Indian Land Case"
[1992] 1 C.N.L.R. 40 41
Mercredi, Ovide and Mary Ellen Turpel. *In the Rapids: Navigating
the Future of the First Nations.* Toronto: Viking, 1993 127
Mills, Antonia. *Eagle Down is Our Law; Witsuwit'en Law, Feasts
and Land Claims.* Vancouver: U.B.C. Press, 1994 39
Morse, B. "By-law enforcement options: a brief survey", [1980] 2
C.N.L.R. 61 150
Moss, Wendy. "Indigenous Self-government in Canada and Sexual
Equality Under the Indian Act: Resolving Conflicts Between
Collective and Individual Rights", (1990) 15 *Queen's Law
Journal* 279 22
Nanahee, Theresa. "Dancing with a Gorilla: Aboriginal Women,
Justice and the Charter", *Aboriginal People and the Justice
System, Report on the National Round Table on Aboriginal
Justice Issues.* Ottawa: Supply and Services, 1993 23
Notzke, Claudia. *Aboriginal Peoples and Natural Resources in
Canada.* North York: Captus University Publications, 1994 269

Parker, A.C. *The Code of the Handsome Lake, The Seneca
Prophet*. 2.5m. Ohsweken: Iroqrafts Ltd. Iroquois Publications,
1990 20

Parker, A.C. *The Constitution of the Five Nations or The Iroquois
book of the Great Law*. 2m. Ohsweken: Iroqrafts Ltd. Iroquois
Publications, 1984 20

Pentey, William. "The Rights of the Aboriginal Peoples of Canada
and the Constitution, 1982 – Part I: The Interpretive Prism of
Section 25", (1987) 22 U.B.C. Law Rev. 21 23

Pointing, J.R., ed. *Arduous Journey*. Toronto: McClelland &
Stewart, 1988 129

Ross, Rupert. *Dancing with a Ghost*. Markham: Octopus
Publishing Group, 1992 380

Rotman, Leonard. *Parallel Paths: Fiduciary Doctrine and the
Crown-Native Relationship in Canada*. Toronto: University of
Toronto Press, 1996 24

Royal Commission on Aboriginal Peoples. *Looking Forward,
Looking Back*, Volume 4. Ottawa: Ministry of Supply and
Services, 1996 . . . . 23, 88, 89, 107, 161, 234

Royal Commission on Aboriginal Peoples, *Restructuring the
Relationship*, Volume 2, Part Two. Ottawa: Supply and
Services, 1996 . . . . 23, 57, 128, 152, 269, 272, 385

Royal Commission on Aboriginal Peoples. *Gathering Strength*,
Volume 3. Ottawa: Supply and Sevices, 1996 . . 151, 152, 212, 234, 237

Royal Commission on Aboriginal Peoples. *Treaty Making in the
Spirit of Co-existence: An Alternative to Extinguishment*.
Ottawa: Canada Communications Group, 1995 42

Salembeir, Paul. "How Many Sheep Make a Flock? An analysis of
the Surrender Provisions of the *Indian Act*", [1992] 1 C.N.L.R.
14 258

Sanders, D. "Prior Claims: Aboriginal People in the Constitution
of Canada". In *Canada and the New Constitution: The
Unfinished Agenda*, (Vol. 1,) edited by Beck and Bernier.
Institute for Research on Public Policy, 1983 21

Sanders, Douglas. *Aboriginal Self-government in the United
States*. Kingston: Queen's Institute of Intergovernmental
Relations, 1985 127

Schwartz, B. "A Separate Justice System?" (1990) 19 *Manitoba
Law Journal* (No. 1) 77 22

Sherrott, Geoff, "The Court's Treatment of the Evidence in
Delgamuukw v. B.C." (1992) 56 Sask. L. Rev. 441 39

Slatterly, B. "First Nations and the Constitution: A Question of
Trust," (1992), 71 Canadian Bar Review 261 . . . . . . 23, 24, 89, 127

Slatterly, B. "The Constitutional Guarantee of Aboriginal and
    Treaty Rights," (1983), 8 Queen's L.J. 232 91
Tehanetorens. *Wampum Belts.* 3m. Ohsweken: Iroqrafts Ltd.
    Iroquois Publications, 1993 20
Trigger, Bruce G. *The Huron: Farmers of the North.* 2d ed. Fort
    Worth: Holt, Rinehart and Winston, 1996 20
Turpel, M.E. "Aboriginal Peoples and the Canadian Charter:
    Interpretive Monopolies, Cultural Differences," (1989-90) 6
    Canadian Human Rights Yearbook 3, ... 22
Venne, Sharon. "Understanding Treaty 6: An Indigenous
    Perspective" in Michael Asch, ed. *Aboriginal Treaty Rights in
    Canada: Essays on Law, Equity and Respect for Difference.*
    Vancouver: University of British Columbia Press, 1997 40
Wildsmith, Bruce. *Aboriginal People and section 25 of the
    Canadian Charter of Rights and Freedoms.* Saskatchewan:
    University of Saskatchewan Native Law Centre, 1988 23
Woodward, Jack. *Native Law.* Toronto: Carswell,
    1998 . . . .   40, 173, 256, 258, 296
Wright, Ronald. *Stolen Continents: The "New World" through
    Indian eyes.* Toronto: Penguin, 1993 20
York, Geoffrey and Loreen Pindera. *People of the Pines.* Toronto:
    Little Brown & Company, 1992 409
Zlotkin, N.K. "Judicial Recognition of Aboriginal Customary Law
    in Canada: Selected Marriage and Adoption Cases", [1984] 4
    C.N.L.R. 1 . . . . 44, 224

Index